SOL LEWITT
100 VIEWS

SOL LEWITT
100 VIEWS

Edited by Susan Cross and Denise Markonish

MASS MoCA, North Adams

in association with

Yale University Press, New Haven and London

Published with the support of the Getty Foundation and the Henry Luce Foundation

Published on the occasion of *Sol LeWitt: A Wall Drawing Retrospective* on view at MASS MoCA from 2008 through 2033 and organized by Yale University Art Gallery, Williams College Museum of Art, and MASS MoCA in collaboration with the Estate of Sol LeWitt

Published by
MASS MoCA
1040 MASS MoCA Way
North Adams, Massachusetts 01247-2450
413.MoCA.111
www.massmoca.org

in association with
Yale University Press
302 Temple Street
P.O. Box 209040
New Haven, Connecticut 06520-9040
www.yalebooks.com

Contributions by Roland Dahinden and Heinz Liesbrock translated from the German by Elizabeth Kieffer. Texts by Jannis Kounellis and Adachiara Zevi, as well as the introduction to Germano Celant's essay, translated from the Italian by Teddy Jefferson. Essay by Christel Sauer and Urs Raussmüller translated from the German by Nadine Scheu and Elizabeth Kieffer. Text by Charles Vandenhove translated from the French by Teddy Jefferson. Text by Alexander van Grevenstein translated from the Dutch by Pond Translations. Text by Roy Villevoye translated from the Dutch by Gerard Forde.

Editors
Susan Cross
Denise Markonish

Design
Dan McKinley

Copy Editor
Laura Morris

Unless otherwise noted, all photographs
are by Kevin Kennefick and are courtesy of the
Estate of Sol LeWitt © The Estate of Sol LeWitt

COVER: *Wall Drawing 1186: Scribbles: Inverted curve (vertical)* (detail). October 2005. Graphite. Collection of Alessandro Maccaferri.

Printed in Belgium by die Keure.

ISBN: 978-0-300-15282-1
Library of Congress Control Number: 2009921050

Contents

**Susan Cross and
Denise Markonish**
Curators, MASS MoCA

Foreword

There is already an impressive collection of essays, writings, and catalogues that address the art of Sol LeWitt. Adding to this will be the forthcoming catalogue raisonné to be published by the Yale University Art Gallery in association with the Estate of Sol LeWitt and PaceWildenstein. What more could possibly supplement this array of information and analysis? Talk to anyone who knew LeWitt or listen to artists who were influenced by his work or helped by his generosity, and it soon becomes clear what has been missing: a book about how LeWitt's ideas, friendship, and generosity of spirit coursed through the art world.

On the occasion of *Sol LeWitt: A Wall Drawing Retrospective*, a twenty-five-year exhibition made possible by a unique collaboration among MASS MoCA, Yale University Art Gallery, and Williams College Museum of Art, we therefore decided it was time to publish a different kind of book, one that documents the wall drawings on view at MASS MoCA and also records what LeWitt meant to the art world as a whole.

Although we limited the list of authors to one hundred, a count based roughly on the number of drawings contained within the retrospective, the assemblage of voices is just a small sampling of the multitudes touched by LeWitt and his work. These contributors include a cross-generational list of artists, curators, museum directors, choreographers, composers, musicians, poets, writers, and architects, as well as LeWitt draftsmen and studio assistants.

While it seemed a fitting tribute to invite those whose lives and art practices have been changed by LeWitt's work, encouragement, and collaboration to contribute to this book, it was also a slippery slope that could easily have led to sentimentality. Those who knew LeWitt recognized that he was a humble man who did not like a fuss. Thus, in organizing this book, we asked the writers to give something other than a personal tribute. As you read through the wide range of texts included here—which illuminate not only LeWitt's wall drawings but the importance and influence of his varied practice, from the structures to photographs to works on paper— you will find that the contributors honor LeWitt by exploring his art and processes, crediting his influence and, not surprisingly, by celebrating his friendship.

In the end, this publication, like the retrospective and like LeWitt himself, is imbued with the spirit of collaboration and generosity. We would like to thank the following people for helping to realize this publication: Carol LeWitt, Sofia LeWitt, Eva LeWitt, Anthony Sansotta, Susanna Singer, Janet Passehl, Joseph C. Thompson, Jock Reynolds, Lisa Graziose Corrin, Dan McKinley, Kevin Kennefick, Laura Morris, Eric Kerns, Paulette Wein, Hallie Scott, Eugene Rutigliano, Elizabeth Kieffer, Teddy Jefferson, Gerard Forde, our friends at Die Keure, PaceWildenstein, Yale University Press (particularly John Donatich, Patricia Fidler, and Carmel Lyons), the Henry Luce Foundation, the Getty Foundation, and, above all, the contributors whose texts and artworks appear on these pages.

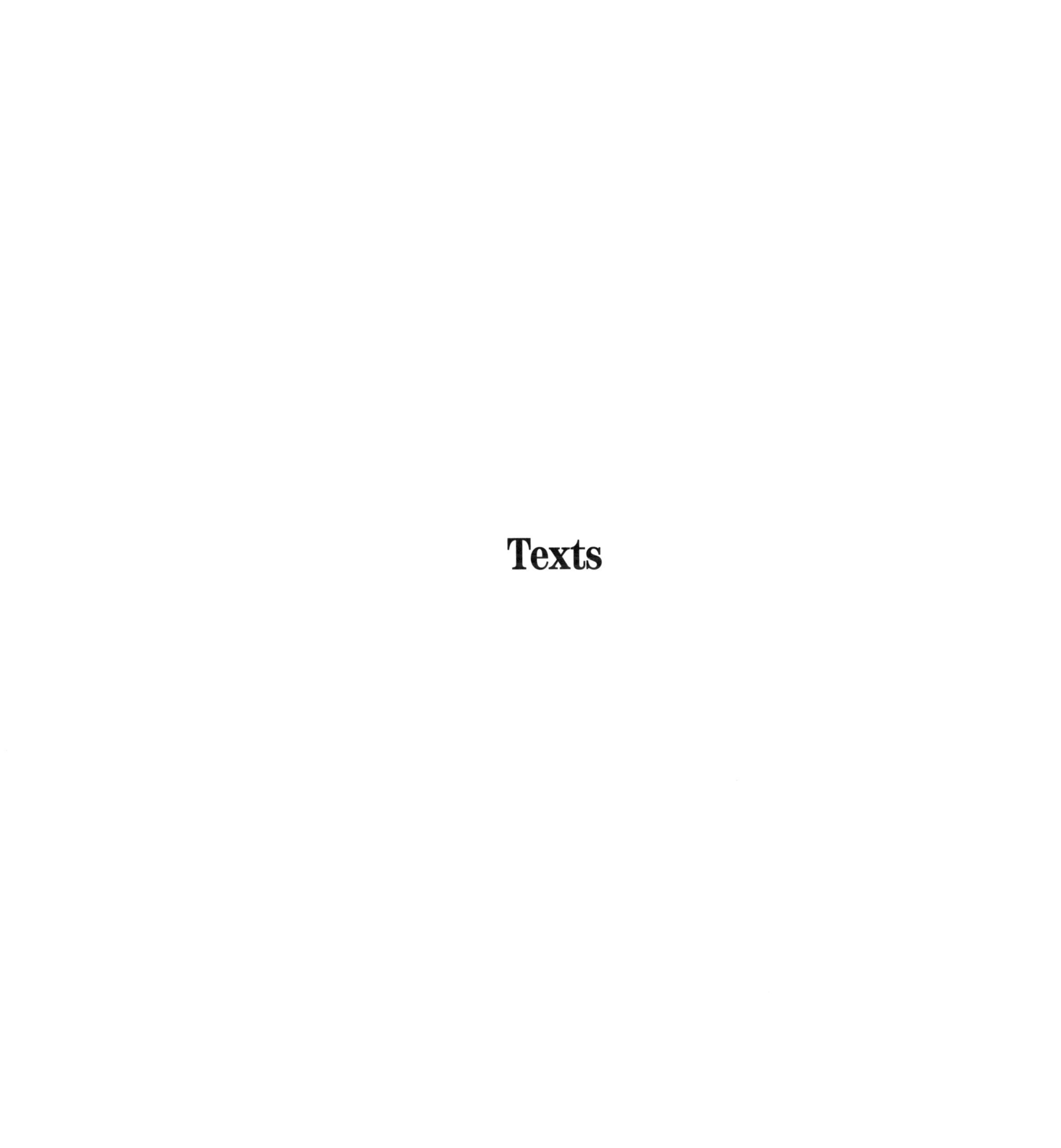

Texts

William Anastasi
Artist

Sol and I were introduced to each other by Virginia Dwan in 1966, the same year he and I would each have our first solo exhibition at her newly opened gallery in New York. I came to consider him a great artist and a great man, a combination by no means common. The friendship continued into the 1970s, after the gallery had closed. Sol's studio was then on Hester Street. Dove Bradshaw, my partner, and I would visit him there.

After he moved to Connecticut lock, stock, and barrel, our contacts ceased for a number of years until I received a telephone call from Janet Passehl, the artist who was by then also the curator of Sol's collection of art. She told me of Sol's having bought a signed certificate that contained a "recipe" for a work of mine, *Incision* (1966), from a man who had years before bought it directly from me. She and Sol were interested in any information on the subject that I could give. I responded as well as memory allowed, and this incident brought about a rekindling of my friendship with Sol, as well as a christening of one with Ms. Passehl.

By that time my son was living with his family in West Hartford, twenty minutes by car from Sol's and Carol's place in Chester. I guess we never visited one home without visiting the other. In 2006, at lunch in New York with Carol, Virginia, Dove, and me, Sol told us that he and Carol would not be going to Italy that summer, and that it would be a shame to have his studio in Spoleto unoccupied. Then he added, "Why don't you and Dove use it?" Virginia practically shouted, "Pounce! It's an incredible place!" We did, and it was. Our first evening there Sol called from Chester to ask how we found everything. Then he said, "Bill, do you see that stack of drawing paper in the studio?" He meant a stack of 22 × 30 inch hot-pressed Fabriano on the floor next to his drawing table— it went from the floor up at least to my knee. Sol continued, "Well, I don't want any of that paper left by the time you leave!"

Carl Andre
Artist

William Anthony
Artist

Sol is our Spinoza.

Sol saved my marriage. As odd as it sounds, it is true.

About four years ago I was feeling long in the tooth and thinking often about the big studio in the sky. I felt the overwhelming desire to display a memento mori—a human skull, in the manner of St. Jerome—in our humble one-room apartment. My wife, Norma, was having none of it and was planning to kick my buns out onto the street, along with the aforementioned egregious object, a dire prospect.

Then, right at that time, Sol came on the scene. We traded art. And I came into possession of three of Sol's gouaches, composed of exquisite, wavelike horizontal lines. They were, for me, a river of life and death, a metaphor that Baba Ram Dass had implanted in my brain back in the 1960s. No longer did I need a skull to contemplate; I had these wonderful paintings. I was happy. Norma was happy. And our marriage was saved.

That is the power of Sol's art.

Stephen Antonakos
Artist

Sol decided. He found his firm ground, and at first it seemed simple. Everybody is familiar with

the idea of a system. It seemed as though by choosing boundaries, Sol had fortuitously been

granted free passage around the tangles of options and involvements that trip or inhibit many.

This ticket, his essential idea—whether Sol chose it, or it chose Sol—proved in his hands (and

in the hands of his friends assisting) huge enough and elastic enough to reveal variations that

no one could say were outside the limits. So, in time, it became clear that Sol's operating structure

embraced forms, materials, colors, and scales of enormous scope—like the little song:

This is the square that Sol drew.

This is the square divided in four that Sol drew.

This is the square divided in four with lines in four directions that Sol drew....

It seemed like a wall at first, then like a room, and, eventually, a magnificent architecture of ideas.

John Baldessari
Artist

Sol LeWitt: Songs My Mother Never Taught Me

I met Sol in the late 1960s. He had invited me to his Chrystie Street loft in New York. He showed me what he was working on: balsa-wood models that would become the *Incomplete Cubes*. What I saw is still imprinted upon my mind. My reaction was "You can't do that!" I could either reject what I saw, or change my mind about art-making. I changed my mind, and his art would subsequently have a large effect upon my work.

His artless photographs of things in his studio bolstered my love of the mundane. I once said to him how beautiful one of his wall drawings was. "That wasn't the point," was his reply.

His idea of making paintings was. Why not work directly on the wall? He continually counseled me to question received wisdom. I've seen painted wall pieces by Sol that are far superior to work by many very good painters.

What has influenced me the most is his idea of having a strategy or ground rules and then following them. The benefit is that one does not have to think about creating something beautiful. Beauty may or may not be a result, but that's not the point. Sol continues for me to be one of the clearest-thinking artists I have ever met.

Robert Barry
Artist

I think my favorite wall drawings by Sol LeWitt are the large ones made with just a pencil, a ruler, and a white wall. Had anyone before made such large drawings?

I do not think they are just about dividing up the space or following the instructions. They activate the space. They create a new kind of space and, sometimes, even a new kind of light. In art this is a very rare thing.

When you see them, you have to really look at them. They may not be there when you come back, but he did give us the plans for making them again. So although the wall drawings may be temporary, they can last forever. They are pictures of time.

Although other people can remake them, I find them very personal. I was fortunate to have traded artworks with Sol. The walls of our house are covered with his drawings. We keep them there because they make us feel so good.

Although written for a different context, I feel Richard Rorty's comment applies: Sol's art is "wonderfully different from anything that has been."

SOL LEWITT

WALL DRAWINGS & STRUCTURES:

THE LOCATION OF SIX GEOMETRIC FIGURES

VARIATIONS OF INCOMPLETE OPEN CUBES

THE JOHN WEBER GALLERY

420 W. BROADWAY NEW YORK

OCTOBER 26 – NOVEMBER 20, 1974

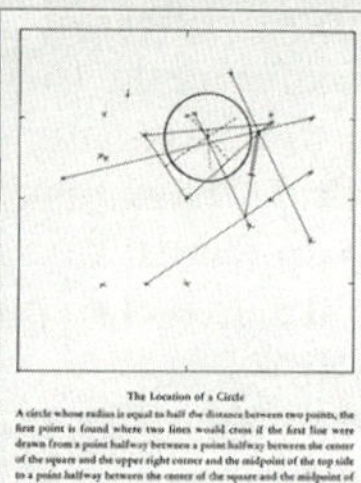

The Location of a Circle

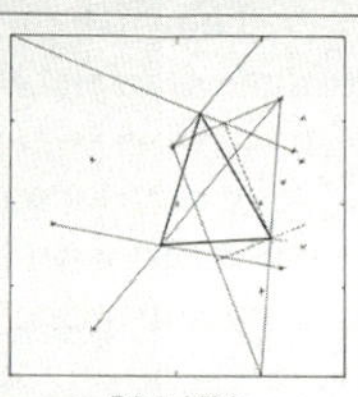

The Location of a Triangle

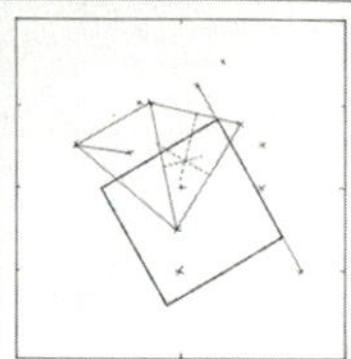

The Location of a Square

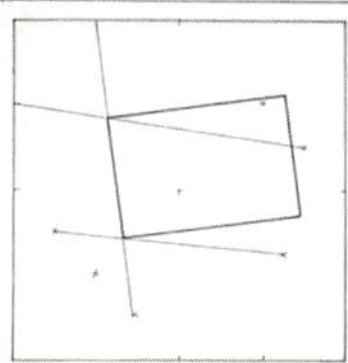

The Location of a Rectangle

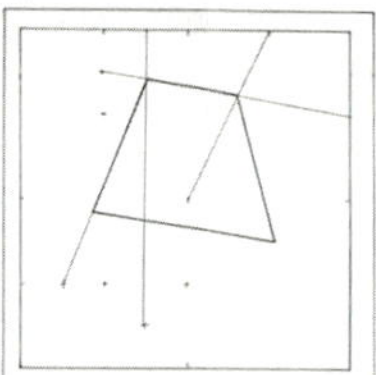

The Location of a Trapezoid

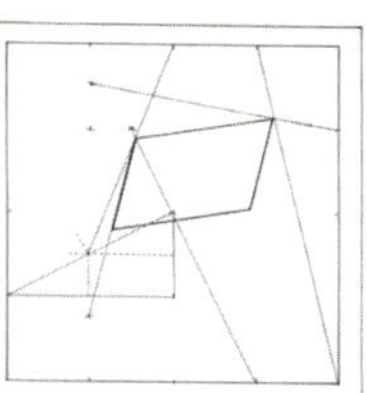

The Location of a Parallelogram

Nicholas Baume
Chief Curator, The Institute of
Contemporary Art, Boston

Lines not short, not uncomplicated, not literature

Concisely descriptive titles are a hallmark of Sol LeWitt's early wall drawings. Consider, for example, *Lines not long, not straight, not touching*. The ideas in such drawings are simple, but the results are not; their formal and experiential complexity belies any succinct terminology. Far from impersonal neutrality, their titles' gnomic density is unmistakably LeWitt. Who else would define his terms with a series of negations? Language was always critically important to LeWitt, and it is impossible to conceive of his art without it. This is nowhere more evident than in his brilliantly incisive body of work on the theme of location. However, in marked contrast to LeWitt's more customary brevity, these drawings often proceed from an astonishing prolixity.

In the context of this retrospective it is worth remembering that many of the wall drawings were first seen in solo gallery exhibitions alongside works in other mediums. Most often, wall drawings and structures (LeWitt's term, which he preferred to the art historically freighted "sculpture") were shown together at LeWitt's galleries in New York, Düsseldorf, London, Paris, and elsewhere. I do not mean to imply that all the wall drawings are formally related to the structures; some are (think of the complex forms of the late 1980s), but many share little family resemblance. For example, in what Lucy Lippard described as "a miraculous display of real, rare, aesthetic energy,"[1] LeWitt's 1974 exhibition at John Weber Gallery presented both a new series of structures, *Variations of Incomplete Open Cubes*, and a new group of wall drawings, *The location of six geometric figures*.[2]

The LeWitt-designed announcement for the exhibition, a work of art in itself, unfolds into a double-sided poster version of the exhibition, with *Variations of Incomplete Open Cubes* on one side and *Location* drawings on the other. At first glance, the two bodies of work have nothing in common but their simultaneous presentation. One of LeWitt's characteristic (and influential) practices was to develop distinct bodies of work in different mediums and follow the logic of each to its conclusion, generating new and often contrary ideas for investigation along the way. The *Variations of Incomplete Open Cubes* are descended from the early serial structures, which had mounted a profound if elegant assault on accepted notions of artistic composition. As LeWitt put it: "The serial artist does not attempt to produce a beautiful or mysterious object but functions merely as a clerk cataloging the results of the premise."[3] Famously, for LeWitt the idea had become an art-generating machine. Similarly, *The location of six geometric figures* was the latest move in his ground-breaking reconsideration of the formal elements of drawing, including its physical support, bringing into play the new concept of location.

While formally dissimilar, these two bodies of work are fundamentally linked and conceptually complementary. They are both radical departures from the very idea of what it means to make art and to express a creative self. Both challenge subjective composition, one by finding a compositional method based on identification rather than imagination (LeWitt did not create, in the conventional sense, the 122 variations of incomplete open cubes; rather he identified them), the other by performing an elaborate deconstruction of composition itself. Both are also based on the conceptualization of basic forms in a complex way. One begins with a simple concept—variations of incomplete open cubes—and ends up with a profusion of different three-dimensional forms; the other proceeds from a profusion of words in order to arrive at six simple geometric figures (circle, triangle, square, rectangle, trapezoid,

---

1. Lucy R. Lippard, "The Structures, the Structures and the Wall Drawings, the Structures and the Wall Drawings and the Books," in Alicia Legg, ed., *Sol LeWitt*, exh. cat. (New York: The Museum of Modern Art, 1978), p. 24.

2. Location was a key theme in LeWitt's work between 1973 and 1977, when he explored the idea in wall drawings, works on paper, artist's books, and prints. LeWitt's October 1974 John Weber Gallery exhibition announcement referred collectively to the new group of wall drawings as *The location of six geometric figures*, although each of the six figures was treated as a separate, independent drawing. Several of them had been first installed in European galleries earlier in 1974. The MASS MoCA retrospective includes two of these 1974 wall drawings, *The location of a rectangle* and *The location of a trapezoid*, as well as the 1975 wall drawing *The location of six geometric figures*, in which all six figures are presented together.

3. Sol LeWitt, "*Serial Project I (ABCD),*" in *Sol LeWitt: Critical Texts*, ed. Adachiara Zevi (Rome: I Libri di AEIUO, 1994), p. 75.

parallelogram). The relationship between these bodies of work reveals much about LeWitt's reinvention of the creative process and his profound originality.

The artist's decision to draw a geometric figure on the wall implies at least some exercise of subjective judgment (to begin with, that decision itself). It may be minimized, mechanized, complicated, or delegated, as in many of the wall drawings, but a judgment has to be made somewhere along the line. In *The location of six geometric figures* LeWitt acknowledged that there was no way to be entirely free from the arbitrary nature of subjective judgment. Instead, he considered to what extent that judgment itself could be codified, systematized, and articulated in such a way that it became integral to, and evident in, the form of the work. Here LeWitt took on the mythic compositional tabula rasa: the artist must make a mark—but where to begin? As usual, LeWitt thought relationally, establishing a series of reference points within a field, usually the entire wall, which led to the final location of the figure. He also turned to language. In the *Location* drawings he incorporated an exact verbal description of the derived location of each figure, the derivation of which was complex, based on the multiple relational elements he had established within the designated space. The detailed spatial relationships that structure the drawings are made literal via language. The results are drawings of extremely simple forms made in an exceedingly complicated way.

This productive tension between the simple and the complex is vintage LeWitt, and it returns us to the comparison with his contemporaneous structures. In its five-word title, *Variations of Incomplete Open Cubes* describes concisely the content of the work,

yet that content, the 122 open-cube variations, is impossible to mentally reconstruct in three dimensions. Conversely, while it is quite easy to imagine locations for the six, two-dimensional, geometric figures, it is utterly impossible to mentally reconstruct LeWitt's locations based on a reading of his written descriptions, unerringly accurate as they may be. His descriptions, which number as many as several hundred words each but are always contained within a single sentence, resist comprehension. Read like an ordinary sentence, the language of each description becomes a hypnotically redundant abstraction. Here is, perhaps, the clearest demonstration by LeWitt of one of his canonical "Sentences on Conceptual Art": "If words are used, and they proceed from ideas about art, then they are art and not literature; numbers are not mathematics."[4]

Consider this brief, relatively simple extract from *The location of a square*: "the second line is drawn from a point halfway between the start of the first line and a point halfway between a point halfway between the center of the wall and the upper right corner and the midpoint of the top side to the start of the first line." LeWitt's language is everyday rather than mathematical; it is not concerned with the economical expression of specialized terms but with the circumlocution that results from using ordinary words. Notice also that he limited the number of different terms used in the description. For example, half is the only fractional measure; quarters, eighths, and other convenient descriptions are excluded, leading to a technically correct yet enormously convoluted piling up of language.

LeWitt made this point quantitatively: "The more information that you give, the crazier it gets until to construct a very simple form or figure such as a circle you could have three pages of text."[5] If, admitting cognitive defeat, we surrender to their striking verbal cadences and rhythms, LeWitt's *Location* works, which he once referred to as his "poetry," may be enjoyed as abstract verbal play.[6]

The *Location* wall drawings might be considered among LeWitt's most disciplined and exacting works, yet they are also among his most absurd and wryly funny. In retrospect LeWitt observed that these drawings were partly a satire on the philosophical pretensions that were associated, by the mid-1970s, with some "advanced conceptualists."[7] Also within this body of work are some of his most intimate and idiosyncratic wall drawings, as I saw for myself on a trip to Spoleto, Italy, a few years ago. From the narrow streets of the old town rises the Torre Vecchio, where LeWitt stayed during December 1976.[8] He left behind an extraordinary profusion of whimsical *Location* drawings, made in his own hand, which map the architecturally irregular interior spaces with all manner of eccentric points, lines,

---

4. LeWitt, "Sentences on Conceptual Art," in *Sol LeWitt: Critical Texts*, p. 89; reprinted from *Art-Language* 1, no. 1 (May 1969), pp. 11–13.

5. LeWitt, "Sol LeWitt Interviewed" (interview by Andrew Wilson), in *Sol LeWitt: Critical Texts*, p. 124; reprinted from *Art Monthly*, no. 164 (March 1993).

6. LeWitt remarked: "These are ways of using language to describe a precise location, like geography. I think of them as my poetry." See LeWitt and Andrea Miller-Keller, "Excerpts from a Correspondence, 1981–1983," in *Sol LeWitt: Critical Texts*, p. 108; Susanna Singer, ed., *Sol LeWitt Wall Drawings, 1968–1984*, exh. cat. (Amsterdam: Stedelijk Museum; Eindhoven: Van Abbemuseum; Hartford: Wadsworth Atheneum, 1984), pp. 18–25.

7. LeWitt, "Sol LeWitt Interviewed," p. 125.

8. LeWitt stayed there at the invitation of his Italian gallerist and friend Marilena Bonomo. The Bonomo family still owns the Torre Vecchio, where the drawings remain.

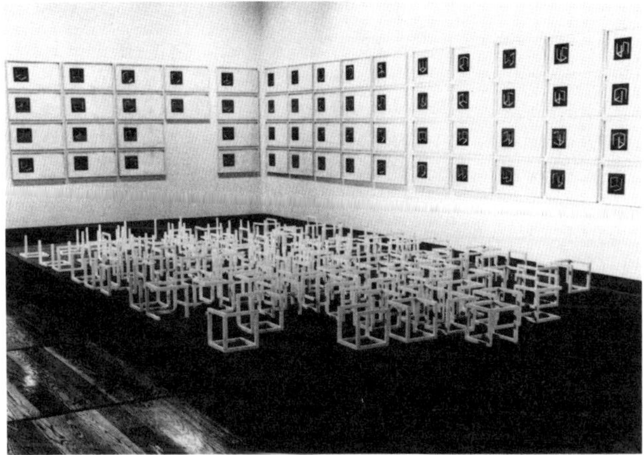

Sol LeWitt. *All Variations of Incomplete Open Cubes*. 1974. 122 white-painted wood structures on a wood base and 131 framed photographs and drawings. San Francisco Museum of Modern Art, Accessions Committee Fund, gift of Emily L. Carroll and Thomas Weisel, Jean and James E. Douglas, Jr., Susan and Robert Green, Evelyn Haas, Mimi and Peter Haas, Eve and Harvey Masonek, Elaine McKeon, the Modern Art Council, Phyllis and Stuart G. Moldaw, Christine and Michael Murray, Danielle and Brooks Walker, Jr., and Phyllis Wattis

and figures and their equivalent verbal descriptions. The playful inventiveness and site-responsive wit of the Torre Vecchio drawings make an intriguing counterpart to the archly deadpan incantations of *The location of six geometric figures*.

LeWitt's *Location* drawings turn composition into a self-reflexive and relational process. As they match verbal description and visual form, they only underline the differences between language and image. Their apparently descriptive purpose defeats itself, pushing language beyond its breaking point. Nevertheless, it must not be forgotten that the *Location* texts do make sense on their own terms. Although I have stressed the linguistic opacity of LeWitt's most elaborate *Location* drawings, there is another side to the story. If, instead of reading the texts, we put pencil to paper and follow them as step-by-step instructions, physically locating the points and lines they describe, we can at least attempt to verify their mad logic. As one of LeWitt's assistants, Tomas Ramberg, explained to me, the only way to make sense of the texts in these drawings is to "perform" them.[9]

LeWitt himself must have staged a kind of performance, working in tandem with language and image in order to create these works in the first place. The text could not be formulated without the drawing; the drawing could not be made without the text.

Let us return one last time to a comparison with the *Incomplete Open Cubes*. The realization of this serial project required the artist to make a similar performative bridge between conception and perception. The task of figuring out all 122 unique variations, being sure to eliminate duplicate forms, was ultimately achieved by making three-dimensional models. Of course, that task could have been accomplished more efficiently by consulting a mathematician or using a computer, but LeWitt was only interested in what he could work out for himself: "I was trying to figure out a way to do it through numbers or letters logically but in the end it all had to be done inherently. I had to build a model for each one and then rotate it."[10] As Jonathan Flatley has observed: "The experience of a gap between apprehension (the sensory perception of the material object) and comprehension (the cognition of the total system organizing that material) would seem to be a recurring theme in LeWitt's art."[11] Despite their dissimilar forms and mediums, both the *Location* drawings and the *Incomplete Open Cubes* operate in this gap between sensory perception and cognition. LeWitt laboriously solved the puzzle he set himself, so that we do not have to, providing us the aesthetic resolution of chaos brought to order. At the same time, his art invites us to experience the pleasures of a particularly active kind of looking, where assumptions are ambushed and intuitions are countered. Finally, LeWitt gives us his ineffably satisfying art. While still wound around itself in a densely knotted tangle, his language of location draws these six geometric figures into a surprising and elegant dance.

The author would like to thank Jonathan Flatley, Carol LeWitt, Mickey Cartin, Tomas Ramberg, and Jen Mergel for their insightful comments.

9. Tomas Ramberg, conversation with the author, July 24, 2008.

10. LeWitt, conversation with the author, August 4, 2000.

11. Jonathan Flatley, "Art Machine," in Nicholas Baume, ed., *Sol LeWitt: Incomplete Open Cubes*, exh. cat. (Hartford: Wadsworth Atheneum; Cambridge, Mass.: The MIT Press, 2001), p. 94.

Gene Beery
Artist

I knew Sol LeWitt for more than forty years. We lived in the same loft building on the Lower East Side of New York City during the early 1960s. We would "shoot the bull" about art and how to beat the fire codes prohibiting artists from living in their studios.

Sol was good-hearted and generous with material things as a man, and was ever productive and original as an artist. He had a wonderful sense of humor and was great at dropping one-liners on the phone, when we talked over the years.

We each had our chosen paths of aesthetic exploration. Sol was a mentor and an enabler in a positive way for me more than he was a specific art influence, although, inevitably, some LeWitt-like effects have shown up in my artist's books and logoscapes, particularly in my ideas for serial work.

I believe Sol didn't want any clones. (This is not to take away from his able and talented artist assistants, who have been essential in realizing the wall drawings and for whom I have only praise and admiration.) Who would have been able to compete with Sol anyway?

While submerged in one of Sol's huge wall works on view at the San Francisco Museum of Modern Art in the 1970s, I realized that he had invented a scientific formula for genuine art. This was good! I imagined that it might somehow lead to his solving the problem of general field theory that Albert Einstein had wrestled with most of his life. Sol's solution would be beautiful to boot!

Heady stuff, it is all there in his art.

I was unaware until this wall-drawing retrospective at MASS MoCA that Sol had made so many wall drawings and proposals for even more: over 1,260 in total. I was shocked to hear that they were usually painted over after their exhibition—and relieved to know that the wall drawings could be resurrected and re-created according to Sol's instructions. What a pleasant moment—eureka!—it must have been for Sol, when he came upon that particular conceptive insight.

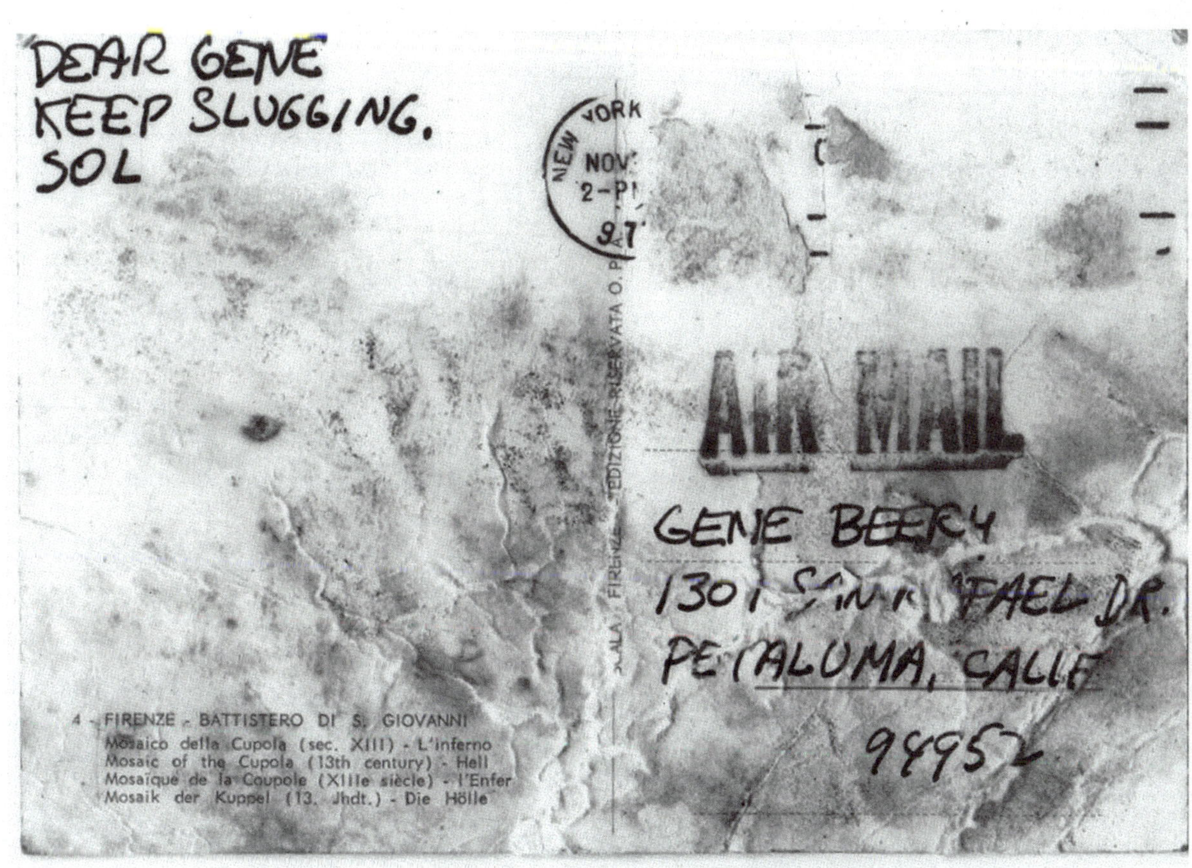
DEAR GENE
KEEP SLUGGING.
SOL
NEW YORK
NOV
2-P
9.7
AIR MAIL
GENE BEERY
1301 SAN RAFAEL DR.
PETALUMA, CALIF
94952
4 - FIRENZE - BATTISTERO DI S. GIOVANNI
Mosaico della Cupola (sec. XIII) - L'Inferno
Mosaic of the Cupola (13th century) - Hell
Mosaïque de la Coupole (XIIIe siècle) - l'Enfer
Mosaik der Kuppel (13. Jhdt.) - Die Hölle

Mel Bochner
Artist

Sol had a restless mind, and never stayed with anything too long because he always saw something new just over the horizon—from sculpture to wall drawing, from black and white to color, from rigid geometry to irrational curves—he kept his work moving and unpredictable. It's for his willingness to take "Loopy Doopy" risks that I admire him most. His relentless questioning of the fundamental grammars of art and his daring in cutting across the conventions of execution and installation helped to divert the stream of art away from object-making toward a more open and democratic vision of art's relationship to culture. For this fact alone all subsequent art is in his debt.

Up until the very end Sol was engaged in what Apollinaire once called "this endless struggle between…order and adventure." Right before slipping into his final coma, he said to his wife, Carol, "If anyone asks, tell them my best work is still ahead."

Dove Bradshaw
Artist

Sol was an extraordinarily sensitive man, as well as a great artist. Surely many of his friends can tell anecdotes about his generosity with both his time and his work. My partner, William Anastasi, had already been exchanging work with Sol in the last seven or eight years, when Sol saw my art and wanted to trade pieces with me as well. When William and I visited his studio one day, he had just been working on a long, horizontal gouache that was pinned to the wall. On his table was a smaller gouache, with gasoline-blue strokes on a burnt-umber ground. I thought that one was beautiful. We talked about a number of things, continuing to look and remarking on works around the studio. When William and I were at the door ready to leave, he asked us to wait. He went back inside and returned with the finished gouache, holding it with outstretched arms.

Sol lent William and me his house in Spoleto, Italy, for the summer of 2006. He was not anticipating coming, but was delighted that it would be used. The effects of Spoleto, a place that has been occupied since around 100 BC, seemed especially apparent in Sol's use of color—even on the walls of his home stateside, painted with yellow ocher, dark turquoise, brick red, and slate black.

Sol's art was included in the exhibition *ONE*, which I organized for Björn Ressle Gallery, New York. It called for several founders and advocates of Minimal and Conceptual art to each execute a work from a single material directly on a wall, floor, or window of the gallery. The selections were made a few months before Sol died. It was natural then to dedicate the exhibition to his memory. I had the wonderful yet bittersweet experience of executing Sol's 1972 work *Wall Drawing 134*, following his instructions: "A not straight line from the left side to the right, drawn at a convenient height." One reviewer wrote that it "reads like an abstract, posthumous signature."[1]

---

1. "Goings On About Town/1: Dedicated to Sol LeWitt," *The New Yorker* 83, no.45 (Jan. 28, 2008), p. 12.

Sol LeWitt. *Wall Drawing 134: A not straight line from the left side to the right, drawn at a convenient height.* April 1972. Black pencil. Private collection. Photo: Jessica Tamson Price, Courtesy Watanabe Studio

AA Bronson
Artist and Director, Printed Matter, Inc.,
New York

1976: Three Paragraphs on Sol LeWitt

In 1976 Sol and a group of like-minded friends founded Printed Matter. Their generosity toward other artists and the wide range of their radical beliefs about and practices in art are revealed in that act: their idea was that anyone should be able to own a work of art, that works of art should be affordable and easily available, and that artists' books were the means by which to accomplish this. Sol's own books run through his life's work like a thread, perpetually drawing us back to his essential ideas. His drawings, sculptures, prints, paintings, and wall drawings are all prefigured in his modest act of making books. His books use the most common means of reproduction to carry his work outward in the world to the broadest possible public. They are a statement in support of democracy, in its purest and most optimistic sense.

In 1976 we began carrying Sol's books at Art Metropole, Toronto, which was an organization that I had founded in 1974 and that, I believe, was the direct inspiration for Printed Matter. At the time, because the Canadian dollar was worth somewhat less than the American, we had to sell Sol's books at a slightly higher price. A book that was $7.00 U.S., for example, would sell for $9.00 Canadian, or perhaps even $9.50. I remember Sol being enraged by this inflation, which he felt was inappropriate and in opposition to his philosophy of books.

In 2006 or so, by which time I was director of Printed Matter, Sol donated an early wall drawing to our cause. Thrilled to install it in our new storefront at 195 Tenth Avenue in Manhattan, we kept it on view for more than a year. It sold and was thus instrumental in supporting the costs of the organization's move and the renovation of the new space. Sol was very ill by then, and was never able to see his drawing on our premises. I hope it would have made him proud to see his ideas for a democratic art form flowering so successfully thirty years later, with the help of his wall drawing from the fateful year of 1976.

Kathan Brown
Printmaker, writer, and founder of
Crown Point Press, San Francisco

Daniel Buren
Artist

One morning in 1971 I was standing at my kitchen sink, looking out the window, and watching my ten-year-old son and his friends building a fort in the front yard, as a taxi pulled up to the curb in front of the house. This was unusual for our neighborhood in Berkeley, California, and I watched as a pleasant-looking man got out. He must be going across the street, I thought, or next door. But he stood for a moment looking up at the house, and then opened our gate and walked up the steps. When I opened the door, my two big dogs raced out, and he had to cling to the railing to keep his balance. "Is this the Crown Point Press?" he inquired politely.

I have recounted that moment, when I first met Sol LeWitt, many times in lectures and writings. It remains clear in my mind, though I can't remember why I didn't expect him that day. Crown Point Press, nine years old in 1971, was in my basement. I had done etching projects with Robert Bechtle, Bruce Conner, Richard Diebenkorn, and Wayne Thiebaud, but LeWitt was the first artist I worked with from outside the San Francisco Bay Area. I didn't know anything about the international art scene. Sol didn't tell me. He just did what he did. What resulted in 1971 were *Lines, not long, not straight, and not touching*; *Lines in four directions, superimposed in each quarter of the square progressively* and *Bands of color in four directions and all combinations*; the latter comprising straight, parallel lines set in wide bands and printed in red, yellow, blue, and black, their sixteen different combinations yielding sixteen different prints. These are still the examples I give when asked to name the most difficult etchings I ever printed: difficult because they were so simple. They set the pace for Crown Point Press for years to come, and opened to me a way of thinking still present in my life.

Sculpture
outshine
line
Locate
endlessly
Wall
imprint
trace
triumph

Ellen Carey
Artist

Color Me Real

In 2004 the Wadsworth Atheneum in Hartford commissioned its final site-specific wall drawing by Sol LeWitt: *Wall Drawing 1131: Whirls and twirls*. Situated at the entrance to the Great Hall, this vivid, room-encompassing work is flanked by white marble staircases, with a stained-glass skylight overhead. LeWitt's drawing transforms these walls, replacing the formerly pale architectural planes with bright, intense color. Large, segmented bands of primary colors coexist happily with segments of purple, green, and orange.[1]

The drawing presents a seemingly incomprehensible puzzle. Yet like proportional harmonies found in architecture (the golden mean), nature (the logarithmic spiral), science (DNA), and mathematics (fractal geometry), it employs parallel systems in a seamless visual logic that blends those complexities with elegant simplicity. The entranceway opens up several f-stops in luminance: the colors are radiant; the figure-ground relationships are pulsing. They command your attention, exulting: "I am here! Color me real!"

The museum's historic second-floor galleries are catapulted into the present, *Back to the Future*–style, with LeWitt's aesthetic boldness, visual intelligence, and fierce commitment to color. The end result is both optical dance and coloristic surround sound, a monumental pattern poured into asymmetrical shapes and orchestrated with larger-than-life hues and full-out saturation.

LeWitt's installation served as the entry point for an exhibition called *Contemporary Art: Floor to Ceiling, Wall to Wall*. In this company the *MATRIX* series mounted an exhibition, *Photography Degree Zero*, devoted to my large-format Polaroid work.[2] The coincidence of *MATRIX 153*, the contemporary art exhibition, and LeWitt's glorious installation was an extraordinary event for me.

Sol and Carol LeWitt came to visit me, and together we viewed the exhibitions. His wall drawing was "totally brilliant!" (as I later overheard a British visitor to the exhibition say), both literally and figuratively, not only for its bouncing-off-the-wall chromatic array, which put color first, but also in its Brobdingnagian scale, dwarfing everything else. In Sol's conception, color is subject *and* object, material *and* meaning, process *and* art. The stately context of the grand staircase met its match in Sol's flamboyant, no-holds-barred, artist-takes-all occupation of what might otherwise have served as a setting for a scene in *Brideshead Revisited*.

Robert Smithson once noted that, "Size determines an object, but scale determines art. A crack in the wall if viewed in terms of scale, not size, could be called the Grand Canyon. A room could be made to take on the immensity of the solar system. Scale depends on one's capacity to be conscious of the actualities of perception."[3]

The fates smiled on me: I had the opportunity to witness the progress of LeWitt's installation in situ. I could never quite get over its enormity, and the arrangement and assortment of colors comprised a symphony in concert with its surroundings. But most of all it was the experience of color that impressed me. It was so real, up-front, and personal.

LeWitt often employed geometry based on the circle and the square: two ubiquitous structures and visual codes. Yet despite that universality, his work always retains a "wow" factor. He was always pushing the parameters, challenging how art was made and what it could be, questioning its meaning.

When the sky is a wall of blue and a huge rainbow appears after a thundershower, I think: "It's nature's wall drawing. Why not?" Robert Thurman, the Buddhist scholar at Columbia University, New York, has stated: "The rainbow body is very common, mentioned frequently in Indo-Tibetan Tantric literature. It is a demonstration performed by an enlightened being to show humans that the enlightened spirit can transcend material elements (yellow earth, white water, red fire, green air, dark blue space) and shape them at will into whatever thing

---

1. Stephen Persing, "Climbing the Walls for Art," *Art in America* 93, no. 9 (Oct. 2005), pp. 146–51, 215.

2. Joanna Marsh, *Ellen Carey/MATRIX 153: Photography Degree Zero*, exh. brochure (Hartford: Wadsworth Atheneum, 2004). *MATRIX* was the first program to showcase cutting-edge contemporary art in the context of a traditional art museum. It was initiated more than thirty years ago by the Wadsworth Atheneum under the leadership of curator Andrea Miller-Keller.

3. Robert Smithson, "The Spiral Jetty," in *Robert Smithson: The Collected Writings*, ed. Jack Flam (Berkeley: University of California Press, 1996), p. 147.

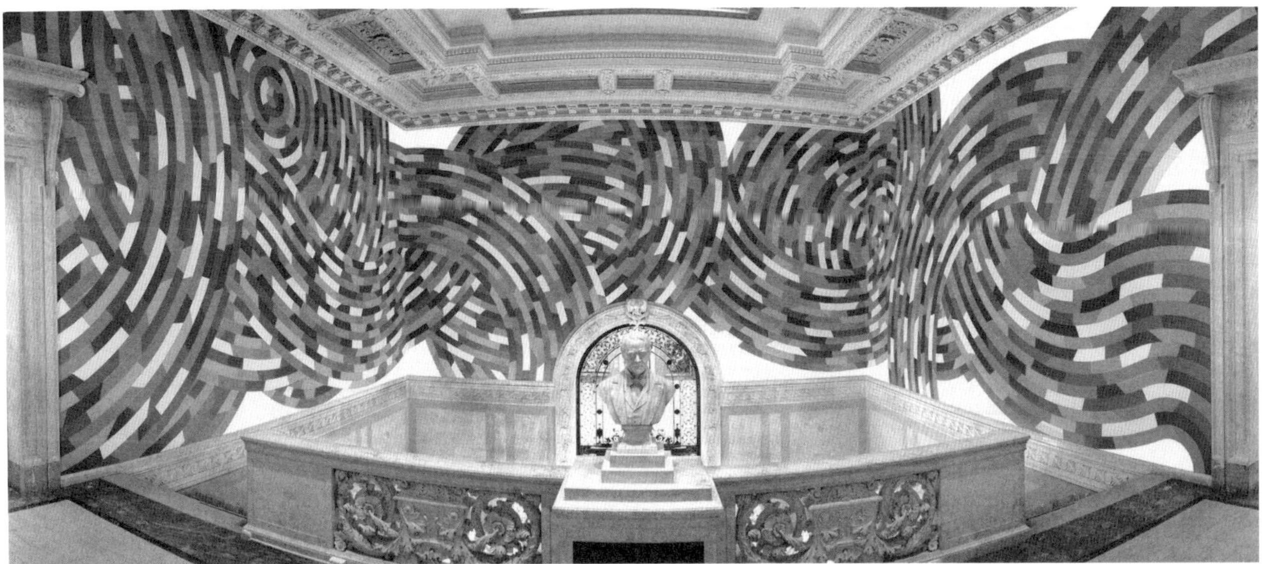

Sol LeWitt. *Wall Drawing 1131: Whirls and twirls (Wadsworth)*. 2004. Acrylic paint. Wadsworth Atheneum Museum of Art, Hartford. The Ella Gallup Sumner and Mary Catlin Sumner Collection Fund. Photo: Allen Philips

of beauty liberates its viewers."[4] The rainbow's colors—red, orange, yellow, green, blue, indigo, and violet—are formed when the sun's rays are reflected and refracted by drops of rain and mist. Forming the basis for LeWitt's work, this palette acts as a connection between his affinities for nature in general and this phenomenon specifically.

Sol's work generously gave me artistic license to move forward, to dig deeper into color's mother lode. By journeying through uncharted territories along a path full of discoveries and surprises, new possibilities and arrangements, I found that my need to rely on traditional photographic colors faded away. They were displaced by imagined, chemically created colors, which I conjured by using gel-colored light (or no light at all), instead of exposing my lens to a view in front of my eyes. In my Polaroid 20 × 24 work called *Pulls*, a process I began in 1996, I mixed and mismatched conventional practices with experimental abandon. What evolved was a menu of inventive techniques and

methods that brought to life colors and combinations of colors never before seen. For me, LeWitt's use of color gained momentum over time, evolving to an ever brighter, bigger, and bolder blowup, to use a photographic term. It was my good fortune to be a witness to this, in essence, to stand under his rainbow.

The author would like to thank Carol LeWitt and the LeWitt family as well as Ethan Boisvert, Gene Gaddis, Janice LaMotta, Robert Lang, Stephen Persing, Patricia Rosoff, and Krystian von Speidel for their patience, editorial skills, and support

4. Robert A. F. Thurman, email message to the author, Dec. 17, 2008. For more on this subject see Sogyal Rinpoche, *The Tibetan Book of Living and Dying*, rev. ed. (New York: HarperCollins Publishers, 2002); and Padma Sambhava, *The Tibetan Book of the Dead*, trans. Robert A. F. Thurman (New York: Bantam Books, 1994).

Mickey Cartin
Collector

I confess that the first time I was in the same room with Sol, about twenty years ago, I felt like I had just seen Babe Ruth. Obviously, this is just the kind of thing that would have pissed him off. I introduced myself, and he said, "Oh yeah, I know you." It couldn't be, I wondered. How could he know me? As time passed, and as close as I grew to him, I discovered that I would always hold him in that kind of awe. Had he known this it would no doubt also have angered him. And when I realized that Sol had become my friend, it was a moment of absolute grace. I can picture his annoyance over all this gushing.

I knew a lot about his work. That pleased him. I knew something about art and ideas, and about how his work was so unique that it never really fit in. I also knew that it was its uniqueness and pure invention that made it so difficult for critics and historians to get it to fit. It didn't matter what they said about his work, or what they called the boxes that they tried to squeeze it into, I always thought that nobody ever seemed to adequately describe what he was up to. That his work was such a modest yet dynamic expression of an over-sized intellect and tireless curiosity has often been why it mattered so much to anyone who thought about his art seriously. It is impossible to define a man like this, one of such particular greatness. That wasn't the fault of those who tried. It was his.

I knew about the thorough injustice in the "art market," and I would frequently have something cynical to say about it. Sol liked that. He would often wonder why the work of so many of his friends would sell at auction for higher prices than his. I knew that he really didn't care about money; in fact, he cared so little it seemed that he was often confused by it. I think he just wanted to know that his work also counted, and I loved the innocence of that questioning. I always felt that rich people who buy art are not the people that should be deciding about quality, but in the art market that is the way it works. "No shit," was all he would say, and that little grin of satisfaction would indicate that we agreed.

The last time I was in Sol's studio he was full of enthusiasm over his new *Scribble* drawings. He had been very ill and in and out of the hospital with very discouraging reports about his health. But he had Carol, Eva, and Sofia around him, and their love and the new direction of his work were clearly sustaining him. As always, there was a long list of destinations for his work written on the wall in his immaculate handwriting: Düsseldorf, Sydney, London, San Francisco, Ghent, New Britain, Kyoto, Paris, Stockholm, Seoul, and more. I'm not clear on the accuracy of this list, but it makes the point. I thought of him still as a driven young artist being drawn into the rabbit hole of his own cavernous mind. What a privilege it is to have known him.

Germano Celant
Independent curator and Artistic Director,
Fondazione Prada, Milan

My first contact with Sol LeWitt's work was in 1969 on my first trip to New York, when Lucy Lippard talked to me about his sculptures and his wall drawings in pencil. It was at Sol's first show in Italy, in Rome, at Fabio Sargentini's Galleria L'Attico, that I had my first real exposure. The following year, in 1970, we met in Turin for the creation of the wall drawings for the exhibition *Conceptual Art, Arte Povera, Land Art*, which I curated for the Galleria Civica d'Arte Moderna and Gian Enzo Sperone. From that point on the dialogue continued, building on our shared passion for art ideas and practices. At the 1976 Venice Biennale Sol made an enormous wall drawing in white crayon on black for my show *Arte/Ambiente dal futurismo ad oggi (Art/Environment from Futurism until Today)*. Then for the 1997 Biennale, which I also curated, he made a cinder-block structure placed at the entrance of the gardens. In 2007 we worked on the planning of a wall drawing in our house in Milan for my son, Argento. Based on friendship, mutual respect, and esteem, ours was an intense relationship, which lasted until Sol's death. I would like to honor our friendship not with an emotional statement but rather a text I began writing in 1972, when we were at the beginning of a shared adventure into both the visible and the invisible.[1] It follows here.

The Sol LeWitt Orchestra

If music is the art form least bound by empirical experience and everyday life, free of any direct relationship with what is represented by language, one could say there is a parallel between Sol LeWitt's work and music. LeWitt's works are visual scores that use two- and three-dimensional signs, unconscious and intuitive exercises in calculation, in which the execution is nothing other than a translation of the conceptual process into surfaces and volumes. The more the execution maintains the precision of the idea or concept—which is the most important aspect of the work—the more accomplished is the communication: entropy of communication is reduced to the ideal state, where there is a correspondence between the concept and the two- or three-dimensional sign. This search for an ideal state, in which the visual event is the exact result of a conceptual process, permits the extreme purification of the idea or concept, to the point at which it is presented for what it is, a rational and objective entity that does not admit those subjective or empathetic additions that are part of the usual aesthetic operation. In this sense, Sol LeWitt's works are visual scores that are based on silent relationships between concepts and processes. They are cognitive events that communicate an idea, and sacrifice to that idea all the intentionality of material and subject.

It is the idea that shapes and gives sense to the work, and it is on the idea or concept that LeWitt works, tending to empty his means of expression of their material nature. In this sense, one could define him as a "musician of concepts," in search of an evermore ideal score. A musician who sees the translation from idea to praxis as itself a kind of contamination, he tries to deny us a visual appreciation of the work, which should instead be given a structural reading. LeWitt's two- and three-dimensional pieces are therefore formulations of an idea and follow a mechanistic rationalism that rejects chaos and leaves nothing to chance. Once the idea is formulated, what follows is not put under any material or subjective control. The work of art is, in fact, a conceptual operation that only happens to be embodied in a material or a form— the object and the trace that derive from it are irrelevant compared to the chosen idea or concept. In this sense, as LeWitt himself says, "Even a blind man can be an artist," because it is the idea that designs the work. The production of the work is nothing more than a process of visualization of the idea, which should not be interfered with by the medium used. One does not therefore have to choose an artistic or aesthetic idea to produce art: it is enough to take any idea and follow through its objective assertion. The idea should be transcribed and not interpreted, given as it is, to communicate what can only be communicated in and through it. The medium, the form, and the material used are nothing other than often dull and banal instruments, and their redundant presence has to be gradually annulled in favor of the concept. Once an idea or concept has been chosen, all decisions on how to proceed have already been made. The execution of the work is only an a posteriori, functional operation, which does not affect the method or the chosen conceptual process. Thus the idea or concept removes what is

---

1. Previously published in *XLIII Esposzione Internazionale d'Arte La Biennale di Venezia. Il Luogo degli Artisti. Catalogo generale.* (Milan: Edizioni La Biennale and Fabbri Editori, 1988), pp. 70–73.

arbitrary, chance, chaotic, emotive, and subjective to emphasize control, clarity, rationality, and sobriety.

In his logical system of the conceptual process, it is clear that LeWitt works with such forms as geometric volumes, which are neither strongly characterized nor evocative. His materials are annulled by the noncolors of black and white, whose simplicity does not change the conceptual whole. In fact, their flatness and insignificance tend to concentrate the intensity of the process that produces them. The attention paid to elementary forms is only of interest insofar as it seems to produce structural and conceptual entities that are not evident but possess independent meaning. Thus even if at a superficial glance LeWitt's works appear formalist, they are, in fact, antiformalist. They are combinations or sequences of two- and three-dimensional signs developed following a conceptual structure that in itself turns out to be the objective component of the work. In LeWitt's work one can clearly see a systematic attempt to eliminate every empirical and emotional element, and the use of method and order is fundamental. Method and order are the work of art; the rigid system of minimal forms in series allows the artist to follow through the conceptual element of the work.

There is, however, a difference between LeWitt's work and that of the pure Conceptualists such as Art & Language or Ian Burn and Mel Ramsden. The difference lies in LeWitt's intuitive and personal choice of the concept, as opposed to the abstract systems of the others. For LeWitt, ideas are discovered through intuition, and it is on the intuition of the idea that one works. His work therefore has a subjective, not an abstract, matrix; it is based on a human, not a technical, apriority. This is why his work becomes musical, starting from a purely conceptual structure that is chosen intuitively and produces a correspondence between that

structure and a sign or group of signs. A parallel in contemporary music might be found in Philip Glass's *Music with Changing Parts*. Glass, like LeWitt, arrives at a musical system on the basis of a conceptual score using combinations of numbers and regular arithmetic progressions. Both Glass and LeWitt work with the unison of sounds and concepts to produce rhythmic, repeated figures, which are spontaneously produced by the conceptual process that formed them.

LeWitt's sculptures are based on the modulation and progression of elementary signs, such as the cube, or else they are sequences developed in two and three dimensions, following a modular structure based on the square. As this square form develops, it becomes an open sign and a closed sign, an open volume and a closed volume, an open structure and a closed structure, the nature and understanding of which lie only in the sequence, in the relation that is created between visual and conceptual logic. LeWitt seems to work within the osmosis between these two systems of logic, once he has made himself a conceptual and procedural vehicle that will allow him to freely develop his intuitions, based on fixed combinations. His constructions eliminate the finality of the work: they are only instruments to emphasize the rational mechanics for analyzing the possible three-dimensional variations of a square, as in *Wall/Floor Piece ("Three Squares")*, 1966, and of three different cubes in *All three-part variations of three different kinds of cubes*, 1969. They comprise an obvious, three-dimensional art that attempts to stimulate and involve the spectator's mind rather than the eye. The mediums used lie at the highest degree of communicative economy: they are capable only of expressing conceptual reasons that can only be expressed in three dimensions, just like the different variations of three cubic volumes in *Variations of Incomplete Open Cubes*, 1974. Finite arrangements and combinations based on the concept of rhythm or space take

on ever-changing forms and dimensions, whose existence serves to show the process of addition inherent in LeWitt's conceptual work. Following a geometric progression, the combinatory and serial possibilities create new, closed, three-dimensional presences; in a linear or centrifugal sequence, they create open ones. The alteration of artistic conventions is clear: "If the artist changes his mind midway through the execution of the piece he compromises the result," and, "The artist's will is secondary to the process he initiates from idea to completion. His willfulness may only be ego."[2] LeWitt's absolutely logical way of working shows this to be true: once the concept has been chosen, the direction and course of the work are already laid down; they are inherent to the concept itself. Every intermediate intervention is arbitrary. The artist can only be an executor of the idea— not an interpreter or adjuster. He who interprets falls into Expressionism.

And so the idea is an object and, as an object, can have two or three dimensions. LeWitt's work is two- as well as three-dimensional; he works with signs on a surface, with lines and their finite combinations of color and form, rather than with volumes. Having set the problem of how to work on a surface that does not become an object, LeWitt has chosen to work directly on walls. Once a system of vertical, horizontal, and transverse diagonal lines has been chosen, along with their specular combinations, the work is transferred directly onto the wall, which, as a surface, becomes part of the work.

Seeing the conceptual process as an object has thus eliminated the third dimension, and has subsumed the material of the wall: its weight, color, fabric, and architecture. From this moment on these qualities become part of the work, their redundancy reduced to a minimum. The various combinations of black

<hr>

2. Sol LeWitt, "Sentences on Conceptual Art," *0 to 9*, no. 5 (Jan. 1969), p. 4.

lines naturally produce different tonalities and combinations. So the discovery of the meaning of their installation is due to their possible combinations. Initially, the lines are straight and overlaid—in a closed system such as the square—into certain, finite combinations. As the lines are inscribed in a rectangle, combinations become doubled, tripled, and quadrupled in innumerable variations.

The amplification of the variations—along with their signs and conceptual richness—continues to eliminate mental and subjective redundancy, even if visual redundancy remains. At a certain point, in fact, the lines break the restrictive scheme of geometric figures containing them and are arranged freely, no longer according to a figure but according to a length or a number. The lines finally reach thousands of examples, as in *Six thousand two hundred and fifty-five lines* or, following a process of arrangement established beforehand, as in *Lines not short, not straight, crossing and touching, drawn at random, using four colors (black, yellow, red and blue) uniformly dispersed with maximum density, covering the entire wall surface.*

As seriality is based on a succession of terms, or on their superimposition and combination, individual personality is excluded. The rigid system of logic itself creates the relations in which signs are symbols of a conceptual orchestration, which is certainly linked to the phenomenology of the signs, but is controlled and controllable, because it is a priori within the mind of LeWitt himself.

Since 1968 LeWitt's wall drawings have aimed to treat the surface even more as a whole—though the idea was already part of the artist's work. In these wall drawings he investigates the various, linear features of the surface, in an analysis that is obviously based on a logical linguistic model, as Filiberto Menna saw clearly: "LeWitt, after all, proclaims a sort of theorem: given a surface implying a series of variations of signs (whether the variations are limited or unlimited is unimportant), find the operational norms necessary to achieve an interrelation of the signs."[3]

The process is purely syntactic, and the solution lies in achieving a mathematical whole or a structure that can be defined in linguistic terms as "an autonomous entity of internal dependencies" (Louis Hjelmslev).[4] The artistic process therefore can be identified with "transformational operations" carried out within a system, and the value of the work lies in the modifications made to the code—a code that foresees such modifications and contains them as possibilities. The surfaces used for the process can be of various types, and so in 1968 LeWitt changed from the modular structures he had used since 1964 (articulating them in a solid, autonomous space) and set himself the problem of linking his works to the environment, the surface of the walls around them. This new investigation moves away from the cellular volumes that are finite articulations, which can be arranged in various ways in different architectural settings, to the wall drawings, in which a grid "adheres" to the wall surface and offers infinite combinations that are nevertheless defined architecturally. The grid of chalk or pencil signs adapts to the surface and produces an arrangement that has a visual and concrete character that is determined naturally by the material and condition of a specific wall. While the wall drawings are traced on the particularities of a wall, they also develop from it as a whole. It is the wall, its geometric irregularities and present physical state, that determines the arrangement of signs to which LeWitt's graphic system adapts itself.

At Gian Enzo Sperone in Turin in 1970, LeWitt traced all the possible "lines between architectural points" in *Wall Drawing 51*, graphically linking all the spatial errors and events that had occurred during the construction of the space and its use as a gallery. The visual space of the pencil lines thus develops in relation to the architectural field. It no longer produces a series of modular traces but an arrangement of lines and connecting courses that arises from the environment itself. The composition of the lines is not based on some a priori conceptual plan. It is determined by the actual nature of the site, which LeWitt does not aim to modify; he wants to use it as a local sign and traces out his own operation on it. The combinations vary, but they are always improvised and thought out on the spot.

At the Tokyo Biennial in 1970 LeWitt found he had to use a setting where the walls had been covered with soundproof paneling full of perforations. The artist could not draw on it, so he proposed: "Inasmuch as the walls of the gallery cannot be drawn on and the artist does not want an artificial wall to be built for this purpose, he would like to propose the following work: on the first wall to the left as one enters, pieces of white paper 4 cm by 4 cm, rolled, would be inserted into each of the holes and cover the surface of the wall; all of the holes would be used. On the second wall, adjacent to the first, white and yellow squares of paper 4 cm by 4 cm would be rolled and placed at random in the holes. The white and yellow pieces should be of equal number, and all of the holes should be filled. On the third wall, an equal number of white, yellow and red squares of paper 4 cm by 4 cm would be inserted into the holes, all of which should be used. On the fourth wall: the same procedure would be used as in the other three, but using an equal number of white, yellow, red and blue rolled pieces of paper. When the project is completed all the holes will have paper projecting from them. The

---

3. Filiberto Menna, "Sol LeWitt: A System of Painting," in Adachiara Zevi, ed. *Critical Texts* (Rome: I Libri di AEIUO, 1994), p. 194.

4. Hjelmslev in ibid. p. 195.

colors would be inserted at random with no thought of arrangement or design." In this case (*Wall Drawing 38*), the procedure that constructs the signs reveals the setting. In other examples, the system develops independently of the location.

Once the artist has chosen a serial group of vertical, horizontal, and transverse diagonal lines, which can be interrupted or joined, semi-circular or irregular, the arrangement on the walls develops in accordance with a modular grid, centered on a square that contains all the possible combinations of the signs chosen. The increase in the number of variations and their richness, however, exclude the restrictiveness of a given architectural figure. These are free series—either in negative or positive, depending upon whether chalk or pencil is used, whether the wall is colored or white. These series cross their settings in a compositional, not dialectical, way—as in *A 40" (100cm) band of vertical and both sets of diagonal lines superimposed, centered top to bottom, running the length of the wall* in Düsseldorf in 1969; or *Arcs from the midpoints of two sides of the wall*, in Spoleto in 1971, or, again, in *Wall Drawing 260: On black walls, all two-part combinations of white arcs from corners and sides, and white, straight, not-straight, and broken lines* at the Venice Biennale and in San Francisco in 1972.

In the most recent works, the potential of color and of the system of lines is explored to the full—so much so that in some cases the lines lose their sense of limit and become a type of chromatic metrics. They start from the center, from the top or bottom, from the left or right , and are inscribed on monochrome walls of black, red, blue, or yellow. The starting point is the same—a flat surface and a line—but, by adding color and setting the arrangement at the center, LeWitt tends to eliminate the crystallization of a reduced system of squares and volumes in combination, replacing it with a whole that oscillates

between zero and infinity, between painting and architecture.

In 1976 the pleasure of making straight lines, diagonals, and curves dance on ceilings and walls—so that joined together or broken, colored or not, they produce fantastic and elegant variations on the initial signs—led LeWitt to add new forms to his range—figures that were born out of the interweaving and coupling of the same elements. And so the circle, triangle, square, and trapezoid appeared on the scene. The lines move, turn, intersect, regroup, and lift lightly. They float on the walls and never tire of improvisation, following a rigid logic of construction and projection; their visual essence is one of abundance, seducing the viewer with their purity of conception and the simplicity of the effects achieved through materials and colors.

Sometimes it is the single, dancing square that does a solo, accompanied by lines and differently colored backgrounds, or the square may interact with a circle or trapezoid to excite the surface of the wall. Thus exquisite environmental effects are achieved, which demonstrate LeWitt's command of all the various architectural contexts that have emerged during his investigations and been offered up for the presentation of art. Sometimes we might take these vigorously pure hollows to be Platonic spaces, true essays of architectural geometry. As has already been underscored, these are not works whose value derives from an expressive creativity but rather from the insinuation of the sensitive and coincidental into their planning—planning that in the course of conceptualization encounters the images' fantastic behavior. This manifestation of excited, kaleidoscopic movement behind the cold, rational figures certainly does not arise from their strict composition but rather out of chance and the correspondence of the figures. Their movements change continually and create an intense rhythm of axial variations, at the center or to the sides. All these variations in the projections

are further complicated by color, be it blue, yellow, red, black, or white.

However, it is always the whole that determines the behavior of each form and part, so that they together move in a precise, rhythmic progression. If the decision is to go to the left or the right, to meet at the center or the sides, all the parts participate as one. It is as if they were moved by an ecstatic and hypnotic power, a sort of dervish geometry that seduces through an excess of life and energy.

The impulse of movement in LeWitt's art is different therefore from monotonous reductionism or the contortions of Expressionist composition; the dance of surfaces and figures is here a mobile and joyful manifestation of the production of art. LeWitt's work emphasizes his enthusiasm for understanding the variations of painting and sculpture possible within a controlled impulse to produce—following an intellectual progression that contains within it both passion and generosity. Since 1979/80 the wall drawings have emphasized that character of chromatic thrill, and the complication of their angular combinations has made them visually richer. They seem to move away from the extreme rationality of his project of the 1960s and 1970s, using intuitions about color and the complexity of angles. They still adapt to the architecture, but express their appearance in a more spectacular way. They aim at an internal connection based not only on geometry but also on interweaving. Compared to the previous works, they are an elegy to unity. They clear the ground of the infinitesimal and turn the walls into a whole, but not one that becomes monumental, rather one adapted to the scale of the working stage offered by galleries and museums. The wonders generated by the interweaving of the "instructions," which are translated into figures and concrete locations, represent a vibrant search for equilibrium between formal perfection and intellectual tension—two features that have always been part of LeWitt's work.

Lucinda Childs
Choreographer

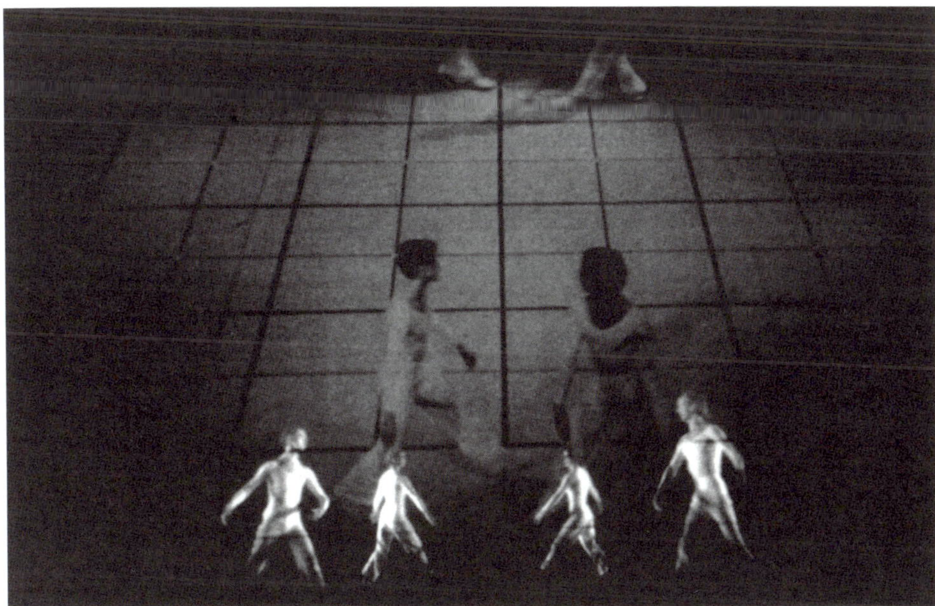

Lucinda Childs
Dance Company.
Dance. 1979.
Brooklyn Academy
of Music. Photo:
Nathaniel Tileston

Dance was commissioned by the Brooklyn Academy of Music in 1979 as a collaborative work by composer Philip Glass, visual artist Sol LeWitt, and myself. It had been initiated by Philip's and my desire to work together on a new collaboration following our efforts together on *Einstein on the Beach* in 1976. Philip had suggested that we ask Sol to design the decor.

Sol's first reaction to our proposal was to question the need for a stage setting for a dance work that would be abstract and in and of itself visually complex. I thought about this for quite a while and came back to him with the idea of a projected film of the dancers dancing, which could be synchronized with the dancers performing live on stage. Pleased with this idea, Sol decided to make a 35-millimeter black-and-white film consisting of passages he would select from the choreography of the three dances comprising the work.

Sol was able to follow the diagrammatic score that I had made for each dance, and was able to create a storyboard for the film directly from the scores. The filming of the dancers was done in a day or two, but the editing took weeks. It is only by seeing the work that it is really possible to appreciate Sol's extraordinary contribution. In performance, the film is projected on a transparent scrim downstage of the dancers in perfect synchronization with the live dancers. Through shifts in camera angle and changes of scale, the spectator's point of view is subjected to a series of ingenious manipulations. The dancers are seen sometimes in close-up and at others in long shots. With split-screen images, the film is projected directly above the dancers on stage at the same scale, creating a perfect double set of dancers. In addition, the images of dancers are shown at certain instances displaced to left or right, with alternating front and back orientations, as images inside other images, and as superimposed freeze-frames.

Dance is still performed and is currently in the repertory of the Ballet de l'Opéra National du Rhin in Strasbourg, France. The work's thirtieth anniversary will be celebrated in July 2009 at SummerScape, Bard College's performing arts festival in Annandale-on-Hudson, New York. I feel truly fortunate to have worked on this project with Sol, who devoted himself totally to our collaboration. Once he had committed to it, no detail, however small, was ever overlooked.

Sachiko Cho
Artist and LeWitt draftsman

Chuck Close
Artist

"Do not do anything that would be a disservice to Sol and his art," is what I always try to keep in mind as a draftsman. I have been working for Sol LeWitt for fifteen years. When he sent me places to make wall drawings, he would often say, with a smile, "Don't work too hard!" That was his way of saying, "Keep it simple; use your common sense; and don't distort the idea by thinking too much." There are decisions draftsmen have to make throughout the course of executing one of his wall drawings, and the artist must always remember to allow room for "interpretation." Sol stated, "The draftsman perceives the artist's plan, then reorders it to his experience and understanding."[1]

Even though Sol also said, "It is difficult to bungle a good idea,"[2] erroneous decisions in the process of implementation can, in fact, lead to disastrous results that do not do justice to Sol's art. A wall drawing should never be seen or executed as just a pretty interior design or, at worst, a parody of the original concept. One of the most difficult problems to avoid is overworking a drawing to a point at which the work becomes sterile through its mechanical execution. On the other hand, a simple line or color can express complex thoughts and inspire a deeper understanding of all the possibilities of universal beauty.

I hope that I have been a good draftsman for Sol LeWitt.

Sol LeWitt would never let me do a portrait of him. He didn't believe in the "cult of the artist;" he only wanted the art to be known. He didn't want to be photographed, didn't want anyone to know what he looked like. This self-effacing attitude masked the fact that Sol was one of the most generous artists I have ever known. Everyone knows about his generosity to other artists of every stripe, many of whom were emerging or overlooked, and to every cause and charity. First and foremost, however, he was generous in his art, laying out for all to see the underlying concepts, rational underpinnings, and logical development within a piece and from piece to piece. He shared his vision, his passion for change, and his belief that following a process wherever it would lead would produce work that even this inventor of Conceptual art could not preconceive. We were free to travel along on this seemingly never-ending journey of discovery and share with him his obvious pleasure in permutation and change.

It is interesting that an artist known for giving over much of the actual process of execution to others made work so filled with Sol himself: his pleasure, his celebration of formal invention, his unique personal vision. Sol's indelible fingerprints are all over works he never physically touched. The wall drawings on view at MASS MoCA, conceived before he died but executed by others—old, trusted hands as well as new recruits—come to life in all their abundant diversity, different apparitions conjured up for our amazement and pleasure by one of the great alchemists of all time.

---

1. Sol LeWitt, "Doing Wall Drawings," *Art Now: New York* 3, no. 2 (June 1971), unpaginated.

2. LeWitt, "Sentences on Conceptual Art," *Art-Language* 1, no. 1 (May 1969), p. 13.

Chris Cobb
Artist and LeWitt draftsman

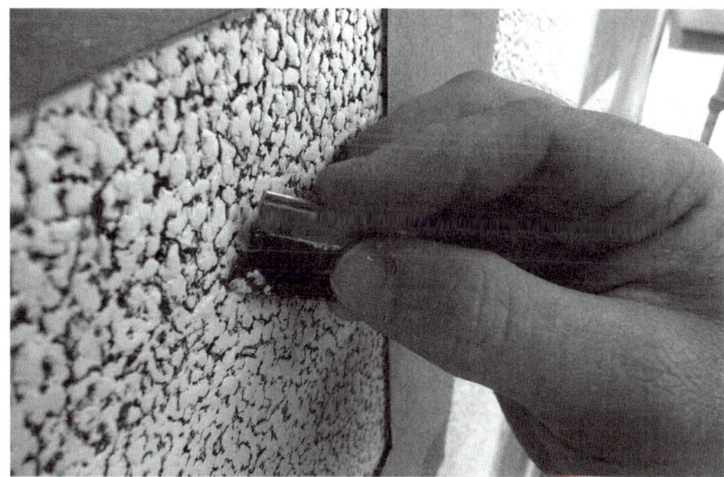

Installation of *Sol LeWitt: A Wall Drawing Retrospective* at MASS MoCA. 2008. Photo: Chris Cobb

It was hard to calculate from the photocopied diagrams we were given at the start of the Sol LeWitt wall-drawing retrospective just how much authority the works would have when they were finished. Some, like *Wall Drawing 343: On a black wall, nine geometric figures (including right triangle, cross, X) in squares,* which I worked on, have large basic shapes. Whether it was the boldness of a 6-foot-high black triangle or the rich blackness of a 6-foot-wide circle, at that scale the figures were transformed from mere shapes into experiences. And that was what was going on all around the galleries as we worked in our teams: those instructions were coming to life, becoming physical experiences.

The experiences, however, extended way beyond the actual artworks. There was also a great deal of preparation that went into what we were doing, long before any marks could be made: masking the walls off, laying paper on the ground, setting up our work spaces, and so on. Then there were the pencils: a crucial task for many of us was to sharpen pencil leads for all the delicate pencil drawings. I can say for certain that when one sharpens over five thousand pencil leads, one really becomes familiar with how a lead feels, how it smudges, how it breaks, and what a needle-sharp pencil lead feels like when it pricks one's finger. I can't say for certain how many leads we sharpened, but if one were to say that "countless pencil leads were sharpened for the project," it would be accurate. The care that went into

just the pencils alone was a good indicator of how the project would look when the works were done.

Similarly, it was clear to me just how much care went into preparing the space before we arrived. Inside the galleries the pristine walls were standing there waiting for us, filling all three floors of the building. For the first two weeks I kept getting lost wandering around in the maze of blank white walls. It took a little while to get oriented.

It was apparent that other professional teams had come before us. They came to clean the aging structure, build and paint the very maze of walls I was getting lost in, do the electrical work, lay the flooring, put in windows, add or remove brickwork, install air conditioning, and, I'm sure, complete many other anonymous tasks that go into making museum shows happen. So all of that labor, plus our five or so months spent installing the wall drawings, added up to an incredible amount of physical, emotional, and psychological energy—all of it invested in realizing Sol's work. Now that it is finished and I have gone through the spaces, I believe this truly can be felt.

Interestingly, as the drawings were being completed and the installation was coming to an end, I noticed that spiders were making little webs on the wall drawings, moving in, so to speak. Some of the bright colors also seemed to be attracting certain kinds of insects: a yellow jacket stayed on a blue star for three days; a moth clung to a grayish ink-wash rectangle (almost perfectly camouflaged, probably thinking that no one could see it); and various gnats seemed to really like walking over the layered surfaces of the crayon drawings (at insect level the built-up areas of crayon must look like giant ice chunks in the Arctic). Watching the insects crawl over the wall drawings reminded me of a joke I heard one child telling another in MASS MoCA's Kidspace: "What did one centipede say to the other centipede? You've got a lovely pair of legs, you've got a lovely pair of legs, you've got a lovely pair of legs, you've got a lovely pair of legs, you've got a lovely pair of legs, you've got a lovely pair of legs…!"

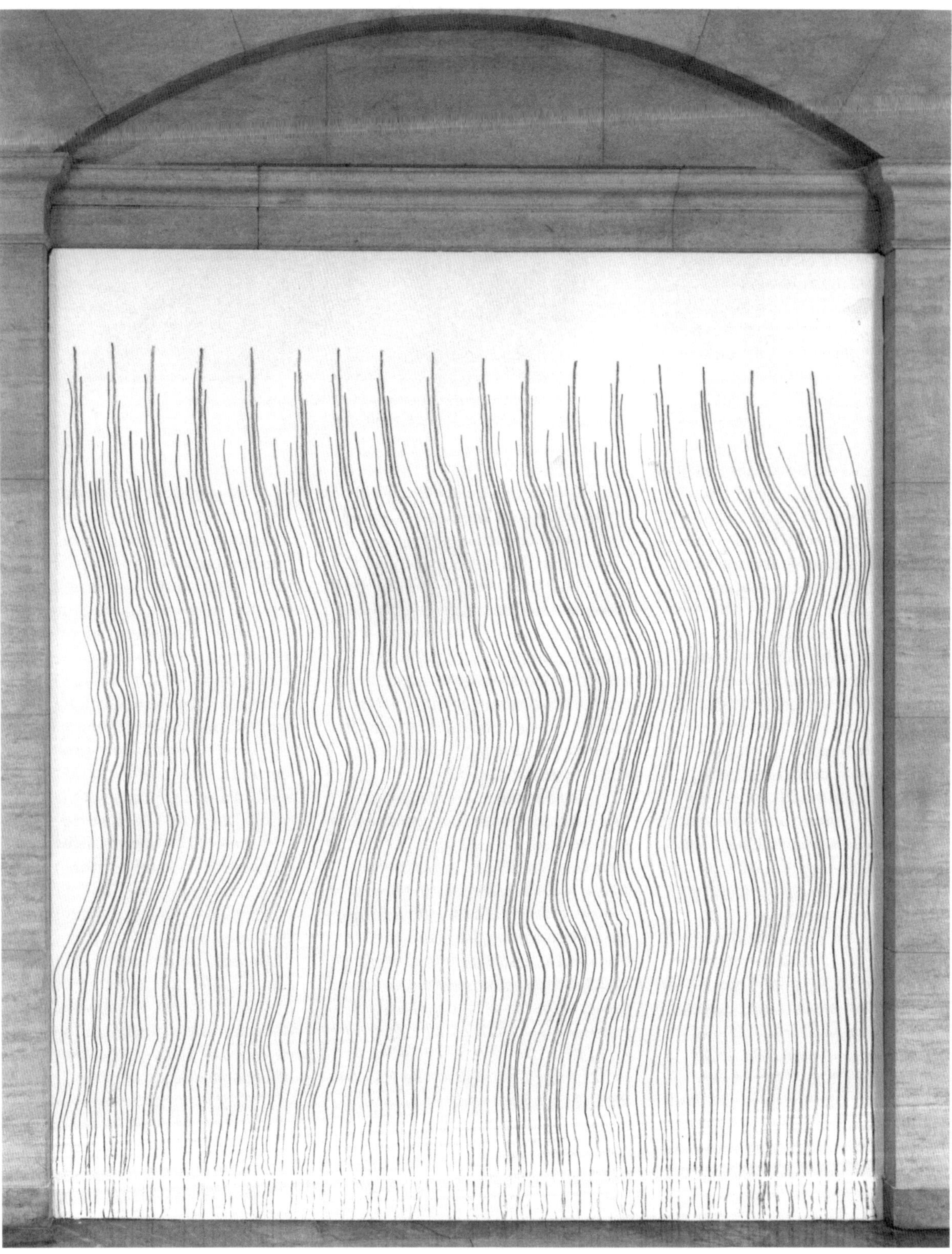

Lynne Cooke
Curator, Dia Art Foundation, New York

Sol LeWitt. *Wall Drawing 123: Copied lines: The first draftsman draws a not straight vertical line as long as possible. The second draftsman draws a line next to the first one, trying to copy it. The third draftsman does the same, as do as many draftsmen as possible. Then the first draftsman, followed by the others, copies the last line drawn until both ends of the wall are reached.* March 1972. Black pencil. Addison Gallery of American Art, Andover, Massachusetts. Gift of the artist, Addison Art Drive, 1991.20. Photo: James L. Sheldon

Wall Drawing 123: Copied lines

By following the set of instructions that are a part of the work's title, anyone, in theory, can execute a Sol LeWitt wall drawing. In practice, however, the artist quickly discovered that skilled draftsmen were required. Thereafter, teams of trained assistants were deployed as needed to install his works in public and private venues alike.[1] The minimal skill set the artist stipulated from his executors was an unemotional, perfunctory manner, but precision, equanimity, conscientiousness, and stamina have also proven to be assets. In carrying out the instructions supplied by the artist, those who draw act as impersonal agents: irrespective of whether ruled or freehand, regular or irregular, their lines never become expressive marks. In LeWitt's practice, ideas are authored, but realizations never signed. Listed on the wall label accompanying any individual work, however, are the names of all who contributed to its making.

The first examples in what was to become a vast corpus of some 1,200 works were comprised of straight lines drawn in graphite pencil. In 1970, barely two years after he had taken up the genre, LeWitt's close friend Eva Hesse died. Within a matter of days he introduced the nonstraight line—as "a bond between us, in our work"—into his spare vocabulary.[2] Since then not straight lines have taken many guises in the wall drawings: quirky and eccentric when they constitute a curling, marbled pattern; regularly irregular when, ten thousand strong, they cover a vast area with equal density. On occasion, randomness may be integrated into a composition, for the work's preset system of instructions will always be articulated in terms that preclude any undermining of its integrity. According to draftsmen who have worked on some of the more monumental, architecturally scaled examples, the rules articulating the work will often inflect the process of making it with a kind of tedium, an almost automatic behavior. A quasi-rote, methodical rendering of the composition's modular unit may result. As occurs elsewhere in LeWitt's art, the ensuing generalization will eliminate any hint of personal handwriting.

In 1967, just prior to beginning this body of works, LeWitt asserted in a manifesto-like statement: "The idea becomes a machine that makes the art."[3] In the case of his wall drawings, if not his sculptures, the impact of rigorously following this axiom proved anything but mechanistic. Even in the presence of some of the grandest, such as *Wall Drawing 1085: Drawing Series—Composite: Part I–IV, 1–24, A+B* (2003), which requires months of strictly coordinated teamwork to execute, the spectator is always keenly aware that the febrile graphite structures were made by hand: far from dry and uninflected, they exude a sensuous, silvery-gray light. Others, which incorporate into their compositions as a formal device the blocks of printed text comprising their verbal instructions, betray a laconic visual wit, their creator's barely disguised delight in the way that the most limpid prescriptions may produce befuddling results—or the converse. Once when a certain, seemingly anomalous, formal decision was questioned, LeWitt answered: "It wasn't absolutely necessary, but some inner urge (aesthetic frivolity, I suspect) caused me to do it."[4]

The instructions for *Wall Drawing 123: Copied lines* (1972) read as follows: "The first draftsman draws a not straight vertical line

---

1. With characteristic generosity, Sol LeWitt devised some works in later years specifically for amateurs.

2. LeWitt in LeWitt and Andrea Miller-Keller, "Excerpts from a Correspondence, 1981–83," in Susanna Singer, ed., *Sol LeWitt Wall Drawings 1968–84*, exh. cat. (Amsterdam: Stedelijk Museum; Eindhoven, Van Abbemuseum; Hartford: Wadsworth Atheneum, 1984), p. 20. The inaugural installation of *Wall Drawing 46* (1970) was at Yvon Lambert, Paris, in 1970.

3. LeWitt, "Paragraphs on Conceptual Art," *Artforum* 5, no. 10 (June 1967), p. 79.

4. LeWitt and Miller-Keller, "Excerpts from a Correspondence," p. 22.

as long as possible. The second draftsman draws a line next to the first one, trying to copy it. The third draftsman does the same, as do as many draftsmen as possible. Then the first draftsman followed by the others, copies the last line drawn until both ends of the wall are reached." The varying heights of the resulting lines reflect the reach of the different assistants; the quirky inflections from the strictly vertical reflect the difficulties of making a continuous gesture from as high as one can reach down as far as possible, in effect, to the floor. Deviations are compounded, as participants attempt to mirror the lineaments of their predecessors' trajectories, while maintaining an uninterrupted flow from their particular line's zenith to its terminus at the base of the wall. As one after another member of the group takes a turn adding to the evolving form, the uppermost points in the cluster of repeating lines limn a meandering, wavelike profile. This rhythmic form, a record of the repeating segue of shorter and taller contributors, at once structures and unifies the composition.

In LeWitt's early wall works the graphite lines are usually made with the hand and wrist; later, when they become more extensive, the arm and shoulder are employed. In *Wall Drawing 123*, by contrast, a full-body stretch is involved; exceptionally, the drafters' corporeal, as well as mental and technical, capacities are drawn upon. Although elsewhere in LeWitt's oeuvre biographical reference is precluded, in this unique instance a collective signature is generated by the group's bodily traces.

Somewhat uncannily, *Wall Drawing 123*, with its "copied lines," calls to mind another collective portrait of an artist's assistants, or their equivalent, through its repeated bodily gestures. Trisha Brown choreographed *Spanish Dance* (1973) for her New York-based company the year after LeWitt devised *Wall Drawing 123*. Brown's notation for *Spanish Dance* takes the form of a diagram with accompanying text: "Dancer A slowly raises arms like a magnificent Spanish dancer and travels forward in time to Bob Dylan's 'In the Early Morning Rain.' When dancer A touches up against the back of dancer B, dancer B slowly raises her arms like a magnificent Spanish dancer and the two travel forward, touching up against the back of dancer C, etcetera until they all reach the wall."[5] While strikingly similar in their compositional structures, these singular works share above all a like attitude, a sly humor, in their creators' address to those who realize them.

When invited to curate an exhibition of his own early wall drawings for Dia:Beacon in 2007, LeWitt included *Wall Drawing 123* on his checklist.[6] Among the many well-known and standout pieces that make up this show, this one seems something of a maverick. Foregoing the technical experience required of LeWitt's devoted team of assistants elsewhere in the installation, it stands apart. Is its inclusion simply a caprice, an "aesthetic frivolity"? Or, more likely, is it a fond homage?

---

5. See Hendel Teicher, ed., *Trisha Brown: Dance and Art in Dialogue, 1961–2001*, exh. cat. (Andover, Mass.: Addison Gallery of American Art, Phillips Academy, 2002), p. 275.

6. Note that when the work was included in 1993 at the Addison Gallery of American Art, Phillips Academy, it was in somewhat related circumstances. *Sol LeWitt: Twenty-Five Years of Wall Drawings, 1968–1993* was a large survey of LeWitt's wall drawings executed by his team of assistants, with students in the institution's art department working under their guidance. *Wall Drawing 123* was realized in two versions there: as *123*, in graphite on a white ground; and, as *123A*, in white crayon on a black ground.

Lisa Graziose Corrin
Class of 1956 Director of the Williams College
Museum of Art and lecturer in art, Williams
College, Williamstown, Massachusetts

Sol LeWitt: Collecting Possibility

I only met Sol LeWitt twice. Once we met to discuss a project that was never realized. On another occasion we walked through the spaces at MASS MoCA in preparation for his wall-drawing retrospective. After he died I wanted a context for understanding his working process and was saddened that I couldn't speak to him directly. So one afternoon I drove to Connecticut to visit the LeWitt collection at his warehouse, as well as Sol's and Carol's home. It might seem counterintuitive, but I thought I could learn much from another facet of Sol's practice: collecting.

Collecting for Sol was as relentless a pursuit as his investigation of the cube. It occupied a great deal of his energy and extended to every corner of his home. On the one hand, there were his spontaneous purchases of an abundance of exuberant fin de siècle Viennese furniture. At the other extreme, a room was decorated not with wallpaper but a systematic alignment of shelves, like a serial wall relief, holding tapes arranged to span the history of music. Sol traded his work with hundreds of artists. Collecting their art was a way for

him to connect the dots between his aesthetic preoccupations, those of his contemporaries, and those of a younger generation.

Curators are notoriously nosy. I began opening innocuous drawers and discovered sheet after sheet of notes dating to Sol's earliest musings. Some were notations made as he worked through variations on a theme within self-imposed constraints. Others included ideas for works and even to-do lists. There were a few rare notebooks with traces of his conceptual meanderings. The drawers provided access to the intimate mental spaces of an evolving intellect. This was Sol's way of collecting his thoughts and collecting himself. He drew, wrote, scribbled, processed, and played compulsively and often preserved this personal history. Like one of his *Location* drawings or one of the rooms of his home, those metal cabinets contained a fastidiously organized arrangement of vectors, a complex rhizomic network of overlapping and interlocking lines of thought.

I took a small pile of manuscripts from a drawer. They had been composed on an old manual typewriter. There were several drafts. At the bottom of a page a confidently handwritten line had been added to the neatly typewritten text: "The idea becomes a machine that makes the art." I was holding in my hands the moment when the generative force churning within these many pages of ephemera had crystallized. In one compact sentence, in one compressed concept, Sol had transformed our thinking about art. The abundance of his ideas seemed to collect in this succinct statement.

Ironically, for this irrepressible collector of all manner of things, repeated, transient manifestations of a process were more highly prized

than the single, fixed realization of an object. On that day I began to decipher the fundamental grammar underlying the "ABCD" of Sol LeWitt.

Underlying Sol's collecting and his art was a passion for suspending elements in contradiction to allow for "rigor and randomness," as my graduate intern Erica DiBenedetto observed. It also let him be both minimal and maximal, clear and opaque, and overdo rules to the point that they subverted themselves and the act of making rules itself. Indeed, Sol created limits so that he could transgress them or overflow their measure. He conveyed a sense of endless possibility inextricably bound to an ethos of endless giving. When subsequent collaborators realize his wall drawings, some of the instructions even allow for the drafters' creative input to intersect with his.

Anyone I asked about Sol always began by telling me that, for him, to be generative and generous were synonymous. As viewers of his wall drawings, we experience profusion amounting to an infinity that empowers us to continue the process beyond the confines of the work. As detached as his cool, white structures might appear, Sol's ardent desire to share makes us, like him, collectors of possibility.

Petah Coyne
Artist

For over thirty years some of the words Sol LeWitt wrote
to Eva Hesse in 1965 have echoed from my studio walls:

Learn to say "Fuck You" to the world once in a while.
You have every right to. Just stop thinking, worrying,
looking over your shoulder, wondering, doubting,
fearing, hurting, hoping for some easy way out,
struggling, gasping, confusing, itching, scratching,
mumbling, bumbling, grumbling, humbling, stumbling,
rumbling, rambling, gambling, tumbling, scumbling,
scrambling, hitching, hatching, bitching, moaning,
groaning, honing, boning, horse-shitting, hair-splitting,
nit-picking, piss-trickling, nose-sticking, ass-gouging,
eyeball-poking, finger-pointing, alleyway-sneaking,
long waiting, small stepping, evil-eying, back-scratching,
searching, perching, besmirching, grinding grinding
grinding away at yourself. Stop it and just DO.[1]

---

1. Quoted in Lucy R. Lippard, *Eva Hesse* (New York:
New York University Press, 1976), p. 35.

Susan Cross
Curator, MASS MoCA

Drawing Restraint

In 2004, at the time of the installation of two Sol LeWitt wall drawings at the Solomon R. Guggenheim Museum in New York, I was walking down the ramps with Sol, when he told me—rather casually but, nevertheless, emphatically—that the museum should install *Wall Drawing 146* (1972). The wall drawing, Sol declared, was one of his most important. I made a note of it, thinking at the time that surely the museum would install the work—which is part of its collection—at some point when Sol was still here to see it. I had forgotten this conversation until I saw *Wall Drawing 146A* (2000) completed at MASS MoCA. Drawn in white crayon on a blue ground, the work, titled *All combinations of arcs from corners and sides, straight, not straight, and broken lines*, is an inversion of the earlier drawing *Wall Drawing 146*, which is executed in blue chalk on a white wall.

As he did in this instance, LeWitt often revisited earlier drawings years later, creating a completely new work from an existing drawing with a simple change in medium or color. *Wall Drawing 146A* was first installed at the Museum of Contemporary Art, Chicago, in June 2000, almost thirty years after *Wall Drawing 146* was first drawn, at the Kunsthalle Bern. At MASS MoCA, however, LeWitt fittingly chose to present the later work on the first floor, alongside his drawings from the 1970s.

With *Wall Drawing 146A* as the sole drawing in the retrospective to fill an entire room, LeWitt seems to be telling us again that this drawing (and its antecedent, *Wall Drawing 146*) is particularly important. To create the drawing the wall is divided into a grid, and in each square of the grid a different combination of two elements is drawn. The elements included are what LeWitt described as arcs from corners and sides and the three basic types of line (straight, not straight, and broken), as well as several permutations of these lines drawn in the four essential directions employed in the artist's earliest wall drawings.

The drawing begins in the upper-left corner of one wall and progressively unfolds over the four walls of the gallery, moving from all arcs to all lines. Although the drawing's composition is made clear (a key to the work, drawn directly on the wall, is incorporated into the drawing itself), when seen as a whole the work becomes much more than the sum of its parts. Viewed from a distance, the grid that forms the underlying skeleton of the work disappears, and the repeated white arcs and lines are transformed into unexpected marks and shapes, reminiscent of hieroglyphs, as they visually transgress the borders of the pencil grid and mingle with neighboring pairs of arcs and lines. The key, however, with all the elements of the completed drawing identified and numbered, ensures that the work's structure and logic are made transparent, and "the viewer," as LeWitt wrote in 1978, "will know that the changes are not capricious, but systematic."[1] The drawing overall is, in a sense, a pictorial alphabet—or "an encyclopedia," in LeWitt's words.[2] With this simple vocabulary, the basis for all his production, LeWitt was able to create an endless variety of work. In even his most extravagant later drawings, such as *Wall Drawing 880: Loopy Doopy* (1998) and *Wall Drawing 958: Splat* (2000), the mix of fluid and agitated lines is rooted in the flamboyant markings visible in *Wall Drawings 146* and *146A*.

The surprising subjectivity of those later drawings, however, is absent in *Wall Drawing 146A*, although even this work illustrates what Robert Rosenblum described as the "crazy extravagance" with which LeWitt's elemental forms proliferated.[3] The florid forms are, in fact, the result of a calculated restraint. Despite themselves—and the organizing grid that fails to contain them—the minimal white arcs and lines against the blue ground impart an impression of irrepressible abandon. The unexpected, sumptuous effect of LeWitt's prescribed system is indebted to the influence of chance—which is always an important factor in his work and is often assisted by the requirements or parameters presented by the architecture of a given site.

---

1. Sol LeWitt, "Illustrations: Works by Sol LeWitt, 1962–1977, with His Commentaries," in Alicia Legg, ed., *Sol LeWitt*, exh. cat. (New York: The Museum of Modern Art, 1978), p. 131.

2. Ibid., p. 129.

3. Robert Rosenblum, "Notes on Sol LeWitt," in Legg, ed., *Sol LeWitt*, p. 16.

Architecture has played an important role in the execution of both *Wall Drawings 146* and *146A*. Although *Wall Drawing 146* (the blue on white version) was first installed in a double-height space punctuated by arch- and entryways in Bern in 1972, it has been installed in spaces of varied characteristics and sizes over subsequent years.[4] In 1975 LeWitt created a version of the same combinations of arcs and lines, *Wall Drawing 260*, in white chalk on one long, black, coved wall at the San Francisco Museum of Modern Art. *Wall Drawing 260* was executed again, at the 1976 Venice Biennale on the four walls of one room. LeWitt wrote of this series' mutability: "The lines make unforeseen combi-nations…. No matter how many times it is done it is always different visually if done on walls of differing sizes."[5] That flexibility is also what makes the drawings so significant. "Even though the system is the same, the space is different, making the combinations of lines different," LeWitt remarked.[6]

While LeWitt's drawings are meant to be ephemeral—drawn, painted over, and redrawn on another wall—a particular work cannot always be accommodated on any given wall. The right size or proportion is often a prerequisite. On the other hand, many of the wall drawings are indeed adaptable, their appearance remaining somewhat similar from installation to installation. With *Wall Drawings 146* and *146A*, however, the works can and do change rather radically with the given architecture. These

drawings can be executed on a single wall or on the four walls of one room, and the height of the walls can vary dramatically. Thus the dimensions of the drawings' grid can change, as do the locations of the varying combinations of arcs and lines and, ultimately, the form and narrative of the resulting works. "In the San Francisco piece," LeWitt wrote, "the movement is read from top to bottom, and in Venice, the movement is read progressively around the room."[7] The ability to create a truly infinite variety of works from a finite system might explain further LeWitt's particular appreciation of *Wall Drawing 146A* and its cousins.

In his article "Wall Drawings," published in 1970, LeWitt stated: "The handicap in using walls is that the artist is at the mercy of the architect." In the same text, however, he conceded that "the physical properties of the wall…are a necessary part of the wall drawings."[8] In the examples of *Wall Drawings 146* and *146A* the architect becomes a collaborator of sorts, introducing into LeWitt's predetermined system certain restrictions and chance elements that make possible additional permutations.

This is likewise true of *Wall Drawing 51: All architectural points connected by straight lines*, another work in the MASS MoCA exhibition. Drawn in blue chalk on a white wall, it has a formal connection to *Wall Drawing 146* and its opposite, *Wall Drawing 146A*. More importantly, *Wall Drawing 51* shares with these works the ability to escape the whim of the architect or, in other words, to overcome the

eccentricities of a given wall. *Wall Drawing 51* uses the demands of the wall not just as a collaborative influence but as the driving logic of the drawing itself. First made in 1970, the piece requires that the drafters draw lines between all the corners, door and window frames, electrical sockets, fire alarms, and any other such elements that break the plane of the wall. The iterations that have resulted—made up of long, overlapping lines—are reminiscent of perspectival grids or airline route maps and belie the simple, objective concept that produced them. Given the long distances between many of the points to be connected, to create the drawing LeWitt used a snap-line, a tool used in construction to draw straight lines in chalk. Not only does the drawing outmaneuver the architect, one might say, it also appropriates an essential tool of the builder's trade. The snap-line technique also made simpler a task that would be more daunting, if not impossible, with the standard pencil and straightedge used for most of LeWitt's drawings of the time.

While the given profile of a wall provides the parameters for *Wall Drawing 51*, the limits of the draftsmen's physical ability also shape this work, necessitating the introduction of this rather unusual method. Indeed, a number of LeWitt drawings are in part shaped by the physical capabilities of the draftsmen, including *Wall Drawing 146*, in which the lengths of the arcs and lines are, according to LeWitt's notes, "determined by the average person's reach to draw an arc (about a yard or meter)."[9]

4. The work has been installed in spaces as varied as the stables of Giuseppe Panza di Biumo's Villa Litta in Varese, Italy, and the large-scale walls of the Guggenheim Museum Bilbao in Spain.

5. LeWitt, "Illustrations: Works by Sol LeWitt," p. 130.

6. Ibid., p. 135.

7. LeWitt, "Illustrations: Works by Sol LeWitt," p. 135.

8. LeWitt, "Wall Drawings," in Legg, ed., *Sol LeWitt*, p. 169; reprinted from *Arts Magazine* 44, no. 6 (April 1970).

9. LeWitt, "Illustrations: Works by Sol LeWitt," p. 130. The form of additional works, including *Wall Drawing 123: Copied lines*, is determined by the draftsmen's physical attributes—in this example, their height and reach.

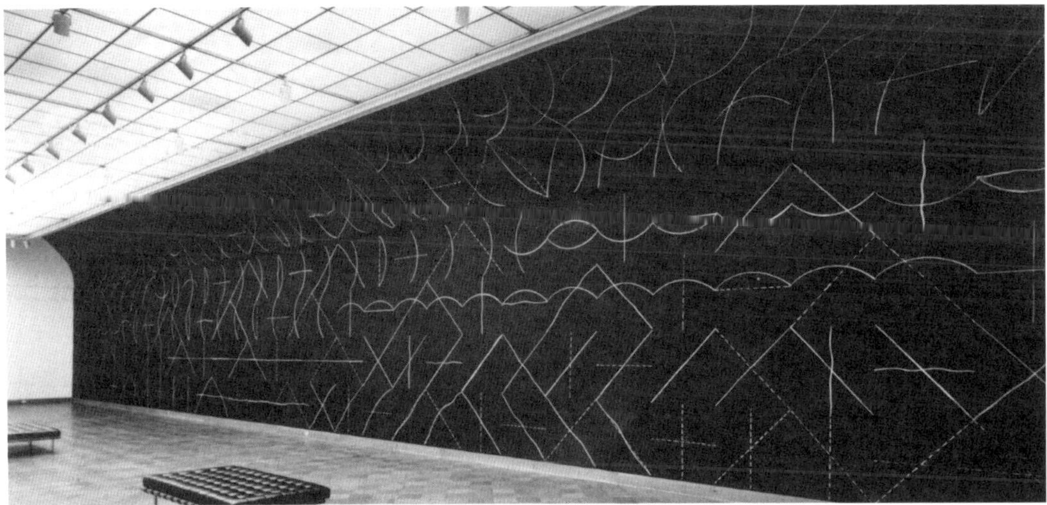

Sol LeWitt. *Wall Drawing 260: On black walls, all two-part combinations of white arcs from corners and sides, and white straight, not straight and broken lines.* June 1975. White crayon, black wall. Collection of The Museum of Modern Art, New York, gift of an anonymous donor. Installation view: San Francisco Museum of Modern Art, 1975. Photo: Rudy Bender, San Francisco

Thus the physical limits of the draftsman and the obstacles presented by the walls themselves are part of the notion of constraint integral to LeWitt's art, seen most notably in his limited vocabulary of forms. His investigation of the relationship between restriction and creativity places him within a long tradition of artists who have imposed on their work a particular set of parameters, whether formal, conceptual, or physical. In this last regard LeWitt's work has an interesting connection to that of a number of performance artists. In his *Drawing Restraint* series (begun 1987), for example, Matthew Barney drew on his studio walls while encumbered by physical restraints. In 1973 Carolee Schneeman had done virtually the same in a performance, *Up to and Including Her Limits,* in which she drew on a wall while hanging from a harness. In 1967 and 1968 Bruce Nauman had filmed himself performing simple, repeated actions within a square area taped out on his studio floor. Even earlier Nauman had created a work on paper that, for me, articulates LeWitt's own strategy. Titled *Brown Crayon Box* (1966), this drawing depicts a single crayon tied to an open-cube form strangely reminiscent of LeWitt's open cubes. Nauman's image of the device for drawing seems to imply some pending action that, if described, might sound like one of LeWitt's instructions: "A line drawn from the corner as far as the string can reach." The line's color would be determined by the attached crayon, and the line's arc or length determined by the string, both elements resulting from constraints much like the size of a wall or the height of a specific drafter for LeWitt.

While a form itself may have limits, its use does not. Embedded in LeWitt's simple vocabulary of forms—characterized by his use of the iconic yet "uninteresting" cube[10]—is the notion of liberation. "Everyone gets into their own box and enunciates principles," LeWitt said in an interview in 2003. "You have your own constraints and your own structure…, and then you realize that what you're saying is 'I can do this, but I can't do that.' And then at some point you say, 'Well, why not?'…'Every wall is a door.'"[11] Acquainted with his sense of humor, I can imagine LeWitt repeating the words of Mae West, another legendary artist and performer: "I like restraint, if it doesn't go too far."

10. LeWitt, "The Cube," in Legg, ed., *Sol LeWitt*, p. 172; reprinted from Lucy R. Lippard, et al., "Homage to the Square," *Art in America* 55, no. 4 (July–Aug. 1967), p. 54.

11. Saul Ostrow, "Sol LeWitt" (interview), *Bomb* magazine, no. 85 (fall 2003), http://www.bombsite.com/issues/85/articles/2583.

Roland Dahinden
Composer and musician

constant motion

take a number
it will determine the number of speakers and pitches
use fifths from string instruments
each fifth sounds in various colors
every color appears in a different light
the sounds are somewhat long and soft
no more than three pitches sound simultaneously
each speaker emits a single pitch or silence
the speakers are arranged irregularly on the floor
the sounds move slowly through the space
they enable silence
use all combinations of pitch, color, and motion
create a logarithm that randomly selects all parameters
all decisions are based on prime numbers
this is a sound installation

Tara Donovan
Artist

Karen Dow
Artist

In thinking about the work of Sol LeWitt, I often find myself focusing less on his role as an originator of Conceptual art practices and more on the subtle details that can be found in specific pieces. While his contributions to the field have clearly provided the aesthetic training and critical language for a whole generation of contemporary artists, myself included, I find the most pleasure in some of the unexpected moments of my experience with Sol's work. His rule-based systems for the creation of his works are something that I have incorporated into my own practice, but I have never subscribed to the idea that his directorial approach was somehow intentionally lacking intimacy. For me, his wall drawings have been particularly influential, because they achieve on a two-dimensional plane through their intense linear repetition what I strive to accomplish in three dimensions with the accumulation of objects. Sol's expansive fields of visual activity, which create seismic perceptual shifts, opened artistic practice and its audiences to an understanding of "installation" as both an extension of the studio and a new form of display that demands the consideration of contingent factors, such as the architectural specifics of a given space. I must contend with his legacy within that expanded context—so successfully articulated by Sol—in order to produce work that continues to challenge received conventions.

The breadth of Sol LeWitt's work is ever inspiring and challenging. One sees in his art the patience to trust in a process that leads, by degrees, to a satisfying completion, a wholeness of aesthetic interconnections.

As a young painter, I found it difficult to trust my impulses toward the accumulative, the geometric, the sublime, and the ordered. The humbleness of LeWitt's vision and the workmanship required to pull off his projects have created a context in which the ordinary can become extraordinary. Simple forms combine to achieve profound beauty. My experience of his work has left me a more confident painter and continually informs my teaching.

In 2001 I was lucky enough to help lead a group of high-school students in the making of four wall drawings. The experience will stay with me always. The transformation of the group in working toward a common goal was beautiful to watch, everyone finding his or her strengths and participating accordingly. I know that the students' experience of the project surpassed their expectations and imbued in them a sense of art-making they will never forget.

Tom Doyle
Artist

Megan Dyer
Artist and LeWitt draftsman

When I think of Sol LeWitt and his accomplishments, I think of J. S. Bach. Their prodigious output and their variations on themes are comparable. LeWitt's work includes so many permutations and transformations, yet he always stayed true to his original concepts. His work, influence, and generosity will continue to go on and on.

The basic structure for draftsmen of Sol LeWitt's works is like this: you get a call about a project, and you pack the necessary clothes and supplies. You arrive at a museum or a private residence with the plan for the piece, and meet the people who will help you install the work, that is, your crew. You have brought very basic tools: a compass, a measuring tape, a straightedge, pencils, drafting tape, and so on. My favorite, seemingly obscure, tool to carry along on projects is a plumb bob, replaced by some draftsmen with a laser level. The work time needed is largely determined first by the piece, second by how precisely the wall preparation was completed in advance, and lastly by the efficiency of the crew that has been hired to assist on the project. Efficiency in this regard is very basic and demands the ability to focus, follow through with instructions, and maintain attention to detail. It is not necessary to have any art background, but it can be helpful with certain kinds of materials used.

The experience of drafting a LeWitt drawing is almost always the same, and, in this way, the drafting is another kind of system that parallels the systems that Sol uses himself. The draftsman's experience in making a piece is all part of this system. As intricate and complicated as a piece may be, it is always based on the same basic system. The fact that this system is essentially foolproof is why I think it is safe to use the term *genius* to describe Sol, and why his work will continue to be made far into the future, something no other artist has been able to achieve. His art operates as actual, functional immortality.

Spencer Finch

Artist

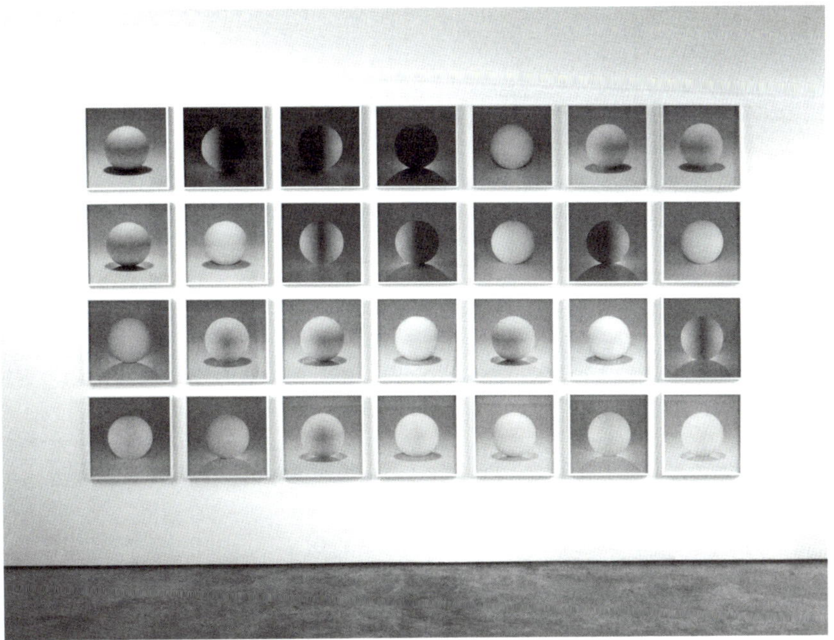

Sol LeWitt. *A sphere lit from the top, four sides and all their combinations.* 2004. Courtesy of the Estate of Sol LeWitt and Lisson Gallery. Photo courtesy of Lisson Gallery, London

It was the worst hangover of my life, and it was Sol's fault. I only met him once, when I had an exhibition in Hartford. I went to Chester with the curator and registrar of the Wadsworth Atheneum, and Sol took us all out to dinner. To be honest, I don't remember too much from the evening, because I went from extremely nervous to extremely drunk somewhere around the salad course. But I do vividly remember Sol being very generous with the wine (it was expensive Burgundy), and my near coma the next day was a testament to that generosity.

I am old enough now to not be embarrassed to say that I have tried over the years, mostly unsuccessfully, to follow Sol's example. His work ethic, his democratic impulse, his range of production, his sensualism disguised as conceptualism, his support of other artists and fledgling institutions, and, yes, his generosity. It is a modus operandi that is known far and wide, yet still very rare and all but impossible to imitate. Of course, in the end, what really matters is the work that rose out of this, and the work is incredible. My experience with Sol's work is consistent with my reaction to all the work that moves me the most and makes me love being an artist. This occurred even recently, when I happened

upon the work *A sphere lit from the top, four sides, and all their combinations* (2004) for the first time. My three-step response is always the same, whether it's Holbein or LeWitt, the same predictable sequence of emotional convulsions:

1. "Wow, that is thought and form combined in pure genius." (Swoon and/or tingle)
2. "Shit, why do I even bother, what's the point in the face of this?" (Collapse)
3. "Fuck him! I'm going back into the studio and do even better, he's not going to have the last word!" (Red face, danger of coronary arrest)

So, if Sol doesn't kill me or make me quit, he will keep me going, spurring me to make better and better work, to try to rise to his level. And I will keep at it, because I know of no other way than to try to use what I have to its greatest effect. I never knew Sol well enough to solicit advice from him, but I can imagine him saying, about wine as well as about talent, "Pour it like you don't own it!"

Alec Finlay
Artist and poet

arc**S**
bec**O**me
Lines

Lines
cub**E**s
Which
Illustrates
concep**T**ual
mys**T**icism

Martin Friedman
Director Emeritus, Walker Art Center,
Minneapolis

Two Sides of Sol

Sol LeWitt was really a romantic. His work took on an increasingly personal tone despite its formulaic basis. For an artist so involved with systems of his own invention, what came forth in his wall drawings transcended mere methodology. Some of these systems were handwritten, step-by-step procedures; others were based on numerical series. These led to such phenomena as vibrant networks of delicately drawn grids overlaid with arcs and circles, and also to cubes, parallelograms, and rhomboids floating in space. Unlike many a fellow Conceptual artist, Sol was never hostage to his systems. Not only did he break their rules whenever it suited him, he also moved freely from one idea to another.

Other things were going on in his mind, I think, beyond form-building: meditations on the nature of space, perception, and the sensory effects of light, line, and color. He played perspectival games with shapes that simultaneously advanced and receded. Despite his disdain for evidence of the artist's hand, his wall drawings, especially those in color, became increasingly subjective. That they were realized for him by artist assistants made no difference. The shift toward the personal is especially evident in his last series, the *Scribble* drawings. Their giant cylinders and arches, drawn in layers of graphite, might be portals to infinity.

Mildred Friedman
Design curator

Sol LeWitt and Design

In the late 1960s Sol became an avid collector of the furniture of Gerrit Rietveld. He admired the collaborative works of Rietveld, Vilmos Huszár, and other De Stijl artists, whose works involved painting colored, rectangular elements on the walls of modernist interiors. These wall paintings predict much that was to follow in Sol's mature work. Although LeWitt was aware that De Stijl was a social movement as well as an aesthetic one, he insisted that in his work, "Forms are only what they are, nothing more or less. When I make a triangle, it is only a triangle."[1] Perhaps most significant to his development was the fact that, like architects, LeWitt eventually hired other artists to execute the constructions and wall drawings he envisioned in innumerable small-scale sketches.

---

1. LeWitt in Martin Friedman, "Echoes of De Stijl," in Mildred Friedman, ed., *De Stijl, 1917–1931: Visions of Utopia*, exh. cat. (Minneapolis: Walker Art Center; New York: Abbeville Press, 1982), p. 211.

Gary Garrels
Elise S. Haas Senior Curator of Painting and Sculpture, San Francisco Museum of Modern Art

When the Sol LeWitt retrospective opened at the San Francisco Museum of Modern Art in February 2000, what was most immediate and stunning was the sense of the extraordinary diversity and fecundity of his work. I am sure that for anyone who sees the more than one hundred wall drawings on view at MASS MoCA the lasting impression will be even more astonishing. The chance to see the wall drawings in a compact and almost kaleidoscopic unfolding over four decades—from the ethereal early pencil drawings to the boldly patterned and colored acrylic late works—is unprecedented. This latest exhibition of LeWitt in Massachusetts offers an encounter with an artistic trajectory of unceasing invention, and is a testament to the constant alertness of this artist's mind and imagination.

To understand how LeWitt might have produced such diverse works, it may be useful to go back to his early declaration of his principles of art, "Paragraphs on Conceptual Art," written and published in 1967, two years before the first wall drawing. At that time LeWitt was focused on making three-dimensional objects that he referred to as "structures." While relatively short, the text holds the keys to approaching and understanding LeWitt's work for the remainder of his career. One of the paragraphs reads as follows:

To work with a plan that is pre-set is one way of avoiding subjectivity. It also obviates the necessity of designing each work in turn. The plan would design the work. Some plans would require millions of variations, and some a limited number, but both are finite. Other plans imply infinity. In each case, however, the artist would select the basic form and rules that would govern the solution of the problem. After that the fewer decisions made in the course of completing the work, the better. This eliminates the arbitrary, the capricious, and the subjective as much as possible. That is the reason for using this method.

By freeing his art from the subjective self—that amalgam of emotion and life experience that underlies expression and thought—LeWitt distanced himself from style. Rather he could work through the implications of an idea and then be free to move on, once he considered the idea to have been explored thoroughly.

Two years later, in the spring of 1969 and just a few months before making the first wall drawing, LeWitt wrote what might be considered an appendix, his "Sentences on Conceptual Art," a much shorter and more gnomic manifesto. Two of those sentences, the first and fifth, also help one to grasp the heart of LeWitt's approach to art:

Conceptual Artists are mystics rather than rationalists. They leap to conclusions that logic cannot reach....
Irrational thoughts should be followed absolutely and logically.

The year before writing these statements, LeWitt, in a private act, had executed one of his most resolutely conceptual works: he dug a hole in which he buried a small cube, documenting the work through a grid of nine photographs, which were mounted and titled *Buried Cube Containing an Object of Importance but Little Value*. From 1964 until 1968 the core of LeWitt's artistic production was related to three-dimensional objects that were variations on cubes and their combinations. While LeWitt would go on over the years to reengage the cube in one way or another, this work bracketed the end of the cube and the three-dimensional structures as the focus of his work. The wall drawings took on that central role the following year.

Throughout LeWitt's work one can find the points at which he exhausted an idea and shifted to a new set of parameters. In most cases these are subtle, and only occasionally are they more abrupt, as in the shift from the structures to the wall drawings. The first forty-five wall drawings were made within a year with various combinations of straight lines; in 1970 in *Wall Drawing 46: Vertical lines, not straight, not touching, covering the wall evenly,* LeWitt introduced the "not straight line" to great effect. Following very direct, simple sets of instructions, all these drawings produced visually rich and complex works. This would generally be the case until 1974, when LeWitt initiated a series of what he referred to as *Location* drawings, in which the instructions became increasingly elaborate to the point of absurdity, often resulting in what appeared to be extremely simple, minimal manifestations. *Wall Drawing 232: The location of a square* (1975) is a prime example. Of course, the greatest rupture in the wall drawings occurred in 1981, when LeWitt drastically changed their materials, from pencil or crayon to ink washes, and introduced three-dimensional illusions. A similar radical shift occurred in 1997 with the introduction of acrylic paint as the medium for the works he continued to identify as "wall drawings," although they could more accurately be called "wall paintings."

Of the many artists active in the second half of the twentieth century, LeWitt was one of the most rigorous in terms of his thought; he was simultaneously one of the most open. His expansive intellect allowed him to find the simplest and most elegant ideas and solutions for art, circumvent dead ends and foregone conclusions, and embrace paradox and contradiction, essential qualities of art for our time.

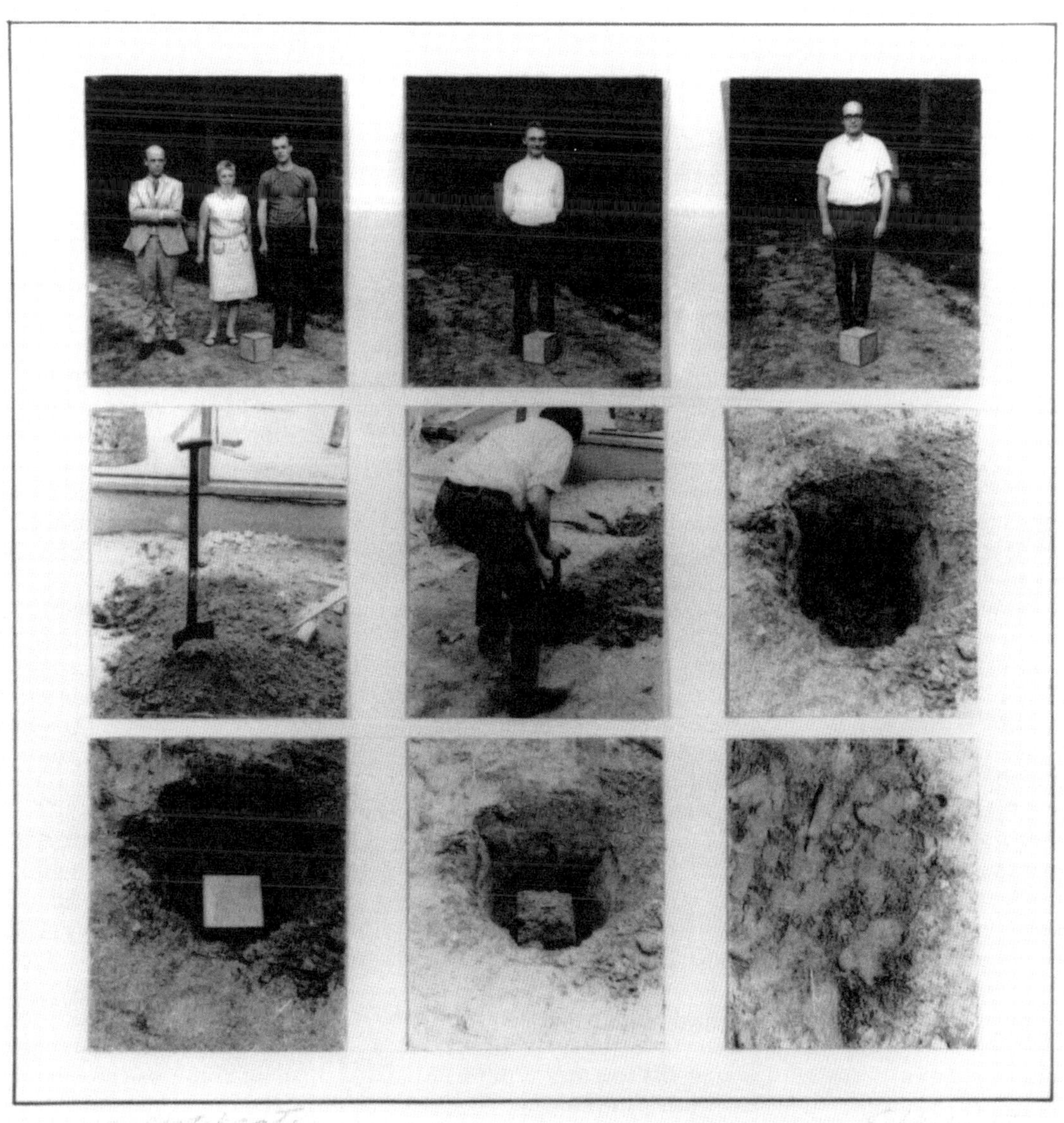

Sol LeWitt. *Buried Cube Containing an Object of Importance but Little Value*. 1968. Black-and-white photographs mounted on paper. LeWitt Collection, Chester Connecticut. Courtesy of the Estate of Sol LeWitt. Photo: Sean McEntee

Mike Glier
Artist

Propagating Wave

What comes to mind when thinking about the art of Sol LeWitt, surprisingly, are images of rivers rippling silently underground and radio waves moving invisibly through space. Like the art of LeWitt, these images exemplify concepts like flow, rhythm, and continuity and demonstrate how energy can move through the world undetected by our senses. But the power that is transported by a LeWitt work is not physical, like a wave of water or energy. It is instead conceptual, and the energy that is released when it encounters resistance is not expressed as erosion or sound but as social transformation.

By establishing a set of elements, say all the permutations of straight, not straight, and curved lines within a grid, and then methodically producing and exhibiting the full set of permutations of these elements, LeWitt proposes that all possibilities within a system are potentially interesting. In the context of art history, which has for centuries created and supported hierarchies of quality and significance, this proposition is radical. Like John Cage's seminal *4′33″*, the art of LeWitt suggests that being open to possibility is in itself satisfying and is preferable to quick judgment, an act that all too often curtails curiosity and experimentation.

But the challenge posed to judgment does not flatten the aesthetic pleasure of contemplating a work by LeWitt. Contrasting experiences, like beauty and ugliness, are not irrelevant in this nonhierarchical art. They are instead experienced as two sides of the same concept, whole, like a coin with two faces. In the case of beauty and ugliness, they form a single idea, the concept of appearance.

The systems established by LeWitt are not utopian. Unlike such systems, which are often closed to variation and, as a result, whither in changing circumstances, many of LeWitt's works of art are adaptive. For example, the instructions for one wall drawing require a number of drafters to make a mark starting high on a wall, their heights determining the outcome of the shape of the drawing.[1] Some works can be resized to accommodate new locations. Like a healthy ecosystem, LeWitt's aesthetic environment incorporates variability as a means to survive the inevitability of change.

This all might sound overly theoretical and irrelevant to daily experience, but the effects of seeing much of LeWitt's art are substantial and transformative. At first, artworks that exemplify

classic design ideas like symmetry, balance, rhythm, subtlety, and contrast appear beautiful, and others that demonstrate anti-design ideas, like irregularity, lopsidedness, asynchrony, brashness, and monotony, are less attractive. But in the full context of his work, these distinctions become confused. "The first question I ask myself when something doesn't seem to be beautiful," Cage once said, "is why do I think it's not beautiful. And very shortly you discover that there is no reason." Experiencing a room of LeWitt work is inevitably a challenge to how each of us determines what is aesthetically pleasing and what is not. Our prejudices, say for a straight line over a crooked one, are brought into consideration, and seem trivial compared to the abundance of possibility that LeWitt presents as an alternative source of pleasure. LeWitt convincingly posits that embracing an array of possibilities is more pleasurable and generative than limiting those possibilities. Difference, in this world view, is not threatening or destabilizing in itself, but is instead a prompt to curiosity, a catalyst for experimentation, and, potentially, a source of delight. This idea, when applied to a world struggling to globalize, is profound.

---

1. The work is *Wall Drawing 123: Copied lines. The first draftsman draws a not straight vertical line as long as possible. The second draftsman draws a line next to the first one, trying to copy it. The third draftsman does the same, as do as many draftsmen as possible. Then the first draftsman, followed by the others, copies the last line drawn until both ends of the wall are reached* (1972).

Dan Graham
Artist

Sol's Humor

I want to mention the humor in Sol LeWitt's work. After his first show at John Daniel's Gallery of wood works, Sol said with characteristic, anarchistic humor that they should be recycled as firewood. Sol's earliest grid structures, he told me, with a dig at the reigning soft humanism, were built as jungle gyms for his cats.

Sol's humor often had a sexual aspect. An early Muybridge-influenced photobox, with peepholes, used an image of a naked woman which spectators could see in a sequence of ever-closer-up shots, each one appearing to come in ever closer to the woman's genitals. The final view was not of her privates, but of her belly button. You could read this work as anti-Duchampian[1] as it wasn't an ironic redo of Courbet's painting *The Origin of the World*—Duchamp's *Given: 1. The Waterfall, 2. The Illuminating Gas*—that is, it was not viewed through a peephole. Sol's work might have been more about the baby Sol LeWitt.

Artists of the mid-1960s often based their work on humor, especially deadpan, banal dumbness, which turned out to be very intelligent. Sol LeWitt's early work, using simple grids, was first perceived as banal.

Many proto-Conceptual artists, such as On Kawara, Stanley Brown, and myself, did work that evoked an anarchistic and/or existentialist sense of humor. In my work I was especially influenced by the ironic humor of two fellow Jewish artists, Roy Lichtenstein and Sol LeWitt.

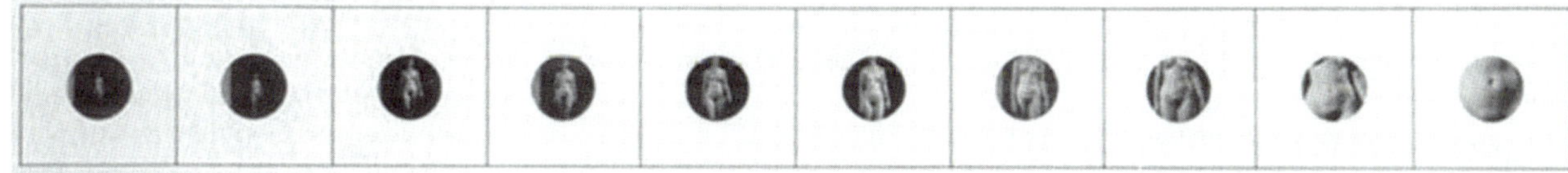

Sol LeWitt. *Schematic for Muybridge I*, 1964/1969. Published in 1970 by Multiples, Inc., New York

1. New York "Minimal" artists disdained Duchamp's readymades, and were more influenced by the often quasi-functional works of Russian Constructivism.

John Hogan
Artist and LeWitt draftsman

The nature of a successful artwork is in its conviction.
The nature of conviction is a belief and an inherent sense of truth.
A truth of one's own device is flawless.

The privilege of working as a draftsman has allowed me to understand and be intimate with Sol's language and the truth that lies within his thinking. For each move and shift— be it from pencil, to crayon, to ink, to paint—the thought that preceded it came as a new form, line, color, or approach, never veering from the first thoughts but only growing and transforming. A new artwork thereby contained the idea and places already visited, yet also had a new context that reaffirmed and moved forward in thought and visualization.

Over the twenty-five years I worked for Sol, there were moments as I was executing a new drawing when Sol's work made a shift. As the draftsman, I would follow his instructions and wonder where the new drawing might be going; as always, through the process of executing the drawing, the idea would reveal itself in the completed work. The work process always stemmed from the direct and specific directions Sol gave without ever stating the why of his decisions. The drawings never wavered from his decisions, relying on the viewer to catch up with the ideas that became the new work.

A pivotal moment in my relationship to Sol's work occurred in 1997, when he began to engage painting in his acrylic wall drawings with flat and glossy forms. My own work as a painter had always been structured by a decision-based approach, relating to composition, content, and material; the tenets of painting. Sol then created a body of work where a single color was brought into a completely new territory, structured by the decision to reference paint's properties and reintroduce his unending engagement with the idea of a square divided into four parts. The decision was both incisive and mystical, qualities he had attributed to artists some years ago. The work seemed to swallow up so much that was seen as painting, yet was now placed in a different light, only needing his idea. The work came alive through the process of rendering it; the acuteness of his thought was ever present. These new drawings became a liberating moment in my own art-making; they became a catalyst of change in my approach to painting. If I were to adapt the often employed analogy of music to Sol's work, for me his new drawings became my insight into a note I had approached over and over, but had never hit the way I wanted to until then. At the same time, I gained further insight into Sol's work.

The thought process that allows the idea to flow freely from one drawing to the next—each recognizing the knowledge of its precedents without invalidating the past, always referencing the earlier premise and reaffirming it with a new perspective and thought—is Sol's truth, yet it informs all art. The wall drawings' unwavering commitment is that the tools and materials always serve the idea, never allowing the idea to become subservient to the tools, as has so commonly been the fashion.

The mental clarity of Sol's work gave artists a new vernacular of idea first and then execution. As a stated truth, the idea became a medium for artists to work with, myself included, in which the first decision creates the conviction of the completed work.

One of the last new drawings that I was able to work on, in early 2007 before Sol's death, was *Wall Drawing 821A: A white square divided horizontally and vertically into four equal parts, each with a different direction of alternating flat and glossy bands*. It was for an exhibition at Sean Kelly Gallery in New York titled *Pure*. Sol called me and, over the phone, told me how he wanted to scale the drawing and how the white was to be done. I spent roughly a week installing it. Once it was completed I was taken completely off guard, deeply moved by the drawing, which created a form I had been intimately familiar with for some twenty-odd years. Somehow here was a new, previously unknown thought as powerful as the earlier one, another iteration of the mystical yet simultaneously direct and simple statement, "Lines in four directions."

I learned many things through my experience as a draftsman for Sol, the most important of which is that the work that succeeds comes from the clarity of the idea and the commitment to the vision of what it is one's art embraces.

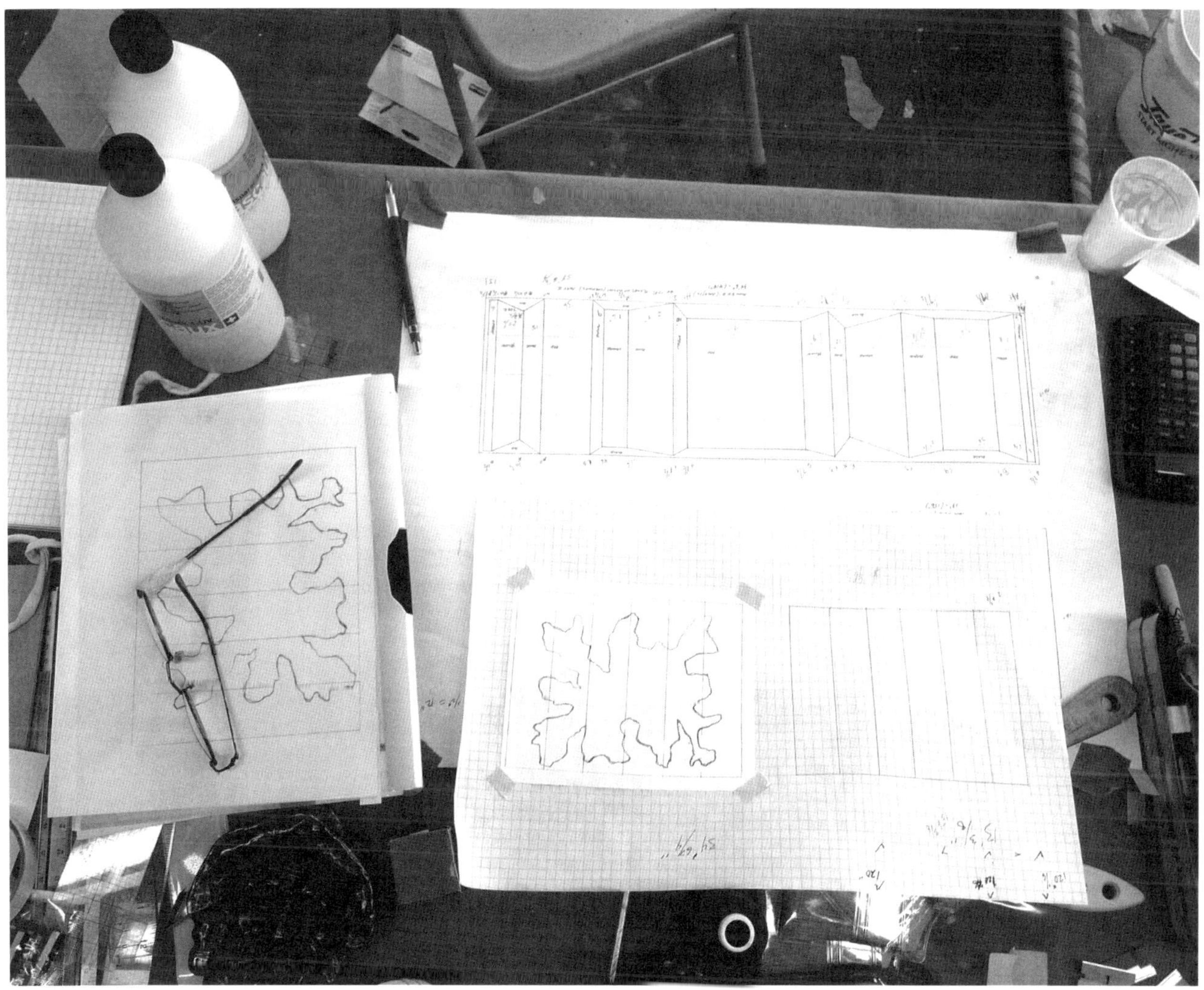

Installation of *Sol LeWitt: A Wall Drawing Retrospective* at MASS MoCA. 2008. Photo: Chris Cobb

Chrissie Iles
Anne and Joel Ehrenkranz Curator,
Whitney Museum of American Art,
New York

Sol LeWitt, Lucinda Childs, and Philip Glass: *Dance*

In 1979 Lucinda Childs and Philip Glass invited Sol LeWitt to collaborate with them on a new work titled *Dance*. The collaboration brought the shared minimalist language of the three artists into a tightly structured dialogue. Glass's musical score formed the framework for Childs's choreography, to which Sol responded by creating a film whose structure counterpointed the dancers' movements in two dimensions. This complex, multilayered, modular form echoed Sol's intent in his *Serial Project 1* (1966) that "the entire work would contain subdivisions which could be autonomous but which comprise the whole," the premise being "to place one form within another and include all major variations in two and three dimensions."[1]

Sol's filmic collaboration extended his wall drawings into three dimensions, his open-cube structures into four dimensions, and his interest in Eadweard Muybridge into an ambitiously scaled form. Applying white lines to form a grid of large squares on the dark stage, he adapted the perspectival floor grid of *ABCD* (1966) and *Incomplete Open Cubes* (1974) to create a framework for the dancers' movements, evoking the graph-like background used by Muybridge in his taxonomic studies of the body in motion.

For two days Lucinda and Sol, with Lisa Rinzler behind the camera, shot the dancers performing selected excerpts of Lucinda's choreography in a studio on Eighth Street. Sol's ability to translate visual structures into temporal form is revealed in his early observation that "regular spacing might become a metric time element, a kind of regular beat or pulse."[2] In two early sculptures, *Muybridge I* (1964) and *Muybridge II* (1964), he had already explored this observation in proto-filmic terms. In each sculpture, a sequence of black-and-white photographs of a naked female body, shot progressively closer to the camera, was pasted into closed compartments inside a long, black, horizontal box, mounted at eye level.[3] The action of the viewer walking along the box, peering through a small hole cut into each compartment, creates the illusion of a figure set in motion, like a three-dimensional flick-book. A lightbulb flashing on and off inside, like a pulse, evokes the interval between film frames.

In *Dance* Sol actualized this illusion of movement. In three of the five sections of the performance ("Dance no. 1," "Dance no. 3," and "Dance no. 4"), the floor was brought into a dialogue with the wall by projecting the black-and-white film of the same sections of the dance onto a large, transparent, vertical scrim, the size of a large wall drawing. The dancers moving across the black-and-white floor grid were visible through the scrim until the projected images of the previously filmed dance obscured them, replacing them with their filmed equivalent. The action of the film and scrim on the visibility of the live performance evoked another core element of *ABCD*, whose structure is predicated on the relationship between the visible and the hidden.[4] Since the closed structures follow the same logical pattern as the open ones in *ABCD*, we know that each closed element contains the same hidden form as its open equivalent.

The scrim in *Dance* produced a similar dynamic between the hidden and the visible. Sometimes the dancers were visible through the scrim; at other times the projected film obscured them; yet the viewer knew that they were there, even when they could not be seen except in a ghostly filmic echo. In one solo passage Sol blew Lucinda's face up on the film to fill the entire screen, while she could be seen dancing the same movement behind it, rendered small by comparison, like one of Muybridge's athletes.

The dialogue between the hidden and visible movement of the dancers was also echoed with the structure of the film itself. Sol split the screen into two, then four sections, placing images shot at different times side by side and guiding the viewer's attention back and forth between the dance projected on the scrim and the movements occurring in real time and space behind it. Sol's technique echoes that of Lucinda, who, as Henry M. Sayre observes, "explicitly explores a geometry of repetition and reflection."[5] In *Einstein on the Beach*

---

1. Sol LeWitt, "Serial Project No. 1," *Aspen Magazine*, nos. 5–6 (1966) item 17, unpaginated.

2. LeWitt, "Paragraphs on Conceptual Art," *Artforum* 5, no. 10 (June 1967), pp 79–83.

3. In *Muybridge I* Sol photographed the woman walking toward the camera. In *Muybridge II* he photographed the same woman seated, as he moved progressively closer to the figure rather than the figure moving toward him.

4. I am grateful to Susanna Singer for pointing this out to me.

5. Henry M. Sayre, *The Object of Performance: The American Avant-Garde since 1970* (Chicago: The University of Chicago Press, 1989), p. 126.

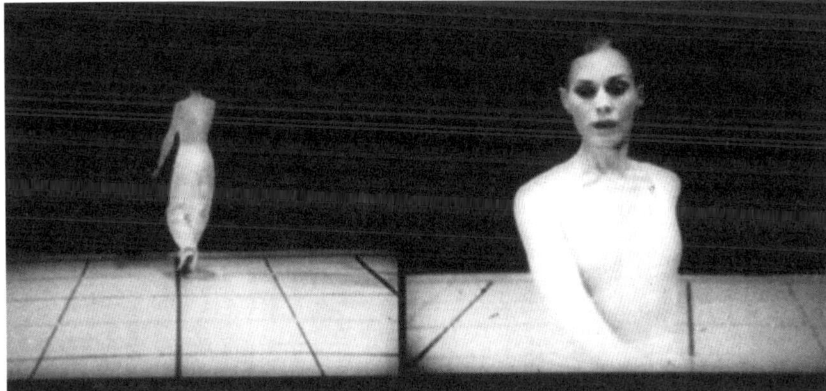

Lucinda Childs
Dance Company.
Dance. 1979. Brooklyn
Academy of Music.
Photo: Nathaniel
Tileston

(1976), another triadic collaboration, out of which *Dance* emerged, Lucinda's dance occurs twice. Doubling, Sayre says, had become Lucinda's trademark. In *Dance* Sol echoes Lucinda's serial doubling. In another kind of mirroring, the dance also occurs twice, but this time simultaneously, in real and recorded time.

In his wall drawings Sol had already rewritten the language of painting by altering its internal structure, eliminating the canvas stretcher, and drawing directly on walls of varying sizes and shapes in predetermined architectural locations. Now he pushed the parameters even further by introducing transparency. In rendering the floor behind the scrim visible, he challenged what Rosalind Krauss has termed "the myths of human erectness and 'pure visuality'" in painting—and also, by implication, in painting's cousin, cinema.[6] Horizontality, a plane outside the axis of the human body, makes the pure visuality of both painting and cinema impossible. Furthermore, the presence of the dancers both on the scrim and behind it dismantled what Yve-Alain Bois describes as the

opposition between representation and action upon which the histories of painting are predicated.[7]

This was made further evident by the lighting of the stage behind the scrim in blue ("Dance no. 1"), yellow ("Dance no. 3"), and red ("Dance no. 5"). The resulting sense of volumetric space contrasted, in no. 1 and no. 3, with the flat space of the black-and-white film projected on the scrim. In the resulting dialogue between actual and filmed space, the frontal movements of the live dancers were contradicted by Sol's use of close-ups, diagonal viewpoints, overhead shots, split screens, and freeze-frames to reveal otherwise hidden perspectives of the dancers' movements, echoing Muybridge's photographing of athletes in motion from the sides and from oblique angles, within a specially constructed box and against a gridded black background.

Sol's ability to translate Lucinda's dance notation into a conceptual filmic composition could already be detected in a diagram he made for the August 1969 issue of *Harper's Bazaar*, in which he laid out the sequence of the action in Samuel Beckett's three-minute

play *Come and Go* (1965), half of which is composed of silence (for which one could substitute, in *Dance*, invisibility). The modular diagram of the three women's precisely choreographed movements anticipates the structure of his film for *Dance* thirteen years later. In both cases, space becomes a unit of time contained within a grid, a format that can imply progressive movement, yet be perceived as a whole simultaneously.

This paradox underlines one of Sol's greatest, and most radical, contributions to art—his assertion in his 1967 "Paragraphs on Conceptual Art" that the idea is paramount. That simple statement, one of the major breakthroughs of the 1960s, rendered the conventions of space, scale, and medium irrelevant. The surface of a wall can be equal to that of a page, and something static, or visible, equal to something temporal, or hidden. This equivalence is clearly evident in *Dance*, where film, music, and dance are brought together in a seamless conceptual whole. To quote Sol: "Conceptual art is good only when the idea is good."[8]

6. Rosalind E. Krauss and Yve-Alain Bois, *Formless: A User's Guide* (New York: Zone Books, 1997), p. 32.

7. Yve-Alain Bois, *Painting As Model* (Cambridge, Massachusetts: The MIT Press, 1993), p. 254.

8. LeWitt, "Paragraphs on Conceptual Art."

Ralph Iwamoto
Artist

The vertical line, horizontal line, right diagonal, and left diagonal, these are the signature elements Sol LeWitt employed in his wall drawings, works on paper, and prints. The hanging wall structures, his standing structures, and his installation work in grid format and in series are all to be admired, but for me it was the hanging wall structures that I came to love. One, an untitled piece from the 1960s, resembling railroad ties or an endless white fence, stands out. The structure is made of an $8 \times 8 \times \frac{1}{2}$ inch plywood panel, to which is attached the ties, or fencelike grid structure, consisting of $6 \times \frac{1}{2} \times \frac{1}{2}$ inch stripping. All parts are painted entirely in white, that is, on the front and sides but not the back of the structure. The top is indicated by the hanging wire on the back on screws. At least eight screws are placed on the back: four to attach the grid structure to the panel, two to hang the work, and two more screws to keep the structure balanced flat to the wall. The paint is flat white or matte, without any gloss. The grid structure is centered on the panel, and the structure, which is like a comb, faces to the left, like a backward, stacked, double E.

Mel Kendrick
Artist

Sol sometimes told students, "Don't worry what it looks like, you'll get used to it." A funny thing to say, and like many of Sol's quietly deadpan statements, it could leave your head spinning.

Think of his "Sentences on Conceptual Art" (1969). I completely misinterpreted them when I first encountered them in the 1970s. They fit easily into the then current dialogue of the end of painting, the death of the art object. An idea alone could be art? This created a dilemma similar to that created by Duchamp's readymades: great for discussion and theory, but how did you continue working?

It is clear to me, reading the sentences now, that they are, in fact, all about working. Sol did not denigrate painting or sculpture. He simply said that to think in those categories was limiting. He did say that new materials do not constitute new ideas, and that you cannot make good art from a banal idea, no matter how well it is executed. How could you disagree with that?

The real directive was clarity. A concept should be carried through to its conclusion. Then if something you have done alters your perception, use it in your next work. If you worry what it looks like, you might never have that luxury.

Robin Heidi Kennedy
Artist

As time goes by, and with it all the people, places, and things that either help or hinder artists in finishing their work, my thoughts constantly return toward how Sol seemed to quite naturally, by a unique disposition of his remarkable brain, conquer the challenges that so plague most of us, posed by stubborn realities like time, space, and matter. While almost everyone else complains about not ever having enough time to prepare a show or complete a commission, Sol would simply get up at 6:00 a.m. every day and get right to work. What is more, he would be done by lunch, often with time left over for a swim, and have the rest of the day for social or professional encounters, his dog, his family, food, wine, and song. It was a wonder to behold, at once inspiring and reassuring. They should teach it in college.

He had the space problem beat as well. Having enough space is a constant, costly, and at times painful pursuit for just about every other artist I know, but the lion's share of Sol's work doesn't even take up any space until it is realized somewhere else. Even then its dimensions have only those distinct limits determined by his spatial conception. Much like an architect or a theoretical scientist, all he seemed to need most of the time was a nice room with a table and a window in the right place.

As a sculptor, I have a special admiration for the way he dealt with matter. While this particularly cumbersome reality of art production has a way of consuming all the time and space you have, along with all your money, all Sol really needed were pencils, a few brushes, some tubes of paint, and paper. His work—copied neatly in diagrams and instructions without the heavy crates, the insurance, the forms in triplicate, duties, and any of the varied customs rules and regulations—flies right over national borders in the form of many capable, devoted assistants who realize his work all over the world. There is something exhilarating, vaguely radical, about all this; I'd say even anarchic, if it didn't show so much simple common sense.

Although I am still lifting weights, glancing at my watch, and dealing with myriad rules and regulations, I know that many artists now enjoy similarly efficient, immaterial art-making careers as the one Sol pioneered. First, however, somebody had to show us that it could be done, while also giving us something really worthwhile. Sol LeWitt did that then, and his work keeps on doing it now. I figure, with regard to conquering time, space, and matter, mortality is no obstacle. In fact, I hear Sol's best work is yet to come.

v. 4, Remember 9/11

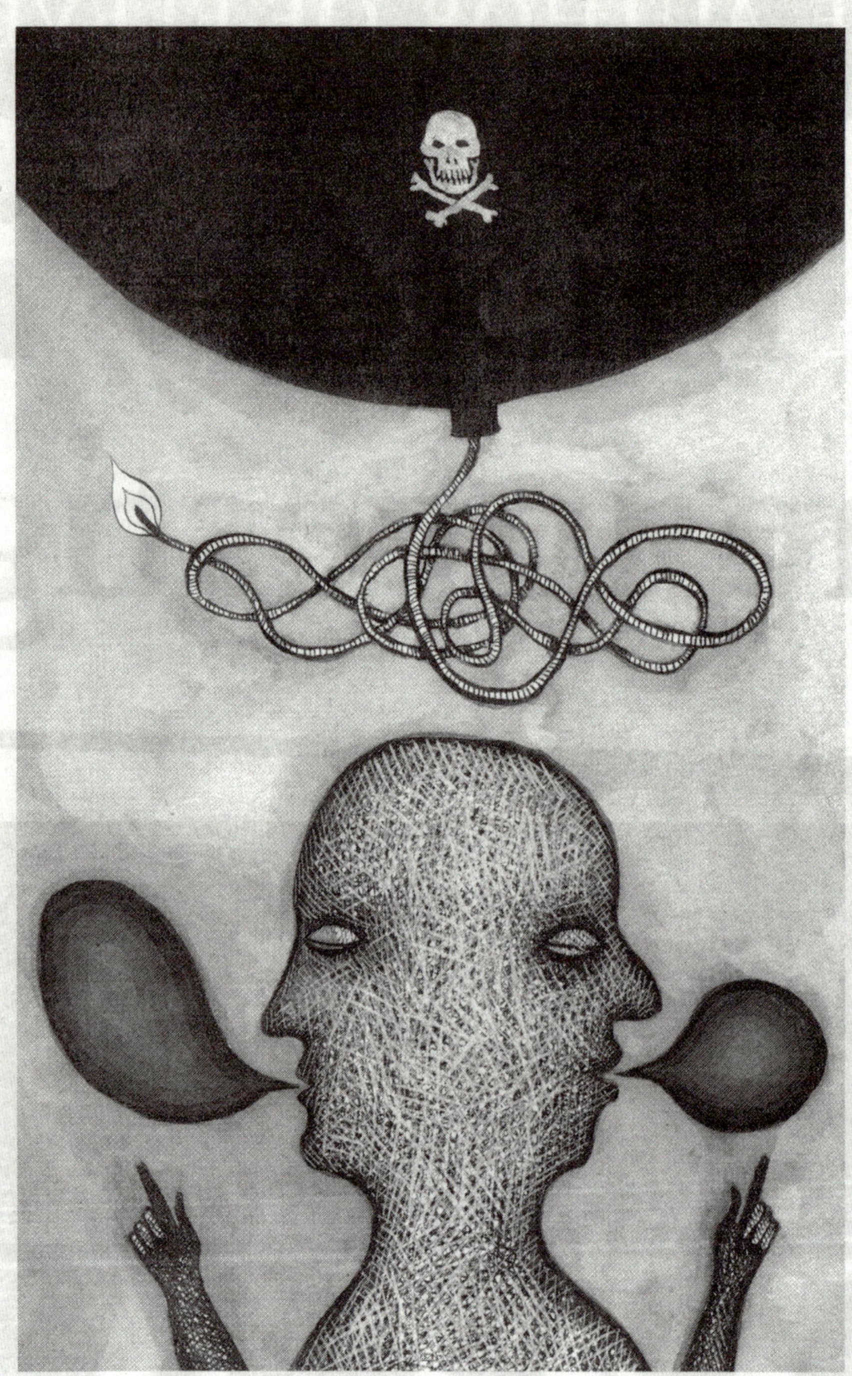

DAVID BROOKS

Surprise Me Most

None of us have ever lived through an election at a time when 80 percent of voters think the country is headed in the wrong direction. But now that we're in the thick of it, a few things are clear. From voters, the demand is: Surprise Me Most. For candidates, the lesson is: Weirdness Wins.

Last winter, Barack Obama succeeded by running a weird campaign. He wasn't just a normal politician aiming for office, he was going to cleanse the country of the baby-boom culture war mentality. In his soaring speeches, he denounced the mores of both the Clinton and Bush eras and made an argument for unity and hope over endless partisan warfare.

But over the course of the spring, Obama's campaign got less weird. The crucial pivot came when he failed to seize on McCain's offer to do a series of joint town-hall meetings across the country. Those meetings would have elevated the race and shown that Obama is willing to take risks in order to truly change the way things are done.

Instead, Obama's speeches became more conventional, more policy-specific and more orthodox. His Denver acceptance speech was different from his Iowa speeches. It was more traditionally anti-Republican and pro-Democratic. In the speech's crucial contrast Obama declared: "It's time for them to own their failure. It's time for us to change America. You see, we Democrats have a very different measure of what constitutes progress in this country."

As David Broder noted, Obama's speech "subordinated any talk of fundamental systemic change to a checklist of traditional Democratic programs."

It is easy to see why Obama might tack this way. Democrats have a huge advantage in a straight-up issue con-

Alain Kirili
Artist

Jannis Kounellis
Artist

Sol LeWitt:
A New Calligrapher

The first times I saw Sol's work, in Germany (in 1969 at the Museum Haus Lange, in Krefeld) and in France (in 1970 at Yvon Lambert, in Paris), I was most strongly impressed by his work's classicism, which could have been my own personal projection. By classicism I mean a meeting between the sophisticated, geometric, abstract forms of the Islamic art and architecture of southern Spain, which I love so much, and the deep connection with the extraordinary tradition of Jewish micro-calligraphy, according to which the Torah should always be written by hand, without any subjective accent.

I felt a deep, sensual rigor in Sol's wall drawings, and that feature of his work stimulated me in the minimalism and voluptuousness of my own early forged sculpture. This work began with regular industrial rod, which was then carefully bent and lightly marked at the top of the sculptures. What appears is a minimal, almost secret, implication of the hand. I have always appreciated this same quality in Sol's work, along with the texture produced by black pencil on the wall; a white wall with black and gray lines of graphite is transformed in my work into space and forged black metal.

I also enjoy sharing the directness of Sol's creation. Drawing and forging are *intimately related*. There is a crucial bit of improvisation in repeated patterns executed by hand: the repetition reveals minute changes in the actions of the hand and the body. We share the dialectic of pattern, repetition, and differences.

Sol wrote about Conceptual art in the May 1969 issue of the magazine *Art Language*:

For each work of art that becomes physical there are many variations that do not....
The words of one artist to another may induce an idea chain, if they share the same concept.

His drawings and my sculptures are a new scriptural world for the twentieth and twenty-first centuries.

What did Sol LeWitt want to say in his early works, where does his work arise from, how close was he to American painting, which is a painting of surface.

Like Pollock and Kline, the visionary Sol had no iconography to tell. His formalization, freed from manual concerns, has no center; it has a musical rhythm that is expanded across a surface. His fundamental square, I believe, has as its target the iconographic excesses of Pop art. It draws its light from an ancient clarity. Maybe its original form was oral. Maybe, the first time, he murmured it into the ear of a passerby on a street near New York harbor, and then he drew it on a wall. Sol's great surfaces, painted on walls, far from involving a merely epidermal concept, awake in us the emotions of the great expanses, the positive epic of America. They constitute a sign of stability without hiding a certain lyricism.

Not long ago he sent me a postcard with a drawing, and on the stamp there was the beautiful face of Billie Holiday. Whether by chance or by design, it is significant, it carves out a space for his work. In the multi-faceted American society, artists design the space that they cultivate in their dreams, and Sol, despite the clear, geometric nature of his style, has a romantic soul in his blood.

Nick Kozak
Artist and LeWitt draftsman

A New Foundation

———

The basement is a space that often represents a fortified foundation for our historical objects, a site of preservation. Its high walls and concrete floor safeguard our earliest memories, shadowing them in evenly subdued light, so that when the magnifying glass is held up to them a crisp and neutral opinion can be rendered. Descending into the basement, we encounter a rich anthology where we discover origins, things that sometimes require the dust to be knocked off. When you wipe them clean and see their underlying sheen, their venerable quality may overwhelm you. It is with this sentiment that the ground floor of *Sol LeWitt: A Wall Drawing Retrospective* at MASS MoCA revealed itself to me. This floor houses some of LeWitt's earliest wall drawings, reaching far back into the history of an artist who accumulated a vast archive of artwork and memories.

With great foresight LeWitt arranged the exhibition's floor plan almost as if it were a reference library, the galleries like bookshelves that group together wall drawings catalogued according to aesthetic and material similarities. As you walk along the hallways, the cul-de-sac-style rooms invite you to meditate over the mathematics of each piece. This plan lends itself particularly well to *Location* drawings like *Wall Drawing 274: The location of six geometric figures* (1975) and *Wall Drawing 305: The location of 100 random specific points* (1977), which necessitate time to digest their concept compounded by labyrinthine geometry. The flow between these drawings invites the viewer to candidly linger from room to room. *Wall Drawing 38: Tissue paper cut into 1½ inch (4 cm) squares and inserted into holes in grey pegboard walls* (1970) eagerly asserts itself with its uniformity, yet still seems delicate. Meanwhile, *Wall Drawing 130: Grids and arcs from four corners* (1972) and *Wall Drawing 138: Circles and arcs from the midpoints of four sides* (1972) stress regularity. Despite how visually overwhelming these two drawings may feel, an undisturbed balance quietly radiates from each concentric arc.

Seriality plays an important role on this floor as well. Across several walls there are combination drawings featuring four colors or basic types of line. *Wall Drawing 47: A wall divided vertically into fifteen equal parts, each with a different line direction and all combinations* (1970) and *Wall Drawing 95* (1971), a variation with vertical, not straight lines in four colors, show fifteen-part combinations of lines in a straightforward format. In both these drawings growth is charted from left to right; it is a logical progression with a natural ascension of layering, from a single type of line to two-, three-, and finally four-type combinations.

Varying in fashion from those drawings is *Wall Drawing 85: A wall is divided into four horizontal parts. In the top row are four equal divisions, each with lines in a different direction. In the second row, six double combinations; in the third row, four triple combinations; in the bottom row, all four compositions superimposed* (1971), also on the ground floor. The previous combination drawings stretch across a wall's surface, unfolding systematically. This drawing, however, expresses a similar idea within an enclosed rectangular expanse. Accordingly, the number of dimensional containers for each permutation is relative to how many permutations result from each combination of lines. Single types of line are divided into a set of four; two-part combinations are divided into a set of six; three-part combinations are divided into a set of four; and there is one four-part combination. In these drawings the single idea is never solitary. Rather a whole unit of related work reinforces it.

The workhorse of the ground floor is *Wall Drawing 1211: Drawing Series—Part I–IV, 1–24, A+B* (2006), the most recent piece

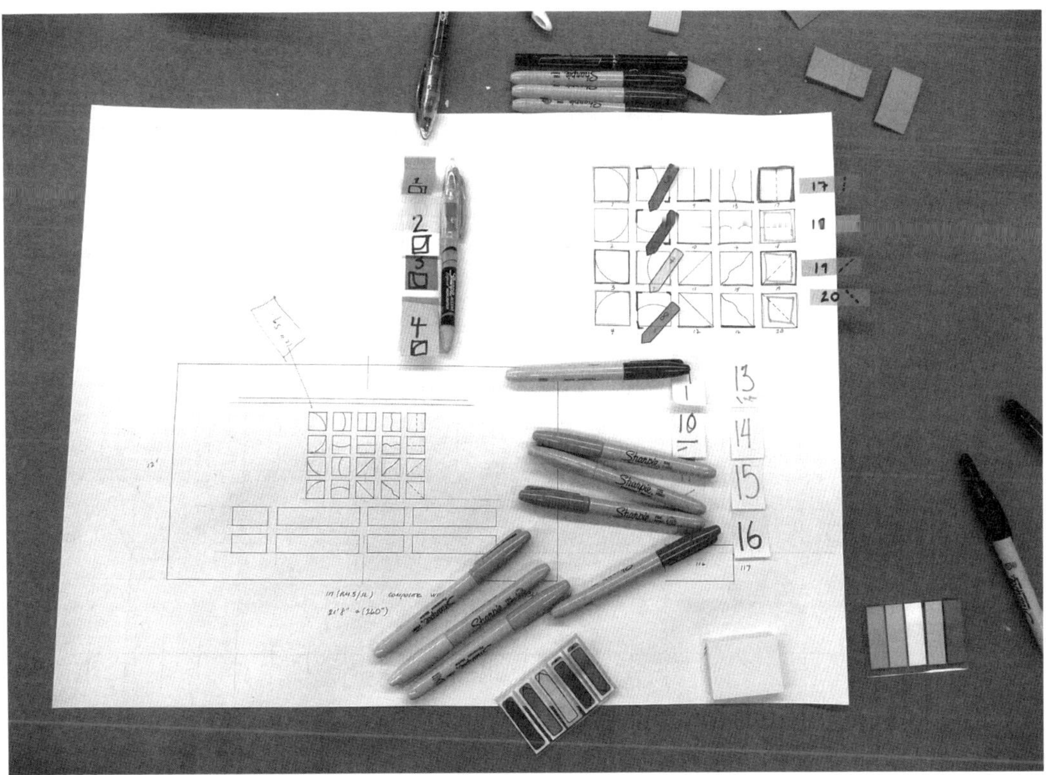

Installation of *Sol LeWitt: A Wall Drawing Retrospective* at MASS MoCA, 2008. Photo: Chris Cobb

on this floor. While this particular iteration of *Drawing Series* comes late in the career of the artist, the absolute seriality and manner of the piece echo the earliest of LeWitt's wall drawings. This drawing is on an entire floor filled with composites and combinations, and it stands as an extrapolated leviathan supported by decades of previous conception and creation. The openness of this room compares to the top two floors of the retrospective. The spacious rooms of the floors above augment LeWitt's endless experimentation and development throughout his career.

The retrospective's layout, with primarily the earliest work at the bottom of the building and the most recent at the top, spreads the drawings out logically and lends to the ultimate balance of the entire installation. It should be noted though that the placement of some of the wall drawings "at the bottom of the house" is not hierarchical. In the LeWitt wall-drawing retrospective the basement becomes a place for history to exist at its finest, a place where these early drawings can exist on their own terms, for it may heighten their intrinsic representations

of time. Thus the journey to the "basement" becomes sacred, as it allows us to travel back in time in order to rediscover the drawings in an environment that conveys their character. There is no competition with the present or future, and we can breathe them in with patience, as they reveal their innate and sometimes clandestine properties.

History will continue to chronicle Sol LeWitt's work, floor upon floor, but we will always return to the foundation brilliant in both vision and conception.

David Lang
Composer

Score based on a detail from a
wall drawing by Sol LeWitt

SLOW TITLE for solo violin — david lang

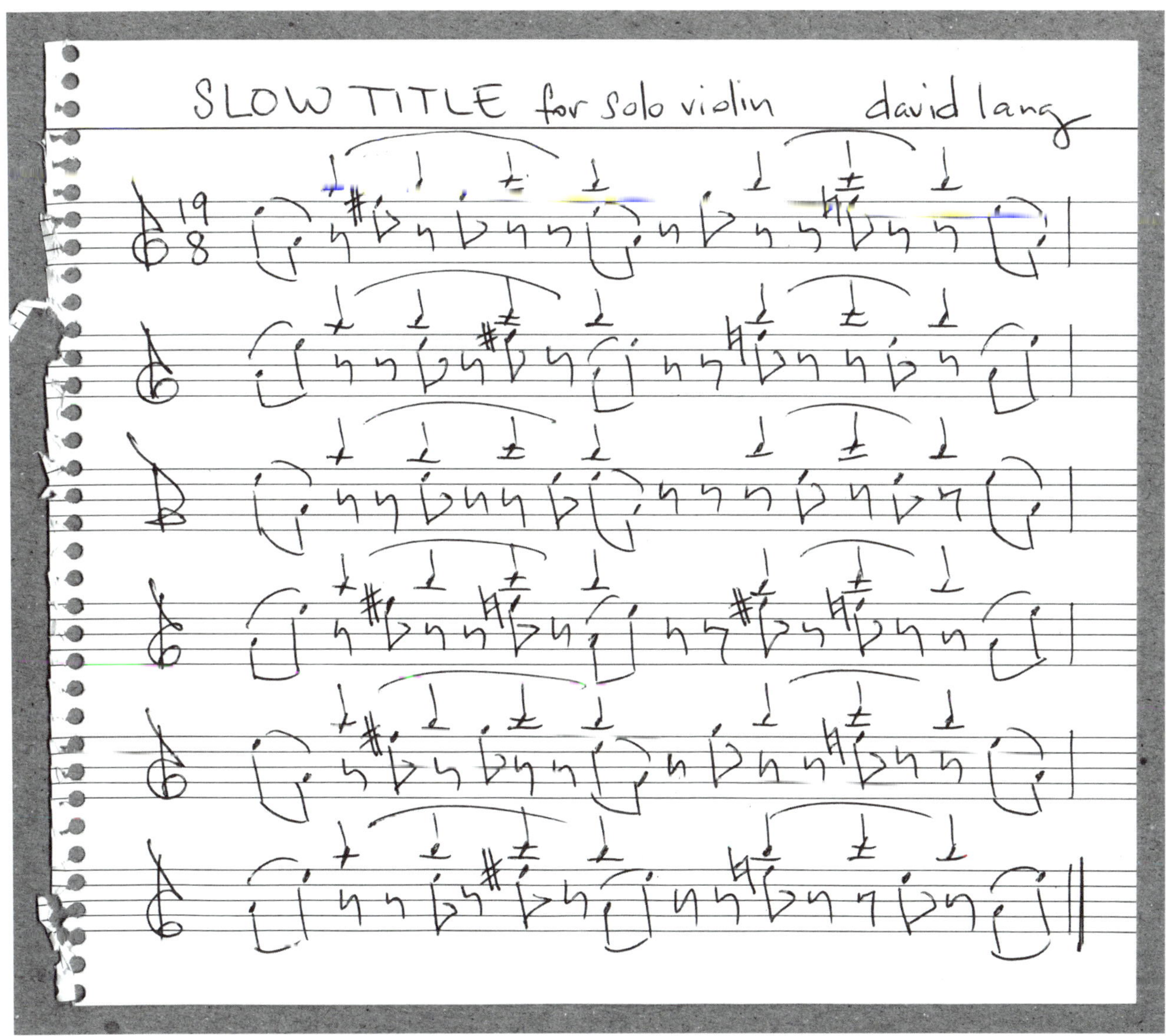

John Lavertu
Artist and LeWitt studio assistant

Sol's grasp and appreciation for art and architecture are well-known, though his interest in Asian art has rarely been discussed. Japanese wood-block prints and vintage hand-colored albumen photographs graced his front room. In addition to owning a sizable number of Asian artworks, he visited Asia. He served in the Korean War, and traveled to Japan and Bali. After my return from a visit to Indonesia, Sol asked me if I had had the chance to see Borobudur. I told him that I had on a previous trip. We then talked a while about this majestic Javanese temple. With the exception of an art historian, I had never met anyone who knew of Borobudur specifically. "I am influenced by all art that I admire (and even art I don't admire). They are all part of history, and of my thinking process once they are assimilated," Sol once wrote.[1]

Certainly, one can draw parallels between his work and Asian art. His later *Dome* works are often compared to Brunelleschi's dome of Italy's Florence Cathedral. However, domes were used often in the Middle East, India, and the Far East. In addition, burial mounds and stupas suggest the dome shape. The stupa is an essential structural and symbolic presence throughout Asian architecture. The Great Stupa of Sanchi in India, built between the third and first century BC, is considered to be the basis for all succeeding temple forms in Asia,

including the pagoda. Structurally speaking, it is essentially a single hill rising from the ground. Sol's *Maquette for Brick Structure, Dome* (2003) is reminiscent of a Jain high cylinder type of stupa.[2] Similarly, *Maquette for Brick Structure, Four Domes, Vertical* (2003) can be compared to a Burmese pagoda, such as the Kuthodaw Pagoda (Mandalay, Burma), in the way LeWitt's white domes are stacked one on top of another. On the other hand, *Maquette for Brick Structure, Three Domes, Horizontal* (2003) suggests burial mounds. Its domes, arranged horizontally, seem to gently emerge from the ground, creating a more topographical appearance.

Sol was once quoted as saying, "I suppose I think about architecture more than I do sculpture," and then continued, "In fact, I probably think of it as a form of sculpture."[3] This idea has roots in India, where wood-carvers led the way in temple-building. The wood-carvers were not only responsible for the finely carved friezes of temples but also the placement of their carved beams. The result is that temples seem to be large-scale sculptures. This idea applies in Southeast Asia as well: Angkor Wat in Cambodia, for example, can be seen as a large sculpture representing the Hindu myth of the Churning of the Milky Ocean. The main tower represents the mountain, while the roads leading to it symbolize the snake featured in the myth. Thus Indian architecture is thought of as living, breathing sculpture.[4]

While LeWitt's essay "Ziggurats" (1966) mentions buildings created between 1916 and 1963 in New York, the title of the essay suggests there is a comparative point of view at work. Indeed, many LeWitt structures and Eastern buildings share a stepped form. Both *Irregular Progression* (2000) and *1-2-3 Tower* (1993) share affinities with Candi Siwa in the Prambanan Temple complex in southern central Java. In the case of Borobudur, the architectural setback was not made simply for structural reasons but for aesthetic ones. Similarly, Sol's choice to use setbacks in these works was made in an artistic spirit rather than out of an engineering concern.

Borobudur, a descendant of Indian architecture, uses the basic forms of squares and circles. From an aerial vantage point, the hill is symbolic as a mandala, the primary shape of which is a circle. As Sol's assistant, I was able to see that many of his working drawings took on a similar bird's-eye view. These design principles are manifest in such works as *Wall Drawing 271: Black circles, red grid, yellow arcs from four sides and blue arcs from four corners* (1975) as well as *Wall Drawing 105: Circles from the center of the wall* (1971). While I am sure Sol was not being specific, I do think that the primary elements of architecture and design are at work here to a similar end.

His own preference for Western or Eastern architecture was never clear. Instead, by using primary forms as building blocks for his structures, he was able to use the power of suggestion, so that the viewer could be open to understanding the object according to his or her own experience. It was Sol's interest in world monuments, including Eastern ones, that allowed him to develop and create his own monuments.

---

1. Sol LeWitt, "Comments on an Advertisement Published in *Flash Art*, April 1973," in *Sol LeWitt: Critical Texts*, ed. Adachiara Zevi (Rome: I Libri di AEIUO, 1994), p. 98; reprinted from *Flash Art*, no. 41 (June 1973).

2. Ananda K. Coomaraswamy, *History of Indian and Indonesian Art*, reprint ed. (Mineola, New York: Dover, 1985), fig. 72.

3. LeWitt in Martin Friedman, "Construction Sites," in Gary Garrels, ed., *Sol LeWitt: A Retrospective*, exh. cat. (San Francisco: San Francisco Museum of Modern Art, 2000), p. 54.

4. Heinrich R. Zimmer, *The Art of Indian Asia*, ed. Joseph Campbell, vol. 1 (New York: Pantheon, 1955), pp. 208–09, 261–63.

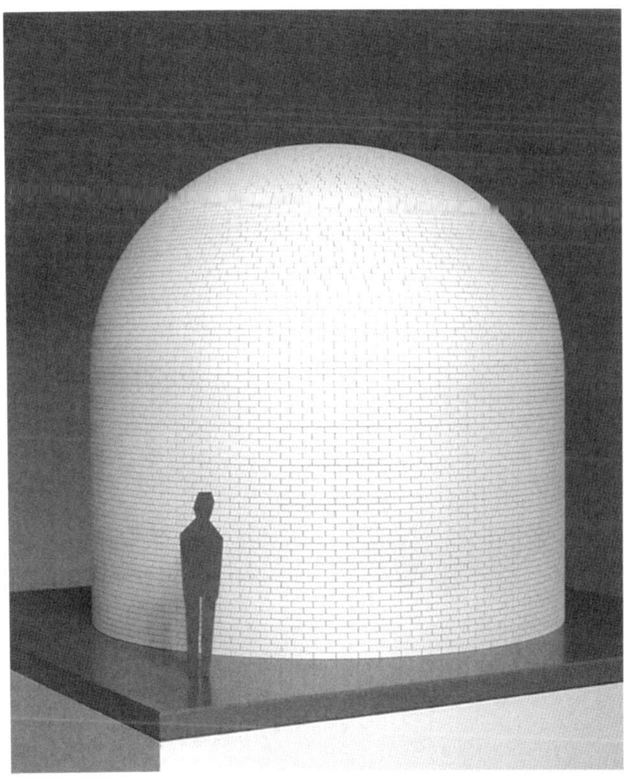

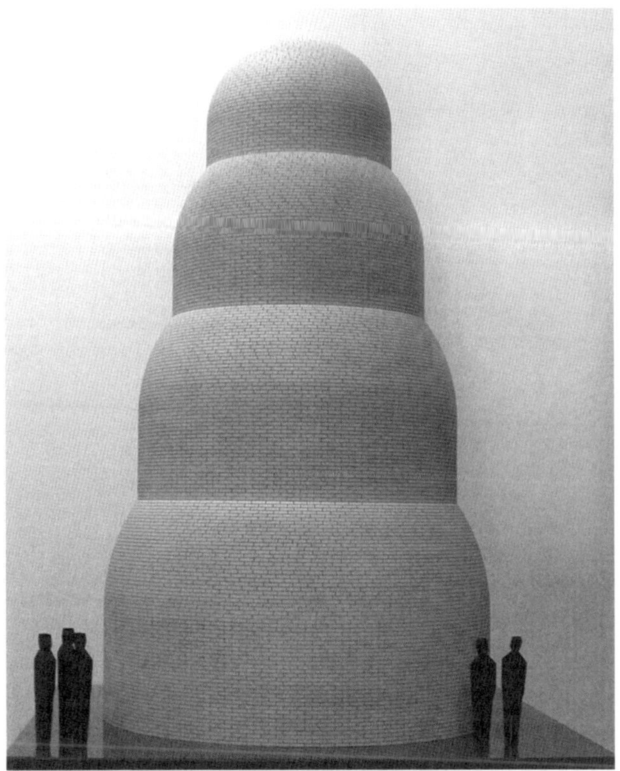

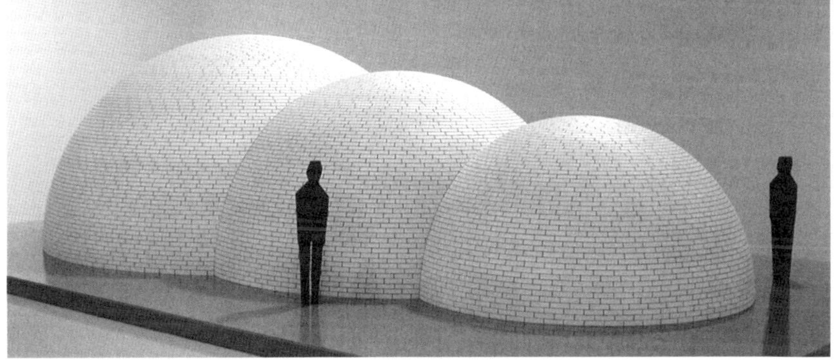

Sol LeWitt. *Maquette for Brick Structure, Dome*. 2003. Painted polyurethane foam, Medex board. LeWitt Collection, Chester, Connecticut. Courtesy of the Estate of Sol LeWitt. Photo: Sean McEntee

Sol LeWitt. *Maquette for Brick Structure, Four Domes, Vertical*. 2003. Painted polyurethane foam, Medex board. LeWitt Collection, Chester, Connecticut. Courtesy of the Estate of Sol LeWitt. Photo: Sean McEntee

Sol LeWitt. *Maquette for Brick Structure, Three Domes, Horizontal*. 2003. Painted polyurethane foam, Medex board. LeWitt Collection, Chester, Connecticut. Courtesy of the Estate of Sol LeWitt. Photo: Sean McEntee

Louise Lawler
Artist

Sun/Sol. 2004/2007.
Cibachrome print

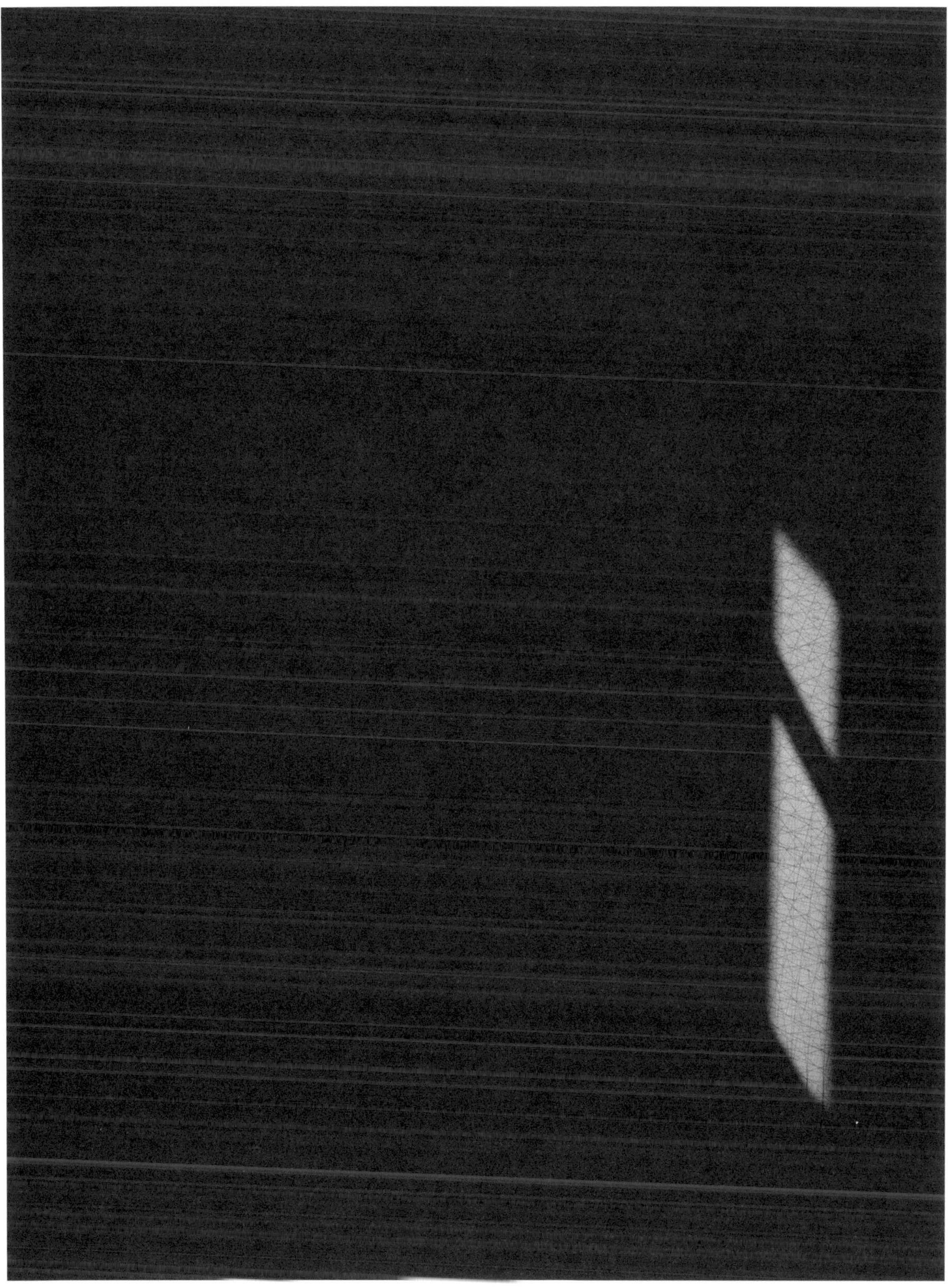

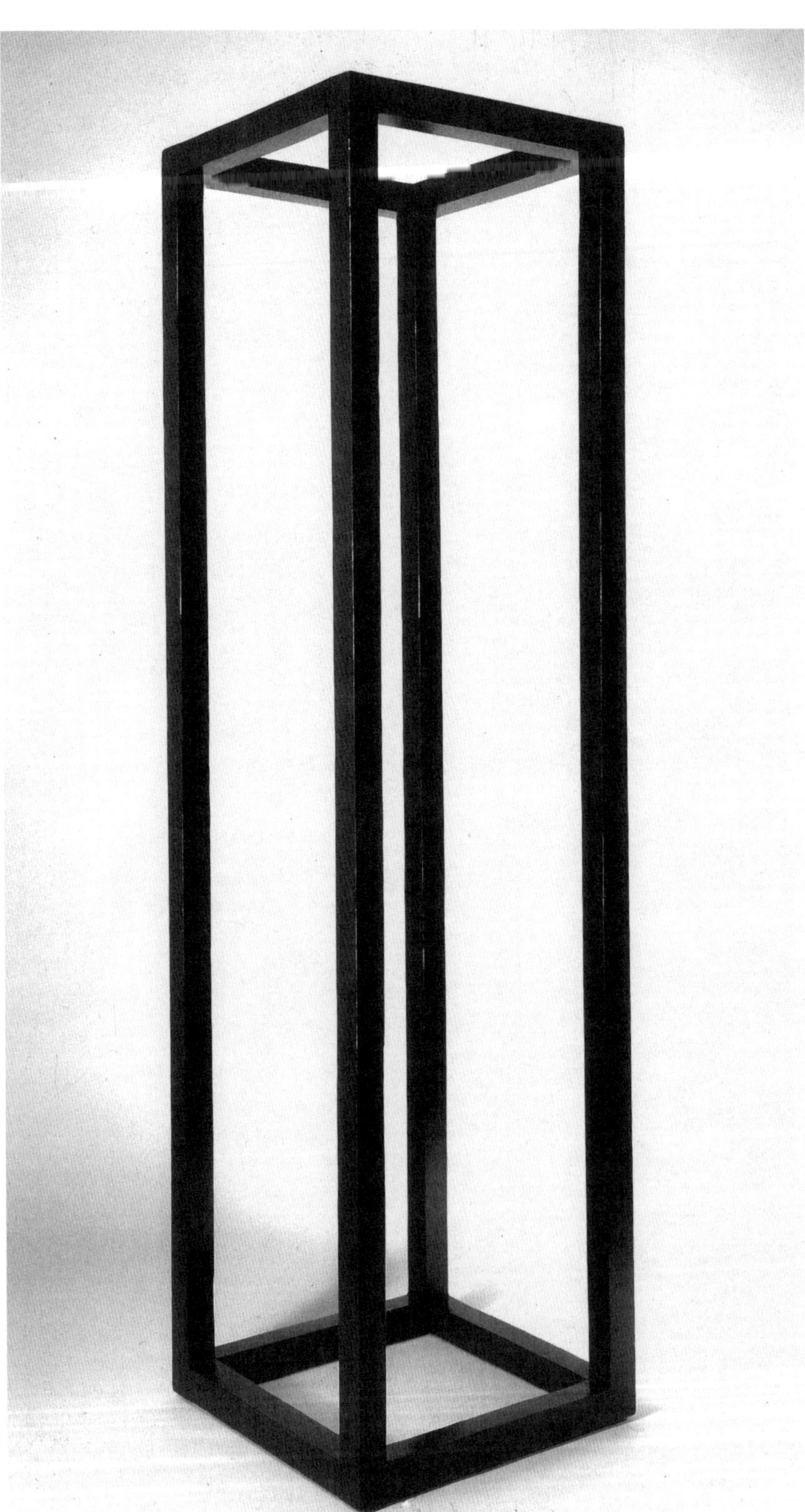

Sol LeWitt. *Standing Open Structure Black*. 1964. Painted wood. Collection of The Museum of Modern Art, Gift of Elizabeth A. Straus (by exchange). Photo courtesy of PaceWildenstein, New York

Robert Lazzarini
Artist

Standing Open Structure, Black

"From the subjective view there is no such thing as nothing."
Robert Morris, "Blank Form" (1960–61)

Sol LeWitt's *Standing Open Structure, Black* (1964) is a work that solicits connections between geometry, the body, and immateriality. It is a vertical, right-square prism with two ends of equal size and a skeletal framework rather than a solid form. By thus reducing the forms of a simple geometry, LeWitt augmented the body's relationship to the object and introduced a different kind of phenomenal subjectivity.

Standing Open Structure elicits a direct, corporeal experience through its formal association to the human body. Its dimensions and shape can be read as a box bounding the upright human figure. The anthropomorphic connotations are reinforced by LeWitt's choice of the word *standing* in the title, as opposed to the more coolly mathematical or objective *vertical*. Similarly, Robert Morris's sculpture *Untitled (Box for Standing)*

(1961), a vertical, rectangular box with one open face, is sized to the dimensions of his body. It resembles a coffin, in which the artist stands. However, in LeWitt's sculpture the bodily presence is not that of the performing artist but that of the interacting viewer.

In keeping with Minimalist philosophy, LeWitt was aware of the necessity for a viewer to circumambulate a work in order to understand its specific geometry. Maurice Merleau-Ponty described the experience of viewing a cube: "As I move round it, I see the front face, hitherto a square, change its shape, then disappear, while the other sides come into view and one by one become squares."[1] But with *Standing Open Structure*'s open form, the viewer has the ability to see through it, immediately understanding the complete geometry from any single point around the object. The viewer is able to conceive of the work simultaneously as a fixed volume and a penetrable space.

LeWitt had already been exploring open, rectilinear forms in 1963 and 1964, when he eliminated planes from and made cutouts in otherwise solid constructions. Yet *Standing Open Structure* is his first sculptural work based entirely on an open framework, a contrivance he would continue to explore throughout his career. By eliminating the viewer's need to

move around it, the open structure creates a new possibility: the idea of entering it. LeWitt's *Floor/Wall Structure (Telephone Booth)* (1964) offers an interesting comparison. A planar, vertical box with a vertical cutout, it not only depends upon the active participation of the viewer's body to navigate around the work in order to understand its specific geometry, but it invites the viewer to enter the work in order to do so. Yet, as *Standing Open Structure* moves away from the material integrity of *Floor/Wall Structure*, it progresses from something toward nothing and suggests a container in which one's body can also make that transformation.

The open structure can be seen as a shorthand representation of the solid: the *idea* of the form in addition to its concrete materiality. It stands to reason that this step toward immateriality and the shift toward a conceptualization of geometry would go hand in hand. *Standing Open Structure* functions as the simultaneous physical and mental apprehension of the rectangular box, an object both experienced and conceived. In this it mediates the concerns of a Minimal sculptor and those of a Conceptualist.

---

1 Maurice Merleau-Ponty, *Phenomenology of Perception*, trans. Colin Smith (London: Routledge, 1962), p. 203.

Heinz Liesbrock
Director, Josef Albers Museum,
Bottrop, Germany

Wall Drawing 1176: Seven basic colors and all their combinations in a square within a square. For Josef Albers

Sol LeWitt and Josef Albers never met in person. Sol, nonetheless, was thoroughly acquainted with the work of the German and found therein hints about answers to the questions that had concerned him in his own art.

When I visited Sol in Chester, Connecticut, in the autumn of 2003 to invite him to participate in an exhibition at the Josef Albers Museum in Bottrop, he expressed his interest in Albers in both congenial and concrete terms. He showed me drawings and illustrations of his own works dating from the early 1960s, drawing from them a direct line to Albers's work. As one example of the suggestions he had gleaned from Albers's art, he cited the tension between the two-dimensionality of the object and its possible expansion into real space, evident in the *Homage to the Square* series, a matter of special interest to him in the 1960s and beyond. At that time he had discovered in Albers's work the ability of color to create depth and spatial movement, and felt himself thereby emboldened to think of color and form in three dimensions.

This artistic affinity was the basis for *Wall Drawing 1176: Seven basic colors and all their combinations in a square within a square. For Josef Albers*, which was realized in 2005 at the Josef Albers Museum. The concept of this work attests to Sol's special generosity and mastery. Although Sol did nothing more than employ elements of his own artistic vocabulary as it had evolved over decades, namely the square and a defined series of colors, he nonetheless simultaneously succeeded in paying homage explicitly to Albers's work. Two original artists freely encounter one another here.

From early on the square was a primary form, fundamental and indivisible, in Sol's work. He employed in this wall drawing the theme of the square within a square in order to refer to Albers. For both artists, the square was a particularly attractive form for its neutrality, its lack of a strong individual identity with which the viewer's attention would otherwise be absorbed. Because it is hardly meaningful in itself, seeming invisible as a form, the square is flexible, versatile in its applications, and leaves space for other things: the actual artistic foci.

For Albers, the square could accommodate unlimited colors without diverting from their interaction. As he once observed of the square: "I'm not paying 'homage to the square.' It's only a dish I serve my craziness about color in."[1] Sol concurred. The squares in the Bottrop wall drawing contained the seven colors he often employed in his art. Each color—red, yellow, and blue, as well as green, orange, purple, and gray—appeared in combination once with every other color as a square within a square. The resulting twenty-one forms coursed through the building like a spiral. Once Sol established the square and the colors as formal elements and clarified their syntactic relationships, the piece developed as if of its own accord. A well-known statement by Sol comes to mind: "The idea becomes a machine that makes the art."[2]

In the Josef Albers Museum work the acrylics lay saturated and luminously on the wall. The quiet pulse from one square to the next radiated silence and majesty. They led viewers through the building and were able to affect them directly; viewers encountered the rooms and simultaneously therein their own presence.

Both Sol LeWitt and Josef Albers strove for simplification and immediacy in their art, from which they developed aesthetic complexity. Albers once summed up that maxim with the following equation: "The measure of art: the ratio of effort to effect."[3]

During my visit with him Sol asserted that one thing was nevertheless crucial regarding Albers. Of course, what separated him from his esteemed colleague, he said, was the conception of beauty based on transcendence, through which, for Albers, the work of art still had its place. To my question as to whether the concept of beauty was not of continued importance for his own work as well, his answer was inimitable. In my memory it vouches for the artist and the person who Sol LeWitt was: "Well, if it turns out to be beautiful, I don't mind."

1. Neil Welliver, "Albers on Albers," *Art News* 64, no. 9 (Jan. 1966), pp. 68–69.

2. Sol LeWitt, "Paragraphs on Conceptual Art," *Artforum* 5, no. 10 (June 1967), p. 79.

3. Josef Albers in Eugen Gomringer, *Josef Albers: His Work As a Contribution to Visual Articulation in the Twentieth Century* (New York: George Wittenborn, 1968), p. 7.

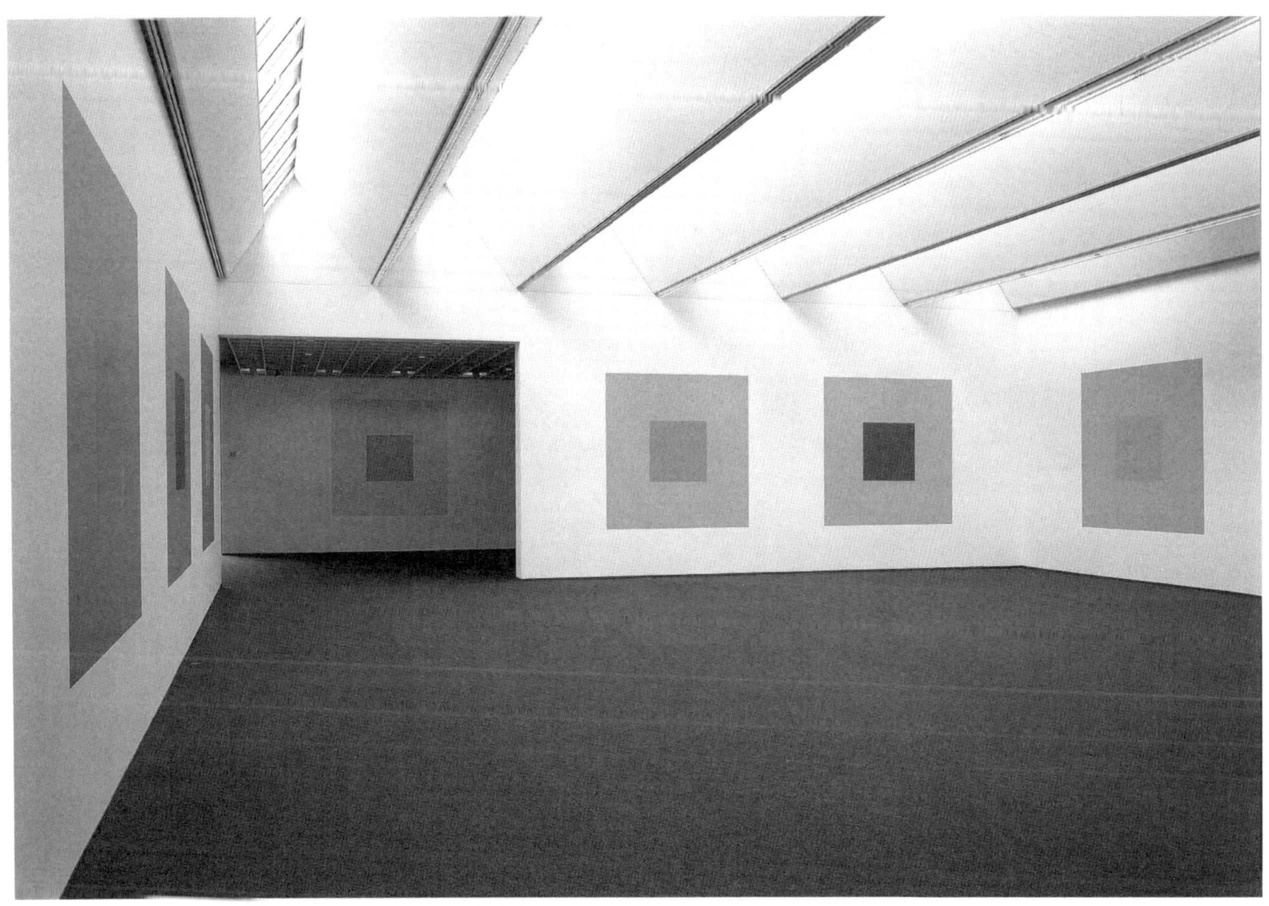

Sol LeWitt. *Wall Drawing 1176: Seven basic colors and all their combinations in a square within a square. For Josef Albers.* Installation at Josef Albers Museum, Bottrop, 2005. Photo: Laurenz Berges

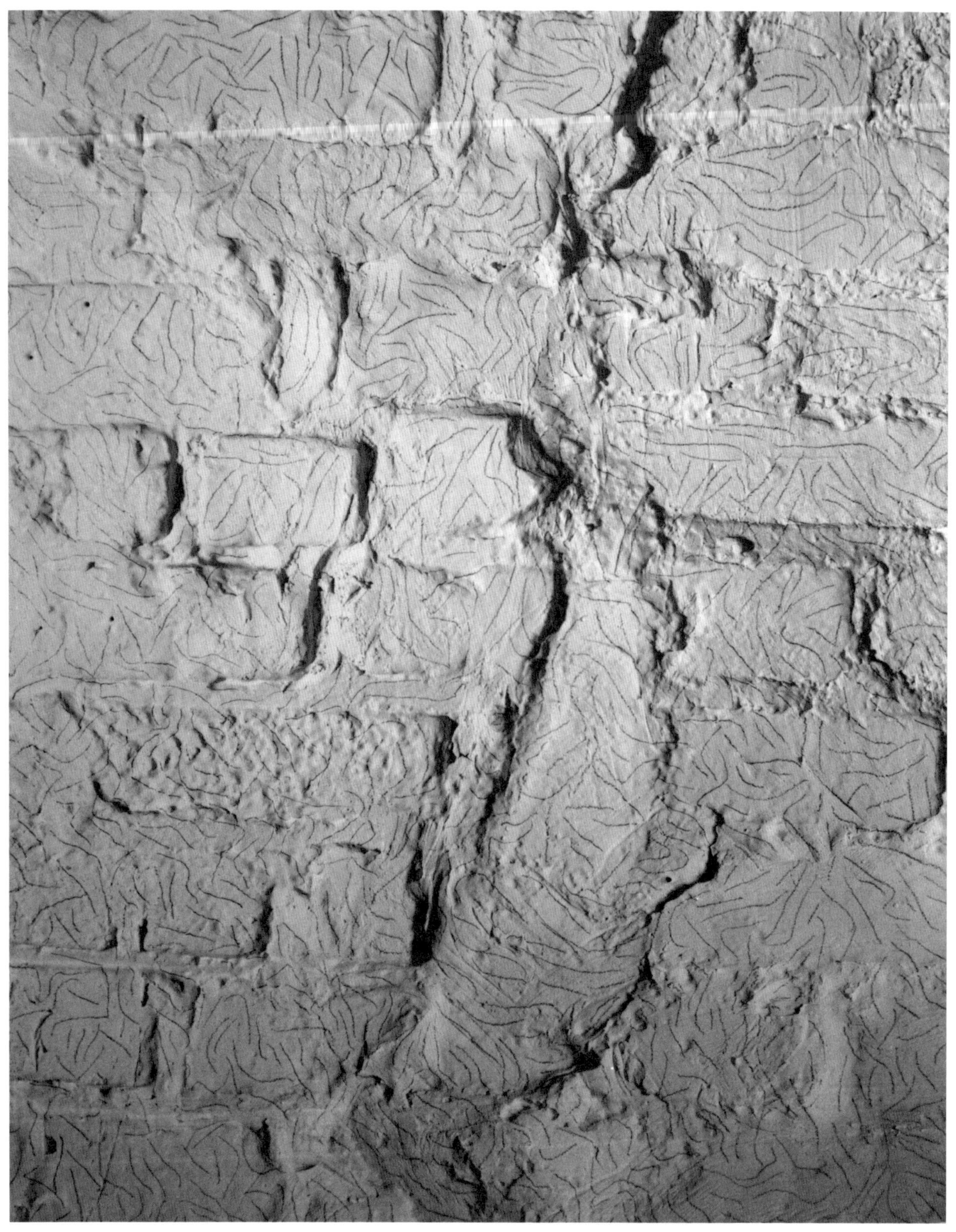

Lucy R. Lippard
Writer and activist

The wall drawing Sol made on the white-painted brick wall in my Prince Street loft in Manhattan in 1971, during the first couple of years he was making works on-site, was perhaps the first he had done on such a recalcitrant surface, which clearly attracted him. The architectural context was probably appealing too. It was on a wide, arched opening that was very roughly bricked up months after my then-three-year-old son, Ethan, and I moved in, in 1968. The archway separated my space from the larger loft on the other side of the building, where Alex, Ada, and Vincent Katz lived. I spent a year trying to make the place livable after moving in the same day the furniture finishing company moved out. The closing of the archway must have meant I finally had a workable bathroom. (We had used the Katzes' for months.)

Nothing straight or geometric would have worked on a surface so lumpy, with globs of mortar and no attempt to be neat. LeWitt's solution was "lines not touching," which ended up having to be wiggly. In those days he made his own wall drawings. He was there day after day drawing in pencil on the bricks, which mightily puzzled my son's friends. "What's he doing?" "He's making a piece." Not being art kids, they concluded this man was making "peace" on the walls of Ethan's living room, peace being much in demand in those days of the Vietnam War.

This was not the only LeWitt we lived with. He had long been part of the family, and the drawing was accompanied by a handsome coffee table made when he first started creating "structures," with highly lacquered colored surfaces, earlier in the 1960s. I asked for orange, and he complied. But my decorating schemes kept changing; he just rolled his eyes when the table became lime green, white, and finally black. In this incarnation it still holds piles of books and magazines in my New Mexico house.

Life and the space on Prince Street changed after a while, and the gorgeous drawing ended up in a dark storage space where a lot of dancing took place during parties. In 1995, when I had left and the place was remodeled for Ethan's own family, the drawing was covered over, though it was temporarily reconstituted at the Museum of Fine Arts in Santa Fe in 1997.

Like all Sol's work at the time, the wall drawings were permutational, and I assume the odd shape and rough surface of the Prince Street piece were eventually explored in other contexts. If his two- and three-dimensional permutations opened windows to increased possibilities, the wall drawings flung open the door to freedom. The premise that they could be remade at the owners' whims and moved around the world by means of a small piece of paper was as "conceptual" as anything made under that rubric, even though Sol insisted he was "a conceptual artist with a small c." And the wall drawings support a whole army of other artists whenever they reappear.

So the Prince Street drawing still lives, as does Sol's endless generosity…. OK, no praise, or I'll be smacked down from on high.

Sol LeWitt. *Wall Drawing 73: Lines not straight, not touching, drawn at random, uniformly dispersed with maximum density, covering the wall.* 1971. Black pencil. New Mexico Museum of Art, Museum of New Mexico, Sante Fe, Lucy Lippard Collection. Photo: Robert E. Mates and Paul Katz

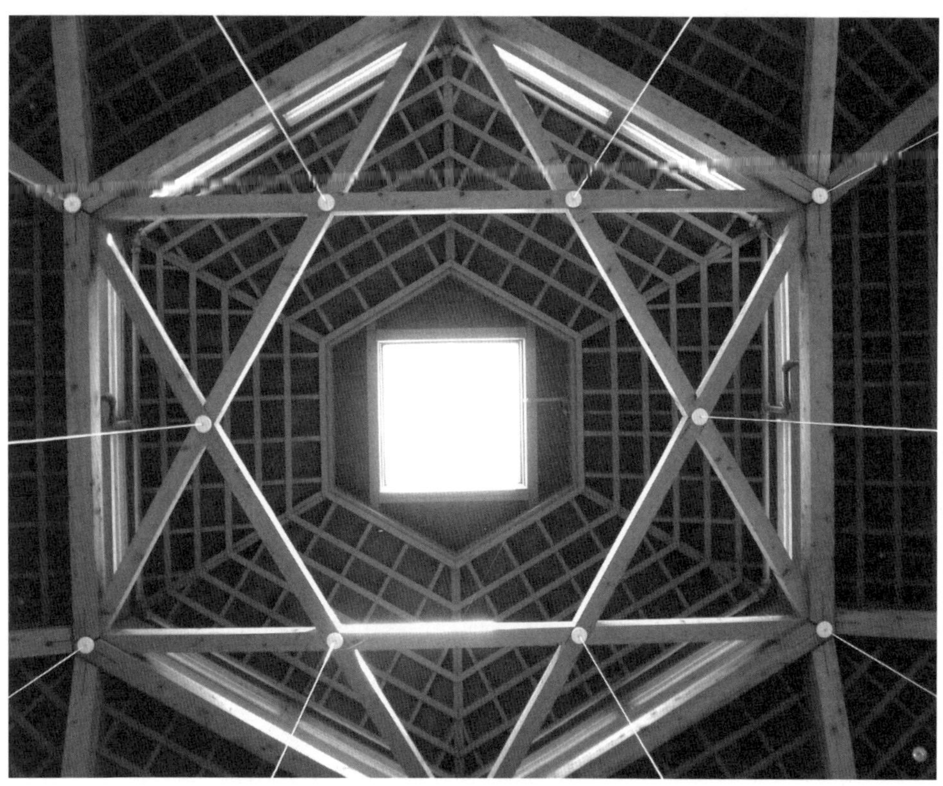

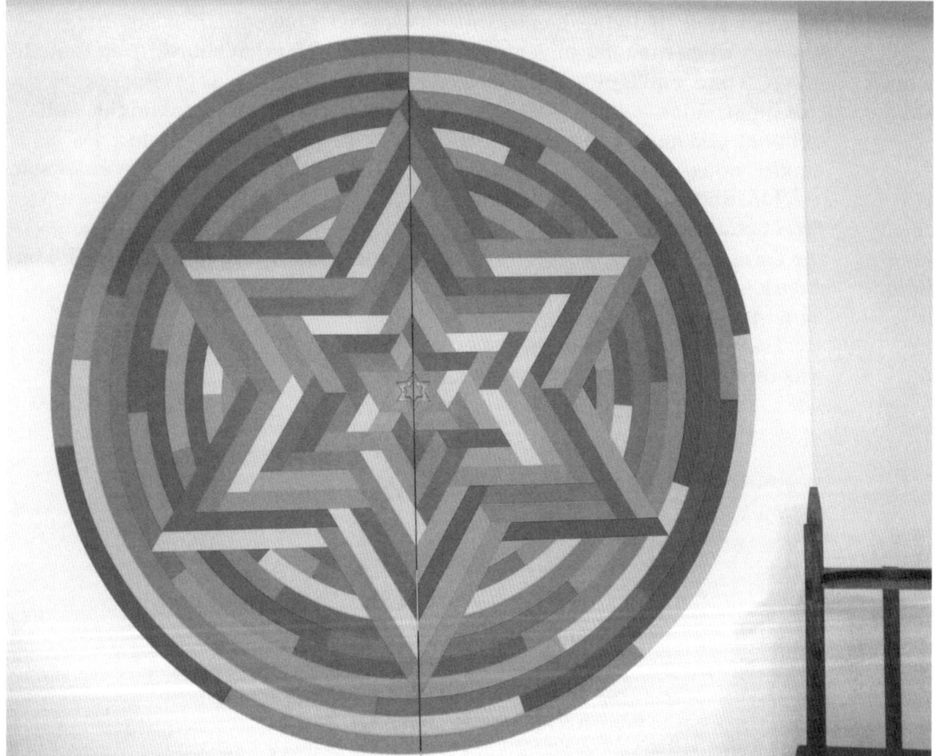

Sol LeWitt. *Ark, Beth Shalom, Chester, Connecticut.* 2001. Acrylic paint on wood panel. Photos: Laurie Kress

Stephen L. Lloyd
Architect

Working with Sol LeWitt on the Design of Temple Beth Shalom Rodfe Zedek in Chester, Connecticut

Artisans and viewers of the wall drawings at MASS MoCA will be very familiar with Sol's use of instructions, on which the works are based. Imagine, then, a set of instructions like this:

On a sixteen-acre site build a structure referring to wooden synagogues of Eastern Europe with clear geometry and perceptible as a sculptural solid to serve as home for a vibrant congregation.

Sol had drawn a floor plan for the synagogue prior to my involvement. He gave me a copy, and I put it aside, focusing on understanding the site and the congregation for myself. Throughout a lengthy process of workshops, rabbi succession, and budget issues, many other schemes were brought forward. As I look back now, I realize that Sol's plan, with its central sanctuary and east-facing courtyard, acted as a graphic set of instructions, even as many other voices and ideas were considered, acknowledged, and incorporated into the whole. Sol granted me and the design team a great deal of autonomy in the realization of the concept. Nevertheless, his set of instructions was powerful enough to guide the result through a complex array of diverse opinions, town regulations, and physical requirements. For a scheme that ultimately was too expensive, Sol carefully drafted the elevations of the octagonal chapel and sanctuary spaces, the latter under a three-tiered roof. In the final design the elevations derived from a quick sketch he made resembling an asymmetrical mountain. The asymmetry had a key functional component, to bring the light from a central skylight toward the bimah, or altar.

The design committee selected the color of the ceiling in the principal spaces: a deep red matching the cover of the prayer books used by the congregation. Sol's remaining interior color choices, a saturated deep blue and a yellow to complete the primary palette, and white for the sanctuary, elicit a complicated response in the visitor. First there is a sense of removal from the world, as one comes in from the outdoors to the deep-blue and red interior; then, as the visitor enters the tall, bright sanctuary, there is a sense of release and expansion, which is tempered by the clear geometry of the octagonal space.

Near the end of the project Sol asked me to visit his studio. He showed me a multicolored drawing of a six-pointed Star of David inscribed in concentric circles. He wondered if I thought it might be suitable for the back wall of the sanctuary. It was a shimmering, jewel-like image filled with energy. It clearly belonged at the front of the sanctuary on the doors concealing the Torahs, and I said so. He asked if I would present it to the committee.

In a meeting in which I was more nervous than at any of the previous presentations to the congregation or the town officials, I felt keenly the responsibility of describing why this image was appropriate to serve as the sanctuary's focal point. In a way it would be the heart of the building, and so it felt like a lot was at stake. I need not have worried. Sol's image spoke for itself: the design committee loved it. Since its installation at the front of the sanctuary, Sol's star has become a symbol of the congregation.

I see the star as a new set of instructions, which in word form might say:

Life is beautiful. Live it.

Of course, Sol would never say such a thing, but I hear it in his work all the time.

Alvin Lucier
Composer and musician

Quadrants

I have often thought of Sol LeWitt as a musician. He removed his hand from the actual production of the work and invited other artists and assistants to draw his work, making it come alive in the same way that composers ask performers to bring their ideas to life. His assistants, including students, were performers. His "scores" were his instructions, which resembled prose pieces that certain composers made in lieu of conventionally notated scores on a five-line staff. I don't mean those of a poetic or purely conceptual nature, but those that consist of real directions for making palpable products. It is not coincidental that verbal scores in music and Sol's prose instructions for wall drawings came about at roughly the same time; examples include La Monte Young's prose compositions of 1960 and Christian Wolff's prose *Collection* created for art students in England.

Last year Anna Hammond of the Yale University Art Gallery invited me to talk about Sol's work and my relationship to it. I had collaborated with him a few times. Once he borrowed a panoramic photograph of the Alps I had used in *Panorama* (1993), a work for solo trombone and piano, as the basis of his *Wall Drawing 730: Zug Mountains* (1993). Later he invited me to provide sound accompaniment for his *Curved Wall* (2004), exhibited in Graz and later at Wesleyan University.

For my talk at Yale, in addition to a few brief remarks in which I mentioned Sol's generosity and openness to the works of others, I presented a short musical work in response to his *Wall Drawing 11: A wall divided horizontally and vertically into four equal parts. Within each part, three of the four kinds of lines are superimposed* (1969), which had been drawn on a large wall in Yale's gallery. The drawing consisted of four simple gestures: descending and ascending diagonal lines and horizontal and vertical ones. In several large squares Sol had combined these lines in various permutations, resembling musical counterpoint. Simply by notating the diagonals as glissandi for a pair of violins, the horizontals as long tones for a clarinet, and the verticals as cello pizzicati (piano clusters would have been more appropriate, but a piano was not available), I was able to fashion a short musical piece called *Quadrants*. Using a simple numerical system, I mixed these gestures in ways similar to Sol's permutations.

I was fortunate to have traded a work with Sol. He had amassed a huge collection of other artists' works simply by trading a piece of his for one of theirs. I gave him the original score of my string quartet, *Navigations for Strings* (1993); he in turn gave me a wall drawing that I executed on an empty wall in my home. All I needed to do to complete and verify the work was to write the words "wall drawing" anywhere on the wall's surface. Perhaps Sol didn't think it necessary for his name to be on it, because, as he was inventor of this genre, there could be no doubt as to who the artist was. Or perhaps he simply wanted to share authorship with the person who drew it.

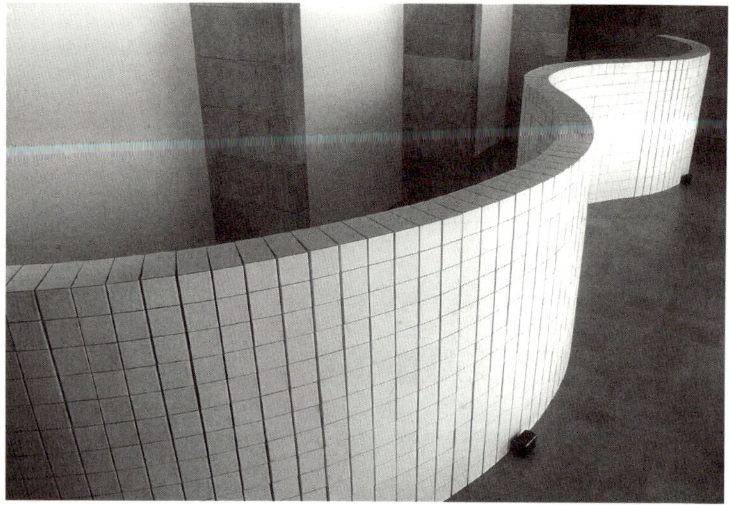

Sol LeWitt and Alvin Lucier: A Collaboration (Main Gallery). 2005 ▪ Sol LeWitt. *Curved Wall (Wesleyan)*. Concrete blocks. Courtesy of the Estate of Sol LeWitt ▪ Alvin Lucier. *Six Resonant Points Along a Curved Wall* ▪ Photo: John Groo

Robert Mangold
Artist

I met Sol in the summer of 1962 at the Museum of Modern Art, where we both worked as guards. My wife, Sylvia, and I had recently moved to New York City after attending the graduate art program at Yale University. Sol became one of our closest friends.

In the early years, when our studios were in the same neighborhood, we saw each other's work frequently. I don't recall long and heated discussions about art issues, but they may have happened. Yet I think through our friendship we developed a supportive admiration and interest in what each of us was doing, and there were some shared ideas in our work.

Sol's art spurred me on to greater efforts. It may or may not have worked that way for him, but in the early or mid-1960s, in New York, there was this rich mixture of diverse ideas and art, which created a fertile working atmosphere for us all.

When Sol published his "Sentences on Conceptual Art" in 1969, they very clearly staked out his interests. These statements were not meant to point the way for all to follow, but rather act as a declaration of the position he had arrived at. It was a solid, formidable position, however, and it caused you to consider and balance your own ideas in relation to it.

Tom Marioni
Artist

Sol LeWitt and His Influence on Me

—

Sol told me something in the 1980s, when he was living part-time in Italy and starting to make wall drawings using ink and sponges. I said to him, "You're not a painter. What do you call these wall works?" Sol said, "I'm an inker." Later I told him he had given me permission to use color, and he said, "You can do anything you want."

In two 1972 action works of mine, *Drawing a Line as Far as I Can Reach* and *Running and Jumping with a Pencil Marking the Paper While Trying to Fly*, and also in the 1989 *Flying with Friends* (others made the drawing), I worked out the idea ahead of time and the execution was, as Sol would say, "a perfunctory affair."

Denise Markonish
Curator, MASS MoCA

Conducting the Library: Seriality and Motion in the Work of Sol LeWitt

---

"The universe (which others call the Library) is composed of an indefinite and perhaps infinite number of hexagonal galleries, with vast air shafts in between…"
Jorge Luis Borges, "The Library of Babel" (1941)

Jorge Luis Borges's story "The Library of Babel," about the creation of an ever-unfolding universe of books, opens with the above description of an infinite building, a serial display of literature. The account could just as well fit *Sol LeWitt: A Wall Drawing Retrospective* at MASS MoCA: a seemingly infinite number of walls, each with drawings that appear to go on in limitless numbers of permutations (not to mention the stairwell/light shaft between floors, or the "vast air shafts in between"). Recently, I discovered that in 1984 LeWitt created an illustrated version of Borges's *Ficciones* in which "The Library of Babel" is published. This

did not come as a surprise to me. LeWitt's twenty-two illustrations for Borges's book are delicate silkscreen prints of isometric forms and repeated lines, akin to many of his early meshlike wall drawings in pencil. These images provide a striking context for Borges's stories of mirrors, labyrinths, and infinity. It makes me imagine LeWitt's notes, instructions, and drawings themselves nestled inside Borges's library of Babel.

Thinking about the indefinite and infinite made me reconsider seriality in LeWitt's work. In 1964 LeWitt made his first homage to Eadweard Muybridge, the nineteenth-century photographer known for his images capturing stages of motion in humans and animals. In *Muybridge I* (1964) LeWitt created a box with keyholes for viewers to look through, inside of which were increasingly closer views of a female nude seen under blinking lights. As the viewer moves through the images, the figure appears to be walking toward him or her. This particular example presents LeWitt's dissection of movement into a system of parts. In most of his work LeWitt took Muybridge's concept and abstracted it. Though other artists addressed serialized movement, most notably in Marcel Duchamp's *Nude Descending a Staircase (No. 2)* (1912) and the experiments of the Italian Futurists, LeWitt's approach was more radical in its combination of stark, abstract imagery with a sense of vibrating motion. In LeWitt's drawings we see not figures but wavy lines, straight lines, and cubes, which shift before our eyes and hum with the energy of movement.

On numerous occasions before the exhibition's public opening, I had the privilege of walking through the LeWitt building at MASS MoCA, where the wall drawings unfolded before my eyes. The process of carrying out instructions, treating walls, taping, marking, and line-

making is in itself a system of parts. In many instances, this system, like Borges's library, seems infinite. However, after I saw one drawing after another being executed, LeWitt's careful attention to individual variation became evident. No two drawings are alike, but they all originate from the same place: that of the serialization of form and motion. Early works, of barely visible pencil marks, lead to colorful patches of stained inks, which give way to bold colors and organic forms, until finally graphite returns in the *Scribble* drawings. These late works contain in them a subtle use of materials, gestural marks, and, most of all, movement and repetition. Here LeWitt's work comes full circle. Even though he is no longer around to continue making permutations, there is the sense that the possibilities go on infinitely in viewers' minds, inside their own libraries of thought.

LeWitt often spoke of his work in terms of music: "The narrative of serial art works more like music than like literature."[1] Literature once written is theoretically finished, whereas music is written and then performed repeatedly, each time bearing the individual musician's mark. This is the essence of what LeWitt borrowed from music for his own work: the idea of passing the physical "making" on to others. By doing so, shifting the execution of the drawings into the hands of his draftsmen, LeWitt opened up the works to controlled variation. Much like John Cage did in his compositions, LeWitt employed a kind of complexity theory wherein simple rules lead to complex patterns, and repetition leads to perceived motion. In providing a

---

1. Saul Ostrow, "Sol LeWitt" (interview), *Bomb* Magazine, no. 85 (fall 2003), http://www.bombsite.com/issues/85/articles/2583.

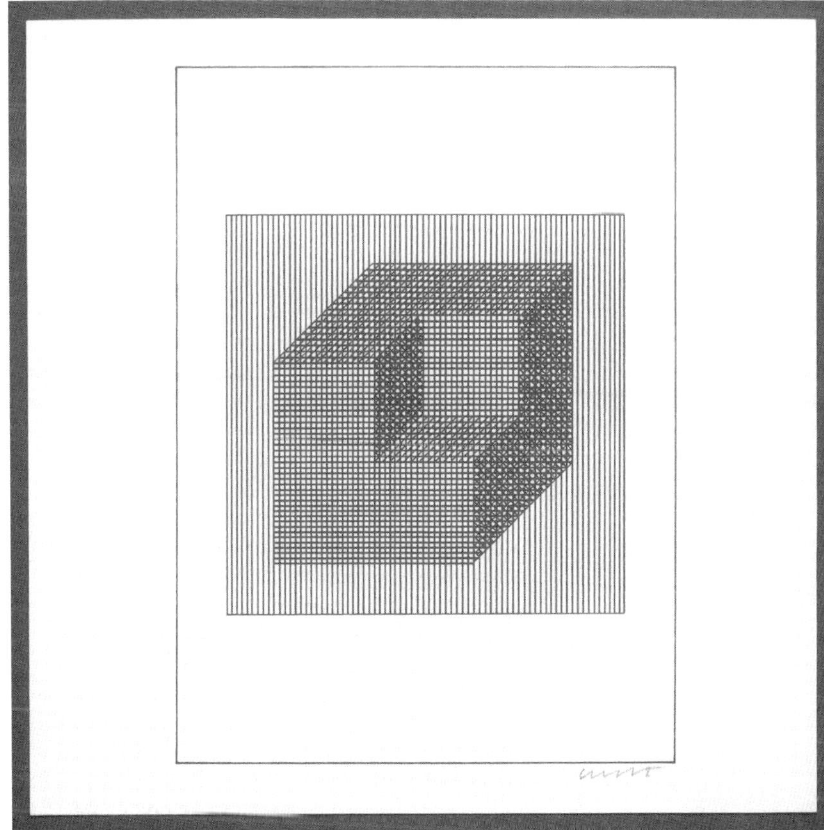

Sol LeWitt. One print of twenty-two from *Ficciones*. 1984. Silkscreen. Published by Limited Editions, New York. LeWitt Collection, Chester, Connecticut. Photo: R. J. Phil

simple "score" or manuscript for others to follow, LeWitt opened up the process and allowed the complexity to grow layer upon layer, from instruction to execution and finally to finished work.

With this concept in mind, I would agree that LeWitt's process is more akin to musical notation than literature—though this conclusion does not come at the expense of his obvious connection to, and practice of, writing. In the end, however, watching the drawings executed on-site seems more like ballet, as the draftsmen move up and down the scaffolding, drawing, painting, and using their bodies. Watching this dance makes me wish Muybridge were around to capture it on film. Now that would be seriality within seriality within a system of parts, surely befitting Borges's limitless library.

Allan McCollum
Artist

Without Sol LeWitt's conceptions of where an artist's touch could end and begin in the making of an artwork, or how an artist's hand and mind could be extended into and through the hands and minds of others—along with the thousands of little decisions that might go into the making of a thousand little marks—there is no way I could be making the work I make today.

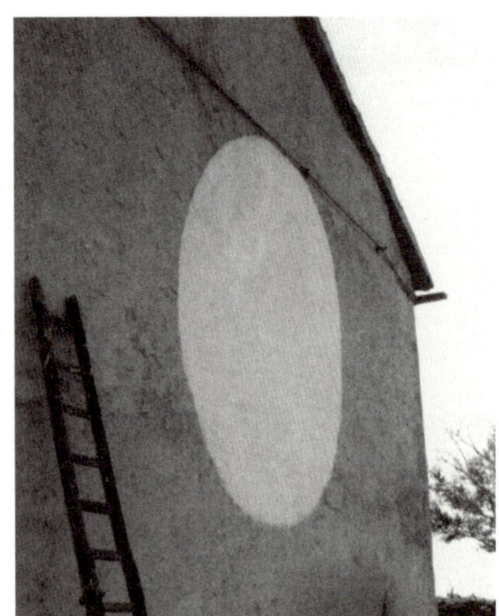

Sol LeWitt. *Wall Drawing 355: A white circle 80" (200 cm) in diameter filled in solid*. July 1981. White paint, brick wall. Courtesy of the Estate of Sol LeWitt

Afranio Metelli
Artist

I met Sol LeWitt in 1978, when my wife, Ann Wood, introduced us. She speaks Italian, and Sol liked to speak with her in order to improve his own Italian. Ann had already met Carol, who would later become Sol's wife. We all began to spend a lot of time together. We would often drive through the hills and valleys around Spoleto to discover little-known parts of this area, visiting castles, churches, farmhouses, and museums and stopping to eat at typical trattorias along the way. Sol and Carol loved Spoleto, and they lived in the house that Sol had bought years before. Both Sofia and Eva were born there.

While Sol was living in Spoleto, it was a natural consequence that he would meet other artists in the city. Spoleto and the surrounding area have traditionally been supportive of activities in the field of contemporary art. Sol was invited to participate in various events, and he always did so with enthusiasm.

One of the places that hosted some of these events was the Castello di Pissignano. Sol visited the castle a number of times, and I think he must have been very fond of it. A piece of sculpture from this period, inspired by a tower of the castle, is dedicated to me. He also contributed to the restoration of some of the buildings inside the castle walls.

Another important work that Sol left in our region is a wall drawing on the exterior of an ancient, restored tower that is now part of a house in the small town of Cancelli in the district of Foligno: a white circle, about three meters in diameter, which you can see from the surrounding hills and plains. His presence in Cancelli has drawn many other artists to the area, and has contributed to the development of a number of art activities there.

James Meyer
Writer and Winship Distinguished
Associate Professor of Art History,
Emory University, Atlanta

The last sentence of "Paragraphs on Conceptual Art" (1967)—"Conceptual art is only good when the idea is good"—is among the most enduring of Sol LeWitt's maxims. The term "conceptual" was widely and loosely applied immediately after LeWitt coined it, encompassing serialism, language art, photoconceptualism, video, performance, book art, mail art, ad art, and those reflexive interventions in the gallery known as "institutional critique." Today "conceptual" remains a free-floating signifier. Used to describe any work that appears "critical," that incorporates text, or that has been generated by a proposal, and ascribed to all manner of photo graphy, video, film, and painting (once conceptualism's great enemy), "conceptual" still implies that a work is more than it appears.

It lends the practice the dignity of an ascribed intelligence. For LeWitt, the conceptual denoted a method, a way of making art (the idea as "machine"). It has become a sort of compliment or, better yet, a wish: the wish that the work has an idea, that it is "smart," that it has something to say.

Forty years after the publication of "Paragraphs," LeWitt's claim that conceptualism is "good when the idea is good" remains useful. Anything goes, says LeWitt, anyone can make an art of ideas. This generous assertion, so typical of the artist, comes with a hook: it is up to each of us to determine whether a work is worth thinking about, whether it is good. His insertion of this proviso at the conclusion of his manifesto is striking, when we recall that the most challenging practices of the 1960s, LeWitt's among them, had set about dismantling the ossified notions of quality and taste then associated with the crumbling edifice of modernism. LeWitt replaced formalist criteria with intellectual criteria, and taste (located, as Clement Greenberg put it, in "vision alone") with thoughtful opinion. At a time when assertions of critical belief are rare, when the market mentality decrees much of what is seen and discussed, LeWitt insists on the necessity of acts of judgment.

Andrea Miller-Keller
Independent curator

Sol and I first met in the fall of 1974. I was a green curator, working on my very first exhibition. The occasion was the start-up of a new program called *MATRIX, a changing exhibition of contemporary art.* Funded as a pilot project by the National Endowment for the Arts, it was intended to be an ongoing, nimble, and low-budget exploration of innovative ideas set squarely in the context of a traditional art museum, the Wadsworth Atheneum in Hartford, Connecticut. *MATRIX* opened in January 1975, featuring three solo shows sharing the same space: *Ellsworth Kelly, Jess,* and *Sol LeWitt.* Sol had been born in Hartford and grew up in nearby New Britain: "I went to the [Wadsworth Atheneum]… as a boy and I enjoyed it. I learned a lot. I also took classes at the Atheneum."[1]

My first visit to Sol's Hester Street loft in New York City was when Sol agreed to design the poster for the new venture. His contribution to the *MATRIX* opening exhibition was a current work, *Wall Drawing 236: The location of a rectangle* (1975). It intrigued our visitors, most of whom tapped into its austere beauty and playfully lengthy instructions.

As we approached the time to paint it out, our audiences were puzzled and even troubled by the option of impermanence incorporated into Sol's concept of a wall drawing. Given the touted flexibility of the new *MATRIX* program, the obvious next step

Detail of *Wall Drawing 46: Vertical lines, not straight, not touching, covering the wall evenly.* May 1970. Black pencil. LeWitt Collection, Chester, Connecticut. First drawn by: Sol LeWitt. First Installation: Yvon Lambert, Paris

would be to paint out the wall drawing, but replace it with another LeWitt wall drawing. This, we hoped, would further instruct our visitors about this perplexing new genre.

And so it was that when the works by Kelly and Jess were taken out of the gallery space, that first wall drawing was immediately replaced by another selected by Sol: *Wall Drawing 46: Vertical lines, not straight, not touching, covering the wall evenly* (1970). By this time I was hooked on the beauty and radical nature of the wall drawings.

Sharing the space with this second wall drawing were two works by Eva Hesse: *Aught* (1968) and *Tori* (1969). Not until six years later did I discern that Sol's choice of *Wall Drawing 46* to accompany Hesse's exhibition in the *MATRIX* series was not at all by chance. This was, in fact, a much earlier wall drawing that he had first drawn in Paris in 1970, immediately upon learning of Hesse's untimely death. In silent tribute to her, it had been the first time Sol—already an established master of straight lines, right angles, and grids—introduced a "not straight line" into his work.

This reticence highlights Sol's well-known sense of privacy. Yet when he did write or speak, his comments were usually pithy and frequently wry. I had the privilege of interviewing Sol many times over the long years of our friendship. He understood that I have always had a strong preference to let an artist speak for him- or herself. And so I will. This is also a cunning way to allow Sol to have the last word.

---

1. Sol LeWitt in Susan Rand Brown, "The LeWitt Riddle" (interview with LeWitt), *The Hartford Courant Magazine*, Oct. 23, 1981.

About the first wall drawing, at the Paula Cooper Gallery in October 1968. Did you think it was a new genre? **Yes.** Did you think it would be so fertile, so useful a new format? **Yes.** Did it seem to you a major move at that time? **Yes. I had been thinking and talking about doing them for some time (over a year). I knew that it was more historical and practical as well as theoretical both for me and other artists. It just made more sense to work directly on the wall than on an object to be put on a wall.**[2]

You have been referred to as the "originator" of wall drawings. **I think the cave men came first.**

About the influence of Eadweard Muybridge's rapid-fire time-lapse photographic studies of animal locution. **[Muybridge] offered a way of creating art that did not rely on the whim of the moment but on a consistently thought-out process that gave results that were interesting and exciting…. [It was] a precise way of making art which was logical rather than rational…. Making decisions the whole time, a circle here, a square there: that is a system. Or else spreading painting everywhere, and that's another system. Muybridge offered a third system for making art.**

About using outside drafters? **Working in an architectural office [I. M. Pei, 1955–56], meeting architects, knowing architects had a big effect. An architect doesn't go off with a shovel and dig his foundation and lay every brick. He's still an artist.**

Unfortunately, architects and visual artists are sometimes mortal enemies (at least many architects think so).

Would a conscientious but unauthorized use of wall drawing instructions be unethical? **No, it would be a compliment.** Would it be authentic? **Yes, it would be authentic.**

Ideas cannot be owned. They belong to whoever understands them…. A work of art, said Gertrude Stein, is either worthless or priceless.

I think of [wall drawings]…like a musical score that could be redone…. I like the idea that the same work can exist in two or more places at the same time.

Was your introduction of the "not straight line" in *Wall Drawing 46* a quiet homage to Eva Hesse and her unique sensibility? **Yes. I wanted to do something at the time of her death that would be a bond between us, in our work. So I took something of hers and mine and they worked well together. You may say it was her influence on me.**

About your *Location* drawings, with their long and complicated instructions. **These are ways of using language to describe a precise location. I think of them as my poetry.**

When presented with the scale that walls have one must begin to engage their physical properties. The theatrical and decorative are unavoidable and should be engaged to emphasize the work.

Some ideas need only to be done one time, others lead to new ideas. Some ideas may lay dormant for some time and then be used in a different context.

I am simply obsessed with making art…. What effect it has on society, or what effect society has on it, I cannot say—but I would accept the premise that it does have an effect and is affected by any number of environmental factors…. I do not make art to change society. If I wanted to do this I would make different kinds of art.

When selecting wall drawings for inclusion in the 1996 *Bienal de São Paulo*, did you take the geographical location or the specific cultural context into consideration? **Not really. Indoors everything looks the same.**[3]

About your early use of preset systems. **[T]he use of dogma was a liberating device.** However, you felt no obligation **to be consistent with past strategies: one can't feel constrained by ideology. If it's a help, it's a help. Otherwise, it's a hindrance.**

[I try] not to be trapped by my own consistencies.[4] Indeed, you put a high value on **always trying to step off into something…not done before.**[5]

To be truly objective one cannot rule anything out. All possibilities include all possibilities without pre-judgment or post-judgment.

Mondrian strived for the direct creation of universal beauty. **I would also like to create universal beauty.**

Many find a spiritual quality in your work. Do you? **One must not exclude anything.**

What do you strive for in your work? **I would like to produce something I would not be ashamed to show Giotto.**

---

2. Unless otherwise identified all quotations by Sol LeWitt are from LeWitt and Andrea Miller-Keller, "Excerpts from a Correspondence, 1981–1983," in Susanna Singer, ed., *Sol LeWitt Wall Drawings, 1968–1984* (Amsterdam: Stedelijk Museum, Eindhoven; Van Abbemuseum, Hartford: Wadsworth Atheneum, 1984), pp. 18–25.

3. LeWitt, conversation with the author, Feb. 21, 1996.

4. LeWitt, conversation with the author, Mar. 30, 1989.

5. Ibid.

Kazuko Miyamoto
Artist, founder of Gallery 128,
and LeWitt draftsman

In 1969 I started assisting Sol LeWitt. I had just finished a four-year painting and sculpture program at the Art Students League in New York. My job was to paint the wood pieces he had constructed. I couldn't paint very well, but Sol was generous enough to give me a second chance, and it worked out fine. Thereafter I, together with other Japanese assistants, fabricated his modular wood pieces. I continued to work on them through 2007. Over the years Sol would give us diagrams for the structures he wanted, and his pieces became larger and more complicated. We learned to build the new ideas he had.

Toward the end of his life, I started to imagine myself working with other assistants on buildings and bridges. I love to watch construction workers in the city. In Japan I once saw, through a glass door, a craftsman busy working wood in a small Japanese-style room. The similarity of the way he was working to what we were doing in New York made quite an impression on me: Sol's wood structures were rooted in Japanese methods!

Twenty-one years ago we transferred the operation to the back room of my gallery on the Lower East Side. I am sure it was very interesting for gallery visitors to see Sol's works in progress alongside those of unknown artists on display in the gallery. Carol and Sol LeWitt supported this gallery policy.

From 1969 to 1979 my own artwork developed contemporaneously with his wall drawings, which I helped install. I gained experience in making art directly on wall surfaces beginning with the first drawing shown at the Solomon R. Guggenheim Museum, *Wall Drawing 69: Lines not long, not straight, not touching, drawn at random using four colors* (1971). This practice freed me from the traditional painting and sculpture I had been making in Japan and the United States. My first artwork influenced directly by LeWitt was a piece in which I stretched black cotton string between two nails, set against the lines of mortar of a white-painted brick wall in my loft. For eight years I continued making similar types of works, which Sol named *String Constructions*.

One time an *Arcs, circles, grid* piece was to be drawn on the wall for Giuseppe Panza di Biumo's collection in Varese, Italy. Whereas Sol had always assigned me to work alone on this type of drawing, with the exception of the first layer, which was a grid, this time I was given a helper. I used to draw like an endurance swimmer doing many laps in a pool: I drew circles and arcs an inch apart from one another, employing a nail, a string, and a pencil attached to the string, as if I were using a compass. On huge museum walls this task could take days and days. In Varese I had to draw not on an empty wall but on one with a mantelpiece right in the middle of it. In order to draw semicircles around this obstacle, I had to move the center points away from the wall and onto the floor. This experience led me to add more depth in my own art, expanding the three-dimensionality of my *String Constructions*.

Now I must dance with the great ghostly faces of those who have passed on but who continue to inspire me.

Jonathan Monk
Artist

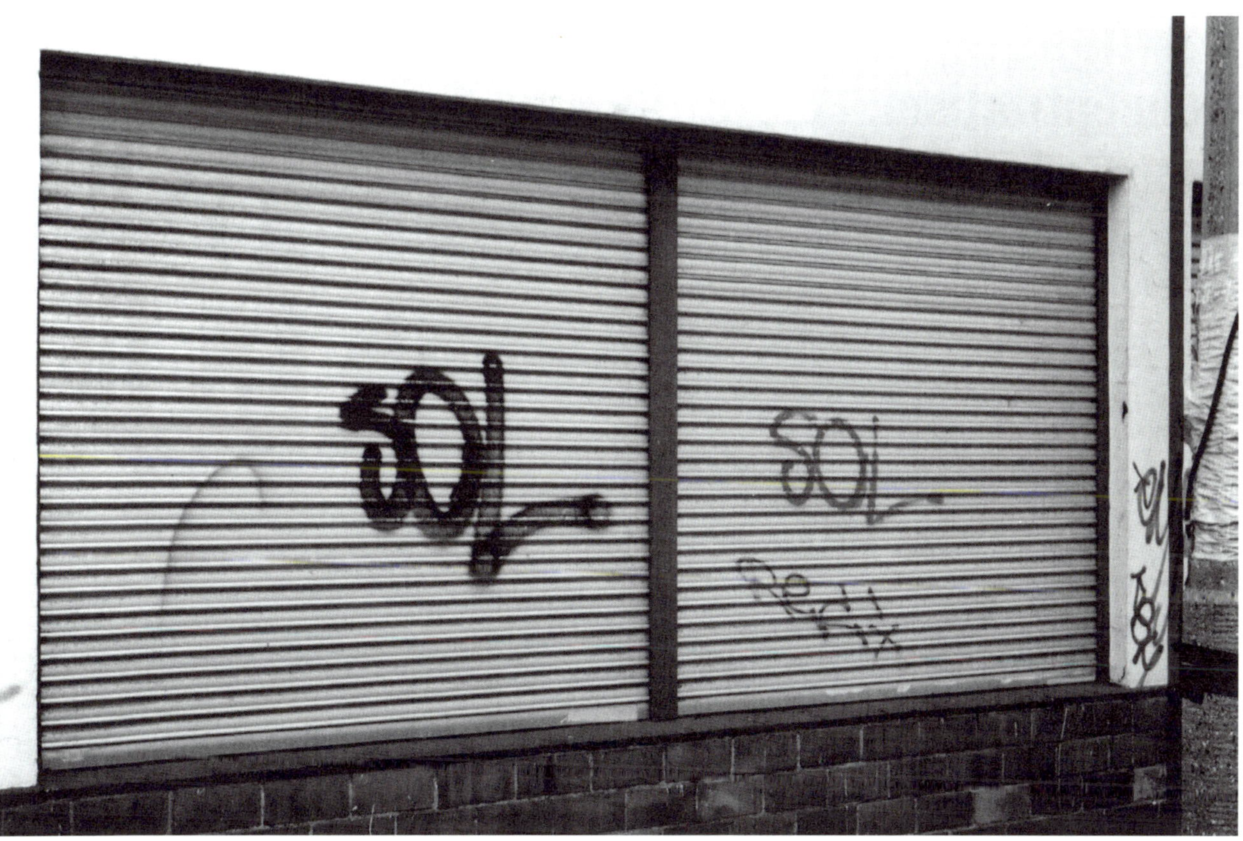

Double LeWitt. 2006. Courtesy the artist and Yvon Lambert, Paris

Saul Ostrow
Writer and critic

LeWitt's Conceptualism: Just Beneath the Surface

Because I knew Sol LeWitt during my student days at the School of Visual Arts, New York, in the mid-1960s and had the opportunity to interview him for *Bomb* magazine in 2003, during which we sorted through our respective memories and views, it is hard for me to write about his work without recourse to personal anecdote. Yet, rather than go down memory lane, I'll use this as an opportunity to reflect upon that interview. In hindsight, it was revealing in terms of Sol's sense of self, as well as his determination to set the record straight, not in any self-aggrandizing manner but for the sake of clarity.

It was during this interview that Sol announced to me that Minimalism—the very movement he is most identified with—was not really a movement at all.[1] Instead it was merely a stop on the way to Conceptual art, which he felt was the most significant thing to come out of the late 1960s. It was in this context that he viewed his work and himself as an artist. One can infer from this that he believed that the historians, critics, and institutions, in sustaining the myth of Minimalism premised on a stubborn insistence to adhere to a canon of their own making, were not only getting his work wrong but were misreading a pivotal moment in the history of late modernism.[2] Such a pronouncement, for an artist of LeWitt's stature, was somewhat bold. The implication was that he desired to have his work reconsidered and evaluated in the context of what he had contributed to Conceptualism.

While such a revision of our understanding of the inner workings of late modernism makes sense given recent events, to ask that one's own work be revised contextually is risky business. Yet LeWitt was willing to submit his work to such a review, even though outwardly it appears to be quintessentially Minimalist in that it is pragmatic, logical, procedural, impersonal, and highly aesthetic. Clearly, he felt that the principles he initially formulated in "Paragraphs on Conceptual Art," published in *Artforum* in June 1967 and from which he never wavered or felt the necessity to revise, could sustain such scrutiny. Apparently, he believed that if we viewed his work in the context of Conceptual art rather than Minimalism, other narratives that form a significant aspect of his work beyond questions of formal intent, aesthetics, taste, and process would become apparent.

When LeWitt's art is viewed from the perspective of Conceptualism, a narrative can be found in his commitment to the idea that everything from the austere and astutely rational to the sensuous can be reduced to a set of instructions (dependent on basic material choices and skills).[3] LeWitt's approach is analogous to that of the computer programmer who constructs narratives that consist of sets of ordered relationships (that form commands), which when read by the operating system set into motion a complex, invisible network of operations. We can view LeWitt's use of mathematical systems and procedural instructions as not only a means of employing modernism's industrial aesthetic but also as a demonstration of how these procedures reflect the underlying structures of our social, cultural, and political systems.

Likewise, there is something Benjaminian in his exploration of the terrain between the fetish and the thing, the original and the mass-produced. A good example of this can be found in the ways that he made available a portion of his work to public institutions through donation or extended loan, and produced an

---

1. Sol LeWitt said: "The problem of Minimalism was that it became an end in itself and what Conceptualism did for Minimalism was to provide an escape from the form-land of the perceptual into the conceptual and the analytic. What I did, originally, was to use the square, cube, and so on, to make a narrative, a narrative in terms of systems, and the narrative had to be understood, it wasn't to be seen. And still people today see things as visual things but without understanding what they are. They don't understand that the visual part is fairly innocuous or boring or whatever. The narrative part is really interesting." From the transcript of an interview by Saul Ostrow with LeWitt, the published version of which appears in *Bomb* magazine, no. 85 (fall 2003).

2. LeWitt: "Well, artists teach critics what to think. They repeat back what the artist teaches them, and if you then say, 'Oh, that doesn't work anymore,' they get terribly upset about that. If you break the covenant that you've had with them, they get very upset [both laugh]. But that's to be expected, too, because they have to learn something else—but they never do and you have to wait for the next change [laughter]." Ibid.

3. "In conceptual art the idea or concept is the most important aspect of the work. When an artist uses a conceptual form of art, it means that all of the planning and decisions are made beforehand and the execution is a perfunctory affair. The idea becomes a machine that makes the art." LeWitt, "Paragraphs on Conceptual Art," *Artforum* 5, no. 10 (June 1967), p. 79.

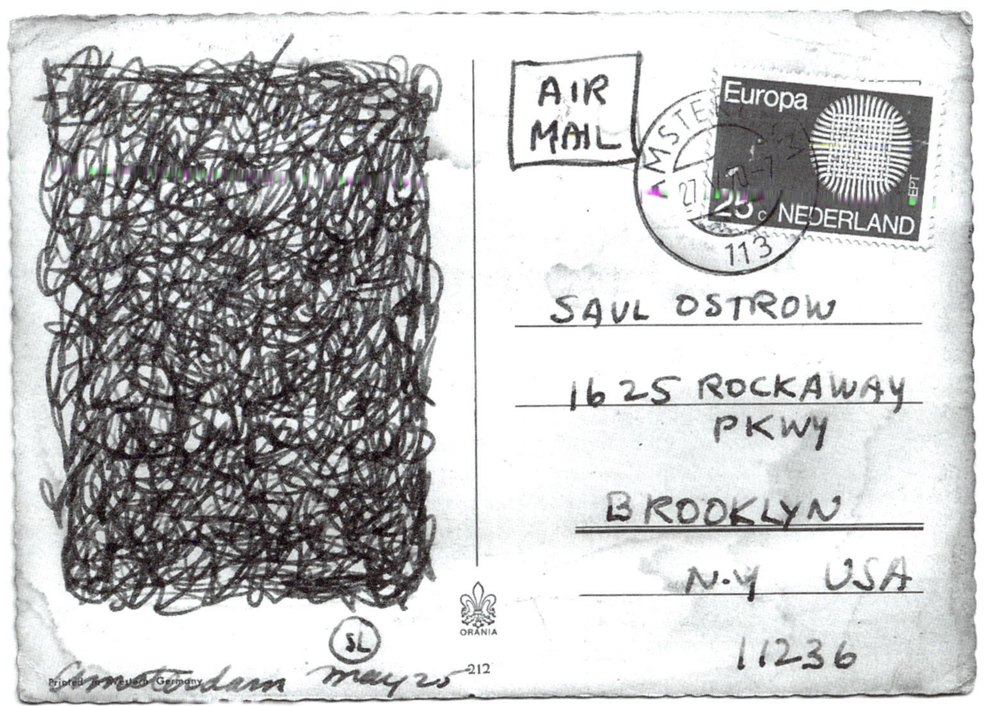

extensive body of work in various print mediums. It is also embedded in the very concept of the wall drawings as well as of the sculptures, which can readily be mass-produced. The underlying notion of art as something no longer unique is made explicit by the fact that anyone who makes the effort can make his or her own wall drawing. But that is not the end of the story: while that one would have no monetary value, it would be no less authentic than the one that came with a certificate. In this simple act LeWitt left us with a reminder that we must appreciate art for the values it represents rather than for its exchange value. Consequently, I own a LeWitt folded-paper drawing of 1972 that I bought from Rosa Esman for $250; it was never intended to increase in monetary value, and to my understanding is today worth no more than I paid for it. Although throughout LeWitt's practice there are many such exemplary enactments of his politics, he never felt it necessary to engage in bombastic art-world polemics or moralizing.[4] He did what he did and trusted that people would, in the long run, understand his work in its fullness.

4. LeWitt: "The reason I think the art of the '60s is valuable in both respects of the Duchampian and the non-Duchampian kinds of Conceptualism, is that it freed art from the formal and aesthetic as a means or an end. It allowed art to move toward narrative, it made an art that was able to create stories. So, instead of the aestheticism and formalism of Modernism, art became politicized, then socialized, then sexualized as we see it today." Ostrow with LeWitt transcript.

Janet Passehl
Artist and Curator of the LeWitt Collection,
Chester, Connecticut

The conceptual artist was a mystic.
The artist was a conceptual mystic.
The artist was a mystical concept.
The conceptual mystic was an artist.[1]

It is 1981, and I am at the Wadsworth Atheneum in Hartford, watching the universe expand. For a young art student, the Sol LeWitt wall drawing exhibition is mind-opening. And in that mystical, karmic way that life has, nine years later my personal universe really does expand, irrevocably, when I am unexpectedly invited by Sol to come to Chester and work for him.

Eighteen years after that I am leafing through very old, handwritten drafts of Sol's published and unpublished writings with Lisa Corrin, director of the Williams College Museum of Art in Williamstown, Massachusetts. We come across a lavishly scribbled page of writing, dated 1965, containing the following:

The total of one's work creates its own philosophy. It emerges from work to work, good and bad, finding its own dimensions.

The total of all past work exerts its influence on the new work. The new work combines the reality of the old and destroys the idea in which it was conceived. It cannot be understood except in context of the other work.

In the course of almost fifty years Sol continually reinvented his work without ever undermining what came before or cutting off the trajectory to the future. In the early 1960s he made canvas-and-wood wall pieces on which wood or canvas squares, painted white, black, gray, or a primary color, recede into holes cut in the main canvas or protrude outward beyond the canvas. These, he told me much later, were attempts to physically manifest the concept of recession and advancement of color on the surface of a painting, a reasonable, analytical move away from the Abstract Expressionist painting he had been attempting in the 1950s. He quickly moved away from painting altogether, because before he could go there again he had to work through the basic skeleton of structure and drawing.

But painting (although Sol rightly never called his works on paper paintings) reappeared in his work of the 1980s, as a combination of complex geometric figures (the pyramid, the star with various numbers of points, the isometric cube) and the exploration of figure-ground relationships. The stars sit deadpan in the middle of the page, usually within a border, while cubes and pyramids first seem to be centered, before seeming to float and bleed off the edges of the paper.

In the early 1990s gouaches called *Brushstrokes* appeared. By this time Sol had been layering primary colors in his wall drawings and the aforementioned gouaches, but the *Brushstrokes* began anew with only red, yellow, blue, black, white, and gray. In a few years he was mixing gouache again to create a greater complexity of color and tone, making the brushstrokes push and pull and vie with one another for optical supremacy and taking a step deeper into the exploration he had begun in the early canvas and wood structures.

In the meantime figure-ground went another round, in the *Irregular Forms*, started in 1992. These are pure, formless forms, free of the reference of geometry, simply "blobs" (his word) floating on a painted ground. The gouaches are neither paintings nor ironic quotations of "painting" as a high art. Instead they are abstracts from the mental idea of painting: a breaking down of the vocabulary of painting into its intellectual components.

After one has explored such elements of art-making, illusionism cannot be far behind. Indeed, for LeWitt it came at the end of his career, foreshadowed by the photographic work *A sphere lit from the top, four sides, and all their combinations* (2004). Illusionism appeared in earnest with the revival of a snippet of Sol's early vocabulary, the scribble, now used in varying densities to create the illusion of three-dimensionality—always within his previously determined geometric vocabulary. The circle became a sphere, and parallel lines took the form of ribbonlike, cylindrical undulations. In the first of these works the forms expand freely to the edges of the page, uninterrupted. Later studies, however, introduce a wry twist: combinations of horizontal and vertical undulations belie their illusory three-dimensionality as they abut one another, hitting a kind of spatial dead end.

It is impossible not to wonder what would have happened next. What aspect of Sol's early work would he have picked up and explored more deeply, richly, and complexly than he had the first time around? But, as Sol liked to say every morning after he'd loaded me up with more freshly painted gouaches, incoming and outgoing mail, books, lists, and instructions than my arms or my day could possibly contain, "That's that for that."

---

1. These lines are adapted from Sol LeWitt's first sentence in "Sentences on Conceptual Art," originally published in *0 to 9*, no. 5 (Jan. 1969); and *Art-Language* 1, no. 1 (May 1969), pp. 11–13.

Adrian Piper
Artist

The Unity of Sol LeWitt's Oeuvre

Think of any object, any event, any state of affairs, anything as it is at a particular moment in time and location in space. Think of that space-time intersection as a point in the space-time matrix. Then think of that thing as it is at a slightly later moment in time, maybe in the same place or maybe in a different one; it doesn't matter. That second space-time intersection forms a second point in the matrix. Then draw a straight line between the first point and the second. Then repeat the operation, as you trace the life of the thing through time and space, plotting its progression from one space-time point to the next with a continuation of your line, which connects each point to the next in the temporal sequence that records its duration and odyssey. That line marks the path of the actual. It marks a section of the journey the thing actually took through time and space.

Now go back to each space-time intersection, and draw an infinite number of lines radiating out through the point that now forms their center, rather like a bicycle wheel with an infinite number of spokes. The line you drew before, the path of the actual, will be one of those lines, but only one of an infinite number. Those other lines, the other spokes of the wheel, are the paths of the possible, the infinite number of possible variations on the actual. The closer each line is to the path of the actual, the more similar that possibility is to the actual life of the thing at that moment. The further away it is, the more dissimilar that possibility is to the actuality of the thing. When the path of the possible is more than 180 degrees distant from that of the actual, it becomes so dissimilar that it begins more and more to resemble the reverse image of the actual.

Sol began at that 180-degree distance, with pared-down geometric forms that at first glance could not have appeared more dissimilar to the actual furniture of the world. But his forms themselves were actual, and each existed in the company of some of its permutations, variations on its actuality, which themselves were also actual. Thus each permutational system—for example, *46 Variations on Three Different Kinds of Cubes* (1967)—implicitly invited us to select further properties of its forms and vary them; to explore the range of the neighboring possibilities in alternative permutational systems; and to gradually and infinitely expand the range of the actual to more distant and dissimilar permutations. A system might have moved, perhaps, from the variability of the closed or open character of each side of a cube, relative to that of the others with which it was conjoined, to the possible variability of the angle at which a bisecting interior side of the cube was placed, relative to those of other cubes with which it was conjoined; or to the degree of curvature of each of the lines that formed its two-dimensional surfaces relative to others, or to the degree of shadow in which each such side was concealed relative to others; or to the color in which each such side was depicted two-dimensionally in a drawing relative to others. The combinatorial function of holding selected properties or parts of the form fixed in relation to others that varied, which in turn would be held fixed in the presence of yet others that varied, was an important feature of Sol's permutational systems, because they uncovered the variability of context and environment in addition to the variability of the forms that inhabited them.

Once Sol saw that the geometricity of forms themselves comprised mere finite variations on the infinite number of possible expansions of line, surface, angle, and color offered by the realm of the possible, he quickly moved past that outer 180-degree point of maximum dissimilarity to the furniture of the world and, in so doing, moved toward the reverse image of the actual. Now each kink and curve in a line drawn as straight as possible revealed variations on straightness; each meeting of lines, whether intended or accidental, revealed variations on bisection and angle; each degree of saturation in the color of a side of a polyhedron revealed a variation on that color and on the shape of that side. Thus LeWitt's systematic investigation of the permutability of line, form, and color expanded to encompass organic line, form, and color as well, and thereby the dizzying variety of line, form, and color found in nature. Now it became clear that no line, no shape, no color, no form, whether alone or in combination—any combination—was beyond the scope of investigation or beyond the scope of systematic permutation. Therefore no thinkable combinatorial possibility was beyond the reach of the actual. The entire infinite range of the visually possible could be transformed sequentially into the actual, progressively pushing the limits of visual and formal possibility further and further with each actualization; linking each actualization not only with previous transformations but with other permutations of form, line, and color produced by other artists in other combinations; and thereby inviting all of us into the game.

John Ravenal
The Sydney and Frances Lewis Curator
of Modern and Contemporary Art,
Virginia Museum of Fine Arts, Richmond

Continual Surprise

One of the defining qualities of Sol LeWitt's career was a commitment to fresh ideas. He rigorously pursued them in his own work and encouraged them in others as well, through his example, his words, and his collecting.[1] Paradoxically growing out of an equally strong commitment to working with a plan and avoiding subjectivity, his commitment to fresh ideas often stretched what we thought we knew about his creative process, at times even seeming to reject the Conceptual basis on which his art was founded. This is especially apparent beginning in the mid to late 1980s, when baroque qualities of exaggeration, attenuation, fragmentation, and rotation began to enter LeWitt's art.

Three works acquired over the past ten years by the Virginia Museum of Fine Arts (VMFA) neatly summarize this development. The collection already included a towering white open-cube sculpture, *1 2 3 4 5 6* (1978), when I arrived as curator in 1998. To represent LeWitt's wall drawings, the first work I added was a four-part ink-wash piece, *Wall Drawing 541: On each of four walls, a fitted form with color ink washes superimposed* (1987), each panel of which features an isometric cube—with superimposed primary colors creating secondary and tertiary colors, plus gray—placed against a ground of a single color. By the late 1980s LeWitt was admitting a hint of irrationality into his repertoire of geometric forms, contradicting the flatness of the wall by tilting his figures to suggest shallow space and cropping them to suggest that they extended beyond the edges.

In addition, when LeWitt installed the piece at the VMFA in 2000—some thirteen years after its first appearance in a gallery in Paris—he decided to alter it by flopping and reorienting the cubes. His motive in this reorchestration was to make the most visually dynamic installation for the new location. In his "Sentences on Conceptual Art" (1969), LeWitt had ruled out such ego-based alterations to an idea once it was formulated—"willfulness," he called it—stating, "The process is mechanical and should not be tampered with."[2] Later he referred to the urge to adjust a work's form as "esthetic frivolity."[3] Nonetheless, he begrudged himself the right. For me, this glimpse into his creative process suggests a subtle shift in the balance between objective and subjective practice, with the visual effect of a work coming to play a larger role in LeWitt's thinking than he had previously allowed.

The next work to join the museum's collection, the large gouache *Wavy Brushstrokes* (1996), extended this trajectory. In the 1990s, at a time when a younger generation of artists was forging a post-studio practice indebted in part to LeWitt's example, LeWitt was reinventing his studio-based practice around the humble medium of gouache. An opaque, water-based medium similar to watercolor but with greater saturation, gouache provided LeWitt with a means of rapid experimentation and immediate gratification. It also allowed him to reintroduce distinctive gesture and individual touch into his work. This painterly practice coincided with and, to a large degree, fostered the change during the 1990s in his wall drawings and sculpture, which became looser and more playful in form and color.

The vocabulary of the VMFA's gouache is consistent with elements found in many of LeWitt's prior works: lines not short, not straight, touching, and stretching from edge to edge of the picture surface; the same width of brushstroke used throughout; primary colors plus black and white; and lines and colors uniformly dispersed to a maximum density. The result of this familiar set of conditions is a remarkably dynamic, expressive, and even personal image whose accumulated tangle of strokes

---

1. It is often noted that Sol LeWitt inspired and encouraged several generations of young artists. I am certain one could also identify a number of museum curators whose contact with LeWitt and involvement with his work at an early stage in their careers significantly influenced their decisions to continue in the field. My own curatorial career began in a 1981 senior seminar at Wesleyan University, Middletown, Connecticut, with Professor John Paoletti in which we organized the first exhibition from the Sol LeWitt Collection, several thousand works of international Conceptual art that LeWitt had placed on long-term loan to the Wadsworth Atheneum, Hartford, with the intention of making them promised gifts. Soon after the exhibition I began working at the Wadsworth Atheneum, where I spent the next three years researching the Sol LeWitt Collection and, with Andrea Miller-Keller, former curator of contemporary art, coorganizing exhibitions from its holdings.

2. LeWitt, "Sentences on Conceptual Art," *Art-Language* 1, no. 1 (May 1969), pp. 11–13.

3. LeWitt and Andrea Miller-Keller, "Excerpts from a Correspondence, 1981–1983," in Susanna Singer, ed., *Sol LeWitt Wall Drawings, 1968–1984*, exh. cat. (Amsterdam: Stedelijk Museum; Eindhoven: Van Abbemuseum; Hartford: Wadsworth Atheneum, 1984), p. 23.

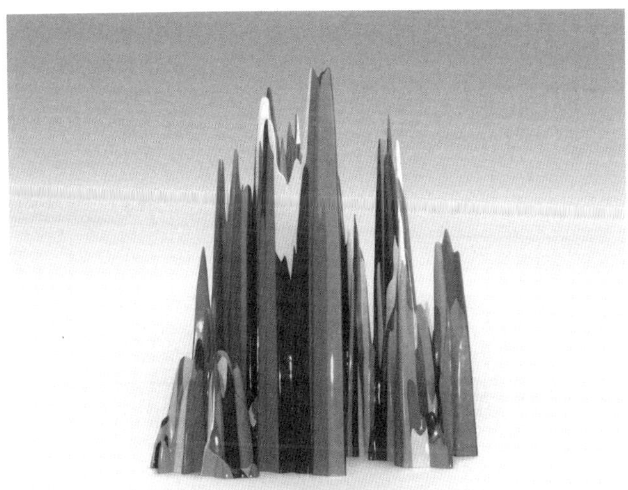

Sol LeWitt. *Splotch 22*. 2007. Acrylic on fiberglass. Virginia Museum of Fine Arts, Richmond. The Sydney and Frances Lewis Endowment Fund, and partial gift of the artist and PaceWildenstein in honor of Frances Lewis and in memory of Sydney Lewis. © Virginia Museum of Fine Arts and courtesy of the Estate of Sol LeWitt

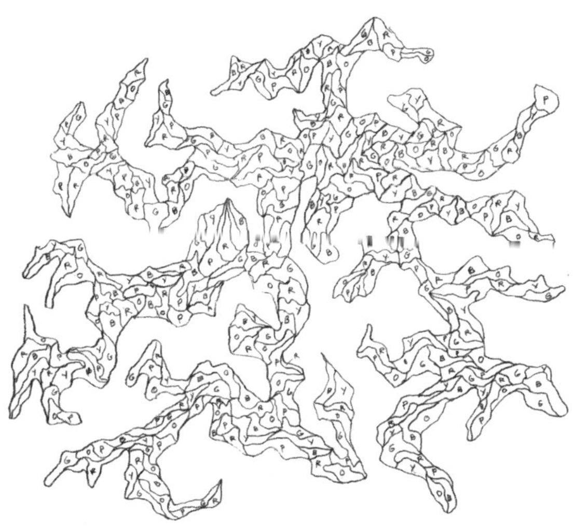

Sol LeWitt. Working Drawing for Nongeometric Form: *Splotch 22* (color). 2005. Ink on paper. Virginia Museum of Fine Arts, Richmond. Gift of the Estate of Sol LeWitt. © Virginia Museum of Fine Arts and courtesy of the Estate of Sol LeWitt

suggests a maelstrom. In addition, one can detect spontaneous choices made during the execution of the work—in strokes that peter out before reaching their destination or veer toward adjacent rather than opposite edges—along with a general sense of joy in the act of painting. LeWitt seems to have relaxed into these works with the confidence of having invented a language that required no further clarification of its rules, and thus could serve as a basis for improvisation.

The museum's third acquisition was the largest and most complex of his sculptures with nongeometric forms, *Splotch 22* (2007), which would prove to be LeWitt's last sculpture. This body of work arose in part from a series of eccentric shapes LeWitt explored in gouaches, which suggested to him the footprints for irregular three-dimensional pieces. To plan the sculptures LeWitt drew free-form contours and then divided the forms into small units, assigning a primary or secondary color and a

height to each cell. No discernible system guided either the placement of colors, except uniform dispersal, or the assignment of heights, other than a general building-up toward the peak. (The VMFA's work rises to more than 12 feet.) LeWitt's fabricator translated his sketches into virtual three-dimensional forms using CAD software, then constructed them in actual three-dimensions from industrial foam coated with epoxy resin and fiberglass. Finally, they were painted with latex.

One could parse the connections between these sculptures and his prior work, but, fundamentally, they represent another one of LeWitt's leaps beyond logic. Their fantastic exuberance—with brightly colored and exaggerated Gothic spires, like a Caspar David Friedrich painting on acid—again suggests an artist secure enough in his approach to admit apparent contradictions and even a hint of the absurd. In conversation, Lawrence Weiner once described LeWitt to me as the

last of the Abstract Expressionists. Hyperbole aside, the comment suggests the paradox at the heart of LeWitt's work, as I believe Weiner was commenting on: his command of monumental scale, mastery of color, distinctiveness of voice, and overall expressive power that, nonetheless, was founded on a rejection of just these sorts of concerns in the Abstract Expressionist generation that preceded him.

If one looks back over LeWitt's body of work and at the thoughts expressed in his seminal writings, it becomes clear that paradox and freedom were always essential elements of his art. He welcomed the surprise of austere descriptions, instructions, and diagrams generating complex and sensual forms—like printed recipes yielding gourmet meals—and the unexpected results that came from following irrational judgments "absolutely and logically." One only wishes to have seen what surprises and delights might have come next.

Steve Reich
Composer and musician

"Once the idea of the piece is established in the artist's mind and the final form is decided, the process is carried out blindly."
Sol LeWitt, 1969[1]

"Although I may have the pleasure of discovering musical processes and composing the musical material to run through them, once the process is set up and loaded it runs by itself."
Steve Reich, 1968[2]

"There are many side-effects that the artist cannot imagine. These may be used as ideas for new works."
Sol LeWitt, 1969

"The impersonal, unintended, psychoacoustic by-products of the intended process…might include submelodies heard within repeated melodic patterns, stereophonic effects due to listener location,… harmonics, difference tones, and so on."
Steve Reich, 1968

"The artist would select the basic form and rules that would govern the solution of the problem. After that the fewer decisions made in the course of completing the work, the better. This eliminates the arbitrary, the capricious, and the subjective as much as possible."
Sol LeWitt, 1967

"While performing and listening to gradual musical processes, one can participate in a particular liberating and impersonal kind of ritual. Focusing in on the musical process makes possible that shift of attention away from he and she and you and me outward toward it."
Steve Reich, 1968

"In terms of idea the artist is free even to surprise himself. Ideas are discovered by intuition."
Sol LeWitt, 1967

"The truth is, musical intuition is at the rock bottom level of everything I've ever done."
Steve Reich, 1974

---

1. All quotes from Sol LeWitt are from Gary Garrels, ed., *Sol LeWitt: A Retrospective*, exh. cat. (New Haven: Yale University Press, 2000). The sources, listed in order, are the following texts in that catalogue: "Sentences on Conceptual Art," p. 372, reprinted from *Art-Language* 1, no. 1 (May 1969), pp. 11–13; "Sentences on Conceptual Art," p. 372; "Paragraphs on Conceptual Art," pp. 369–70, reprinted from *Artforum* 5, no. 10 (June 1967), pp. 79–83; "Paragraphs on Conceptual Art," p. 369; Garrels, "Sol LeWitt: An Introduction," p. 33, reprinted from Garrels, "A Conversation with Sol LeWitt," *Open: The Magazine of the San Francisco Museum of Modern Art*, no. 1 (winter–spring 2000); Martin Friedman, "Construction Sights," p. 59.

2. All quotes from Steve Reich are from Reich, *Writings on Music, 1965–2000*, Paul Hillier, ed. (New York: Oxford University Press, 2002). The sources, more specifically, are: "Music As a Gradual Process," p. 34, reprinted from Marcia Tucker and James Monte, *Anti-Illusion: Procedures/ Materials* (New York: Whitney Museum of American Art, 1969); "Music As a Gradual Process," p. 35; "Music As a Gradual Process," p. 36; "Author's Introduction to Writings about Music (1974)," p. x, reprinted from Reich, *Writings about Music* (Halifax: Press of Nova Scotia College of Art and Design; New York: New York University Press, 1974); "Second Interview with Michael Nyman," p. 95, reprinted from *Studio International* 192, no. 984 (Nov.–Dec. 1976); "Second Interview with Michael Nyman," p. 94.

"Sometimes inadvertent and casual things can set my ideas into another direction.… I started using curved lines and bright colors, everything that was completely different than what I was doing then.… That turned into what I'm doing now and a new way of thinking."
Sol LeWitt, ca. 1998

"The difference between the sixties and now is that those years were a time of very strong ideology, politically, aesthetically, and every other way. In order to break with the past and make new things, you had to begin with some kind of ideological framework… I could never have made a colored sculpture. It was something I just couldn't do.… But now I say, so what? If it seems to promise some kind of interesting result, why not do it?"
Sol LeWitt, ca. 1999

SR: It's very important for me to work with different kinds of instruments.… Mallet percussion and [clapping] bare hands produce short tones, whereas voices, bass clarinets, and strings can produce longer ones, and that leads to basic decisions about duration of notes, the human breath, and so on. Plus, the sheer beauty of sound these instruments can produce, especially in combination.

Nyman: You're not interested in genuinely minimal music?

SR: No, I'm not. I'm interested in music in a more traditional sense of that word, and I really always have been.
Steve Reich and Michael Nyman, 1976

"When you discover a new idea, It may be very important to present that idea in a very forceful and pared-down way. My early pieces are very clear examples of a strict working-out of certain musical ideas that were new.… But once you've done that for a while—you can't write the same piece over and over again. The artists I admire are the ones that move on."
Steve Reich, 1974

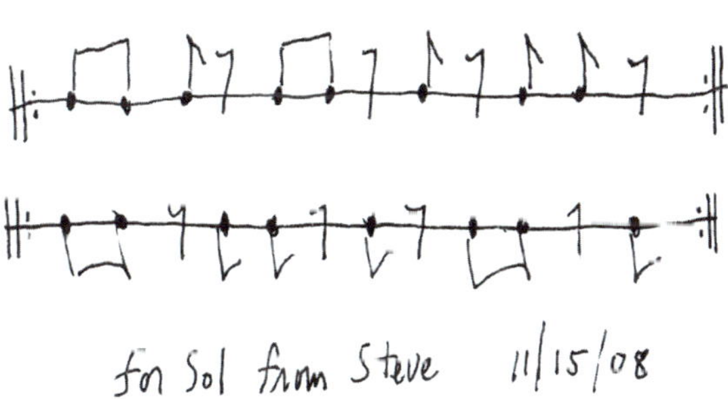

Jock Reynolds
The Henry J. Heinz II Director,
Yale University Art Gallery, New Haven

Wall Drawing 146A: All two-part combinations of arcs from corners and sides, and straight, not straight, and broken lines within a 36-inch (90 cm) grid

This particular wall drawing now occupies a large room of Sol LeWitt's own design within some 27,000 square feet of gallery space devoted to his retrospective at MASS MoCA, and it is a first cousin to his *Wall Drawing 146* (1972) and *Wall Drawing 260* (1975). These two wall drawings reside in two major public collections. The former is in the collection of the Solomon R. Guggenheim Museum, New York, but for a long time belonged to one of LeWitt's earliest patrons, Italian Count Giuseppe Panza di Biumo; the latter is now owned by the Museum of Modern Art, New York, the institution that gave the artist his first retrospective and where he once worked as a guard.

Coming upon *Wall Drawing 146A* (2000) for the first time (which differs only from *Wall Drawing 146* and *Wall Drawing 260* in the crayon and wall colors LeWitt designated for each), a viewer might be a bit puzzled at first. Although you have entered an environment of stunning visual beauty and find yourself literally surrounded by a vast, lyrical array of simply combined lines dancing together with all the elegance of a late Matisse cutout, it is not immediately apparent how this large system of lines came to be conceived, drawn, and presented as a single work of art within a very subtle graphite grid registered upon a bright-blue wall. But not to worry, for to readily comprehend the conceptual thinking LeWitt employed in this wall drawing, one need only step outside the big room it inhabits and take a good look at a smaller blue wall, upon which has been written and diagrammed the complete visual vocabulary the artist used to set forth his aesthetic intention for this work. For those of you equipped with some knowledge of science, the way LeWitt chose to illustrate the twenty different kinds of lines in *Wall Drawing 146A* may remind you a bit of the periodic table of elements. Below the basic graphic representation of his line elements, LeWitt also set forth another visual key, the full set of one hundred ninety-two possibilities for how these twenty types of lines can interact with one another in two-part combinations. For some viewers this may call to mind the conceptual elegance of the double helix that James Watson and Francis Crick first used to visually describe the basic elegance of DNA to the world.

The artistic medium most truly comparable to LeWitt's visual interests, however, is music. It may be even easier for a viewer of *Wall Drawing 146A* to think of its twenty different kinds of lines as twenty different notes that are to be played serially in closely related variations and sequences, much as Steve Reich and Philip Glass began doing as pioneering Minimalist composers in the 1960s (and whose work LeWitt held in high regard and supported early on in its development by purchasing a number of their scores). The directions LeWitt provided for his wall drawings are essentially scores, comprised of concise, verbal language and explicit diagrams that readily transmit his concepts and visual ideas to others, much as musical composers pass on their compositions to those who would play their music.

In the more than 1,260 wall drawings LeWitt created between 1968 and 2007, he sometimes offered chance operations and other choices for his assistants to make as they realize his art, while in other works he clearly set forth the exact systems of lines, geometric forms, colors, and other visual elements that comprise the totality of particular wall drawings, along with descriptions of which materials are to be used in their creation. And thus no matter where throughout the world a well-prepared individual, ensemble, or large orchestral group of LeWitt assistants may be called upon to site-specifically create a wall drawing or group of wall drawings on his behalf, it is always clear how each of LeWitt's works is to be realized, be it upon a single wall or on all walls of an entire room, as the artist stipulated for MASS MoCA's installation of *Wall Drawing 146A*. And now that LeWitt is gone, his wall drawings will need more than ever to be continuously studied and

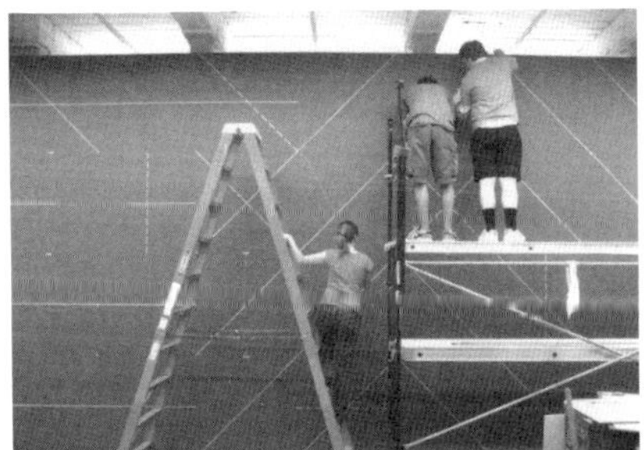

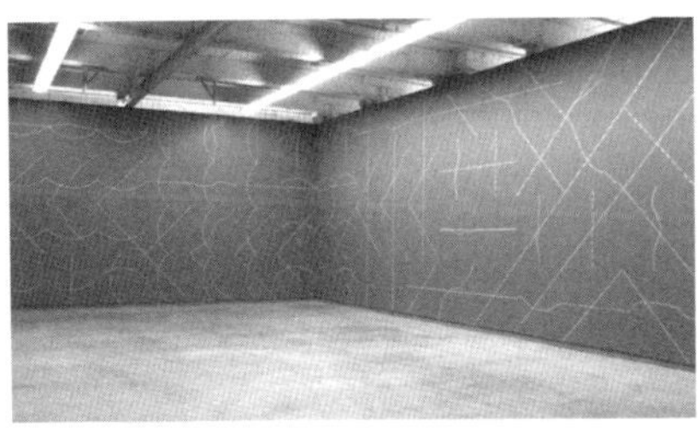

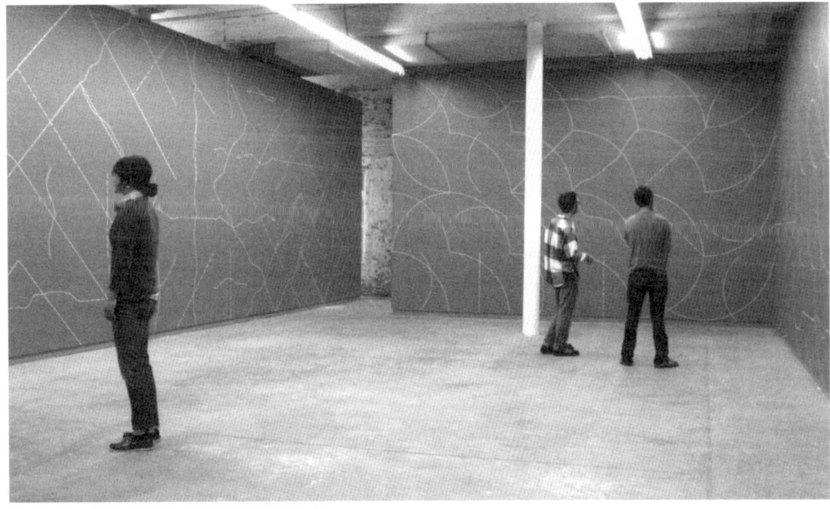

Sol LeWitt. *Wall Drawing 146A: All two-part combinations of arcs from corners and sides, and straight, not straight, and broken lines within a 36-inch (90 cm) grid.* June 2000. White crayon on blue wall. LeWitt Collection, Chester, Connecticut. Photos: Will Reynolds

executed by others—especially new generations of students and artists—if this unique oeuvre of Conceptual art is to be kept alive for audiences to enjoy, both now and in the future.

It is also worth knowing that *Wall Drawing 146A*, with its multiple offering of two-part line combinations drawn over an expansive grid, is directly expressive of LeWitt's early interest in the work of nineteenth century photographer Eadweard Muybridge. Muybridge was the conceptual and visual pioneer who fastened together and then triggered banks of cameras in rapid succession to record discrete, sequential images of animal and human locomotion. During the 1960s, as LeWitt was finding his

way as a young artist, he adopted what his good friend and fellow artist Mel Bochner described as the "serial attitude." LeWitt became deeply interested in Muybridge's experiments, especially how they enabled motion—the gait of a horse, the flip of a gymnast, the twirl of a dancer—to be perceived in elegant, visual passages that dramatically expanded human perception and thought, when recorded before austere, black backgrounds skeined with carefully drawn grids of white lines. And it also did not escape LeWitt's attention that it was another artist he deeply admired, Thomas Eakins, the great American painter, draftsman, photographer, sculptor, and teacher, who helped extend the invitation Muybridge received

to conduct his advanced studies of *Animal Locomotion* at the University of Pennsylvania in Philadelphia. Over time LeWitt became as comfortable creating in all visual mediums as Eakins did in his day, reveling in a continuous production of images and structures that often seem very simple at first viewing but then reveal themselves to be enticingly complex and visually poetic upon further examination and contemplation. *Wall Drawing 146A*, just one example of LeWitt's unique and exceptional oeuvre, offers visitors to MASS MoCA a very rewarding encounter with a masterpiece of Conceptual art produced by one of America's greatest artists.

Matthew Ritchie
Artist

Sol LeWitt's Secret

Much has been made of the notion that Sol LeWitt's work is not about the object itself but the ideas behind the object. This is, of course, an almost meaningless statement, since ideas, objects, and the world they belong to have meaning "only because the human urge toward meaning is what makes the world a place at all."[1] We are also encumbered by LeWitt's own pragmatic modesty, making it impossible to gauge the artist's true ambitions.

But let's play the game and pretend there are actually ideas or systems that can somehow hide behind objects, and that these can be distinguished from ideas or systems that can only be found in objects. I like it. Then let's take this notion one step further, and try to imagine there is a correspondingly real state between an idea and its manifestation, a space where latent forms and emergent systems drift, waiting to be summoned by the eye. I imagine this as a larger, extra-dimensional space, somehow isometric to our own. This space, if we grant it exists, is actually a grand and terrifying prospect, quite far in its implications from the cozy theorizing of late 1970s Conceptual practice, closer by far to the shadow space that T. S. Eliot described in "The Hollow Men": "Between the idea/ And the reality/Between the motion/ And the act/Falls the Shadow/… Between the conception/And the creation/Between the emotion/And the response/Falls the Shadow."[2]

Doesn't that seem like a perfect description of what LeWitt, despite his generosity and his modesty, was doing all along? One of his hopes was "to re-create art, to start from square one."[3]

What if what we saw of the LeWitt project, with its sly humor and vast appetite for public and private projects, was just a mask for an even more enormous shadow project, this deduction of higher forms, this vast transcendental argument for immanence? I like to imagine that he didn't want us to simply revere the Minimal severity of his early "shape without form, shade without color, paralyzed force, gesture without motion" (from the same Eliot poem), or later to just dreamily revel in the gorgeous consequences of that same geometry lushly veiled in ecstatic colors seemingly salvaged from Giotto's palette.

I like to imagine that all along LeWitt harbored an even more extraordinary ambition; that implicit in his venture are not only all the LeWitt works that might have ever been but the promise of all possible combinations of line and color, hovering between the super-sensible noumenon, the thing in itself, and the manifold, the field of as yet unsynthesized presentations.

Wouldn't it be a fitting tribute to house a project like that in a magnificent and unending procession of glorious chambers, collectively memorializing and celebrating the premise and promise of all human perception? Wouldn't that be a fine thing?

---

1. Kenneth Baker, "Keith Sonnier at the Modern," *Artforum* 10, no. 2 (Oct. 1971), p. 80.

2. T. S. Eliot, "The Hollow Men," in Eliot, *Poems, 1909–1925* (1925; repr., London: Faber and Faber, 1930).

3. Sol LeWitt in Martin Friedman,"Construction Sights," in Gary Garrels, ed., *Sol LeWitt: A Retrospective*, exh. cat. (New Haven: Yale University Press, 2000), p. 51.

Dorothea Rockburne
Artist

"Logic can take you from A to B, but imagination encircles the world."
Albert Einstein

Often when I'm filling out official forms and I come to the part designating religion, I am tempted to fill in "geometry" (not the kind one learned in school but the magic kind, Plato and Pythagoras, etc.). Sol and I talked about that kind of geometry and often shared insights.

I find Sol's geometry to be generous, while often wonderfully goofy. Once, a long time ago when I was in his New York studio, I admired as a work of art the sheet of paper on which he was casually making small lines to clear his pen. The lines went this way and that, making little formal sense, but all the while they were very Sol, very accurate. As I commented on the casual and beautiful geometry this sheet of paper presented, Sol threw his head back and laughed. Then, in a few days, this small work arrived at my studio as a gift, signed and framed. I think this drawing of Sol's was perhaps the origin of the later *Scribble* drawings. I have it, and I love it.

James Rondeau
Curator and Frances and
Thomas Dittmer Chair,
Department of Contemporary Art,
The Art Institute of Chicago

Wall Drawing 1: Drawing Series II 14 (A&B)

Sol LeWitt's first wall drawing, made five years after the artist began showing his sculptures, was realized in October 1968.[1] Using sharpened sticks of graphite, LeWitt executed the composition directly on the wall in two parts, side by side, each of which measured 4 square feet. The two halves were divided into quarters (separated by thin bands of exposed white wall), and each of these four areas was quartered again, resulting in eight distinct sections each made of four parts. Each subdivision displayed the motif that was to become a foundation of LeWitt's mature art: lines in four directions—horizontal, vertical, and two diagonals. The elimination of any mediating support—a sheet of paper or an expanse of canvas—between the drawn mark and the surface of the wall emphasized the purely two-dimensional quality of the work and, at this early stage, demanded impermanence, precluded

a conventional sale, and opened up the possibility for multiple draftsmen each time the piece was installed.[2] LeWitt's concept was revolutionary.

Wall Drawing 1 was made for a collective, activist enterprise organized by the prominent, young art critic and curator Lucy Lippard, the Minimalist painter Robert Huot, and the political advocate Ron Wolin as a benefit for the Student Mobilization Committee to End the War in Vietnam, an alliance formed in 1966 as a coalition of various national antiwar groups.[3] The exhibition, held from October 23 to 31, 1968, was the inaugural show at Paula Cooper Gallery, located in a third-floor 5,000-square-foot space at 94 Prince Street in SoHo. The benefit featured the work of fourteen artists, including LeWitt and Huot, as well as Carl Andre, Jo Baer, Robert Barry, Bill Bollinger, Dan Flavin, Will Insley, Donald Judd, David Lee, Robert Mangold, Robert Murray, Doug Ohlson, and Robert Ryman. All the contributors were relatively young and clearly identified with Minimal art.

The presentation at Paula Cooper Gallery was novel in every conceivable way. Although Minimal art was at that time reaching a critical apex, it was not the dominant mode in the Midtown commercial-gallery system.[4] In SoHo in October 1968, Cooper's space was then the only gallery in an industrial neighborhood interspersed with artists' studios. Both the location and the interior of Cooper's large, rough, loftlike space were self-consciously modeled after those studios, the places where art was made and an environment that was in direct opposition to the traditional and polished interiors of the modestly scaled commercial emporiums uptown. Cooper's gallery—soon to become an archetype emulated by countless dealers in the United States and abroad over the next two decades—thus carried a bohemian, even exotic, tinge when it opened.

The installation at Paula Cooper Gallery was also the first New York antiwar benefit to feature abstract art, unlike most of the other protest exhibitions presented in the late 1960s, which tended to include figurative, even propagandistic, art. As Lippard wrote on the announcement card for the exhibition:

These fourteen non-objective artists are against the war in Vietnam. They are supporting this commitment by contributing major examples of their current work. The artists and the particular pieces were selected to

---

1. The idea was first documented among other linear permutations as *Drawing Series* in Seth Siegelaub's exhibition *The Xerox Book* (1968). When first drawn, Sol LeWitt's work was untitled; only later was it catalogued as the genesis of a larger serial operation he called "wall drawings."

---

2. Andrea Miller-Keller recounts: "Paula Cooper recalls that the first wall drawing was imbued with a 'quiet authority' and that she was 'impressed most of all by its beauty.'… Cooper was deeply troubled by LeWitt's specifications to paint out the work when the exhibition closed. When the time came, she was unable to bring herself to destroy something of such beauty. In the end, she prevailed upon LeWitt to return to the gallery to paint it out himself. Interestingly, LeWitt does not remember this incident at all." See Miller-Keller, "Sol LeWitt: Twenty-Five Years of Wall Drawings," in *Sol LeWitt: Twenty-Five Years of Wall Drawings, 1968–1993*, exh. cat. (Andover, Mass.: Addison Gallery of American Art, Phillips Academy; Seattle: University of Washington Press, 1993), p. 42.

3. The coalition's activities consisted principally of distributing leaflets, holding meetings on campuses and in communities, organizing street demonstrations, and conducting student strikes. The exhibition's proceeds were divided equally between the organization and the artists.

---

4. On view simultaneously in other New York galleries, for example, were solo shows by Anthony Caro (at Andre Emmerich), Alex Katz (at Fishbach), Larry Poons (at Leo Castelli), Antoni Tàpies (at Martha Jackson), Wayne Thiebaud (at Allan Stone), and Jack Youngerman (at Betty Parsons). Only Dan Flavin (at Dwan) shared a general conceptual and aesthetic framework with LeWitt. Flavin was included in Lippard's selections at Paula Cooper Gallery.

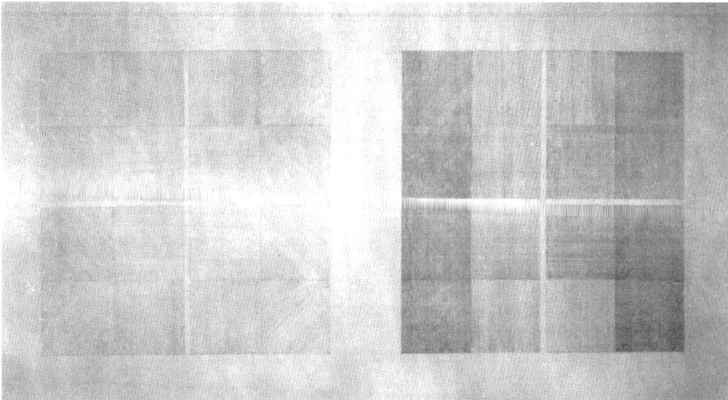

Wall Drawing 1: Drawing Series II 14 (A & B) (detail). 1968. Black pencil. Mr. and Mrs. Donald Fisher, San Francisco. Photo: Walther Russel

represent a particular aesthetic attitude in the conviction that a cohesive group of important works makes the most forceful statement for peace.[5]

In a more explicit vein, Lippard described the venture as "a kind of protest show against the potpourri peace shows with all of those burned dolls' heads. It really looks like an exhibition first and a benefit second." The curator went on to characterize the innovative nature of highlighting socially engaged abstract art. During the 1960s, she noted, "an increasing number of abstract artists have found it morally necessary to protest the political climate, their art-for-art's sake position notwithstanding."[6] In presenting nonobjective Minimal work, Lippard and her collaborators were as interested in advancing a new formal agenda differentiated from the prevailing aesthetics of protest art as they were in the antiwar effort itself. This "peace show of Minimal art," Lippard pointed out,

brought a "new constituency to the context of 'politics and art.'"[7] (LeWitt's "writing on the wall" almost could be understood in this context as a gesture that formalized and intellectualized the transgressive nature of graffiti.)

In LeWitt's work, abstraction is indeed coextensive with acute social consciousness. He was, somewhat contradictorily, an essentially apolitical artist who believed deeply in equity, fairness, and social justice. A few months before first executing *Wall Drawing 1*, LeWitt had summarized some of his views on art and politics:

I don't know of any art of painting or sculpture that has any kind of real significance in terms of political content, and when it does try to have that, the result is pretty embarrassing…. Artists live in a society that is not part of society…. The artist wonders what he can do when he sees the world going to pieces around him. But as an artist he can do nothing except be an artist.[8]

This modest demurral notwithstanding, LeWitt, according to Lippard's authoritative retelling, "supported endless 'radical' causes with art and money, supported the goals of the Art Workers' Coalition… picketed the Museum of Modern Art, the Whitney and the Guggenheim… and has withdrawn or withheld work from those institutions displaying 'arrogance' to artists or oppressed groups."[9] Indeed, throughout his entire career LeWitt remained a profoundly ethical artist who did not shy away from inherently political acts when and where his honorable values met the larger world. His lifetime of work—coupled with his eminently pragmatic humanity—offers a model in which creative innovation and the exercise of citizenship are not mutually exclusive propositions. It is perhaps useful to be reminded that his singular contribution to the history of art—a body of work that is vanguard, independent, oppositional, and wholly transformative—first emerged, in the crucible of the late 1960s, both in and apart from the intersections of social activism and advanced art.

5. A photograph of the announcement card appears in Sébastien Delot, "New York 1968: Une exposition de groupe manifeste à la galerie Paula Cooper," *Les cahiers du Musée du national d'art moderne*, no. 99 (spring 2007), pp. 83–95.

6. Lucy R. Lippard in Grace Glueck, "A Party That Includes You Out: Art Notes," *The New York Times*, Oct. 27, 1968, p. D26.

7. Lucy R. Lippard, *A Different War: Vietnam in Art*, exh. cat. (Bellingham, Wash.: Whatcom Museum of History and Art; Seattle: Real Comet Press, 1990), p. 18.

8. LeWitt in Lucy R. Lippard, "The Structures, the Structures and the Wall Drawings, the Structures and the Wall Drawings and the Books," in Alicia Legg, ed., *Sol LeWitt*, exh. cat. (New York: The Museum of Modern Art, 1978), pp. 28–29; quoted from *Metro* (Venice, June 1968), p. 44.

9. Lippard, "Structures," p. 30, n. 41.

Bernice Rose
Chief Curator, Menil Drawing Institute and Study
Center, The Menil Collection, Houston

Nancy Rosen
Independent curator and adviser

A Paragraph for Sol LeWitt

Once, while I was riding through a heavily industrialized part of Italy in the backseat of Sol LeWitt's car, he looked around at me as he drove and remarked, "They lost the plan in 1610." LeWitt never lost the plan. His first plan, "Paragraphs on Conceptual Art," which was published in 1967 and laid out his territory, was followed by terser guidelines for implementation in his "Sentences on Conceptual Art" of 1969. Embracing paradox, his rules liberated our sight. They returned to basic elements to realize his vision. The wall, as the new site of drawing, and the floor, as the new site of sculpture (wherever they might be found), became universal spaces for reinventing our possibilities. His rules for locating vision were the product of a beautiful mind. As the realization of his works required no particular manual skill, not even for executing the drawings, something remarkable happened: art could be and was made by all. LeWitt's art evolved as a traveling show made by others. Numerous people everywhere were enlisted as surrogate artists. Even experiencing the agonies of artistic labor, they collaborated not only with LeWitt but with others from the whole history of the artistic construction of vision, beginning with the most basic mark-making. This unique collaboration, as Robert Storr has written, takes LeWitt's art beyond the limits of his mortality and connects his sight to an eternally renewable present.[1]

Aharon Appelfeld, Altona, Androccio, arc, Bach, Bauhaus, Benozzo Gozzoli, Beth Shalom, casella postale, Chinatown, circle, Cleveland Indians, *Consequence (WD #720)*, cube, Davenport, Deep River, Deruta, Eva, Fabriano, *Ficciones*, Gemeentemuseum, Giotto, gouache, graphite, grappa, Holocaust, ink, *Isozaki (WD #667)*, James Ingo Freed, Joyce Carol Oates, Korean War, Las Cruces, Lippi (father and son), Lower East Side, Monteluco, Muybridge, Nabokov, NBA, New York Cultural Center, Oskar Schlemmer, Pinturicchio, postcards, Printed Matter, pyramid, Quirinale, relatives, Richard Strauss, *Scribbles*, Sofia, sphere, square, strangozzi, swimming, tee shirt, triangle, typeface, Umbria, Villa Celle, Wadsworth Atheneum, Wiener Werkstätte, working drawings, *X (WD # 1247)*, Yiddish Book Center, zigzag

---

1. Robert Storr, "Darkness Tangible," in
Sol LeWitt: Scribble Wall Drawings, exh. cat.
(New York: PaceWildenstein, 2007), p. 10.

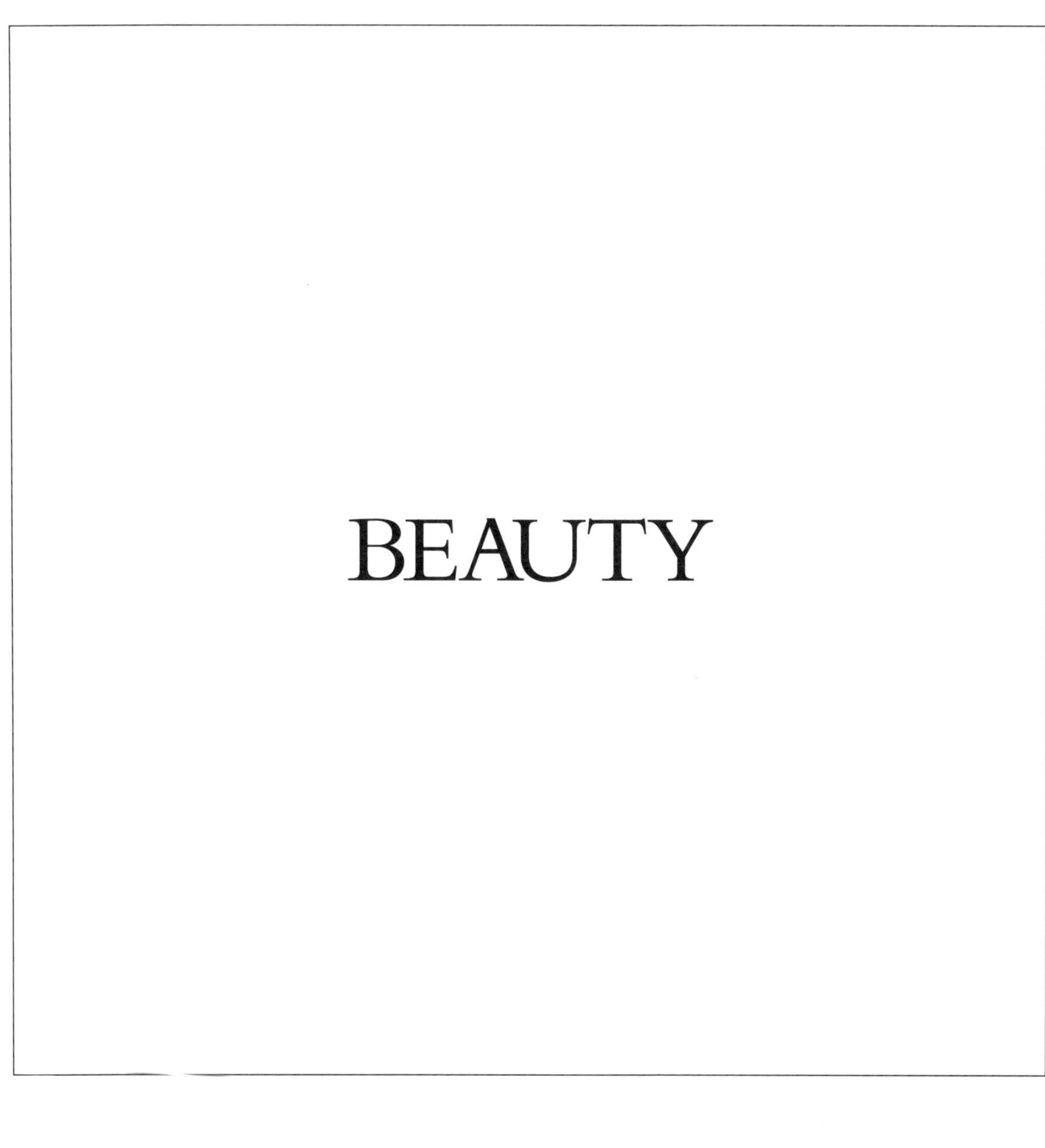

BEAUTY

**Christel Sauer and
Urs Raussmüller**
Founders and artistic directors,
Raussmüller Collection,
Hallen für Neue Kunst,
Schaffhausen, Switzerland

Sol LeWitt and the Hallen für Neue Kunst, Schaffhausen

In Schaffhausen we have been privileged to live for the past twenty-five years with an impressive group of works by Sol LeWitt. We are showing sculptures and wall drawings dating from 1967 through the 1990s in a permanent installation, and have been delighted to see that the fascination with these works persists despite recent artistic trends and technical innovations. Indeed, as new possibilities for pictorial production have become ever more complex and their usage more prominent, LeWitt's works stand apart all the more strongly through their unpretentious presence. Due to the simplicity of their materials and forms, as well as the physical directness of their production, they seem to possess a natural timelessness.

It was above all the intelligence of LeWitt's concepts that originally appealed to us in his artistic approach. Here was someone who finally had disposed of the age-old distance between artwork and viewer in a straightforward way. He placed simple geometric structures directly on the floor and drew lines with a pencil right on the wall. He emphasized the space with clear, three-dimensional edges and used the quality of two-dimensionality on planes of all sizes. Over the years we increasingly perceived the complexity of the effects resulting from Sol's choice of materials, his determination of the works' dimensions, and their exactly specified execution. We marvel to this day at the fifteen squares of the pencil drawing from 1970: how subtly the gray tones contrast with the white wall, how colorfully the graphite shines in the sunlight against the matte ground, how ingeniously the progressive number of lines affects the impact of the work, and to what degree the skillful execution animates an apparently simple geometric principle.

Among the qualities of the installations at Schaffhausen are the number and importance of the works by which each artist is represented. From the very beginning in 1982/83 the presentation of comprehensive groups of works has been intended to enable even inexperienced visitors to gain access to the ideas underlying and shaping the artworks' character and appearance. Moreover, the works at the Hallen für Neue Kunst not only find the space they need but also have sufficient time to unfold in impact through a long-term presentation. We determined the selection of Sol LeWitt's works together with the artist, as we did with others, before building the walls and spaces for their presentation. Since then LeWitt's works have asserted themselves generously and remarkably serenely in their bright surroundings that overlook the green water of the Rhine flowing past.

Even more than the sculptures, the wall drawings at the Hallen für Neue Kunst have proven to be particularly riveting for their physical directness. They offer surprisingly different solutions to the problem of how to convincingly structure essential linear patterns in combination with the primary colors (plus black), and thus constitute a constant visual and intellectual challenge. Viewers move from the early serial pencil drawings, whose almost monkishly disciplined execution makes a strong impression (particularly against the background of the digital techniques available today), to the *Wall Drawing 354 A–E: Isometric figures* (1981), whose strikingly three-dimensional feel is barely understood given the (seeming) simplicity of its construction. Finally, when visitors approach the *Wall Drawing 308: Three-part drawing* (1978), they are confronted by the explosive energy of its superimposed rays of red, yellow, and blue. The artwork's intensity becomes physically palpable and thus narrows any intellectual distance the viewers may have in favor of a more emotional appeal.

LeWitt repeatedly visited the Hallen für Neue Kunst, at times alone or with his family or assistants. He knew he had the liberty to intervene in and make changes to the existing installation. In 1994 he took the decisive step of designing new works for the group that he in the meantime had come to regard as "classical." He played with the lateral light source from the large windows, capturing the reflection of the light in wide wall drawings that juxtapose matte and shiny blacks. Like massive clouds, two forms float on the dark background, each the inversion of the other. In addition, LeWitt filled the three sides of a room next to these irregular forms with a colorful, cubic pattern of strong, three-dimensional effect. Visitors who sit in this room cannot get enough of the diversity and equality of the color tones. As with other works by LeWitt, viewers try to decipher the guiding, logical principle of organization, which cannot be found here, because it does not exist. Instead the viewers

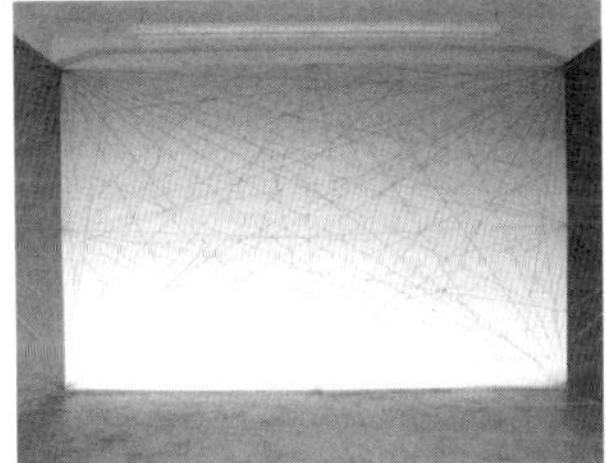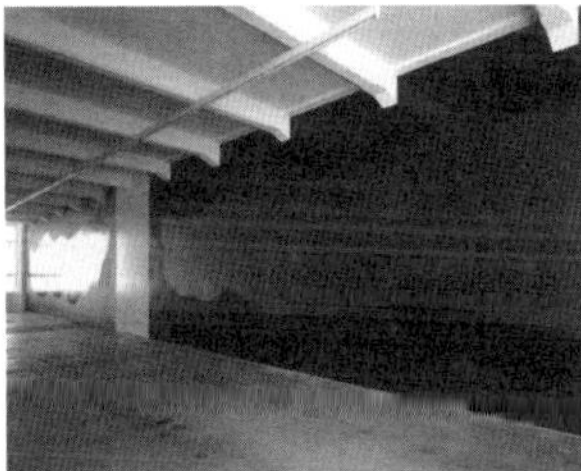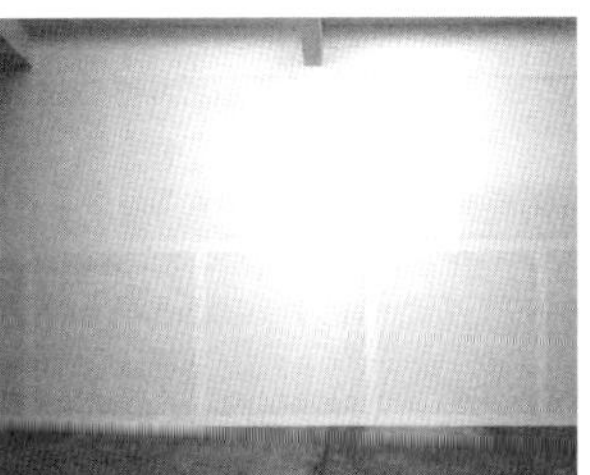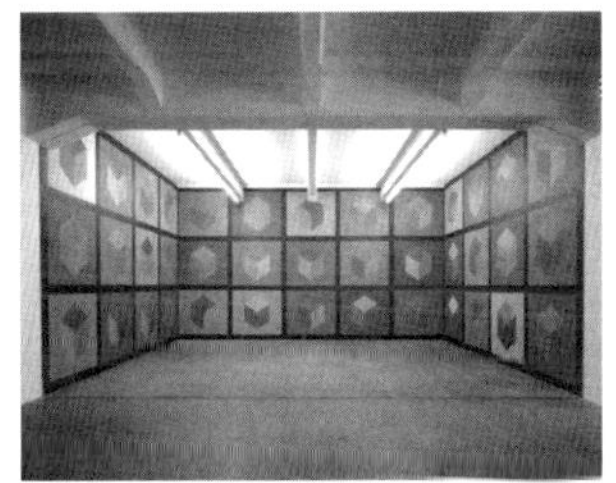

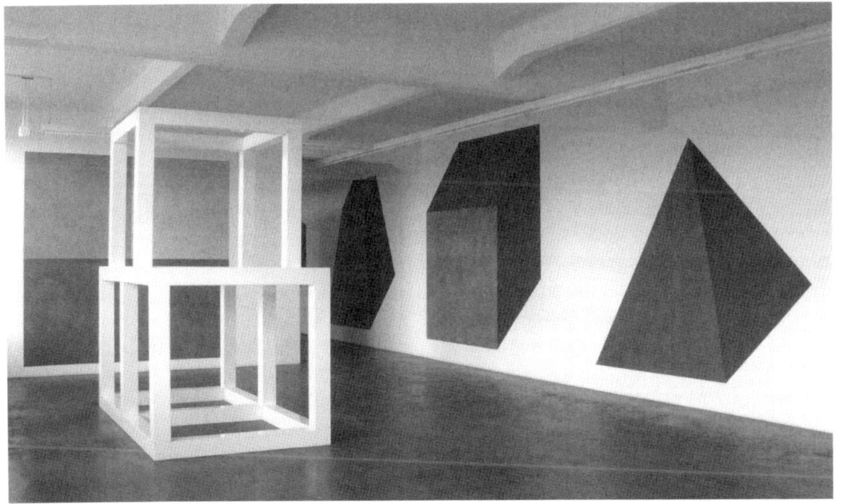

CLOCKWISE FROM TOP LEFT:
Sol LeWitt. *Wall Drawing 308: Three-part drawing: red, yellow, and blue.* 1978. Red, yellow, blue crayon, black pencil, red, yellow, and blue walls ▪ Sol LeWitt. *Wall Drawing 749: Irregular black shape.* 1994. Acrylic paint ▪ *Wall Drawing 61: All one-, two-, three-, and four-part combinations of lines in four directions, each within a square,* 1970. Black pencil ▪ Sol LeWitt. *Wall Drawing 746: Cube with color ink washes superimposed.* 1994. Color ink wash ▪ Sol LeWitt. *Wall Drawing 354 A–E: Isometric figures.* 1981. India ink wash ▪ All works: Raussmüller Collection, Hallen für Neue Kunst, Schaffhausen. Photos © Raussmüller Collection, Hallen für Neue Kunst, Schaffhausen

perceive with rising admiration the process of production that allowed a result of great complexity and power to develop simply through the reduced means LeWitt employed and the precision of the work's execution.

Adding to all these sensations is the impact of the visible absence of any hierarchy. Having no primary or secondary emphases, favored or unprivileged areas, the works of LeWitt are clear statements of a democratic world-view. As such, they are open to all. In order to experience their expressiveness one need possess neither background knowledge nor an ability to discriminate. The works encounter the viewers openly and without reservation, but still maintain their unmistakable individuality. The intensity they communicate is already contained in the first idea and ultimately takes form in its execution. That LeWitt involved others in the realization of his works from an early point in his career underscores the intellectual principle of his approach: he qualified authorship (which manifests itself sufficiently in the idea before the execution) to favor the dissemination of knowledge about the procedures of production, combined with a disciplined engagement. These are the conditions of a great oeuvre whose vitality is ensured far beyond the artist's own generation.

Joe Scanlan
Artist

Credit Where Credit Is Due

In April 2008, within a larger article in *Artforum* on the subject of art and money, I expressed admiration for Sol LeWitt's wall drawings, works of art that exist as ideas until someone wants to produce them locally at his or her own expense.[1] In any wall drawing the network of idea, institution, local draftsmen, and LeWitt (by proxy, if not in spirit) determines how the work will be materially produced, all the while that the idea (*Wall Drawing 69: Lines not long, not straight, not touching, drawn at random using four colors,* for example) is hovering in the vicinity of the actual drawing without ever becoming fixed by it. Thus LeWitt's instinct for how an artwork might "be" in the world proposed a fundamental shift in how and where it might be produced, as well as in the extent and form it needed to exist in order for us to assign it value. Whereas the value of most artists' work still depends on the quality of their personal output, the value of the wall drawings is that they can be made by many people in different places simultaneously and repeatedly. Thus, like the best aspects of the information economy, LeWitt's wall drawings collect and make sense of diverse points in space without privileging any one of them, creating art (and meaning) out of the relations between things rather than in the things themselves.

This is not to say that LeWitt's wall drawings are produced collaboratively, however much agency their producers have; nor is it to suggest that the process of making a wall drawing is democratic, that the people with pencils who are physically drafting the image are somehow equal to the artist. In writings and interviews throughout his career, LeWitt was quite clear: he appreciated the work that everyone did, but didn't think the people who made his art were necessarily artists, nor did he think that "anyone" could make his work. LeWitt also wrote that his ideas were based on his experiences and that they were subject to change as his experience changed. It's fair then to think that his authority in the wall drawings grew as he gained fame as an artist and, over time, came to realize that unequal power relations were a necessary dynamic for ensuring their sublime commitment and beauty. I also suspect LeWitt shared Max Weber's view of the division of labor, meaning that he did not see disparities in responsibility or status as unjust; rather he saw them as a way of recognizing and protecting the particular credit that each participant was due. Serving as pencil sharpener every day is not an occasion for bitterness or envy; it is an opportunity to be the best pencil sharpener you can be until the day you get asked to draw some lines—at which point you are free to accept or reject that opportunity, because the dynamic allows even a "lowly" pencil sharpener the illusion of being able to choose one's station in life. Consequently, whatever surplus distinction might accumulate in the process of making a wall drawing gets distributed by osmosis: the communal glow that equalizes diverse people who are engaged in benevolent work.

Still LeWitt's attenuated version of authorship did not preclude the possibility that all the participants could follow all the guidelines and still make an artwork that wasn't "good enough." Even though this seldom occurred in LeWitt's lifetime, how could it happen at all? Isn't the premise of the wall drawings that the idea produces the work, meaning that if everyone performs in accordance with the idea's parameters a satisfactory artwork should result?

Apparently not, as was the case after *Wall Drawing 271* (1975) was first executed at Dia:Beacon in spring 2007, when the sandpaper and rollers were brought back out, the wall roughed up and repainted, and the *Black circles, red grid, yellow arcs from four corners, blue arcs from the midpoints of four sides* had to be drawn all over again. Why? Because Sol said so.

I can only conjecture how this rare fiat affected the otherwise rosy social scenario of making a wall drawing, as the increasingly hagiographic treatment of LeWitt's draftspersons in exhibition catalogues attests.[2] Perhaps LeWitt's fiat was a way of countering a burgeoning sentimentality around his work, a way of complicating the caricature of the artist as the quintessential nice guy. Given his elegant taste for mischief, maybe LeWitt rejected a wall drawing from time to time just to keep everybody on his or her toes. More likely, given his love of music, I would aver that LeWitt thought that a group functions best not only when it connects and tolerates as many different participants as possible, but also when one of them occasionally has the wisdom and the audacity to tell the rest of the group what to do.

---

1. Joe Scanlan, "Modest Proposals," *Artforum* 46, no. 8 (April 2008), pp. 312–19, 390.

2. It would seem that the desire to organize survey exhibitions of Sol LeWitt's wall drawings engenders a desire to document their various drafters over the years as well. See, for example: Susanna Singer, ed., *Sol LeWitt Wall Drawings, 1968–1984,* exh. cat. (Amsterdam: Stedelijk Museum; Eindhoven: Van Abbemuseum; Hartford: Wadsworth Atheneum, 1984); *Sol LeWitt: Twenty-Five Years of Wall Drawings, 1968–1993,* exh. cat. (Andover, Mass.: Addison Gallery of American Art, Phillips Academy; Seattle: University of Washington Press, 1993); and *Sol LeWitt,* exh. cat. (La Coruña, Spain: Fundación Pedro Barrié de la Maza, 2002). This trend seems unique to the wall drawings as compared to, say, the various fabricators of Michael Asher's installations over the past four decades or, more recently, the collective participants of a Relational Aesthetics event. It is even unique within LeWitt's oeuvre, since no one has yet endeavored to catalogue the names of LeWitt's sculpture fabricators or his printers. The exceptional character of the desire to document workers using pencils to make art, but not workers using machines, deserves greater analysis than space here allows.

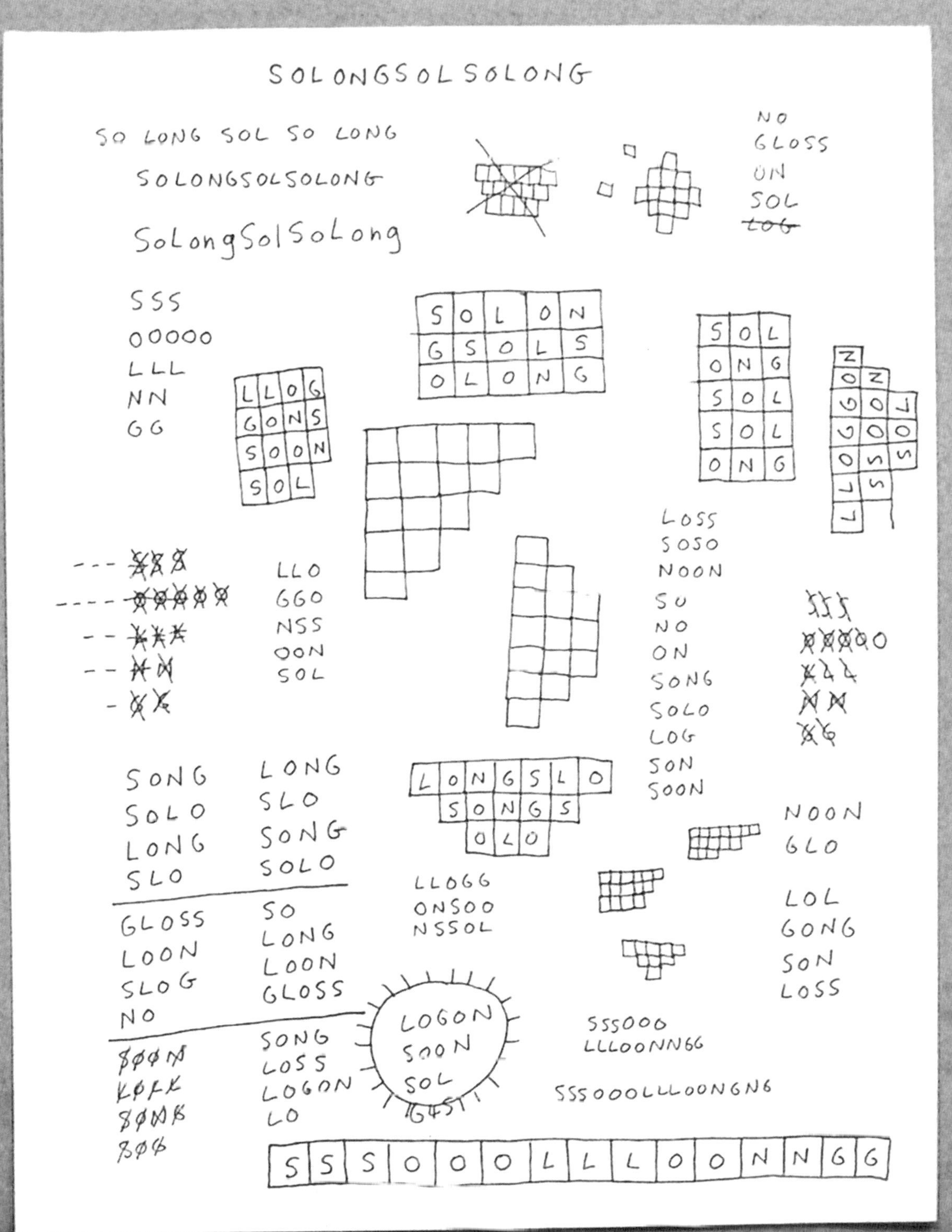

SOLONGSOLSOLONG
SO LONG SOL SO LONG
SOLONGSOLSOLONG
SoLongSolSoLong
NO
GLOSS
ON
SOL
LOG
SSS
OOOOO
LLL
NN
GG
SOLON
GSOLS
OLONG
SOL
ONG
SOL
SOL
ONG
LLOG
GONS
SOON
SOL
LLOGGON
SSOON
SOL
LLO
GGO
NSS
OON
SOL
LOSS
SOSO
NOON
SU
NO
ON
SONG
SOLO
LOG
SON
SOON
SONG
SOLO
LONG
SLO
LONG
SLO
SONG
SOLO
GLOSS
LOON
SLOG
NO
SO
LONG
LOON
GLOSS
SONG
LOSS
LOGON
LO
LONGSLO
SONGS
OLO
LLOGG
ONSOO
NSSOL
NOON
GLO
LOL
GONG
SON
LOSS
LOGON
SOON
SOL
G
SSSOOO
LLLOONNGG
SSSOOOLLLOONGNG
SSSOOOLLLOONNGG

Stephen Schermeyer
Artist

I met Sol through a mutual friend in 1988–89. I was making minimal—pardon the word—steel tables. They were archetypical really and were extremely basic and unadorned, almost styleless. Sol saw these and had an inspiration—as was customary for him—to make a table of the same material. He had—a number of times—made tables out of wood, but not for a while. He sent me a drawing by mail. It was a small piece, a table but in the shape of a bench. It was his iconic "lines in four directions," and comprised four, approximately 12-inch-square modules. Made of one-inch-square stock, they were arranged in a row. He requested, emphatically, that he wanted his table's surfaces to be kept the same way as mine were: in the raw without extensive finishing. The welds (the joins where the pieces meet) were to be exposed, just as the mechanic in question would have left them. He asked that two tables be fabricated. One went off to Italy, and the other would be kept by Sol in his house in Chester, Connecticut, for many years.

Not soon after that and without prior warning, I received a call from my shop that there was a lengthy fax waiting for me. The fax machine at that time was a relatively new invention—to send an image immediately!—and Sol used it with gusto. The fax, the caller said, was of all "these images." Sol had liked the small table so much that he decided to do an extensive series of "coffee tables," which were 14 inches high and had tops 49 inches square, in a number of his hallmark Conceptual motifs: triangles, cubes, arcs, lines in four directions, even some with colored-panel insets. It was as if his drawings came alive in another medium, a functional one no less, with the material making the drawings far more vibrant and the method far more expressionistic in its final rendition.

While under normal circumstances one would expect some advance notice for a project of this scope, this was not the case with Sol. He drew you into his work and his life, and, in my case, it is quite impossible to divorce work from the personal. He exuded a quiet and studied enthusiasm, had many varied interests, and was very much a person who cared about the people he worked with. That said, Sol assumed I would take this project on and would begin work immediately. He asked for a complete set of drawings for a catalogue, and said he wanted the workers to fabricate some tables right away.

Whenever there was a question regarding materials and possibilities, Sol was there—always—and took the utmost pleasure in the give and take, never being at odds with the material, never seeking an unreasonable resolution, never demanding. Although Sol never visited the shop in person, solely because of distance, he was always excited to receive a packet of photographs of work in progress and, better, a finished piece on its way.

James Siena
Artist

I first saw Sol LeWitt's drawings when I was a student at Cornell University in the mid-1970s. The exhibition was small and modest; it consisted of perhaps twenty works. I remember studying a drawing whose title included the words "ten thousand lines." Measuring about 7×5 inches, the drawing was done in ballpoint pen. Looking at this drawing, I was struck by many things. First there was the patience required in its making. Second there was the rigor in the precise and very large number of lines, completely unverifiable of course (an example of the element of the absurd in LeWitt's work). Thirdly and most importantly for me, there was the depth of feeling in the drawing.

In spite of its evident conceptual specificity, I felt a person behind it, a very interesting person, in fact. So my way into LeWitt is by way of the solitary explorer at his drawing table, a curious individual for whom the idea is, of course, paramount, but for whom the physicalization of any given idea completes it and makes it real and human. In the years that followed he became a major influence on me, though I view him as more Apollonian to my Dionysian.

When it comes to his wall drawings, I'm a huge fan. I love the fact that they are "in" the wall, not "on" it. They engage architecture beautifully, as its equal. They have a tenderness and humility that go against their large scale and grandeur.

It's no surprise then, despite my memory of the intimacy of those early drawings, to see LeWitt writ large in this exhibition at MASS MoCA. As I walked through the galleries while the works were still being executed, I was acutely aware of his curiosity, his relentless desire to explore a range of approaches to any given mode, and his sense of play within his world of limits. Most of all I felt his humor and love of the absurd. Though we all know that to exhaust any given idea is an impossibility, if we look, and think, closely enough, we see that that is precisely his point. LeWitt's relentless quest to go as far as possible (and, against the odds, he went light-years) may be his greatest contribution to art and his most inspiring quality for me. Art is inexhaustible.

John F. Simon, Jr.
Artist

When I was an ambitious student searching for ways to bridge computer graphics and painting, I encountered Sol LeWitt's statement, "The idea becomes a machine that makes the art,"[1] and instantly connected with his work.

"Of course," I said, "It's obvious the idea becomes a machine: that's software!" It seemed perfect and easy. I could write the code and let the machine iterate every possible picture. And it worked for me…in theory.

Reality was more complicated. There was something deeper in Sol LeWitt's art-making process that I had yet to grasp. I noticed that my experience with a LeWitt drawing ran counter to my ideas about the drawing's logical premise. I tried to pinpoint how the work's complexity emerged from its succinct description. Then while viewing a beautiful wall drawing, I realized that the concept used to generate the drawing fell away in the presence of its materials.

My reasoning mind finds pure beauty in LeWitt's diagrams of all possible combinations of lines, arcs, shapes, and so on. My love of mathematics resonates with small sets of things grouped in a large number of ways. The programmer in me admires the softest of software—words written on paper—being turned into wall-sized murals by teams of assistants (with minimal debugging, I'm sure).

But if the system is objective, how does it gain so much power in individual artworks?

My understanding came when I shifted my focus from the machine that made the art back to the idea. Executing the idea brings the work into being. The choices made in how to convert the logical idea into something physical reveal the decisions of the system's creator. This is how an objective system becomes personal.

My favorite example of this is *Incomplete Open Cubes* (1974), because it is not possible to display in a gallery all potential incomplete open cubes. For example, we could assemble four wood bars in a square for the top of the cube, but in the installation they would have to be floating in air. (In my work *Endless Bounty* [2005] I used three-dimensional computer graphics to display the gravity-defying parts.) Because he recognized this limit in shaping the piece, a specific group of 122 white-painted wood pieces became LeWitt's subset of the infinite.

---

1. Sol LeWitt, "Paragraphs on Conceptual Art," *Artforum* 5, no. 10 (June 1967), p. 79.

Susanna Singer
LeWitt Studio Manager

"Recently there has been much written about minimal art, but I have not discovered anyone who admits to doing this kind of thing. There are other art forms around called primary structures, reductive, rejective, cool, and mini-art. No artist I know will own up to any of these either…. Mini-art is best because it reminds one of mini-skirts and long-legged girls. It must refer to very small works of art. This is a very good idea. Perhaps "mini-art" shows could be sent around the country in matchboxes. Or maybe the mini-artist is a very small person…"

Sol LeWitt, "Paragraphs on Conceptual Art," 1967

The Sol LeWitt I knew and worked with for over thirty years was among the most ethical, loyal, trustworthy, trusting, disciplined, democratic, witty, and amusing people I have known. He was steadfast in his beliefs and, although shy and unassuming, possessed a self-assurance that rarely wavered.

Sol made me laugh every day, and his sense of humor and wit can be seen throughout his work. Among the many examples are the paragraph quoted to the left; his titles like *Loopy Doopy*, *Splat*, *Splotch*, and *Blob*; and *Wall Drawing 84*, a 12-inch square filled in by using all of the Crayola crayons in a box of twelve.

His democratic principles are perhaps best exemplified by the drawings that were never to be sold for more than $100, thus allowing any-one to own an original work of art.

A voracious reader of both fiction and nonfiction, Sol gave the all-time best book summaries. His love of language is evident in the *Location* wall drawings, which he referred to as his poetry.

He listened to all kinds of music (especially classical) and likened the role of the Conceptual artist to that of a composer, and the role of the fabricator to that of the performer.

With few exceptions, Sol rejected requests to be interviewed or to speak in public, refused awards, rarely published his writings (after 1971, that is), believed that a discussion of his work should be exempt from an examination of his persona, and would never have allowed this book to be published.

That said, his beliefs and character are easily found in his art.

That Sol was an avid sports fan (the Cleveland Indians and the New York Mets and Jets were his favorite teams) may be the only thing about him that one cannot discern from his oeuvre.

Ingrid Sischy
Writer and contributing editor for
Vanity Fair USA and co-international
editor for Vanity Fair Europe

It is fitting that, in the beginning, Sol worked at the Museum of Modern Art in New York as a guard. And it's not surprising that he loved the gig. Even though he went on to become an important artist, being a guard is a perfect metaphor for Sol's critical place in art history and in the art world. I don't mean the kind of militaristic guard whose function is to ensure that people "Do Not Enter" places or things. Not at all. It was the opposite with Sol, whose role as a protective spirit of art—against its trivialization and commercialization—and of other artists remains a book yet to be written.

There is a quote by Gertrude Stein that Sol used in the 1978 catalog for his exhibition at the Museum of Modern Art, which goes something like this: "A work of art is either priceless or worthless." As Sol himself famously said, for him it was the *idea* behind the art that was either worthless or priceless. And here's the kicker: for him, ideas belonged to everybody. "If there are ideas in my work that interest other artists, I hope they make use of them,"[1] he wrote in a letter to *Flash Art* in 1973. "If someone borrows from me, it makes me richer, not poorer. If I borrow from others, it makes them richer but me no poorer."[2] The generosity that is embedded in this perspective is also deeply embedded in his work. Not only is his art a collective enterprise, it cuts through time and space. "Need to move?" "Take the plan for the wall drawing with you, and we'll do it again in the new place." His generosity went beyond his own work. So many artists describe him as a guardian angel, because of how he was there for them when they needed a push for their work or a hand for the rent. Sol may have hung up his museum guard's uniform when he started to be able to earn a living from his art, but his shift never ended.

---

1. Sol LeWitt, "Comments on an Advertisement Published in *Flash Art*, April 1973." *Flash Art*, no. 41 (June 1973) p. 2.

2. LeWitt, interview with the author, 2006, unpublished.

Pat Steir
Artist

Sol LeWitt:
An Artist

"Conceptual Artists are mystics rather than rationalists. They leap to conclusions that logic cannot reach."
Sol LeWitt, "Sentences on Conceptual Art," 1969

Without doubt or ambivalence Sol LeWitt set out on an intuitive journey that had no end.

In 1969 Sol wrote his "Sentences on Conceptual Art."

They were not rules, and he did not follow them.

He never looked back.

He never ever stopped making art.

He never questioned his intuition.

Never questioned the art while he was making it.

Never judged the work or selected good work from less good.

Never judged one venue as superior to another.

The result of this nonhierarchical way of thinking and being was a life work that grew organically like a plant that permutated and mutated, endlessly growing and changing with nothing to prove, existence being the proof.

Although not a geometrician, Sol loved the clarity and beauty of geometry and platonic forms. He intuitively knew the relationship of musical instrument and musical invention to geometry. Sol was particularly inspired by the structural geometry of Bach and Mozart, and sensed deeply and with lucidity the ratios that underlie musical harmony. Sol's romance with music and the mathematical construction of harmony inform all of his work.

Enhanced and supported by his deep feeling for structure and clarity, LeWitt's art seems to embody the Pythagorean discovery that numbers in geometry represented by form reveal the mystery of the universe, and that logic does not always prevail.

As though reinventing geometry, Sol began with the line and the line in four directions, which became the not-straight lines, which became the arcs, circles, and grids, which became the cube. As time went on his cubes permutated into circles, triangles, and all forms derived from the cube, both as three-dimensional structures and as wall drawings.

A forerunner of his later art, the *Location* drawings—linear work done early in Sol's practice—have long and totally complete descriptions of each location of various points, expressing absurd hilarity and playfulness, as well as enormous visual beauty.

The later work is even more lyrical and visually lighthearted. There are blobs, multicolored lines, and endless permutations of lines and geometric forms in two- and three-dimensional space. Although this work looks more expressionistic, it seems to me that Sol was at play, teasing order and logical sequence, creating with humor the appearance of disorder. Order, however, is always the underlying subtext. In fact, he always returned to his drawings of cubes and his lines in four directions.

Sol's work was never completely rational; that departure from a dogmatic attachment to the rational or logical is in large part what makes this work *Great Work*.

When he began Sol felt anyone following his written directions and interpreting them in any way could make the wall drawings. The wall drawings were and are fine art made in an artisanal way. Art made by hand by artisans, possibly, but not necessarily, executed by the artist. It is this sense of democracy that contributes to the depth and poignant beauty of the wall drawings. Although the wall drawings were rarely made by the artist's hand, they are certainly handmade; the names of the artisans are always listed on the wall beside the drawings. The handmade quality of the work gives it resonance. Reminding me of prehistoric cave drawings, the drawings seem to say *someone* was here.

Sol defied the prevailing system of exclusivity. The wall drawings are inclusive in every way.

Allowing his wall drawings to be done and exhibited anywhere and everywhere, he accomplished his one and only goal: to have his work realized and seen. While being everywhere, they are not anywhere; they can be bought and sold but not possessed; although works are sold, they can be realized in many places if the second, third, or fourth place does not claim ownership.

Sol sent thousands of postcards with drawings and few or no words on them, a sort of precomputer email, mail art that he didn't claim as such.

Sol was making drawings and sending postcards with drawings on them until a few days before he passed away.

His last work, made in the final weeks of his life, is a symphony of freedom, control, and clarity.

For Sol there was no life without art.

George Stolz
Independent curator and critic

Reading the Wall

————

"Wall drawings are to be considered ideas rather than objects," Sol LeWitt once instructed.[1] But in practice the immediate, physical presence of the wall drawings themselves can present something of an obstacle to the scrupulous carrying out of those same instructions. The wall drawings surround us; they fuse with the architecture we inhabit and partake of its tangible solidity; they are as capable of overwhelming us as entrancing us with their scale, their color, their complexity, and oftentimes their beauty: how can we consider them anything but "objects"?

Ideas rather than objects: it is perhaps helpful in this context to recall that for LeWitt, walls were akin to pages of a book; by extension, wall drawings, like words on a page, not only are "written" by their author in the sense of having been conceived prior to their physical manifestation but are also intended to be later "read" by the viewer, both in the sense of grasping the information contained within that is transmitted by the set of codes and signs immediately at hand, as well as in the sense of arriving at a certain interpretation, evaluation, or response. "It is only by reading the wall that the viewer understands it fully," to cite LeWitt again on that format to which he gave so much care and devoted so much thought.[2] The lines or bands of color or scribbles in a wall drawing are, like words on a page, undeniably visual objects; yet at the same time, like words on a page, they also operate on a different level. They are possessed of agency; they convey something beyond themselves, something that is apprehended—by the intellect or the emotions or, ideally, a combination of the two—through faculties based in, but ultimately distinct from, vision alone. Thus the mental exercise of considering the wall drawing physically before one's eyes as an idea, of attempting to "read" and understand its more atemporal components, is not *not* to see the object that conveys the idea: it is, arguably, to perceive it more fully.

1. Sol LeWitt in Alicia Legg, ed., *Sol LeWitt*, exh. cat. (New York: The Museum of Modern Art, 1978), p. 95.

2. Ibid., p. 164. See also p. 139.

Robert Storr
Artist, critic, curator, and
Dean of the Yale University
School of Art, New Haven

First Things First

It is a quiet declaration, but a resounding one still. It comes first in a long series of concise, clear, uncompromising statements and so initially seems to have pride of place. Published in *Art-Language* in 1969, those statements bear the collective title "Sentences on Conceptual Art." However, after one reads the thirty-four other texts—some entries, including the initial one, consist of more than a single sentence—it almost seems as if the opening lines had been slipped in, given that there are no direct references to them in any that follow. Nor is there an argument developed from or around them that could explain their presence or enlarge their meaning in the terms they explicitly, but in context anomalously, employ, although the methodological concerns spelled out in the balance of the thirty-five statements do frame the conditions within which that declaration is intended to be understood.

Whether readers stop cold at the up-front position of this unexpected philosophical assertion or hurry past it in order to immerse themselves in the systematic exposition of the artist's core ideas about the necessary conditions and procedures for Conceptual art, Sol LeWitt spoke plainly about the a priori predicate

for all the other rules he laid down, and did so fully aware of how jarring his choice of words was bound to be.

> 1. Conceptual Artists are mystics rather than rationalists. They leap to conclusions that logic cannot reach.[1]

Of course, the troublesome item is LeWitt's forthright affirmation that "Conceptual Artists are mystics." After all, this was the 1960s, when "scientific" models of thought generally prevailed over those less grounded in verifiable facts or, worse, those with otherworldly preoccupations. Mainstream formalism, in the eyes of Clement Greenberg, its leading American exponent, was avowedly "positivist." In tension with this tendency were other formalisms, notably that of Donald Judd, who was committed to empiricism.

In the minds of the majority of LeWitt's contemporaries, mysticism in the visual arts was a throwback to pre-World War II movements and a cluster of modern masters with an embarrassing weakness for the esoteric. Most problematic were the greatest of them all, Vasily Kandinsky, Kazimir Malevich, and Piet Mondrian; the consensus within the rising New York avant-garde was that the less said of their metaphysical leanings the better. By the same token, the highly influential linguistic theories of Ludwig Wittgenstein were discussed without much mention of his spiritual quest. The 1960s was a hard-headed no-nonsense era.

Yet such attitudes only amplify the resonance of LeWitt's claim and underscore his corresponding warning against unwarranted and, in his estimation, unfruitful reliance on logic and rationalism. They were, he posited, not only the foundations of formalism but the basis for its pre-

dictability and consequent aesthetic sterility. "Rational judgments repeat rational judgments," goes the second of his statements, which is also to say that formalism operates by extrapolating one set of formats and formulas from the previous ones with ever-diminishing returns. Thus while LeWitt insisted that once a working premise or process had been decided upon it must be rigorously adhered to, he was equally adamant that an artist's starting point should not merely be a reasoned extension of the stopping point of a previous project.

Instead the artist must make a leap of faith, an intuitive jump to a new premise rather than to a foreseeable destination based on an old one. For conclusions arrived at in advance of making a work demand nothing more of the artist than illustration and nothing more of the viewer than preordained acceptance. True discovery for both artist as well as viewer requires active curiosity about the unknown. That in turn presupposes a willingness not to know or to pretend to know the situations or phenomena before we have apprehended them conceptually and experienced them perceptually.

Such faith involves no smoke and mirrors, no eyes wide shut, no secret erudition, no solemn creed, in short none of the apparatus or obscurantism of nineteenth- or twentieth-century mysticism. To the degree that LeWitt's mysticism seemed to fit the pattern of anti-modernist antecedents in taking a stance against reason, the aim was not to advocate unreason. LeWitt's object was simpler and of an entirely different, almost tangibly immanent, sort. It was to make something that renewed the world around it. Doing this took a flight of the imagination, but it also meant landing squarely in reality and working with the utmost discipline. It was a radical idea then, and it is a radical idea now.

---

1. Sol LeWitt, "Sentences on Conceptual Art," *Art Language* 1, no. 11 (May 1969), p. 11.

Mary Temple
Artist

Sol LeWitt's process requires that a wall be lavished with as much attention as necessary to fulfill his rigorous formal requirements. His wall drawings may take days, weeks, or months to complete, regardless of how long they will be exhibited. Conceivably, the drawing could be painted or sanded away immediately following the making of the last pencil mark, and would then exist in a material sense for a fraction of the time taken to construct it. I love how this relates to LeWitt's conviction that it isn't necessary for an idea to become a physical object to be an artwork. His model has helped me to sustain an extremely labor-intensive practice, while keeping a philosophical outlook when the sanding begins.

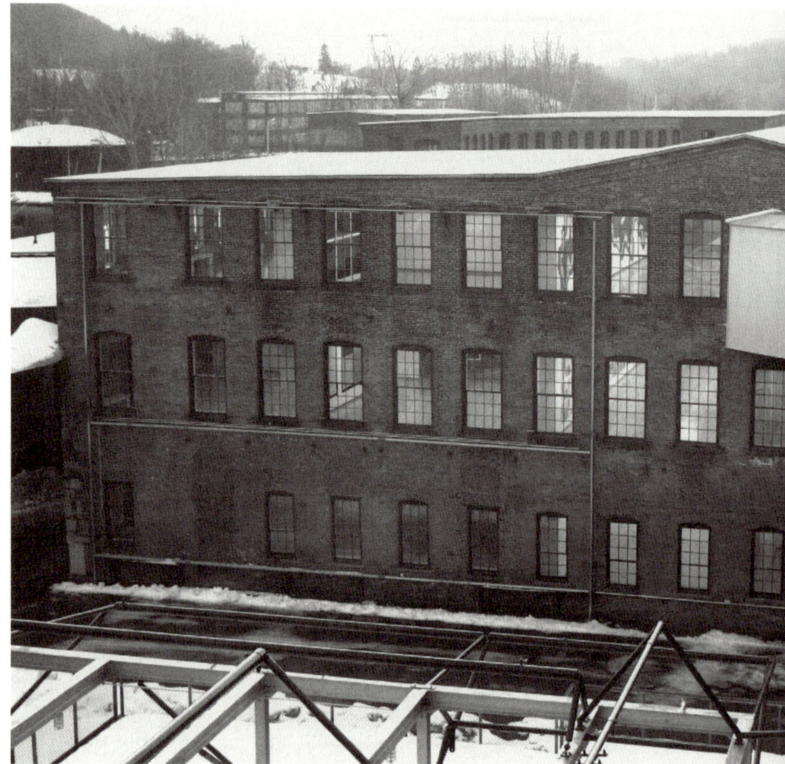

Building 7, MASS MoCA

Joseph C. Thompson
Director, MASS MoCA

Two Surprises That Should Not Have Been

1.

Sol LeWitt's stature as one of the pioneers of Conceptual, Minimal, and Serial art somehow obscures a fact that this retrospective makes dramatically evident: from his fine early pencil drawings to the lush color washes of his mid-career, and through the almost incomprehensible density and luminosity of his last *Scribble* works, Sol's drawings are just plainly beautiful, gorgeously rendered, and exquisite in visual effect.

For some of Sol's peers, beauty and good design fell under the negative sign or were, at the very least, suspect. Sol's various writings and interviews have little to say about aspirations of formal beauty, or equivocate between disinterest and dismissal. But not disdain, however, and walking through this exhibition is an object lesson in thought rendered beautiful. The taut skein of pencil marks; the very tooth of the wall and the subtle textures created by the nap of a well-chosen paint roller; the vibratory, almost riotous pleasure of complementary colors placed in radical contact; the sense of human touch and time imbued in hand-sanded walls: all these conjoin to create pictorial spaces of stunning depth and visual richness not captured under such frigid labels as "Conceptual" and "Minimal."

2.

A not-so-closeted designer (who also created handsome books, scarves, and pottery), Sol was a natural architect, a fact which was often obscured by his ability to work so congenially with found spaces and in architectural situations handed to him. His strategic selection and activation of Building 7, for example, radically transformed the visitor circulation path of the entire MASS MoCA complex, replacing our former "spine" of galleries with a grand loop. Building 7 immediately became the new heart of the rearranged campus, connecting to MASS MoCA's existing galleries through elevated tunnels, ramps, vertical light-wells, and other arterial paths. (Some of these were in place, but others were invented by Bruner/Cott & Associates to magnify the circulatory possibilities suggested by Sol's selection of Building 7.) The rehabilitation of Building 7 almost guarantees the subsequent development of the 120,000-square foot Building 6 for future artists' projects, which is to say that Sol's future reach in space and time will take many forms, still unknown. As Building 6 develops, Building 7 will become the point of inflection for a great figure-eight circulation path.

Inside, the practical-minded Sol accepted the building's post-and-beam grid system as the structural basis for the placement of interior-wall partitions, much as many of his drawings are generated from a predetermined grid. Cladding the relatively dense forest of support columns with carefully placed new partitions for his art, he welcomed the raw, paint-flecked, outer masonry, also leaving in place the large windows that yield exuberant side lighting together with extraordinarily generous views onto MASS MoCA's industrial courtyards and rolling hills beyond. Although there is nearly one mile of interior partitioning winding through the galleries, one never feels lost in a maze, the reassuring presence of the building's perimeter and views to the outside always in plain sight.

Marco Tirelli
Artist

The first time I encountered the art of Sol LeWitt was at the Venice Biennale in the 1970s. It was like being struck by lightning! I entered a huge, square space painted completely black with a subtle pencil-drawn grid that contained every possibility of how to draw a line with white chalk. Infinite white marks floated in a black abyss: like a planetarium of luminous stars, daughters of a mental big bang so potent and precise, crazy and perfect, that it made one think of a challenge to Creation itself, or like a sort of cosmogony, a medieval model of the universe in which one could search for the hidden order of things beyond the apparent disorder.

I always considered Sol a mystic artist as opposed to a cold formalist, as some would like to frame him. Moreover, Sol himself, in his famous "Sentences on Conceptual Art" (1969), wrote of Conceptual artists as being not so much rational as mystical. I say this as I am thinking as well that a man who spends his life listing all the "possibilities in the world" is closer to God than to bookkeeping. Sol LeWitt's art is a metaphysical one because it speaks of the absolute. It manifests itself in fragments, but only so as to display the infinite. Through the visible it tells of the invisible. This is great art.

In time Sol became a dear friend. A thousand pages would not be enough for me to write of his integrity, sweetness, and generosity. His humanity is a treasure that I, along with others who had the fortune to know him, will carry in my heart. I like to think of him now among the stars as he measures the distance from one to another, imagining new configurations for the constellations.

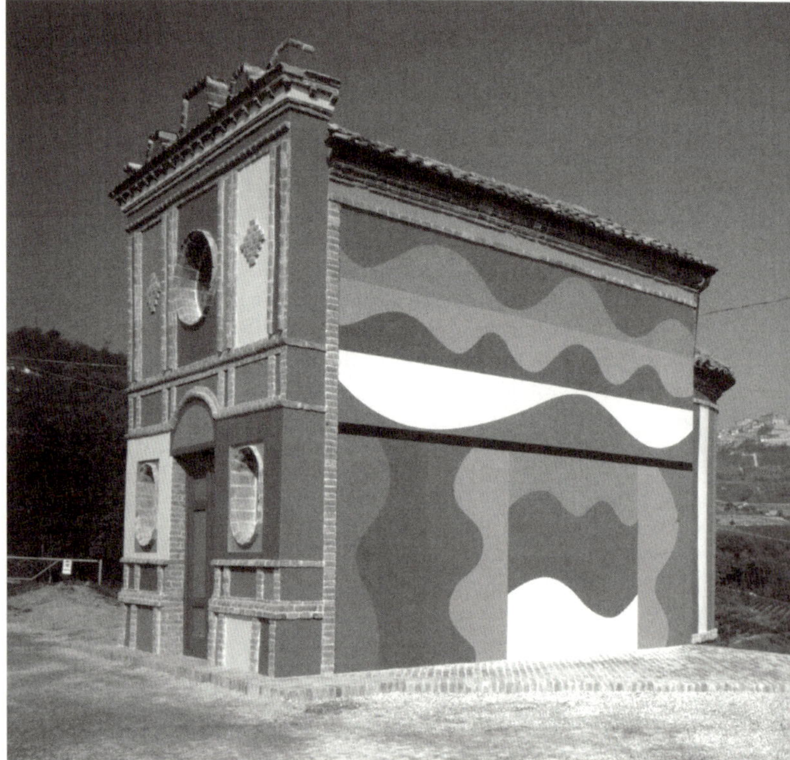

Sol LeWitt. *Wall Drawing 913: Ceretto Chapel.* Acrylic paint. August 1999. Bruno Ceretto, Alba, Italy. Photo: Roberto Cecato

David Tremlett
Artist

Alexander van Grevenstein
Director, Bonnefantenmuseum, Maastricht

"He was a friend of mine." [1]

I'm not too sure where we met, either in Düsseldorf (Germany) or Bari (Italy), places with galleries we both showed at, around the years 1973–74. Then it was in Italy where most of our brief, good times were spent: Spoleto, where Sol and Carol had a house, or Rome, from time to time, or Naples, at venues where some sort of exhibitions were occurring. In Spoleto we would swim lap after lap. Sol would have worked out a method, rhythm, and a particular number of laps to be done, and I generally watched the last few from poolside.

But the project we shared at a former chapel, known as the Madonna del Barolo, in the vineyards of La Morra, just outside Alba (in Piedmont), was to be the most memorable. We both had a love for the wall surface, and managed to complete the little chapel without a fight: Sol decided to cover its entire exterior—he had a superior knowledge to mine of working on building exteriors—and I went to work on the interior walls and floor. The results, as Sol said of the project, showed that: "The outside has to do with the perception of the eyes, while inside the main concern is the perception of the mind." [2] Afterward we would live to drink another bottle of Barolo for many years to come.

Sol was a great and generous artist who left much behind. He had a wry smile for the good and bad of the art world, but remained a tireless "art worker," an inspiration to us all.

1. This is the title of a traditional song that has been attributed to Mark Spoelstra.

2. Sol LeWitt in "La cappella del Barolo" (interview with LeWitt and David Tremlett by Alessandro Allemandi), Il giornale dell'arte, Sept. 1999, p. 6.

Sol LeWitt undeniably belongs to a select group of artists who have shaped the twentieth century. Besides making prints, drawings, and photographs, he expressed himself with the greatest of ease in sculpture as well as painting, without following the beaten tracks of either Expressionism or gestural brilliance. He was therefore not a sculptor or painter in the classical sense. He had no penchant for expressive subject matter or material whatsoever, instead closely approaching the degree zero of visual means.

LeWitt was a draftsman able to spread his interplay of line and color over the continents, with works executed in several places at once. He directed things at a distance. His visual means are therefore reduced to a depersonalized state, in which the execution of his "designs" is not hindered by the personal interpretation of those carrying out and mediating the work. LeWitt's work has more to do with economy of means than personal signature. His guidelines and results are so closely linked to simplicity, frugality, and minimal intervention that recurrence and repetition alone produce a state of unbridled exuberance. In a LeWitt wall drawing the large quantity of the same kind of lines and layers of color, and yet more lines and layers of color, often takes on astronomical dimensions in order to achieve the desired result. It takes many hands working for days or weeks to complete a wall drawing. The genius of LeWitt lies in this working practice, which in concealing the "invoking" ritual makes the person (or persons) carrying out the work the "chosen" one.

LeWitt's wall drawings do not age; they possess eternal youth. They can be carried out again and again without the dilemmas involved in reconstruction or restoration, as the preconditions have already been set. The spectator, although kept at a certain distance, is not abandoned. Always amazing, the result is one that has never been seen before.

Charles Vandenhove
Architect

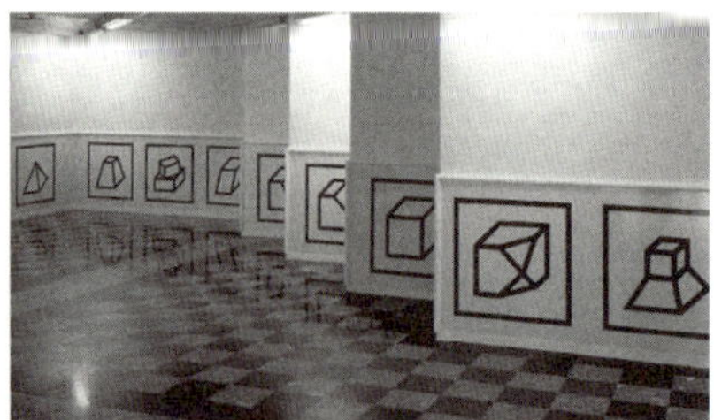

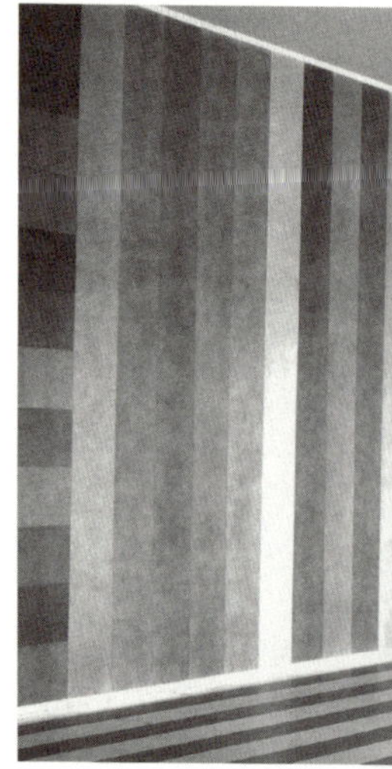

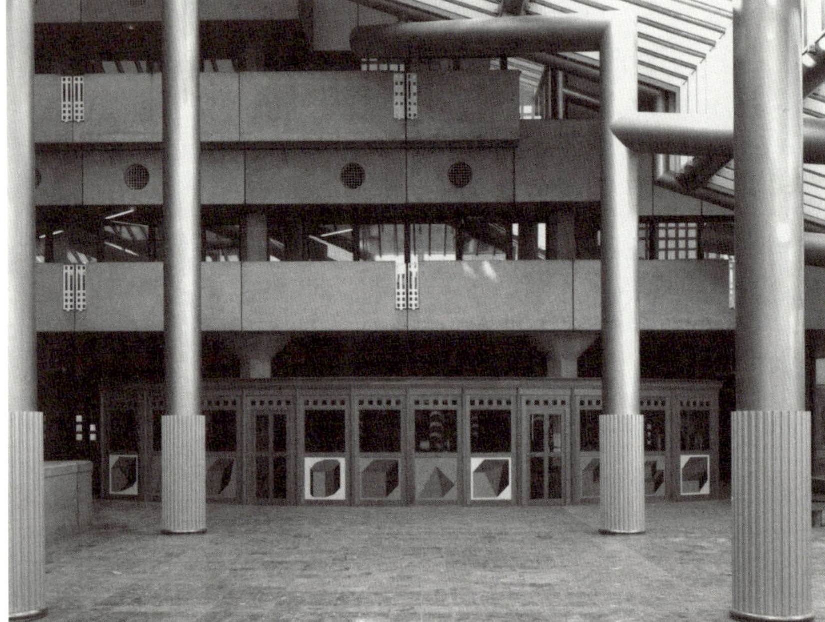

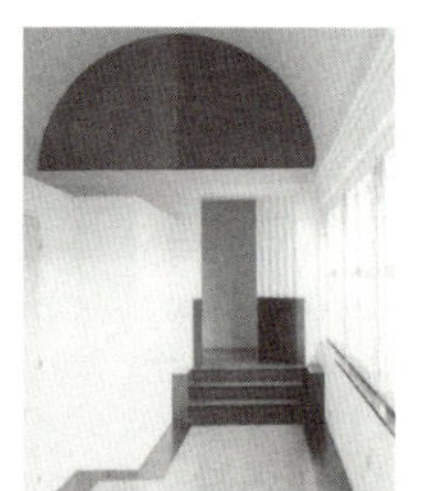

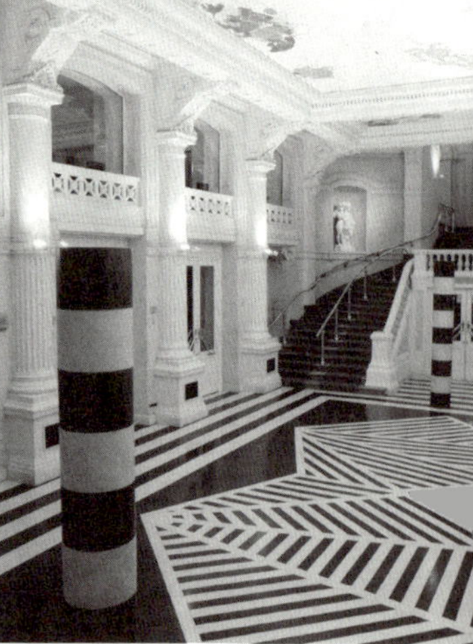

It was Yvon Lambert who introduced me to Sol LeWitt in Paris in 1980. At the time I was designing the one thousand-bed Centre Hospitalier Universitaire in Liège, I asked Sol to do a project for me on the wainscoting of the walls of the patients' rooms and the hallways. I asked for a design with no hierarchy. I had made the same proposal to Daniel Buren, Niele Toroni, and other artists. Sol immediately made two proposals, one in black, the other in color. The drawings were blown up, traced onto steel panels, enameled, and baked in an oven at about 900 degrees. I was with my wife in Spoleto, Italy, when I showed Sol the first proofs of the panels.

For the Maison Heureuse, a charitable shelter for young children in Ans, near Liège, a project completed between 1988 and 1991, Sol made original drawings to decorate the end walls of the vaulted corridors. The drawings were applied using a very specific technique devised by Sol.

For the Théâtre Royal de la Monnaie in Brussels in 1986, Sol's drawing was reproduced in the floor in black and white marble, facing a monumental painting by Sam Francis on the ceiling.

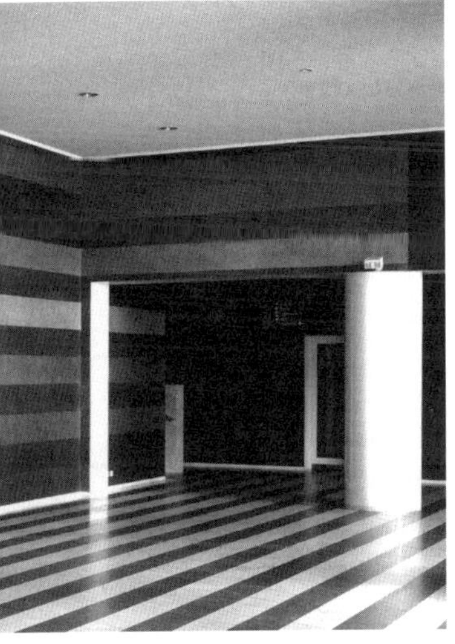

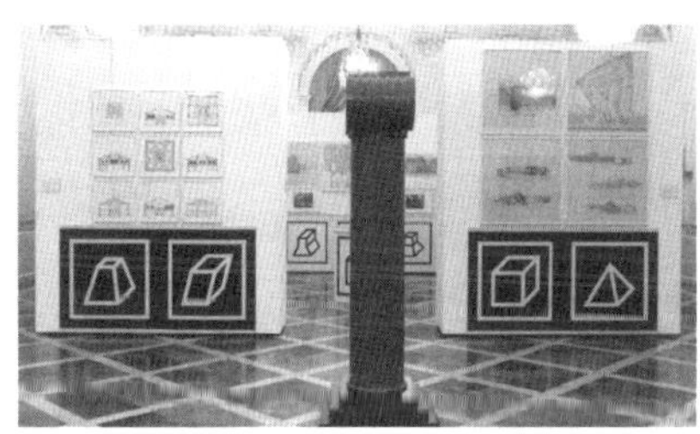

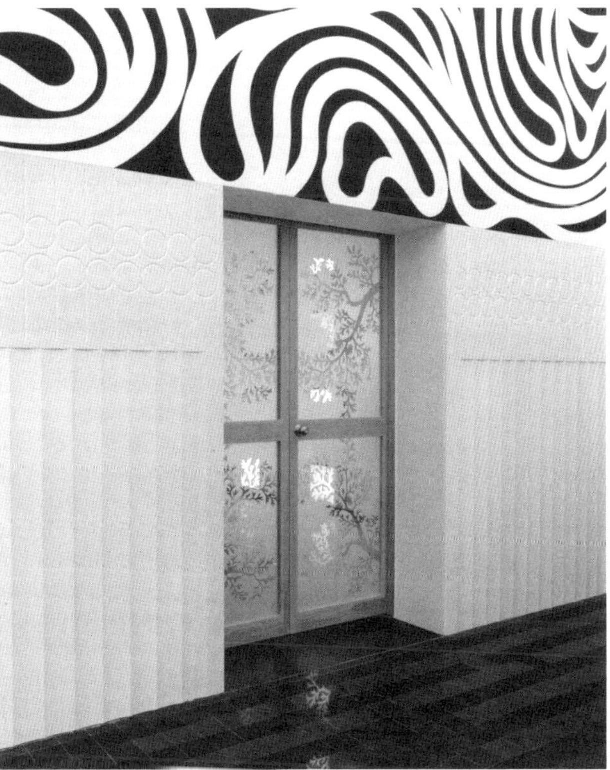

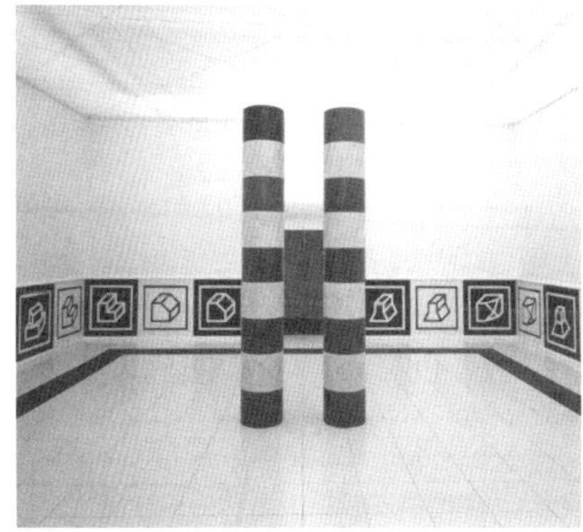

In 1991 Sol created a very subtle drawing for the entrance hall for the Koninklijke Schouwburg (royal theater) in the Hague.

In 2000, for the Bonne Fortune house, a private residence in Liège, Sol made a monumental drawing in black and white for the salon. Buren decorated the entrance hall of the same building in black and white marble and mirrors.

In 1985 in Aachen, Germany, at the Neu Galerie-Sammlung Ludwig, as part of a solo exhibition of my work, some of the panels designed for the Centre Hospitalier Universitaire in Liège were presented along with a project in homage to the artist: a house for Sol LeWitt.

The Palais du Beaux Arts, Brussels, mounted an exhibition of the models for the University Hospital Center's enameled panels in 1986.

FROM LEFT TO RIGHT ■ Sol LeWitt. *Forms derived from a cube (color)*. 1980. Enamel on steel. Centre Hospitalier Universitaire de Liège ■ Sol LeWitt. *Forms derived from a cube (black and white)*. 1980. Enamel on steel. Centre Hospitalier Universitaire de Liège ■ Sol LeWitt. *Wall Drawing 467: Double asymmetrical pyramids drawn with 4" (10 cm) wide alternating parallel (to left side or bottom) bands*. February 1986. India Ink. Théâtre Royal de la Monnaie, Brussels ■ Sol LeWitt. *Wall Drawing 536A: Four pairs of semicircular walls; divided into two, three, four, and five equal parts, respectively. The areas are filled in with color ink washes superimposed*. 1991. Color ink wash. Maison Heureuse, Ans, Belgium ■ Sol LeWitt. *Wall Drawing 696: Horizontal and vertical bands with color ink washes superimposed*. 1992. Ink wash. Koninklijke Schouwburg, the Hague ■ Sol LeWitt. *Wall Drawing 962: Parallel Curves*. February 2001. Acrylic paint. Collection: Alalunga Anstalt di Valuz—Mr. M. Delmentico, Liège ■ *Maquettes of Forms derived from a cube (black and white)*. 1980. Designed for the Center Hospitalier Universitaire de Liège. Collection of Charles Vandenhove ■ *Maquettes of Isometric figures (black and white)*. 1980. Designed for the Center Hospitalier Universitaire de Liège. Collection of Charles Vandenhove ■ All photos courtesy of Charles Vandenhove

Carol Huebner Venezia
Artist

We swam together. Laps. Outdoors in the Spoleto Olympic-sized pool. One afternoon as we lounged in the late summer sun, enjoying the sounds of our kids splashing in the water, Sol asked:

"Would you do a project with me?"

"What?"

"Photograph a cube."

"How?"

"A white cube with lights directed on each corner and each face, every possible combination."

"How many photographs would that be?"

"I guess about one hundred."

"OK."

A few months later a small white cube arrived at my studio in New York, and the rest was up to me. This project became the book *CUBE* (1990), comprising 511 images, in fact, once the math was done.

In my understanding this was Sol's process: the idea first, a question formed, and then the offering of the manifestation of that idea to someone else, an artisan working in wood, clay, or stone, or his trusted assistants, photographers, students, rug weavers, or whomever was appropriate. In that space between the concept and the actual work ran a bridge of faith in, respect for, and curiosity about the artists or artisans he collaborated with.

Sol did not, in my experience, collaborate on his ideas. Those were private considerations. As generous and collaborative as Sol was, he was also extremely private, internal, and silent. No small talk. In Italy every day he would rise at 5:00 a.m., walk from his home into Spoleto, buy a newspaper, get a coffee at "his" bar, and enter the studio.

There Sol painted the gouaches. Classical music flowed out the open studio windows. Our children, Carol (his wife), and I would go about our business in the spaces outside the studio, but that was his private world. This combination of disciplined, internal creativity and enormous generosity of spirit is the Sol LeWitt I knew.

Michael Venezia
Artist

It would be truly a feat to separate our love for Sol and Carol, Sofia and Eva, from Sol's life as an artist. That is not to imply that his was not the life of a steadfast artist. It was. But I will leave a discussion of Sol's practice to those who knew Sol primarily through his art. If you knew a person as we knew Sol, and know his family, you would understand that it is impossible to separate out his work from my feelings about our son's dedicated guardians, our first travels together in 1979 from Spoleto to the Amalfi Coast, my first casual meeting with Sol in 1959, together with Dan Flavin and Robert Ryman, all of them staff at the Museum of Modern Art.

There are too many emotional ties. Suffice it to say that Sol is an artist of the highest quality, of the first rank. In a few words: a line, a mark, a piece of color, without history…the sublime aspiration reached.

Roy Villevoye
Artist and LeWitt draftsman

Wall Drawing 429: The wall is divided vertically into seven parts. All one-, two-, and three-part combinations of three colors

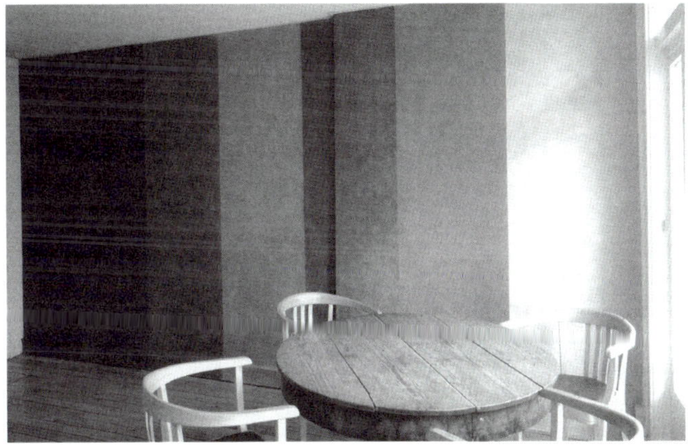

Sol LeWitt. *Wall Drawing 429: The wall is divided vertically into seven parts. All one-, two-, and three-part combinations of three colors.* 1985. Color ink wash. LeWitt Collection, Chester, Connecticut

My wife, Fransje Killaars, and I got to know Sol in the spring of 1984. Along with other young artists we were invited to assist him in setting up the major retrospective exhibition of his wall drawings at the Stedelijk Museum in Amsterdam. After the exhibition we were happy to remain at his service as freelance assistants. In September 1985 he sent us the instructions for a wall drawing to be carried out at the Musée d'Art Moderne et d'Art Contemporain in Liège, Belgium: "Divide the wall into 7 equal parts (from left to right): yellow, red, blue, yellow red, yellow blue, red blue, yellow red blue." For the rest, the instructions contained only the curator's address and telephone number, as well as the work period.

This drawing seemed to sum up all the excitement I had felt and the insight I had gained into making art since I had come into contact with Sol's work. The astounding and compelling simplicity, the profound beauty of his formula, and the looming impression of the form the work would soon take when executed in ink brought on a great euphoria in me. Beside the impression that I had reached the heart of art-making, I also felt an uncontrollable sense of covetousness. I wanted to live with this work. And I imagined that for the rest of my life I would have everything that I believe art has to offer me—endless pleasure, beauty, mystical insight—and also a work that, while apparently simple, continues to reveal itself anew from within a logical system.

Originally Sol had proposed for Liège a wall drawing of abutting pyramids; however, while discussing the work on-site, I realized there was a problem with the proportions in relation to the wall surface available. So Sol came up with a new wall drawing. Eventually though the wall was adapted to enable the execution of the original design with the pyramids. Back home I could not restrain myself, and together with Fransje I carried out *Wall Drawing 429* on the only suitable wall in our small living room in Amsterdam. When we had finished it, I telephoned Sol and told him how important it was for me to be able to live in such close proximity to his work. He laughed and said in a friendly and certain tone: "I owe it to you." I didn't give much thought to what that might mean, but I felt enriched.

Some time later Sol and his family visited us in Amsterdam, and we served him his favorite Dutch pea soup. He was very excited when he found out that we lived in an Amsterdam school building, the typical style of social housing of the 1920s. This fascinated him enormously. At that time our apartment contained only the most essential items of furniture; the wall drawing in the living room therefore took on a very prominent role. When he entered the living room, he looked briefly at the work and said, "Thank you, I consider this a compliment."

This room later became our bedroom, and since then we have had a panoramic view of the work from our bed. It is with us at the most important moments of each day: as we awake, and as we prepare to greet the night. It glows continually throughout the day. The work's richness has grown for us as we have developed as artists. A permanent benchmark, the drawing has guided us both mentally and visually. Through Sol's personal generosity in wanting to share it with us, each day we see and feel his presence in our lives as a master, unique colleague, and a very kind man.

Ursula von Rydingsvard
Artist

Sol's poetic logic and mathematical systems had a tremendous influence on me when I first came to New York in 1973. Within a way of thinking that seemed rigorous there was always the mythical and the unexpected.

I reacted to his work and thought he had purged all that was emotional, that he had cleansed and sanitized it. Perhaps what is closer to being true is that Sol's work offers emotional options—options that don't have prejudices—many options, enabling one to enter into a wide-open arena.

I interviewed him once about Eva Hesse for a lecture that I was preparing. I can remember very few spoken words, but I do recall clearly a painting made by his daughter Eva that he gave me, which consisted of thickly outlined circles arranged in a loose grid. In my mind this was a gift summarizing his connection to Eva Hesse, a gift that enabled me to better understand her work.

Recently, in looking at Sol's wall drawings at Dia:Beacon, I especially marveled at the parallel lines that quiver slightly as they run down vertically from ceiling to floor, each line subtly different in color from the others. These very slender lines, which interact with the most graceful anonymity, lacking in any eccentricity, fluttering downward, seem to barely touch the wall. In backing up from this wall, I felt that I was seeing the loose weave of a fine fabric or an environment connected to some kind of lightness.

What seemed always evident about Sol was his perpetual search, as he unearthed so many different ways to talk about so many closely related ideas. His was the mind of a brilliant little boy who uses logic as his base and deviates from that logic for the joy of doing so.

Adam D. Weinberg
Alice Pratt Brown Director,
Whitney Museum of American Art,
New York

Drawing is one of the most fundamental and personal gestures in art, recording the artist's most intimate sensations and ideas. Yet in the wall drawings of Sol LeWitt the act of drawing is depersonalized, or seems to be. I am hesitant to relate the wall drawings to the person of Sol LeWitt, as he never wanted the work to be about himself. Nevertheless, this contradiction, inherent in the wall drawings, was a reflection of the man. LeWitt was quiet and soft-spoken. One often had to strain to hear him. His manner, combined with the fact that he was hard of hearing—or at times selectively so—lent him an air of reserve.

However, when in conversation, he focused his full and warm attention on you. You knew he was fully there, completely present. LeWitt had presence, neither regal nor authoritarian but human, ethical, and intellectual. Without seeming the least bit evasive or off-putting, LeWitt typically revealed only what was necessary whether in dinner conversation or in an interview (although emotional, witty, and often humorous reactions to certain subjects periodically erupted). In certain social situations LeWitt had a way of being with you and not being with you simultaneously. It was not uncommon in social circumstances for him to pick up a book and start reading or get lost listening to a piece of music.

LeWitt's wall drawings have great presence. They are direct, unaffected, logical, and comprehensible. They are also alchemical, seductive, sensuous, and, yes, so very intimate. Yet it is quite the contradiction that he never directly touched these walls or the materials to create the wall drawings. How can it be that these rooms resonate with such immanence? The notion of contradiction is at the heart (and mind) of LeWitt's wall drawings: complexity/simplicity, consistency/diversity, intellectual/visceral, rational/intuitive, surface/layers. The success of this work, its contradictory character, is that despite its presence it seems to be out of reach, existing on another plane, in every sense of the word. In the end the more we know the work, the more we know the work, not the man. Sol LeWitt believed that who he was as a person was irrelevant to his art. It was the art that mattered.

Lawrence Weiner
Artist

<u>A LINE IS A LINE FOR ALL THAT</u>

IT IS NOT ABOUT A SYSTEM
IT IS AN ATTEMPT TO MARK A REAL POSITION
OF THE ARTIST IN RELATION TO THE STRUCTURES
EMCOMPASSING US ALL
EACH DRAWING   EACH SCULPTURE   EACH PRINT
IS BASED UPON WHATSOEVER AWARENESS RESULTED
FROM THE LAST ENCOUNTER
THE FASCINATION WITH MUYBRIDGE WAS NOT ABOUT
THE FAMILY OF MAN BUT ABOUT THE INHERENT
MEANING OF MOTION
EACH LINE   EACH COLOR   EACH FORM
IS ABOUT THE INHERENT MEANING OF WHAT WE
FIND WHERE WE FIND IT AT A SPECIFIC MOMENT OF STASIS
METAPHOR IS OBVIATED AS LEWITT MARKS
WHERE WE ARE AT THE MOMENT
OFTEN SURROUNDED BY THE DETRITUS OF WHERE
WE HAVE BEEN
IT IS NOT ABOUT BEAUTY OR HUMANITY
IT IS HUMAN IN SCOPE & SCALE
CARL ANDRE WRITING UPON THE OCCASION OF A
LEWITT EXHIBITION IN DEN HAAG LIKENED SOL
TO SPINOZA
A SPINOZA IT WOULD SEEM OF OUR TIME
POISED BETWEEN BELIEF & EXTENSION
PERHAPS THE BODY OF WORK ALLOWS THE
DIGNITY OF SPINOZA & THE HUMILITY OF
GALILEO CONTENT IN THE KNOWLEDGE THAT
WE ALL REVOLVE AROUND A CENTRAL CORE
& THE MARKING OF WHERE IT IS
IS THE ROLE OF THE ARTIST

<u>A LINE IS A LINE FOR ALL THAT</u>

Mark Williams
Artist and LeWitt studio assistant

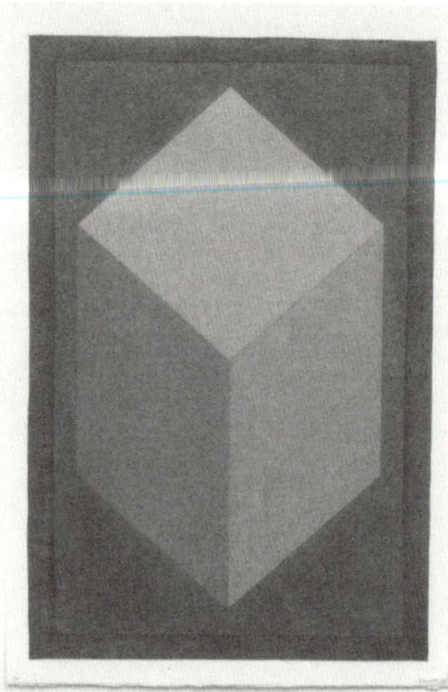

Sol LeWitt. *100 Cubes*. 1989.
Gouache on paper. LeWitt Collection,
Chester, Connecticut. Photo: R. J. Phil

I worked as a studio assistant for Sol LeWitt for about two and a half years up until the time of his death. Part of my duties was to check the condition of Sol's works upon their return from various exhibitions. The process involved studying the works in minute detail to see if anything was wrong with them after they had been returned. After seeing all of the cube gouaches from the *100 Cubes* project (1991; there are actually 101 cubes), I became more interested in using different color combinations within paintings of the same image. I decided I needed a copy of Sol's book *100 Cubes* (1996) and got one. It has been in my studio ever since, and I page through it to find inspiration. Sol's subject matter was a cube in three colors, with a colored background or negative space surrounding it, and a border—five colors in all. My own paintings have often dealt with five colors as well. I have a background base color, an image repeatedly silkscreened in another color, and then the same silkscreened image hand-painted larger in three colors over that. Instead of a cube, I have been using images of toy soldiers partially covered by various playful forms.

Sol had written that once the subject matter was arrived at—the cube, in this case—he was free to think about other concerns such as size, technique, and color. I know he found this process of working liberating, and I do as well. For the past few years I have been making paintings, followed by sculptures, prints, and light drawings, of fourteen images. I simply pick one of these images and then paint it using different colors, techniques, textures, sizes, and so on. The work becomes about just doing, painting, trying out new things, while adhering to a structure or rule. One painting isn't really better than another.

There is a certain simplicity to some of Sol's work. That's okay with me because I like simple things. I am reminded of the film *Painters Painting* (1972), in which Willem de Kooning says, "I don't think painters have particularly bright ideas.... Not such a bright idea for Monet to paint his haystacks."[1] One man's haystacks are another man's lines in four directions. Exhausting all the combinations of how lines in four directions can be depicted within a square may not be a fantastic idea, but I like it. To take this idea and then make prints, drawings, and wall drawings is an idea I like even more. I also enjoy how one's own personal preference becomes important when admiring Sol's work. Who's to say which combination of lines in four directions is the best or which *Incomplete Open Cube* is the best? So much of Sol's work exists in relation to other work, and I enjoy that. It is almost like a puzzle. One piece is satisfying, but when they are taken in all together they really make an impact.

I admire how Sol meticulously plugged away at his work. For a while, toward the end of his life, he was making gouaches of horizontal,

wavy bands. Once I watched him working on a fairly large one in his studio. He loaded up his brush and then painted a wavy horizontal line. When his brush ran out of gouache, he dipped it back into a jar and then picked up where he left off, continuing the line. Each line was more or less the same—very democratic. He was sitting there all the while, taking his time. Sol struck me as someone who was very comfortable in his own skin, and I believe it was evident in his work. To me much of his work exerts itself softly and just is—very Zen. In his series one piece may not be better than another, but taken as a whole they really add up to more than the sum of their parts. I think this deliberate way of working, exhausting all the possibilities of a given idea and working toward a larger whole, is the aspect of Sol I will keep with me the most.

---

1. Emile De Antonio, *Painters Painting: The New York Art Scene, 1940–1970* (1972)

Adachiara Zevi

Architect, art historian, and President of
the Bruno Zevi Foundation, Rome

"The Most Impressive Show That I Didn't See But I Wanted To"

Sol LeWitt told me it was the Jannis Kounellis show of January 1969, which inaugurated the "garage" of Fabio Sargentini in Rome with twelve horses placed in the space at regular intervals. He said this during the last interview I had the honor of conducting with him, a year before he passed away. He had requested the meeting with the specific and generous objective of elaborating the fundamental role Italian art and artists had played in his work for more than fifty years. That relationship began in 1950, when he was still a student who made sporadic trips to Florence and Rome, and continued with greater regularity from 1969 on, when, at the invitation of Sargentini, he came to Rome in May for his first show in Italy at Galleria L'Attico, a fact often left out of biographies. The Kounellis show was no longer up, but the repercussions from it were still being felt, as the photographs of those horses, nervous and pawing the ground as they ate, defecated, urinated, and desecrated this space dedicated to art, made their way around the world in the

catalogue to a different exhibition, *When Attitudes Become Form*, in Bern the same year.

What is it that struck Sol so deeply that even in 2006 he referred to it as "one of the best shows in the last fifty years…. The most impressive show that I didn't see but I wanted to"? He continued, "You should do it here in some place…. People don't even know about that show here."[1] The answer is essentially this: an approach to art that is more sensual than ideological/philosophical/mental; the disruptive and liberating freshness of the image; the dialectic with the totality of the space.

"Leaving New York was for me at that time a good move because I thought that the American artistic scene was very narrow, and what I found in Italy was something much larger and bigger…. [The American scene] was narrow in its kind of ideology that had a lot of Calvinism [underlying it]…. It was moralistic," Sol stated.[2]

During the interview he made an insistent reference to what he called the French Academy, those artists and art critics who privileged the trajectory running from Marcel Duchamp and leading, via Jasper Johns and Robert Rauschenberg, to Pop art. Minimalism—to which he contributed starting with his modular structures of the mid-1960s—from his point of view, moved into a new formalism. On the opposite side, "Arte Povera was a really interesting new idea. It didn't relate to the French School," Sol said.[3]

His agreement with statements by Kounellis is surprising: "When you talk about Italian painting," Kounellis stated, "you are talking about possible diversity within the ironclad

logic of the square. Our work threw the square into crisis." Kounellis also insisted: "There are two possibilities: either you have a single image, or you represent a cultural situation. The single image is idealist, tied to the Puritan or Calvinist world."[4] With respect to Piet Mondrian's square, and Kazimir Malevich's white one, sullied by Byzantine gold, Kounellis specified: "The Minimalist square lost its attraction by losing its initial raison d'être" and translated the idea of history "into a matter of mere measurement."[5] For this reason, in an *Untitled* work of 1967, bird cages with live birds frame a canvas that has white roses attached to it; despite the identicalness and the regular intervals among the cages, they challenge Minimalist seriality and self-referentiality and look instead to the structure of the medieval icon in which the saints, absorbed in their daily tasks, surround the sacred figure of the Madonna.

In spite of such syntony, the difference between the horses of Kounellis and the delicate, pencil wall drawings of LeWitt could not be greater. Kounellis's work had definitively claimed the space beyond the painting in 1967; LeWitt, on the other hand, had returned in 1968 to the wall, tracing by hand the first wall drawing. Both worked, curiously, in the name of Jackson Pollock. Let's take a step backward.

In his canonical text "Specific Objects" (1965), Donald Judd proclaimed: "Except for a complete and unvaried field of color or marks, anything spaced in a rectangle and on a plane suggests something in and on something else," and indicated

1. Sol LeWitt, interview with the author, 2006, unpublished.

2. Ibid.

3. Ibid.

4. Jannis Kounellis, "L'epos contemporaneo" (interview with Germano Celant), in Celant, ed., *Kounellis,* exh. cat. (Milan: Fabbri Editori, 1992), p. 30.

5. Kounellis, "Omolia" (Dec. 1984), *I Libri di AEIUO*, nos. 12–13, 1985, p. 63.

that the sole alternative to such illusionism is three-dimensional objects because, "Three dimensions are real space. That gets rid of the problem of illusionism and of literal space."[6] These objects may resemble sculpture, but their roots are in painting, in the compact and anti-relational surfaces of Pollock, whose "drip paintings" defeated the residual illusionism of Cubist geometry. It was, in fact, Pollock who showed Kounellis the path beyond the painting. "The problem is understanding what pushed us to go beyond the painting. My first dialectical moment was with Art Informel. I lived through the tail end of it and was trying to break out. So I understood the depth of Pollock and the inconsistency of Jean Fautrier. The centralizing scheme of Fautrier seemed to me phantasmagoric. It wasn't real. Pollock, meanwhile, had tried to break centrality," Kounellis wrote.[7] In the name of Pollock then, both Kounellis and LeWitt gained or reached real space. But while Kounellis called himself a "painter" in an attempt to reconstruct with real fragments "the centrality of a humanist text in a society that prefers serialism"[8] (this is how the dialectic between the "ground" of the garage and the "figure" of the horse is to be read), LeWitt described himself as a "realist" when he returned to the wall to challenge Judd's anathema.

"I think that what I do is realism and that the use of several lines is more real than a picture of objects or a person…. I don't think it's abstract," said LeWitt, adding, "My work has a lot to do with architecture because it doesn't exist without architecture. A lot of the ideas come from the same source, which is geometry, and

therefore I can say that I'm closer to Brunelleschi than to Cézanne."[9]

This statement is crucial. If the divide between idea and execution set out in the opening of his "Paragraphs on Conceptual Art" (1967) is a mainstay of architectonic practice, and if his *Modular Structures* are rooted in architecture and the urban grid, it is in the isometric drawing, newly architectonic, antiperspectival, and therefore real and anti-illusionistic, that LeWitt found the connection between the sculptures of the 1960s and the wall drawings.

The first wall drawings, including those on the corrugated surfaces of the Galleria L'Attico space, in effect take up only part of the walls; they simply expand the dimensions of a sheet of drawing paper to fit the size of the room. The faint, delicate webs of lines completely fuse with the wall to make them "as two-dimensional as possible."[10] They are mindful of the stratification of Pollock's dripping, but carry it over the threshold of possible combinations offered by the *Modular Structures* and the *Drawing Series*. It was not until 1970, the year following Sargentini's Kounellis exhibition, that LeWitt found the courage to take on "the entire wall." It was at the Galleria Civica di Torino, Italy, where "lines connecting architectural points" crossed the wall to connect elements of the architectural space, such as beams, electrical outlets, and conduit in *Wall Drawing 51*.

In this way LeWitt moved through stages, from one wall to four walls to the entire space. Just as with Kounellis's horses in the garage, from this point on in LeWitt's work, architecture determined the size of the wall drawings. "The idea of using the total space of the gallery or any other architecture was something that the Italians were involved in….

None of the Americans dealt with the ambiente (environment) the way we are talking about. It was all so much more object based…. My work was like a combination of what I was seeing in New York and what I had experienced in Italian art," Sol said.[11]

Thus came a synthesis of tradition and modernity, of wall painting and contemporary architecture. Of the fresco cycles that LeWitt had the chance to admire in Arezzo, Assisi, Florence, Orvieto, Padua, and Spoleto, he preferred those in which the representation extended over the surface without violating its flatness with perspectival illusionism: "They had made a strong impression on me because they were very forceful paintings, and even at the time they were done with that sort of religious statement…. Their aesthetic statement had little to do with religion, and still it had something of that Byzantine frontalism, and so… I mean it was that kind of directness and simplicity that greatly impressed me."[12]

Therefore, if the Minimalist structures are limited to acritically echoing the "white cube" of the gallery space, Sol, on the other hand, used lines, arches, simple and complex geometric figures, circles, undulating bands, and "loopy doopy" lines to build visual sermons in a dissonant and dialectical relationship with the neutrality of the architecture.

A final hint: invited in 1995 to work in a space completely frescoed by LeWitt in Paliano, Italy, Mario Merz introduced, winding through the room, a sinuous and frugal table that he defined as "an altar in a Byzantine space."[13] But that is another story, or rather another chapter in the same story.

6. Donald Judd, "Specific Objects" (1965), in *Donald Judd: The Complete Writings 1959–1975* (Halifax: The Press of the Nova Scotia College of Art and Design; New York: New York University Press, 2005), pp. 182, 184.

7. Kounellis, "L'epos contemporaneo," p. 12.

8. Kounellis, "Omelia," p. 65.

9. LeWitt, interview with the author.

10. LeWitt, "Wall Drawings," *Arts Magazine* 44, no. 6 (April 1970), p. 45.

11. LeWitt, interview with the author.

12. Ibid.

13. Mario Merz in Adachiara Zevi, "Sol LeWitt e Mario Merz sotto lo sguardo di Jan Dibbets," in Rudi Fuchs, *Accumulazioni: Jan Dibbets, Mario Merz, Sol LeWitt*, exh. cat. (Catania, Italy: Carte and Zerynthia, 1996), p. 21.

Jeremy Ziemann
Artist and LeWitt assistant

My first execution of a wall drawing for Sol took place within my first year after high school, in 1989. I had taken a year off to "make things," in the words I have come to use to describe "what I do." I assisted Anthony Sansotta on one of Sol's ink-wash wall drawings for a private client. Beginning with that first drawing, and for the next eighteen years, I had the privileged opportunity to maintain a relationship with Sol and his work.

Throughout college I mostly worked on wall drawings for Sol; afterward I set up a studio in Ivoryton, Connecticut, for producing my own works and for building furniture and cabinetry to pay the bills. Sol would periodically check in: "Are you doing anything for me?" Usually, whether I said yes or no, a day or two later my fax machine would push out a working drawing from Sol for some structure.

My own works typically are geometric constructions that explore relationships of light and shadow or reflectivity. When I first met Sol I was making small structures of fiberglass paper that had perforated lines on opposing sides. These pieces were a study of light and the shifting of moiré patterns; they had as much to do with surface as transparency.

I had, and still have, an enduring respect for Sol's use of form, and I felt privileged for the opportunity to be in my own studio making decisions about the best way to construct a requested project. Sol would give me the freedom, without the oversight, to make such decisions. He showed a respect for my space, time, and working process, even when I had to tell him "not yet" or "maybe in a few days," before having him to my studio for a visit. To me, the challenge and excitement lay in taking his ideas and realizing them in a manner that felt right, or that appeared to me as the appropriate construction. I never tried to influence his idea or suggest a change based on my opinion; I always felt the strength or success of the work was his game, not mine. That said, sometimes there were misinterpretations of a drawing, or Sol had drawn something that could not be realized in three-dimensional space. Once he looked at a finished maquette and said, "That was not what I was thinking,…but… maybe I'll like it better."

As his designs for concrete-block structures became more technically complicated to realize, Sol would send me to work in the field and oversee construction. On one visit to Syracuse University, where there was far too much pomp and circumstance for Sol, he said, "I want the pieces to curve like this on the hill." As he gestured with his arms, he handed a plan to me and said, "Jeremy will answer the rest of your questions," as about a dozen people surrounded me, among them structural engineers, hydroengineers, and construction foremen. On our way home, Sol said, "You will have a degree in block."

One project that we worked on together in 2004 was *A sphere lit from the top, four sides, and all their combinations*. Sol asked me to meet him at his studio in Chester one morning. We walked to the center of town to get the paper he needed. He asked me, "You know that photo book I did on the cube?" I said yes. "What about doing that with a sphere?" I said I thought it could be nice. "Why don't you think about it?" he responded. About a month later he called me at my studio: "You know that thing we were talking about?… Why don't you do it?" A few weeks later I had him visit my studio to see the progress; from that point forward I would go to his studio with printed options to discuss.

The chance to work with Sol in so many phases of his career while honing my own skills was amazing for me, someone who likes to make things.

Plates

Wall Drawing 11: A wall divided horizontally and vertically into four equal parts. Within each part, three of the four kinds of lines are superimposed.   1969   (detail opposite)

Wall Drawing 16: Bands of lines 12 inches (30 cm) wide, in three directions (vertical, horizontal, diagonal right) intersecting.   1969

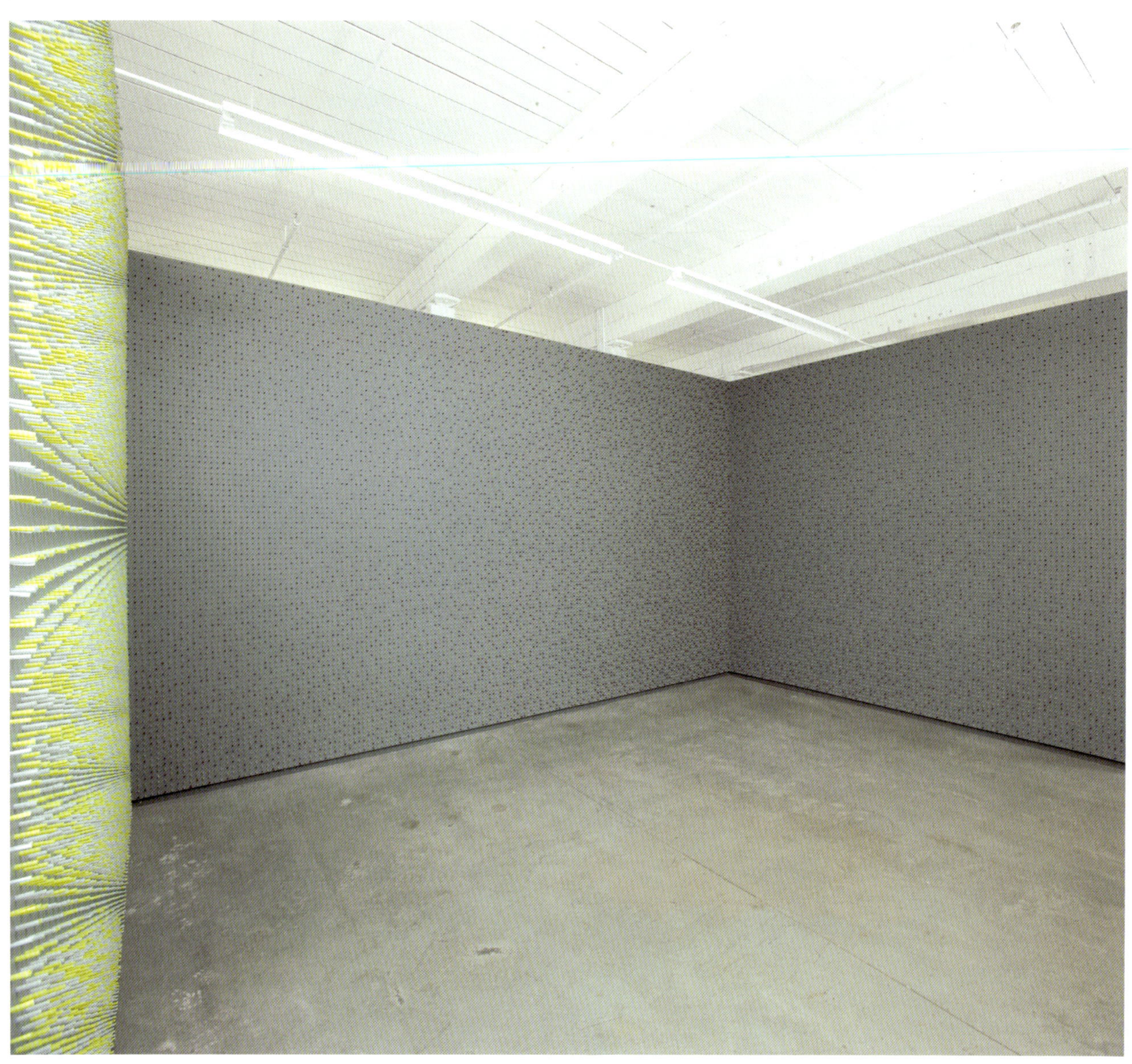

Wall Drawing 38: Tissue paper cut into 1½-inch (4 cm) squares and inserted into holes in the gray pegboard walls. All holes in the walls are filled randomly.   1970   (detail opposite)

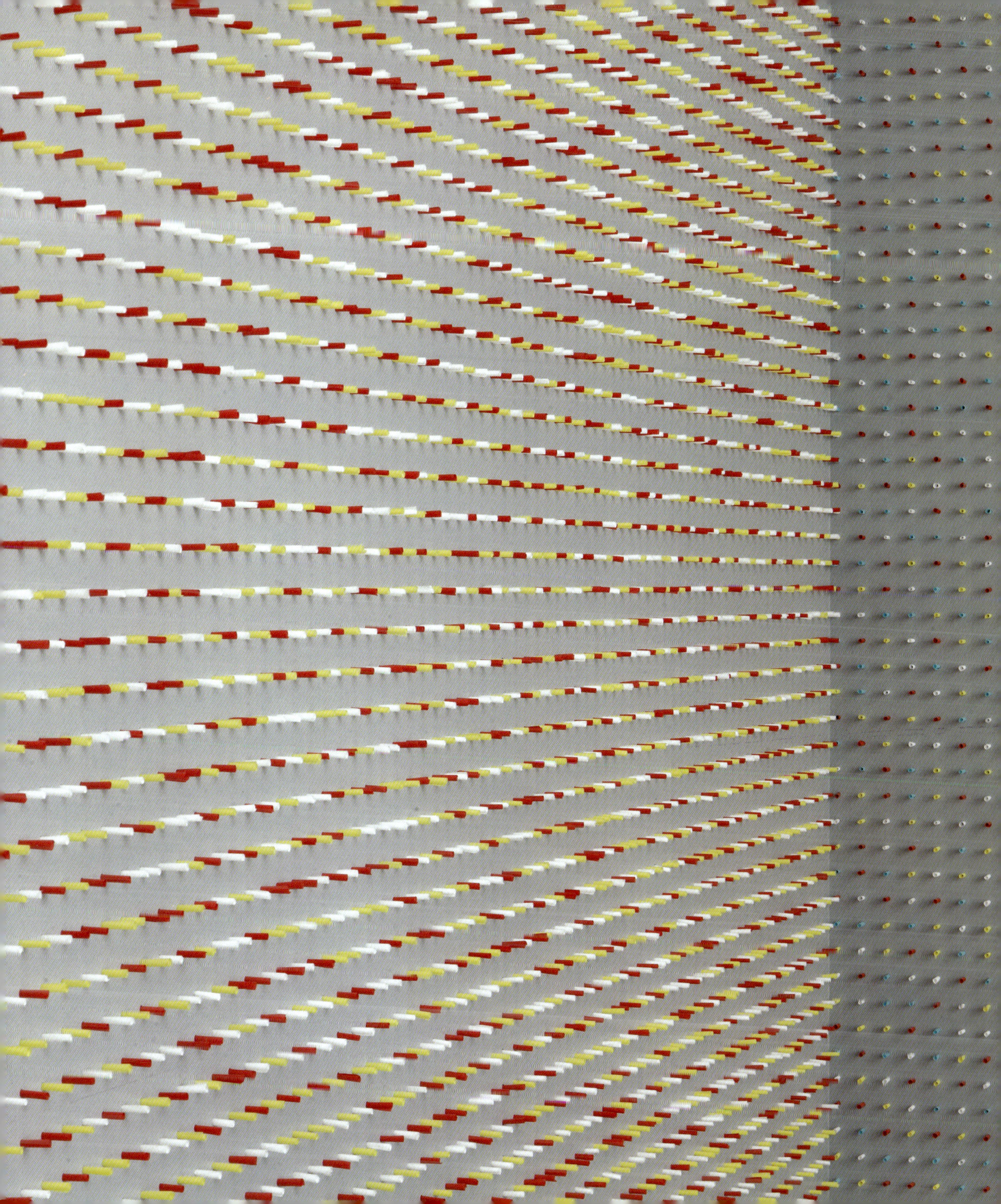

Wall Drawing 46: Vertical lines, not straight, not touching, covering the wall evenly.   1970   (detail opposite)

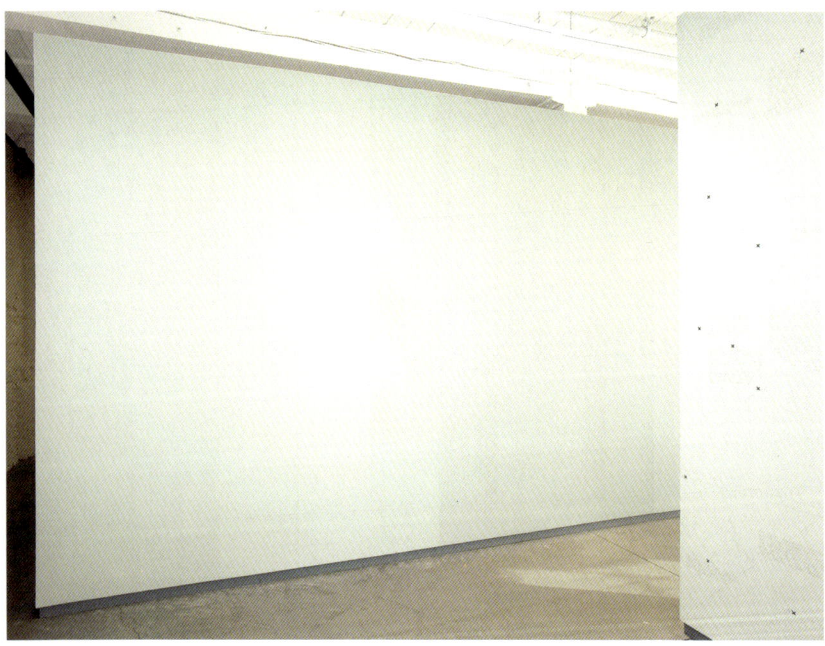

Wall Drawing 47: A wall divided vertically into fifteen equal parts, each with a different line direction, and all combinations.   1970

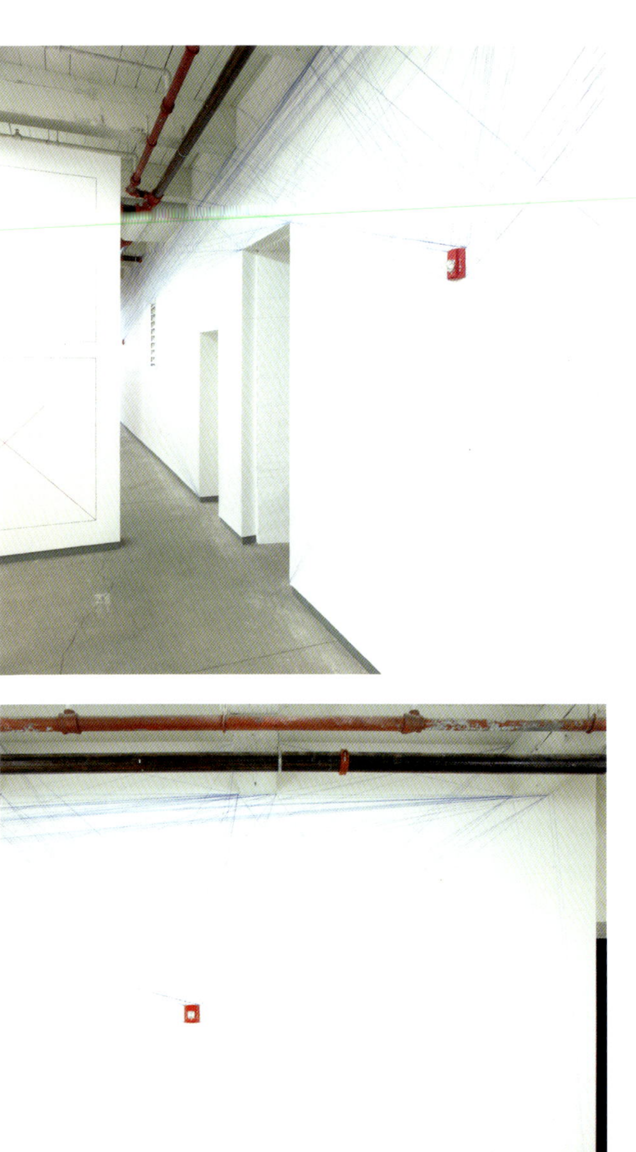

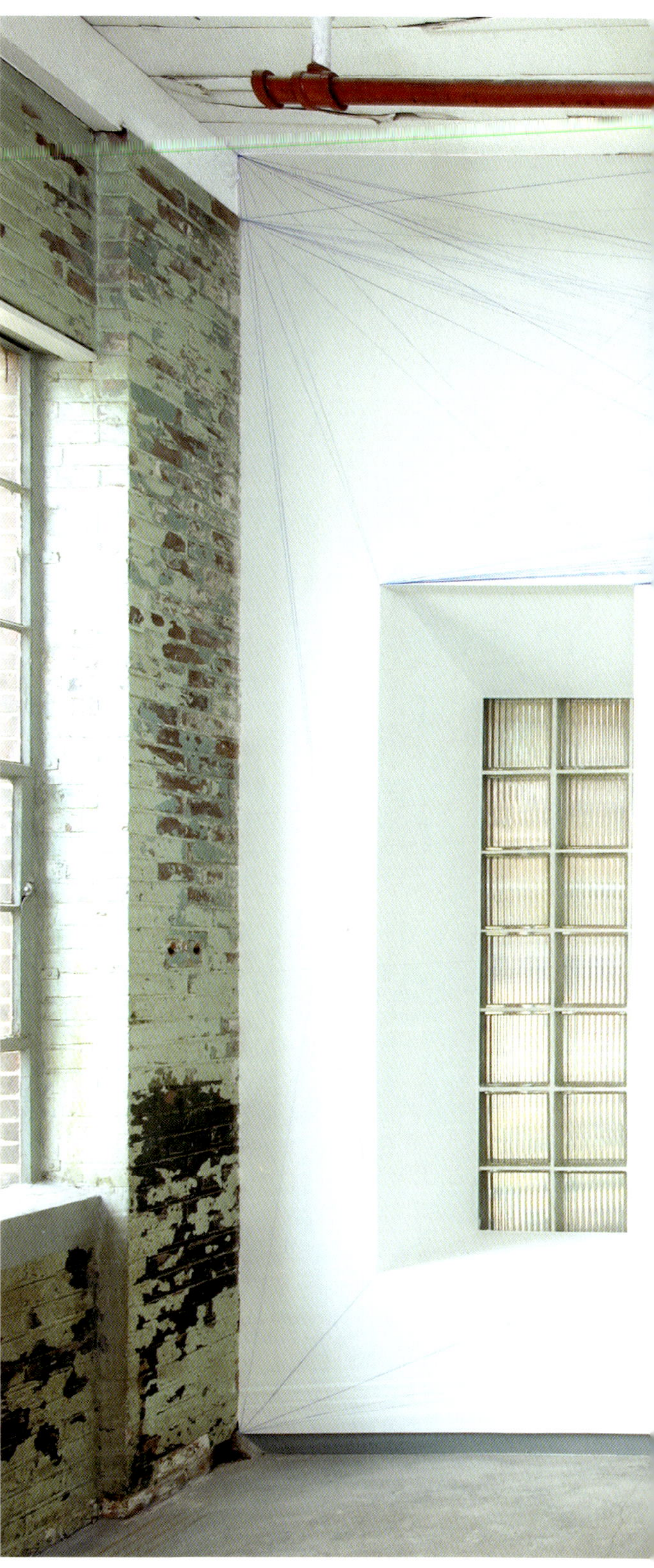

Wall Drawing 51: All architectural points connected by straight lines.   1970

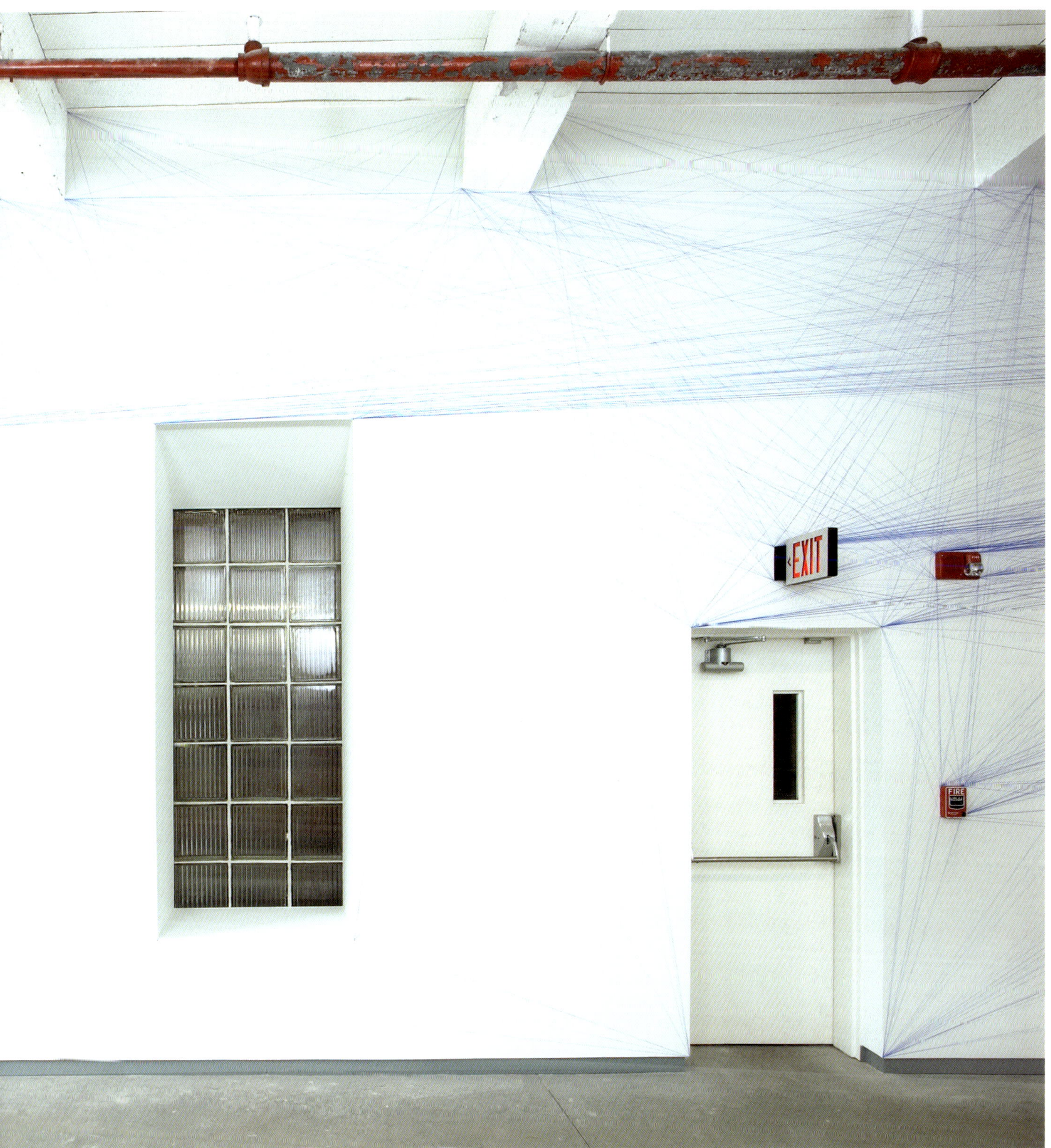

EXIT
FIRE

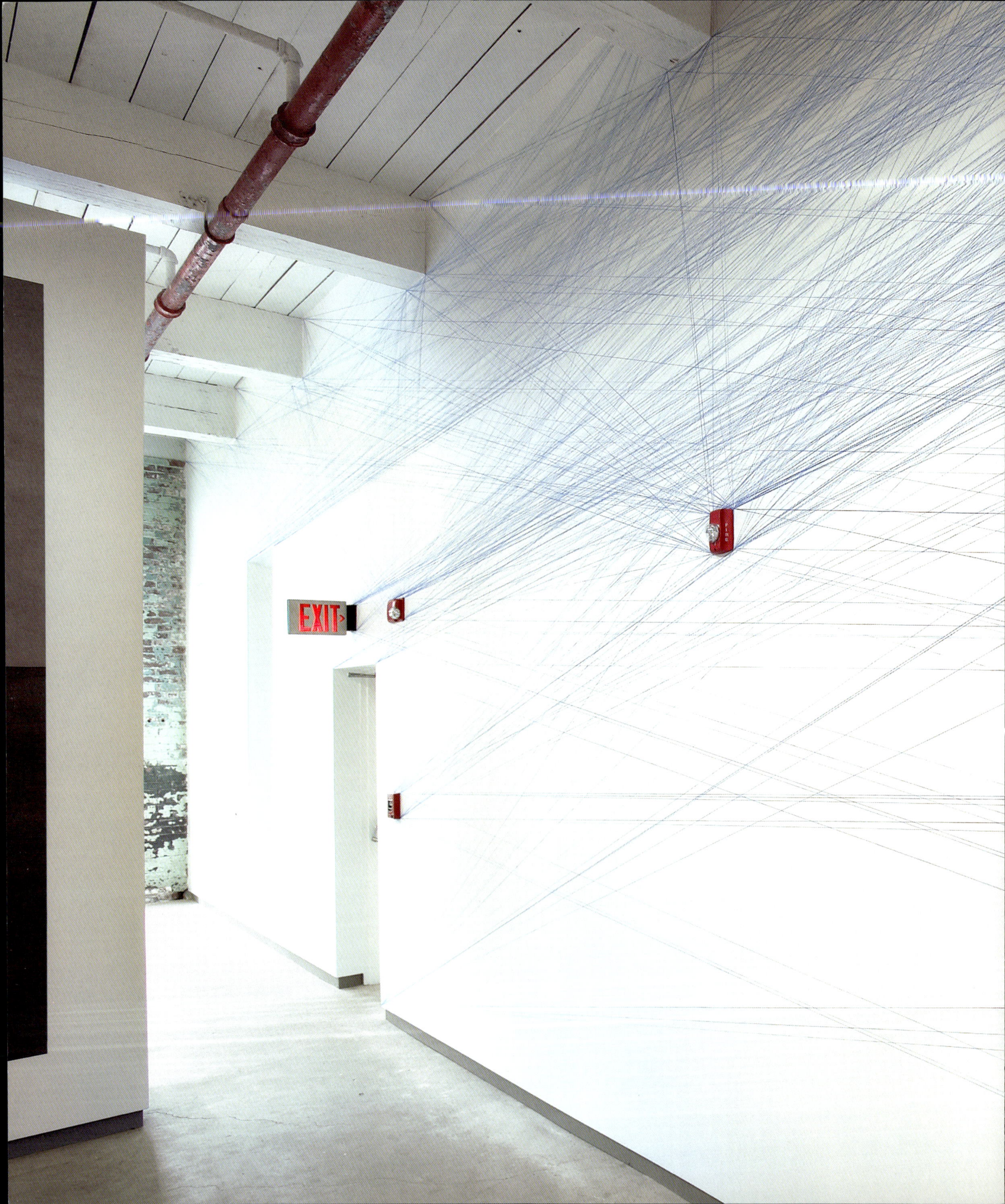

EXIT

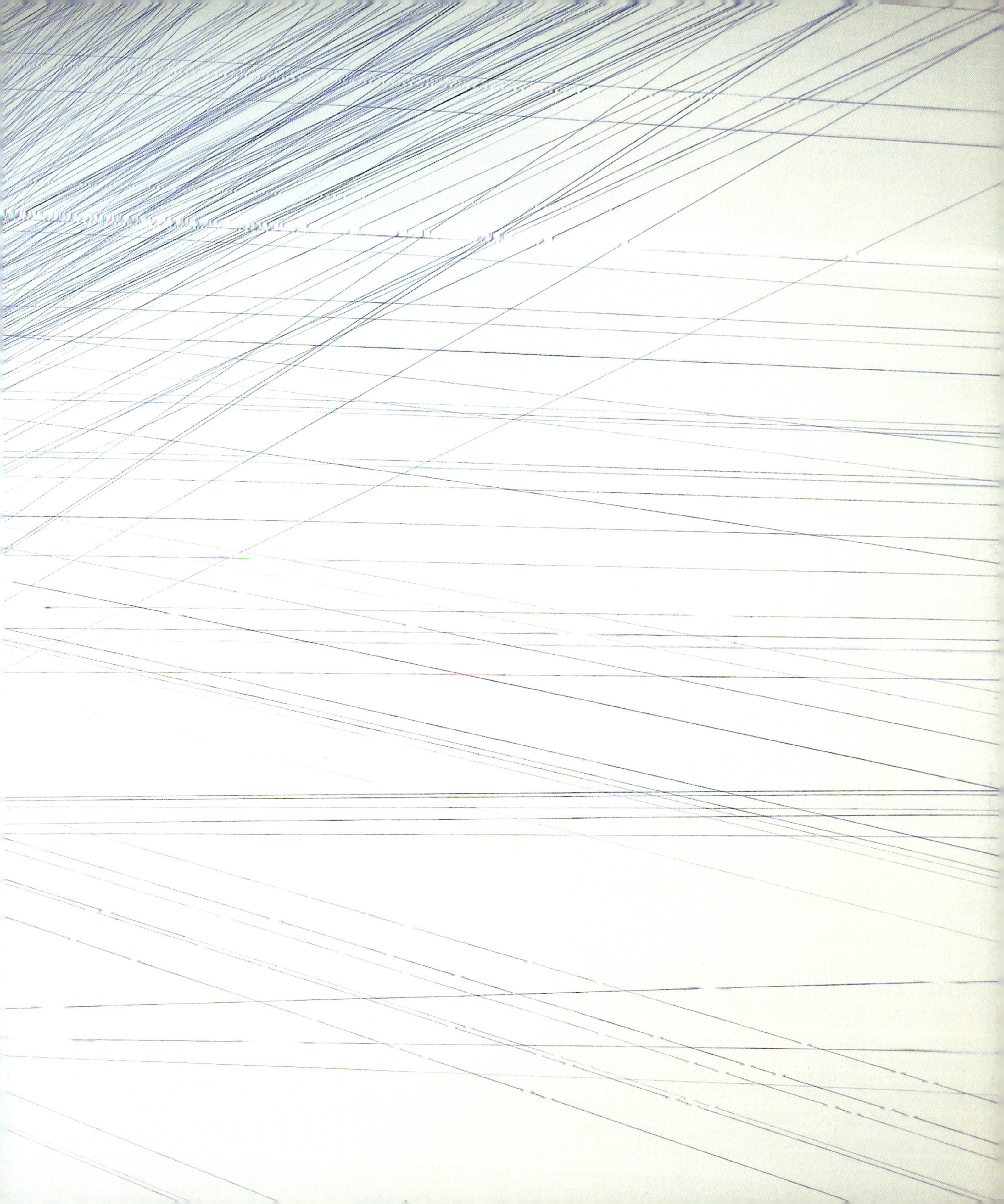

Wall Drawing 56: A square is divided horizontally and vertically into four equal parts, each with lines in four directions superimposed progressively.   1970   (detail opposite)

Wall Drawing 85: A wall is divided into four horizontal parts. In the top row are four equal divisions, each with lines in a different direction. In the second row, six double combinations; in the third row, four triple combinations; in the bottom row, all four combinations superimposed.   1971

Wall Drawing 86: Ten thousand lines about 10 inches (25 cm) long, covering the wall evenly.   1971   (detail opposite)

Wall Drawing 87: A square divided horizontally and vertically into four equal parts, each with lines and colors in four directions superimposed progressively.   1971   (detail opposite)

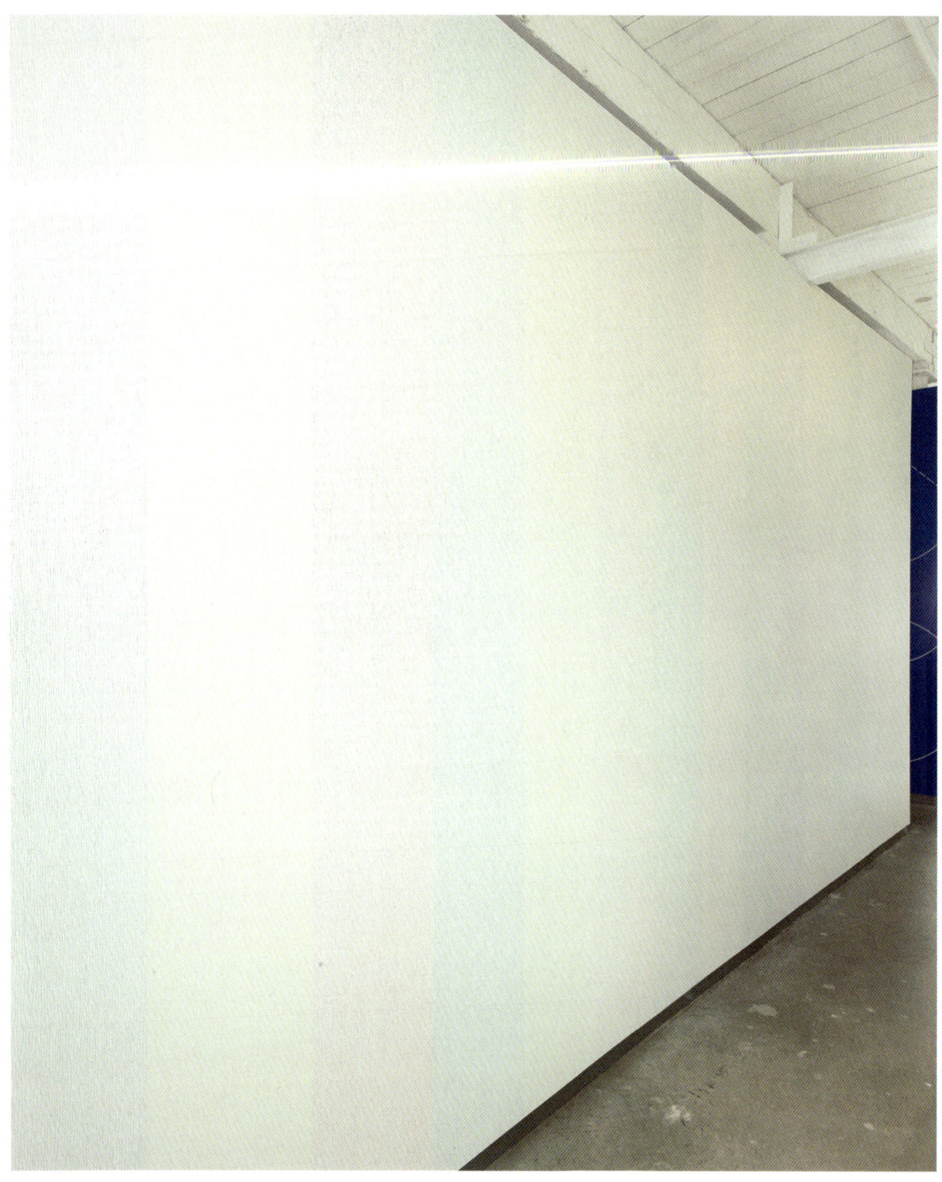

Wall Drawing 95: On a wall divided vertically into fifteen equal parts, vertical lines, not straight, using four colors in all one-, two-, three-, and four-part combinations.   1971   (detail opposite)

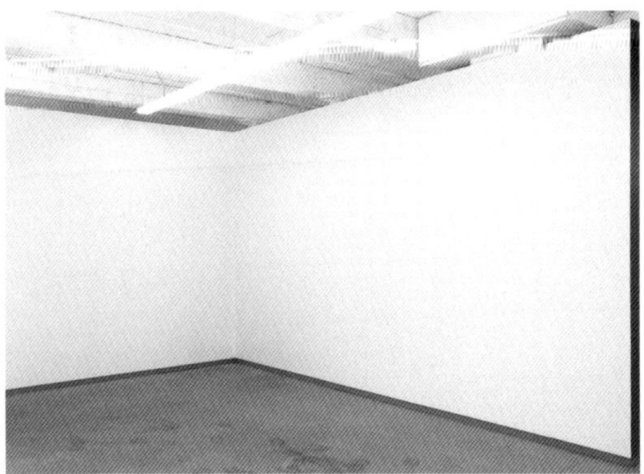

LEFT WALL: *Wall Drawing 130: Grid and arcs from four corners (ACG 103).* 1972

RIGHT WALL: *Wall Drawing 138: Circles and arcs from the midpoints of four sides (ACG 59).* 1972 (detail opposite)

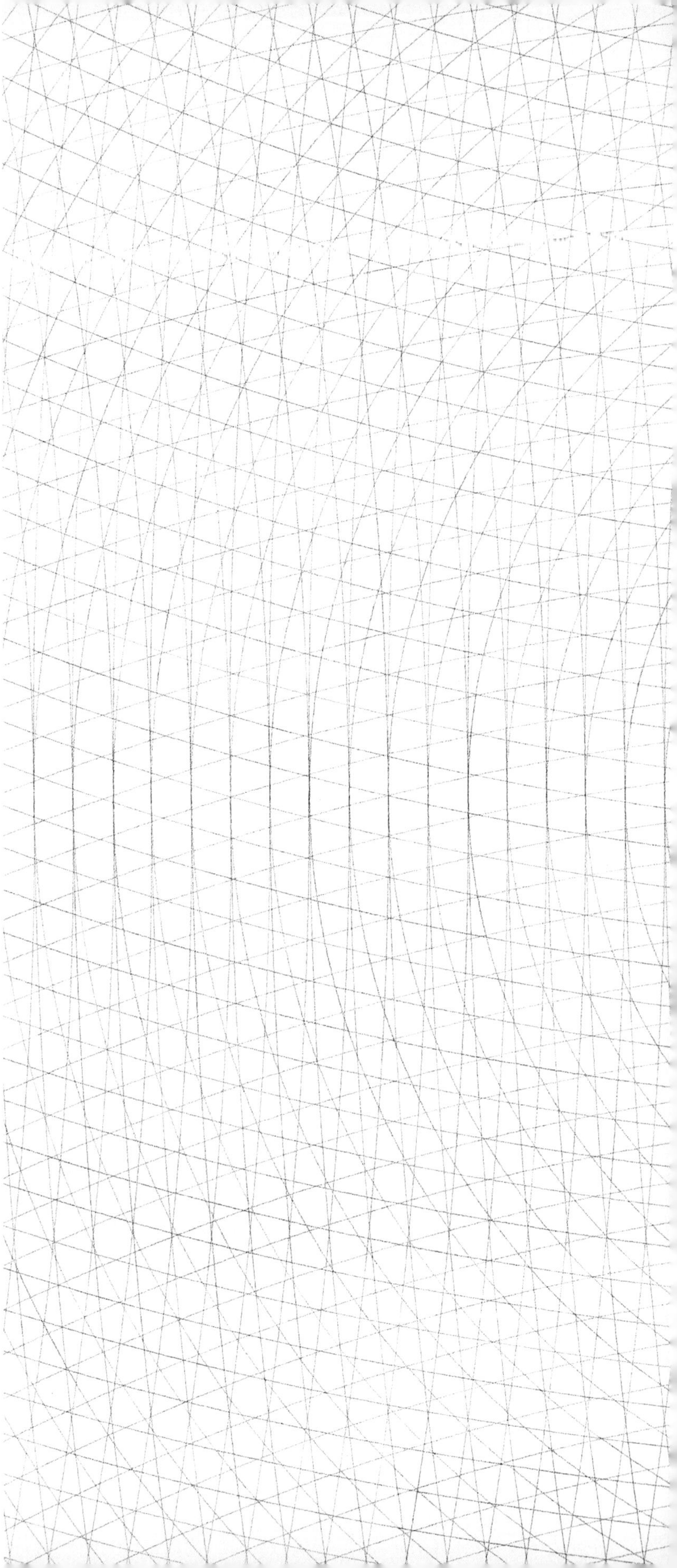

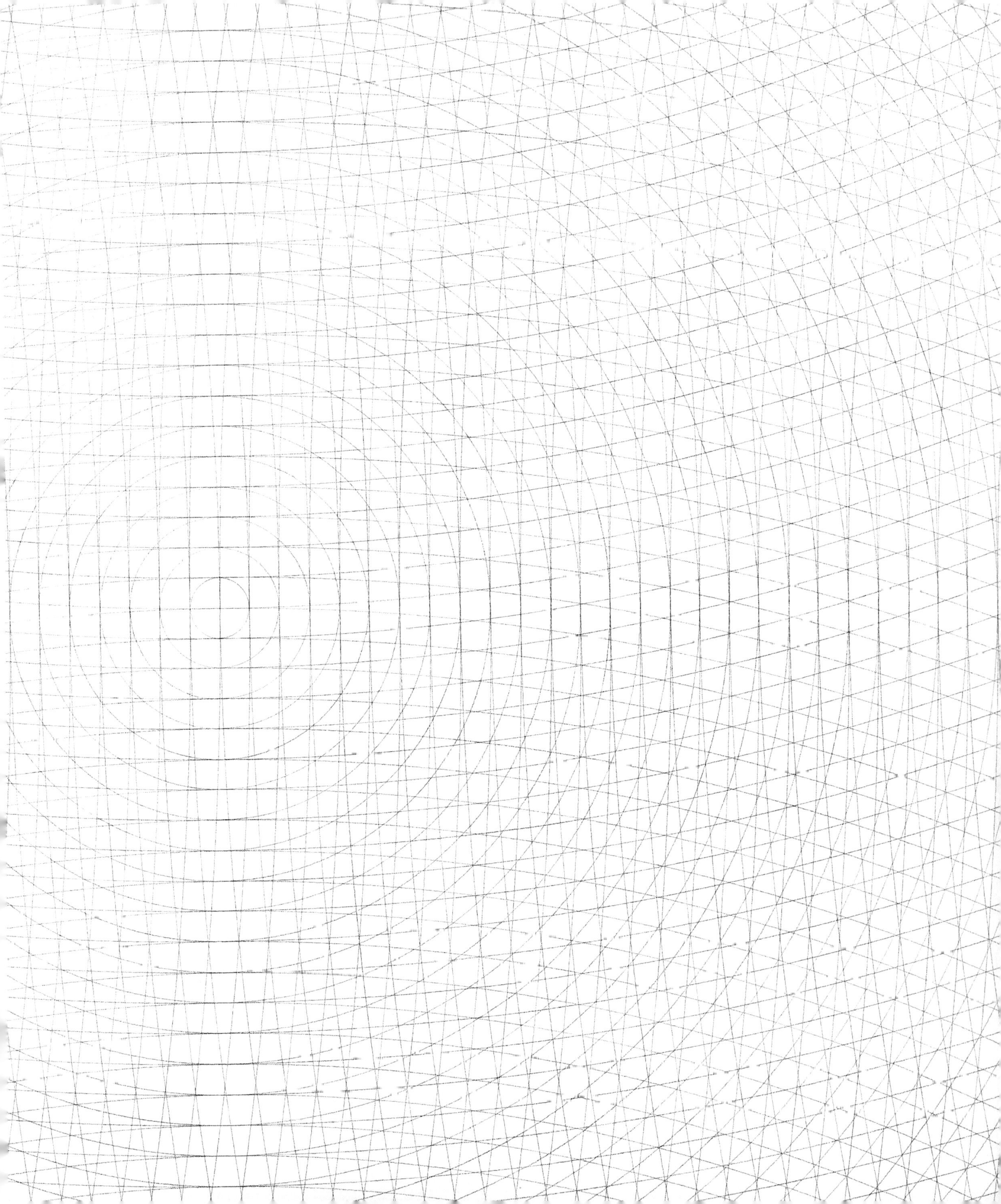

Wall Drawing 142: A 10-inch (25 cm) grid covering the wall. An increasing number of vertical not straight lines from the left side and horizontal not straight lines from bottom to top, adding one line per row of the grid. All lines are spaced evenly based on the number of lines, filling the last row of each direction. 1972 (detail opposite)

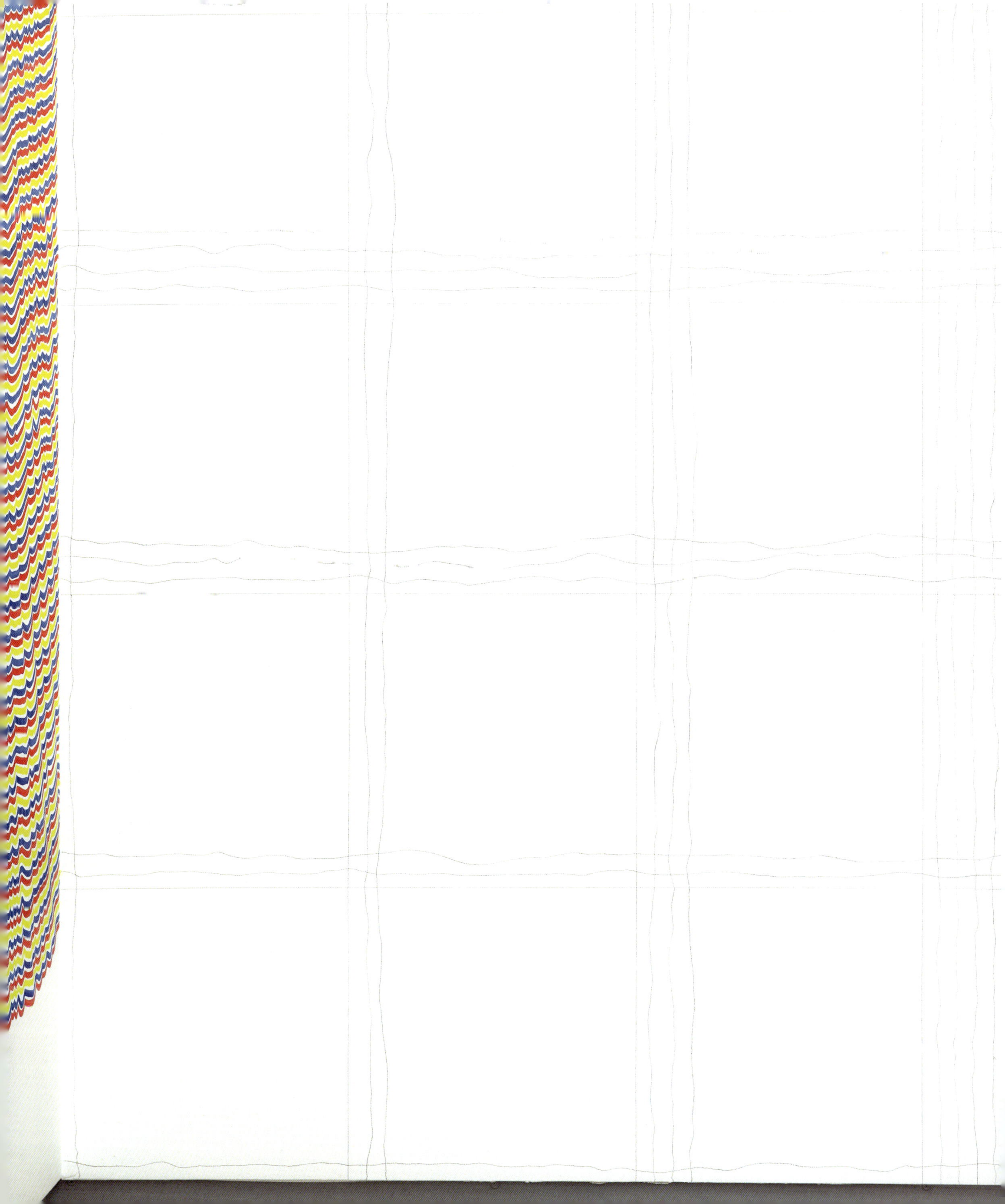

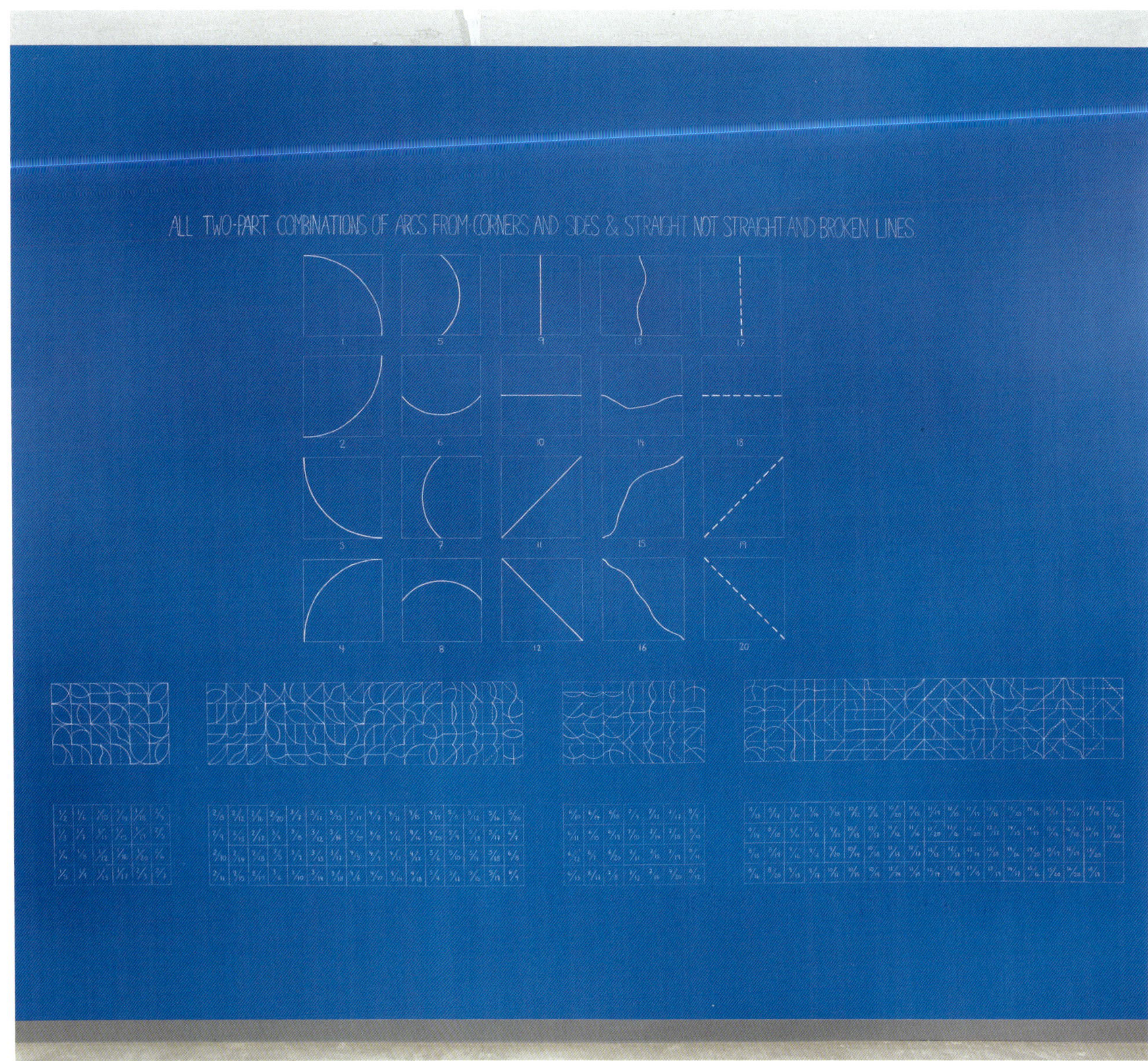

Diagram for *Wall Drawing 146A: All two-part combinations of arcs from corners and sides, and straight, not straight, and broken lines within a 36-inch (90 cm) grid.* 2000

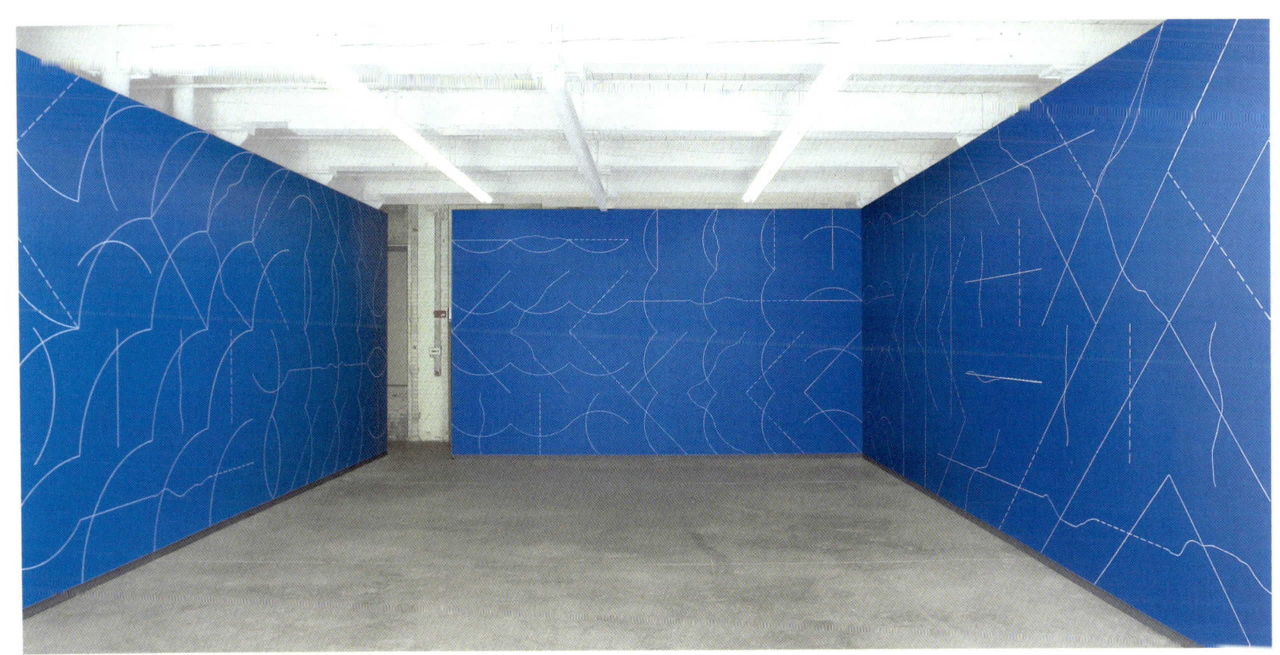

Wall Drawing 146A: All two-part combinations of arcs from corners and sides, and straight, not straight, and broken lines within a 36-inch (90 cm) grid. 2000 (detail)

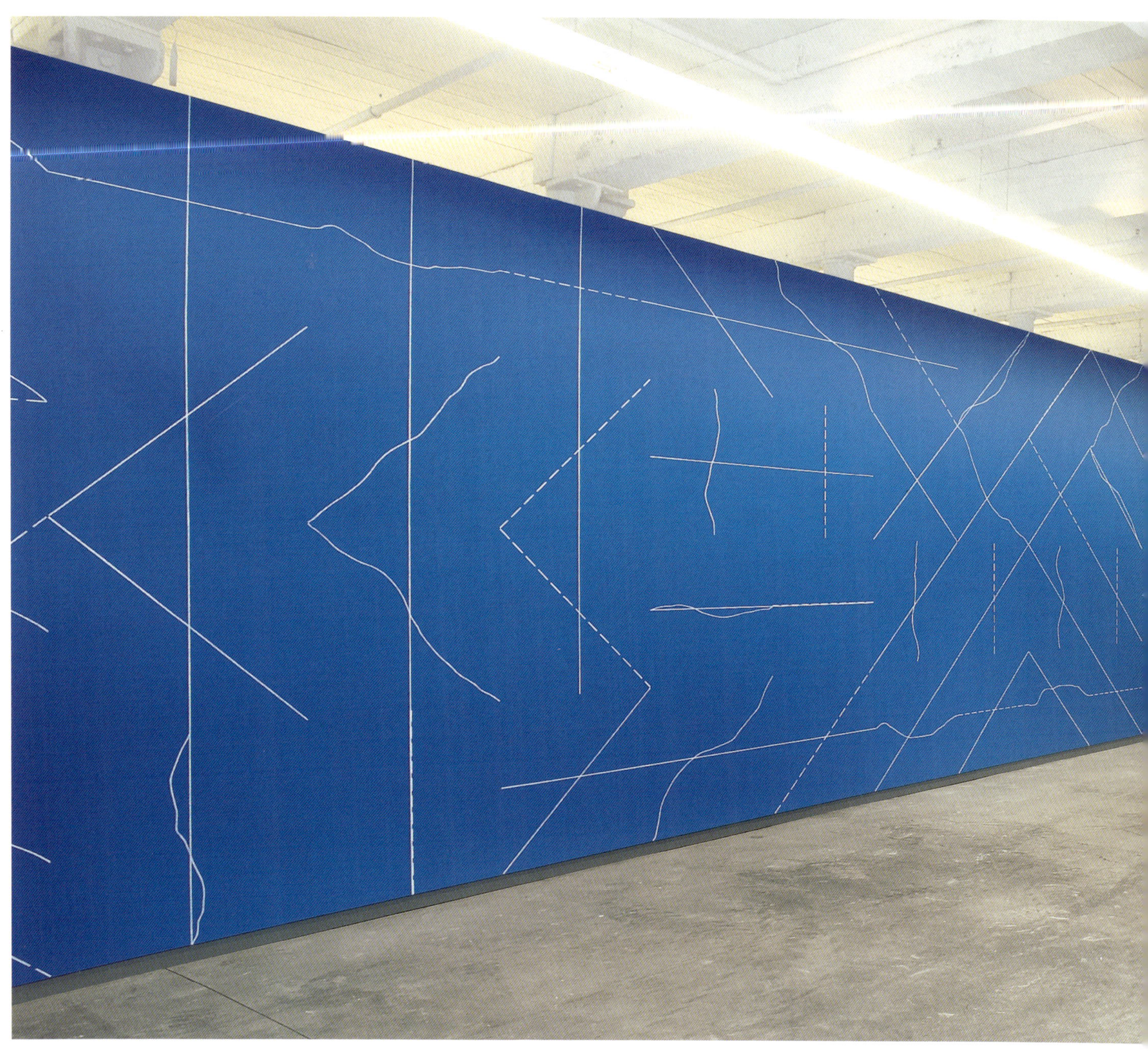

*Wall Drawing 146A: All two-part combinations of arcs from corners and sides, and straight,
not straight, and broken lines within a 36-inch (90 cm) grid.   2000   (detail)*

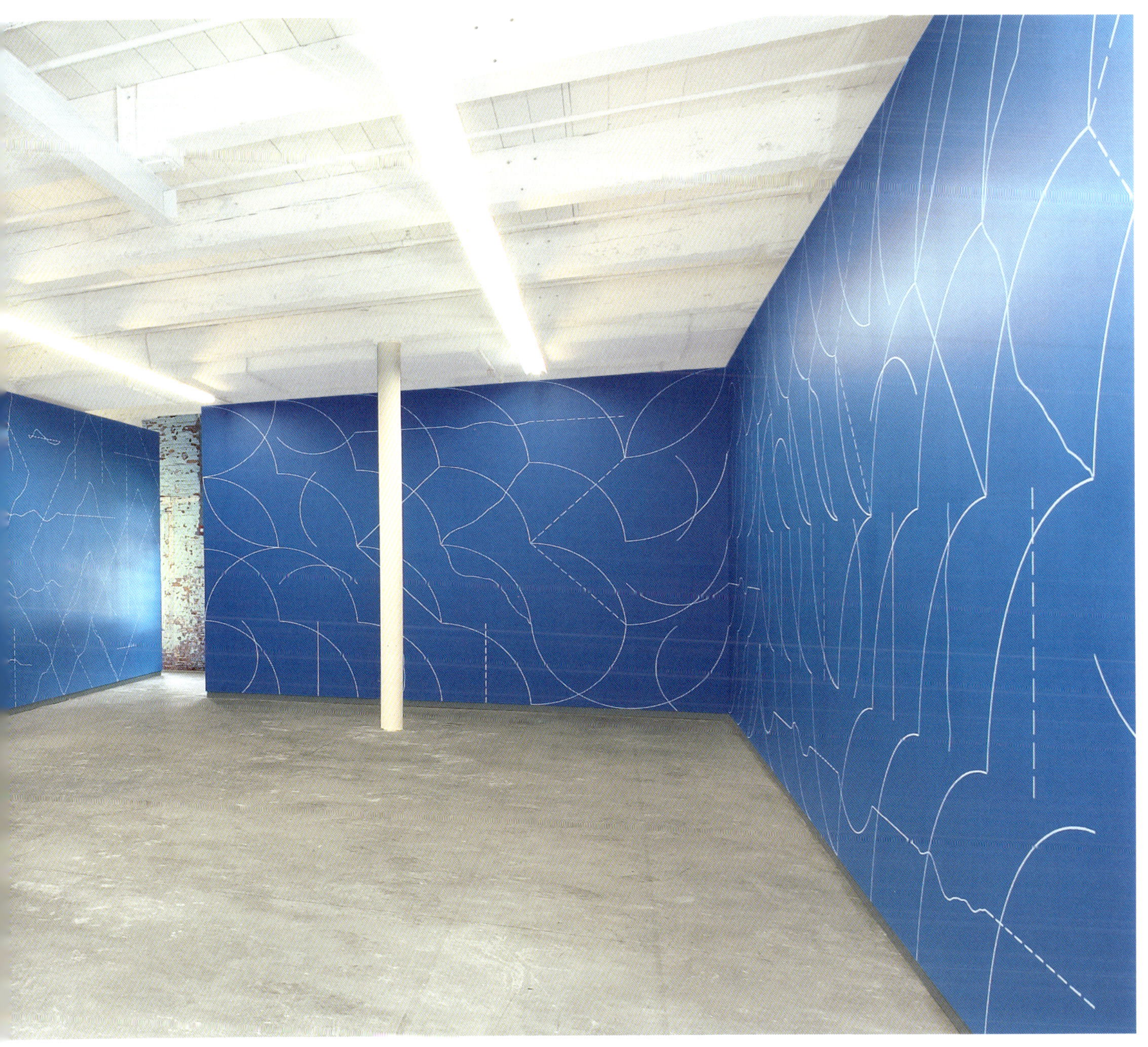

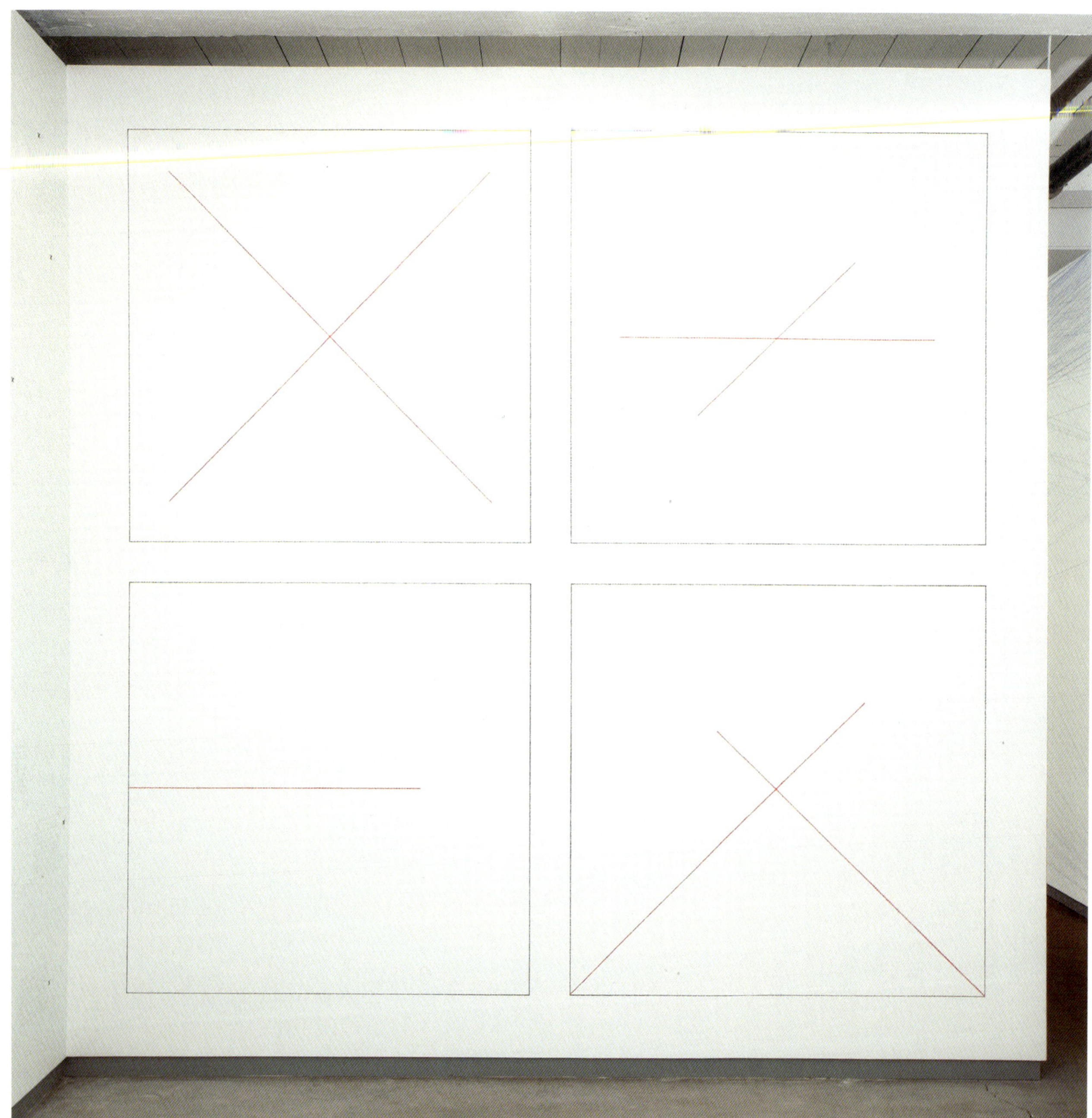

Wall Drawing 160: A black outlined square with a red diagonal line centered on the axis between the upper left and lower right corners and another red diagonal line centered on the axis between the lower left and upper right corners.   1973

Wall Drawing 164: A black outlined square with a red horizontal line centered on the axis between the midpoint of the left side and the midpoint of the right side and a red diagonal line centered on the axis between the lower left and upper right corners.   1973

Wall Drawing 159: A black outlined square with a red diagonal line from the lower left corner toward the upper right corner; and another red line from the lower right corner to the upper left.   1973

Wall Drawing 154: A black outlined square with a red horizontal line from the midpoint of the left side toward the middle of the right side.   1973

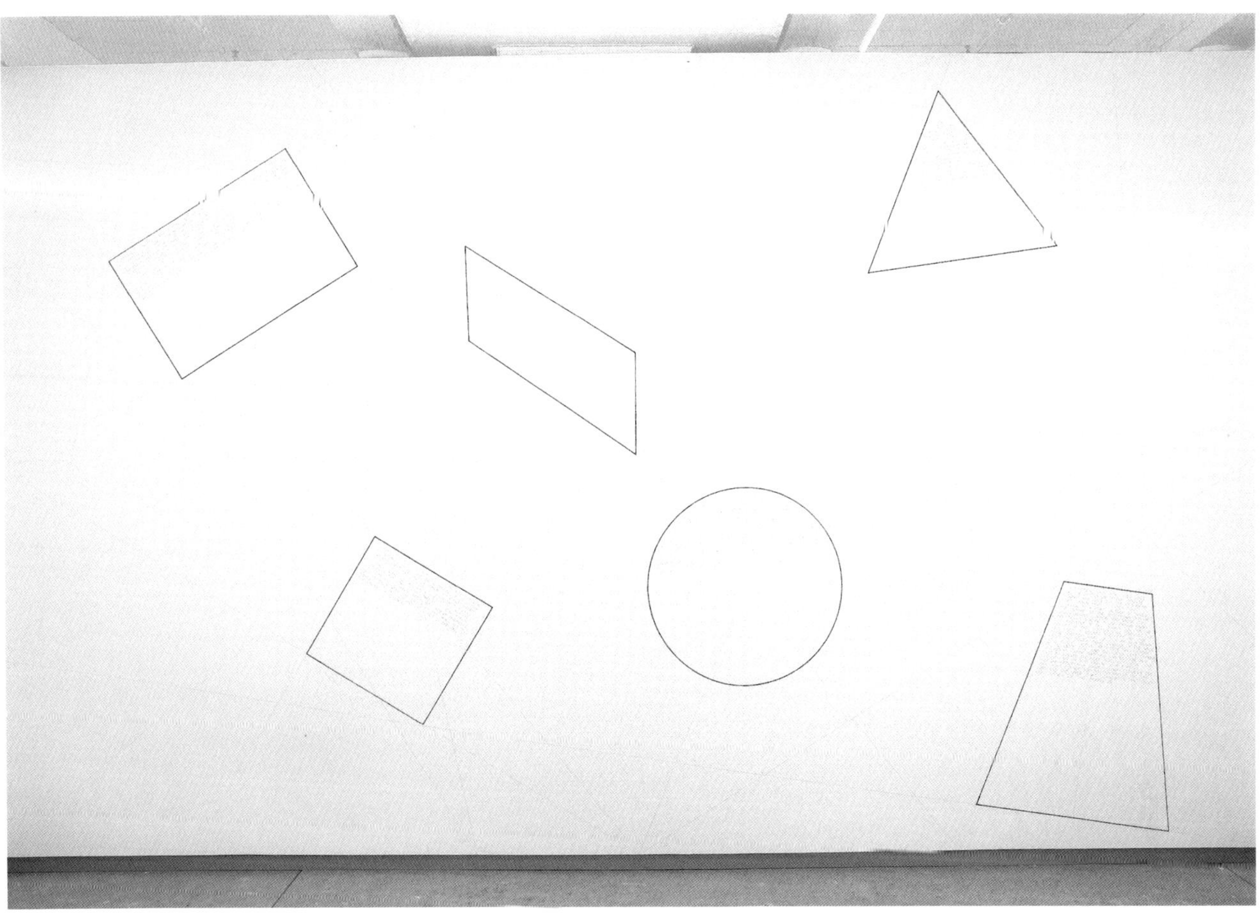

Wall Drawing 274: The location of six geometric figures. (The specific locations are determined by the draftsman.)   1975

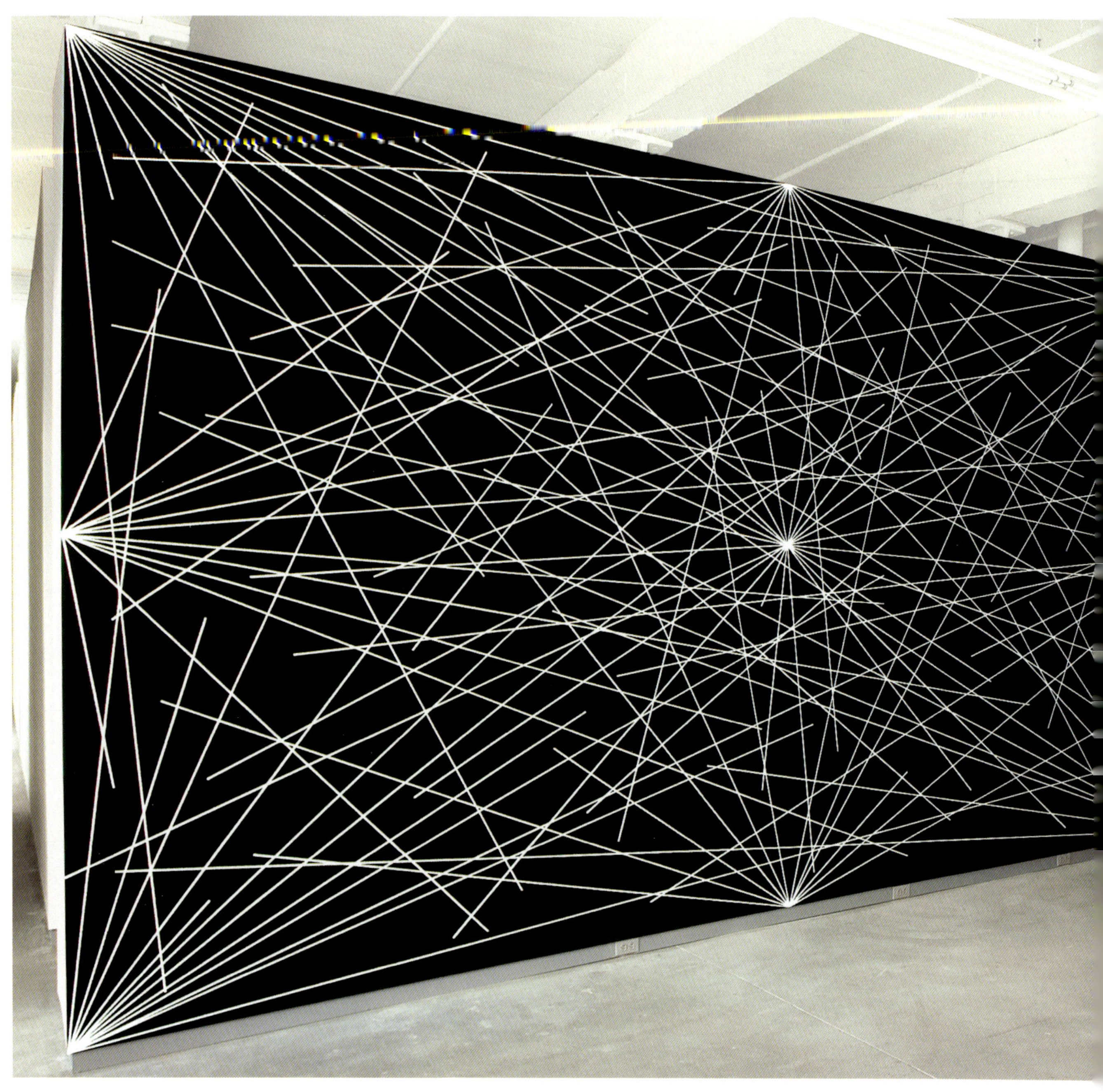

*Wall Drawing 289: A 6-inch (15 cm) grid covering each of four black walls. White lines to points on the grids.
Fourth wall: twenty-four lines from the center, twelve lines from the midpoint of each of the sides, twelve lines
from each corner. (The length of the lines and their placement are determined by the draftsman.)* 1976

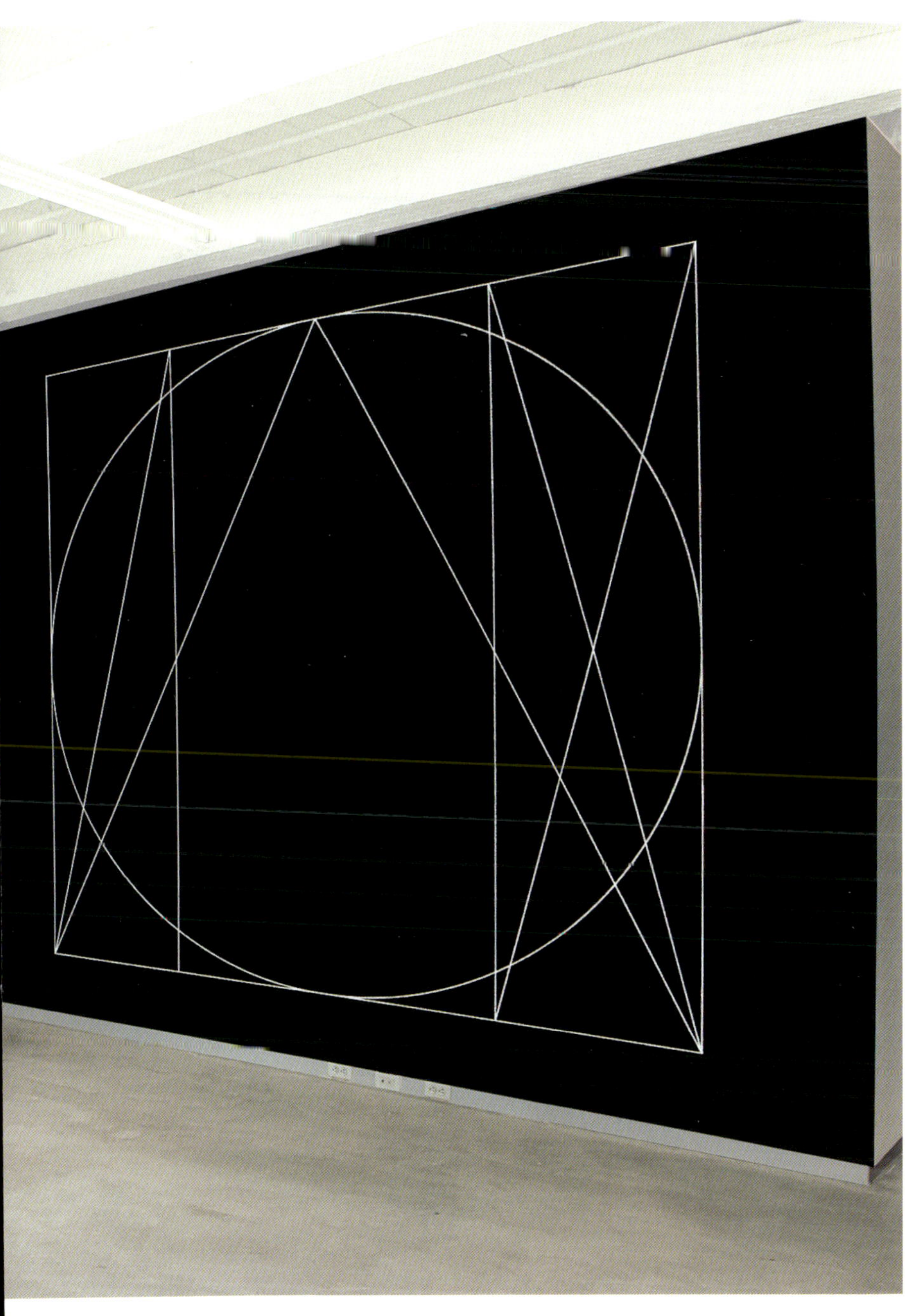

Wall Drawing 295: Six white geometric figures (outlines) superimposed on a black wall. 1976

Wall Drawing 305: The location of one hundred random specific points.
(The locations are determined by the draftsman.)   1977   (detail opposite)

50.
THE FIFTIETH POINT IS LOCATED
HALFWAY BETWEEN A POINT HALFWAY
BETWEEN THE TWELFTH AND THE THIRTY-
SECOND POINTS, AND THE TWELFTH
POINT.

10.
THE TENTH POINT IS LOCATED
EQUIDISTANT FROM THE NINTH POINT,
THE THIRD POINT AND THE MIDPOINT
OF THE TOP SIDE.

21.
THE TWENTY-FIRST POINT
IS LOCATED AT THE CENTER
OF THE WALL.

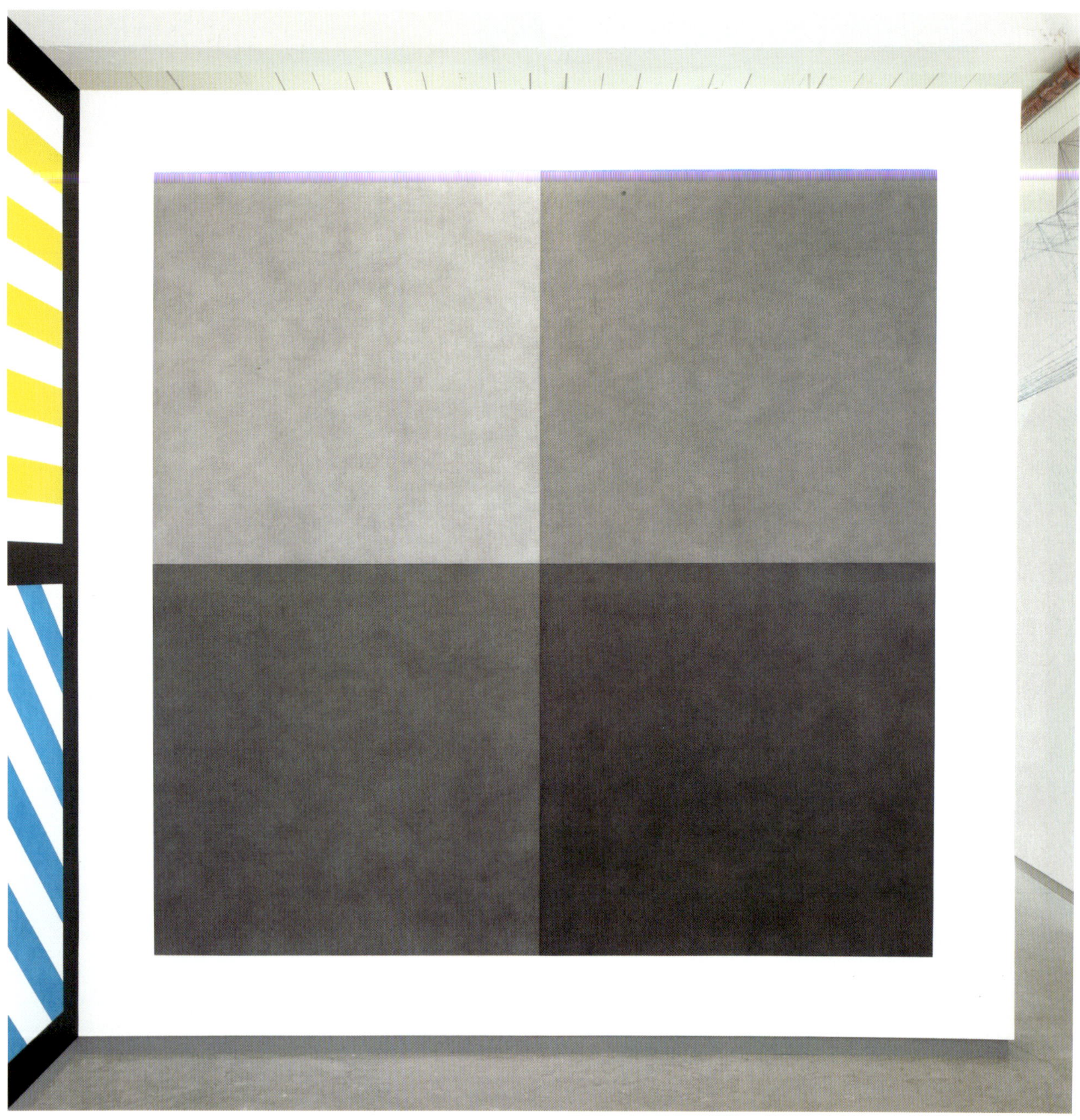

Wall Drawing 365: A square divided horizontally and vertically into four equal parts, each with a progressively darker gradation of gray.   1984

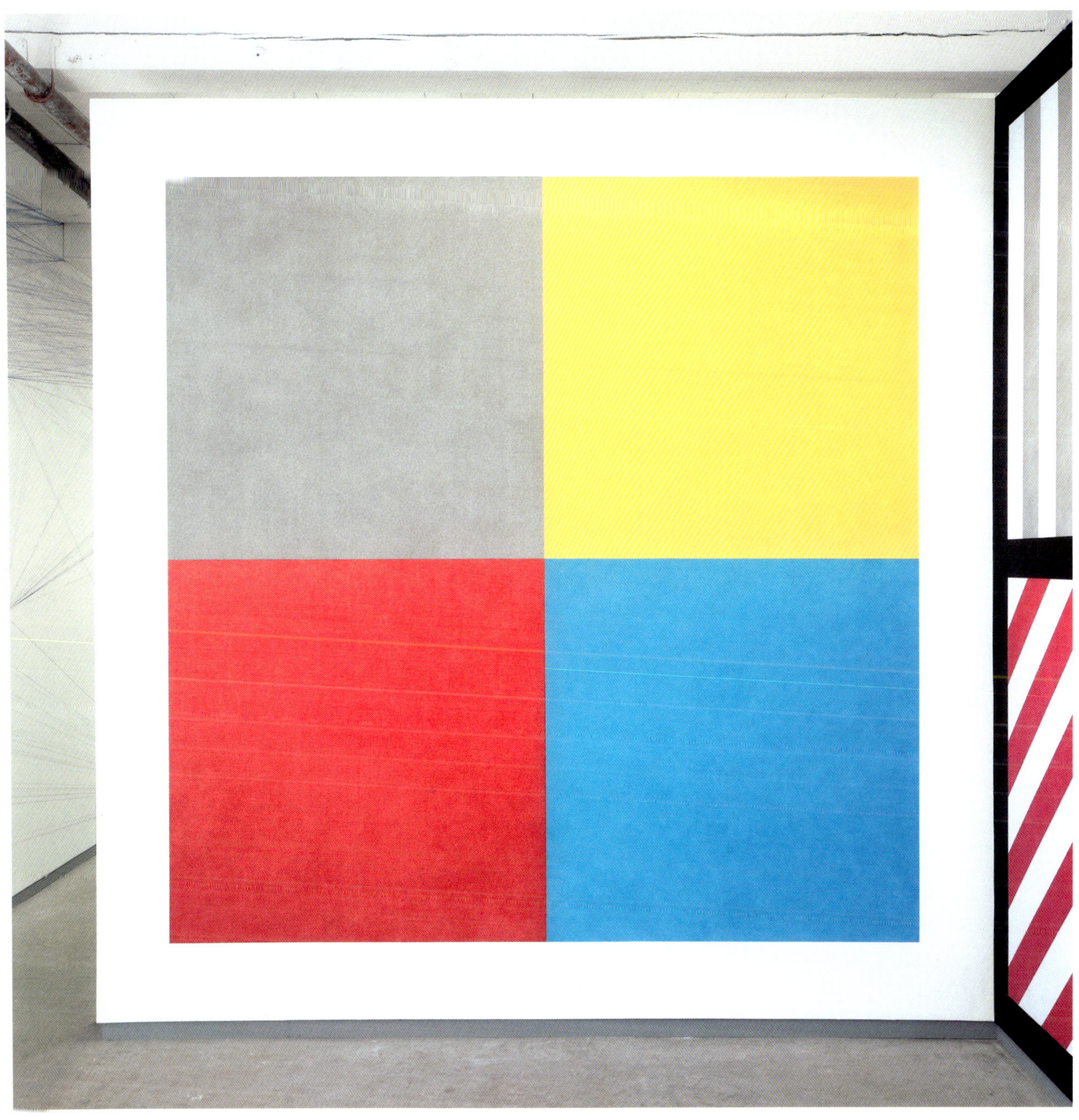

Wall Drawing 381: A square divided horizontally and vertically into four equal parts, one gray, one yellow, one red and one blue, drawn with color and India ink washes.   1982

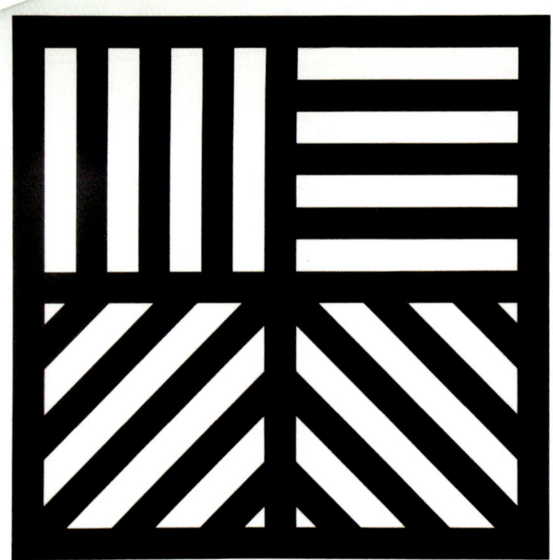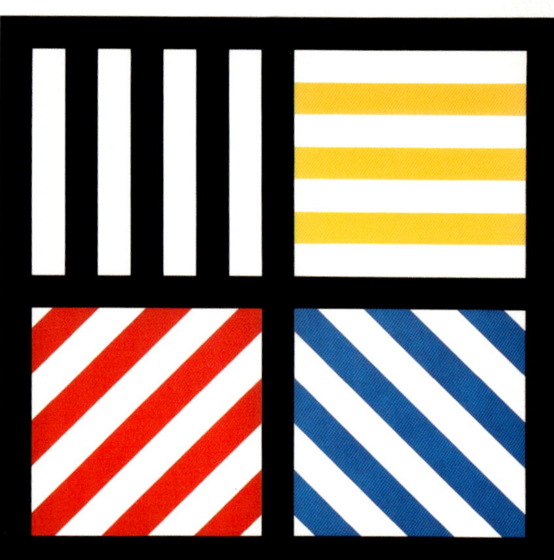

Wall Drawing 391: Two-part drawing. The two walls are each divided horizontally and vertically into four equal parts. First wall: 12-inch (30 cm) bands of lines in four directions, one direction in each part, drawn in black India ink. Second wall: Same, but with four colors drawn in India ink and color ink washes.   1983

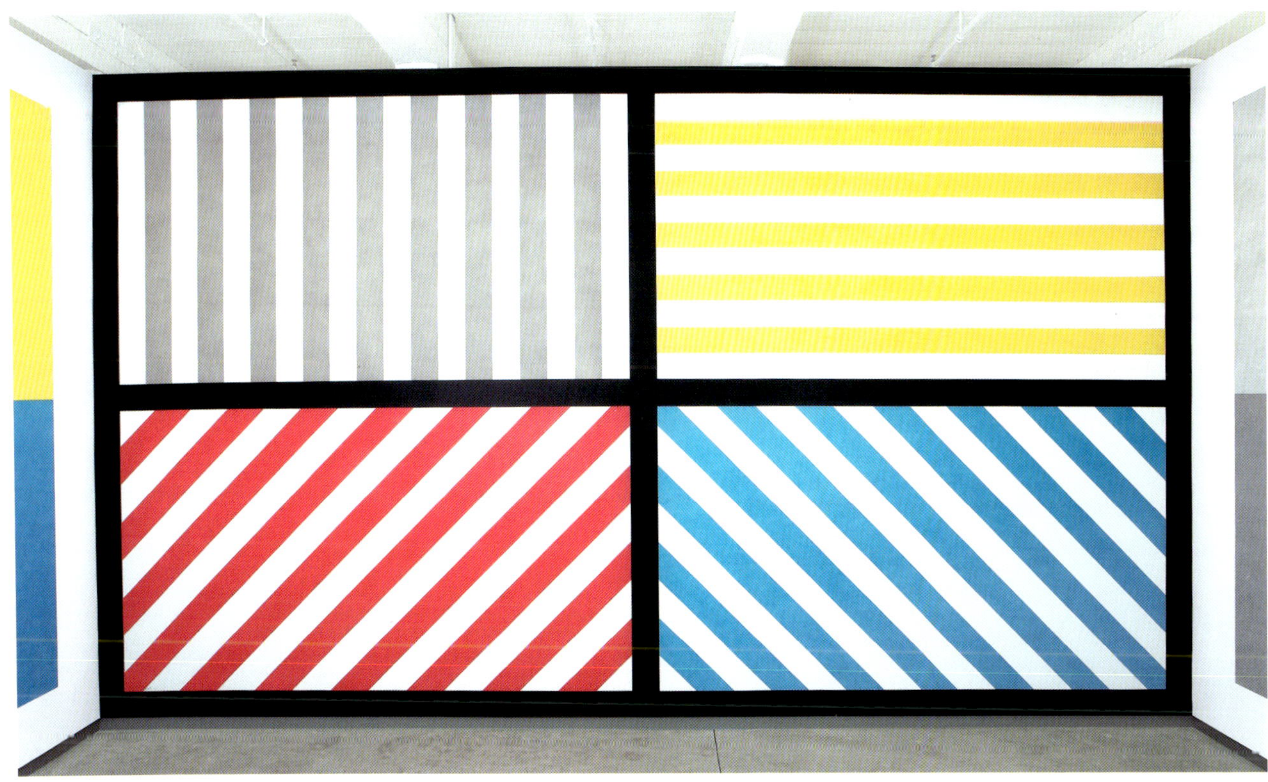

Wall Drawing 419: The wall is bordered and divided horizontally and vertically into four equal parts with a 6-inch (15 cm) black ink band. Each quarter has alternating parallel 6-inch (15 cm) bands of white and color ink bands. Upper left: gray; upper right: yellow; lower left: red; lower right: blue. 1984

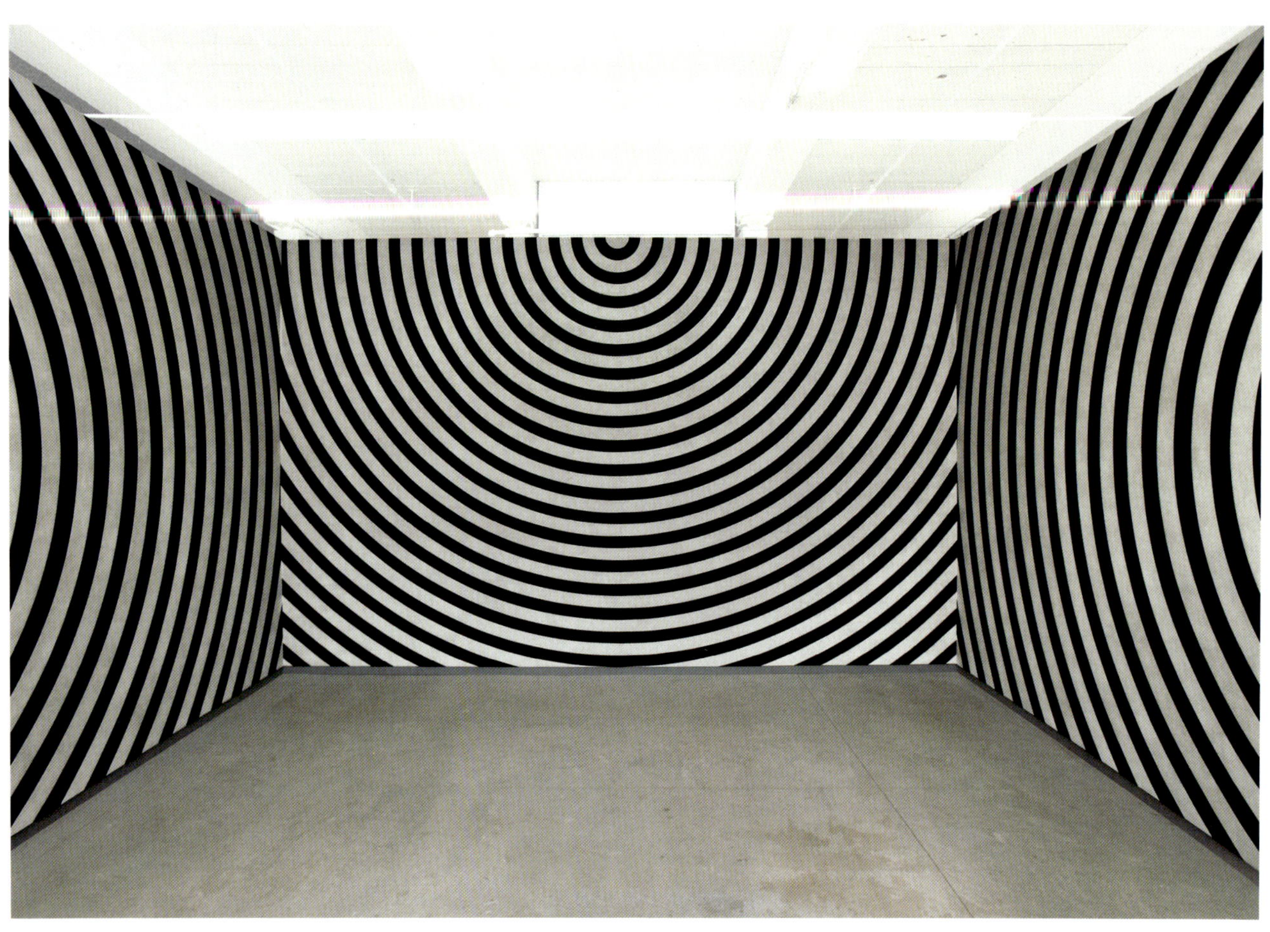

Wall Drawing 462: On four walls, one room, arcs 4 inches (10 cm) wide, from the midpoints of four sides, drawn with alternating bands of gray and black ink wash.   1986   (detail opposite)

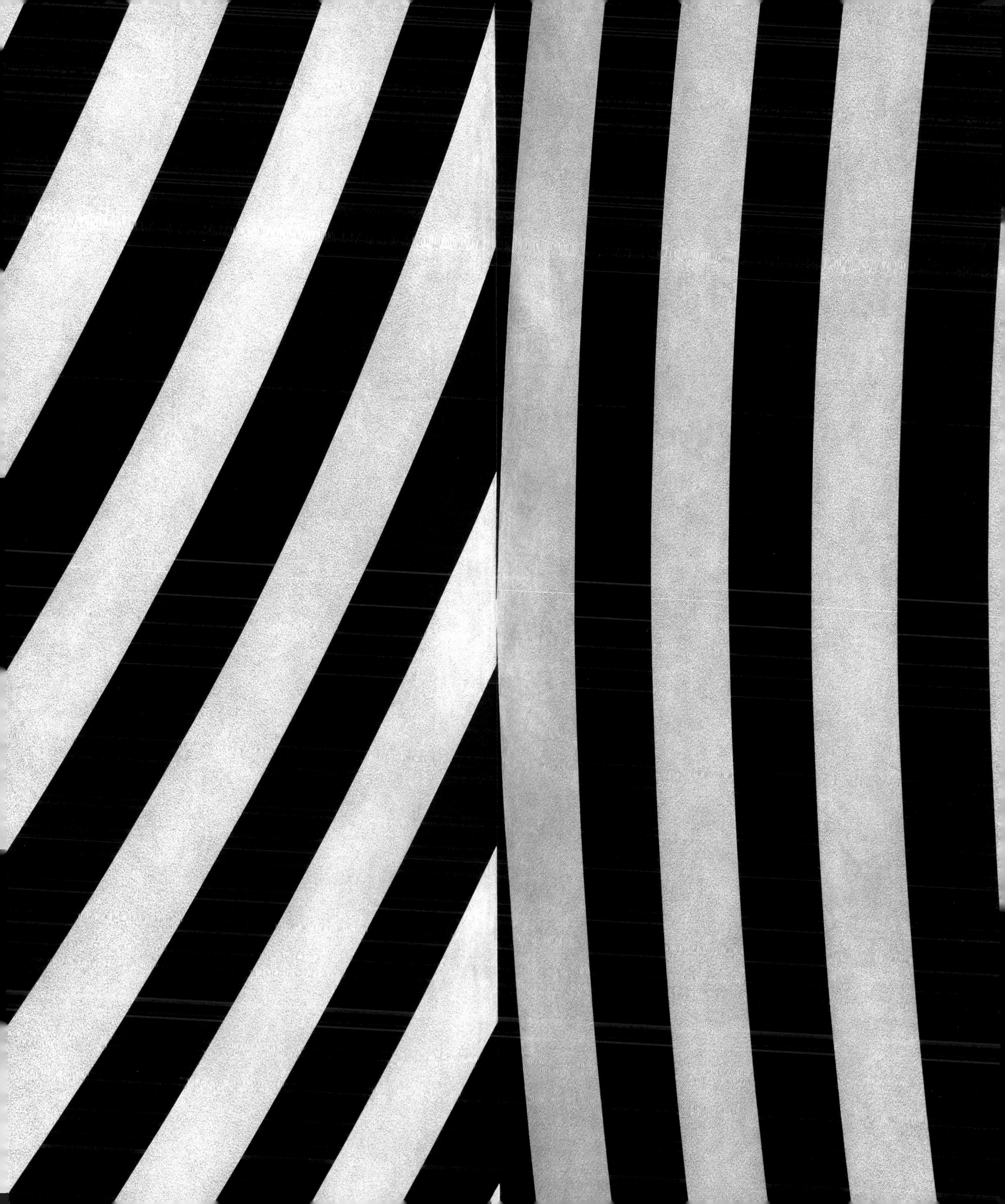

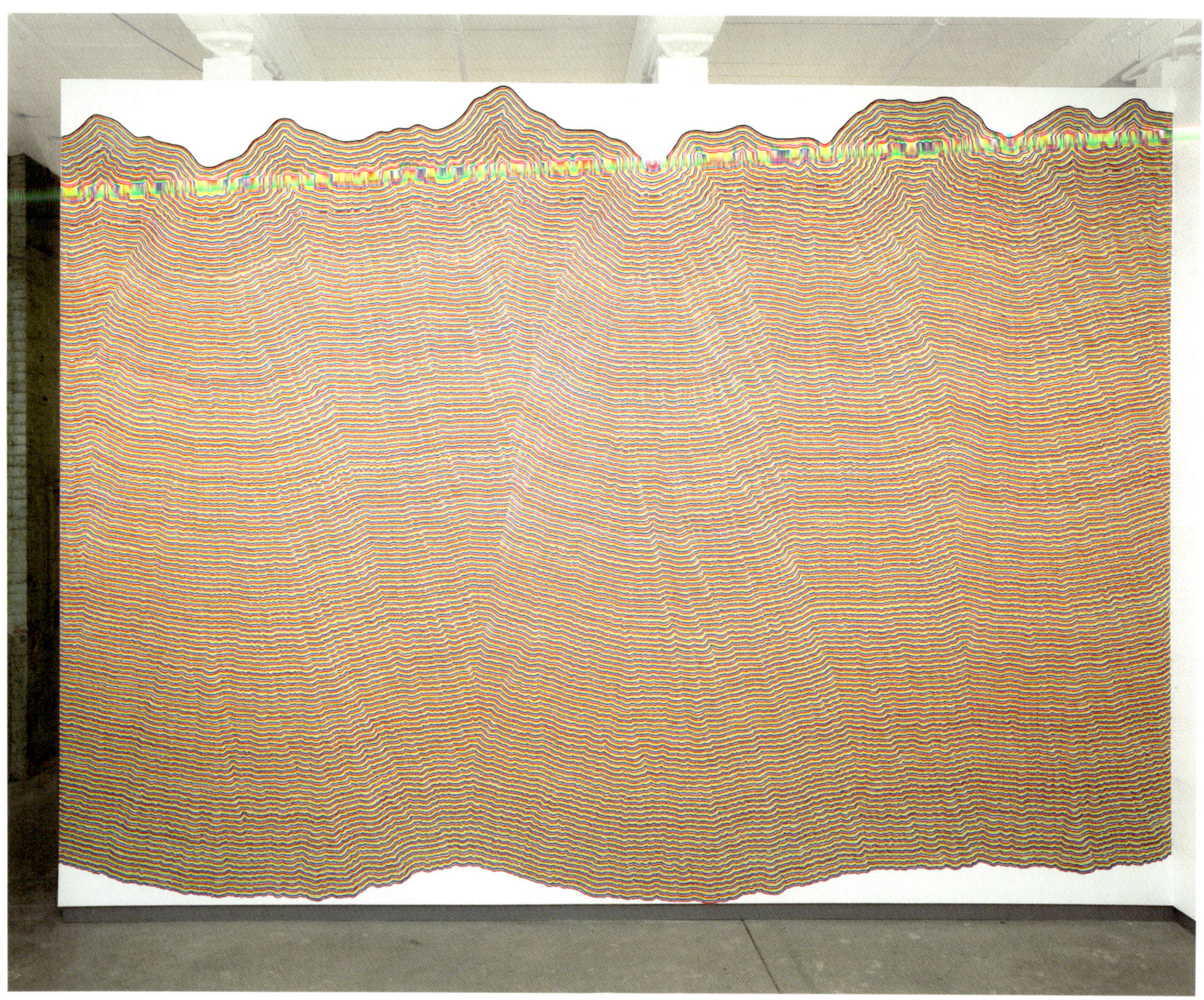

Wall Drawing 797: The first drafter has a black marker and makes an irregular horizontal line near the top of the wall. Then the second drafter tries to copy it (without touching it) using a red marker. The third drafter does the same, using a yellow marker. The fourth drafter does the same, using a blue marker. Then the second drafter, followed by the third and fourth, copies the last line drawn until the bottom of the wall is reached. 1995 (detail opposite)

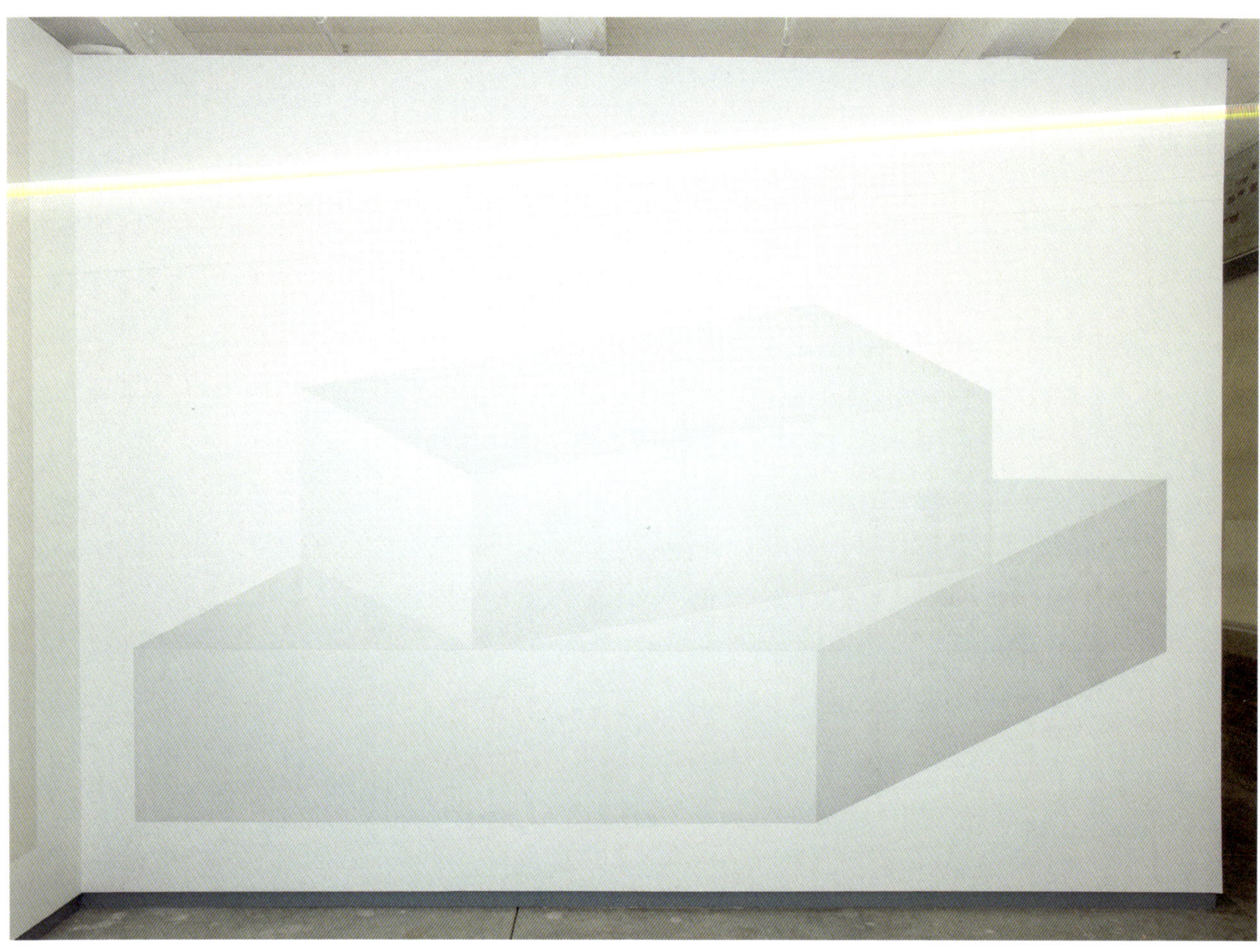

Wall Drawing 957: Form derived from a cube.   2000

Wall Drawing 1094A: Projecting form.   2003

Diagram for *Wall Drawing 1211: Drawing Series—Part I–IV, #1–24, A+B (192 Drawings)*   2006

Wall Drawing 1211: Drawing Series—Part I–IV, #1-24, A+B (192 Drawings)   2006

Wall Drawing 1211: Drawing Series—Part I–IV, #1–24, A+B (192 Drawings)   IA-1/1234   2006   (detail)

Wall Drawing 1211: Drawing Series—Part I–IV, #1–24, A+B (192 Drawings)   IB-1/1234   2006   (detail)

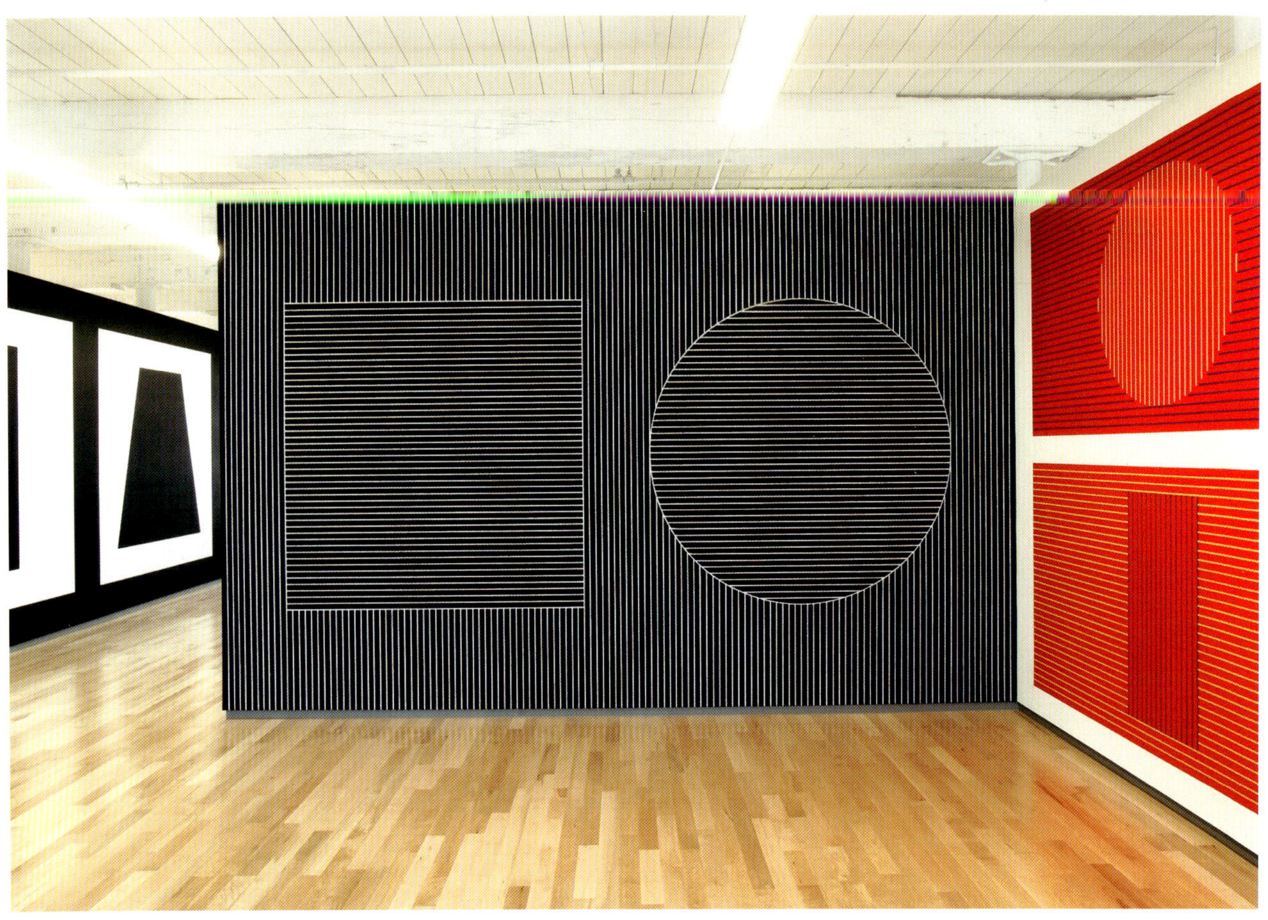

Wall Drawing 335: On four black walls, white vertical parallel lines, and in the center of the walls, eight geometric figures (including cross, X) within which are white horizontal parallel lines. The vertical lines do not enter the figures.   1980   (detail opposite)

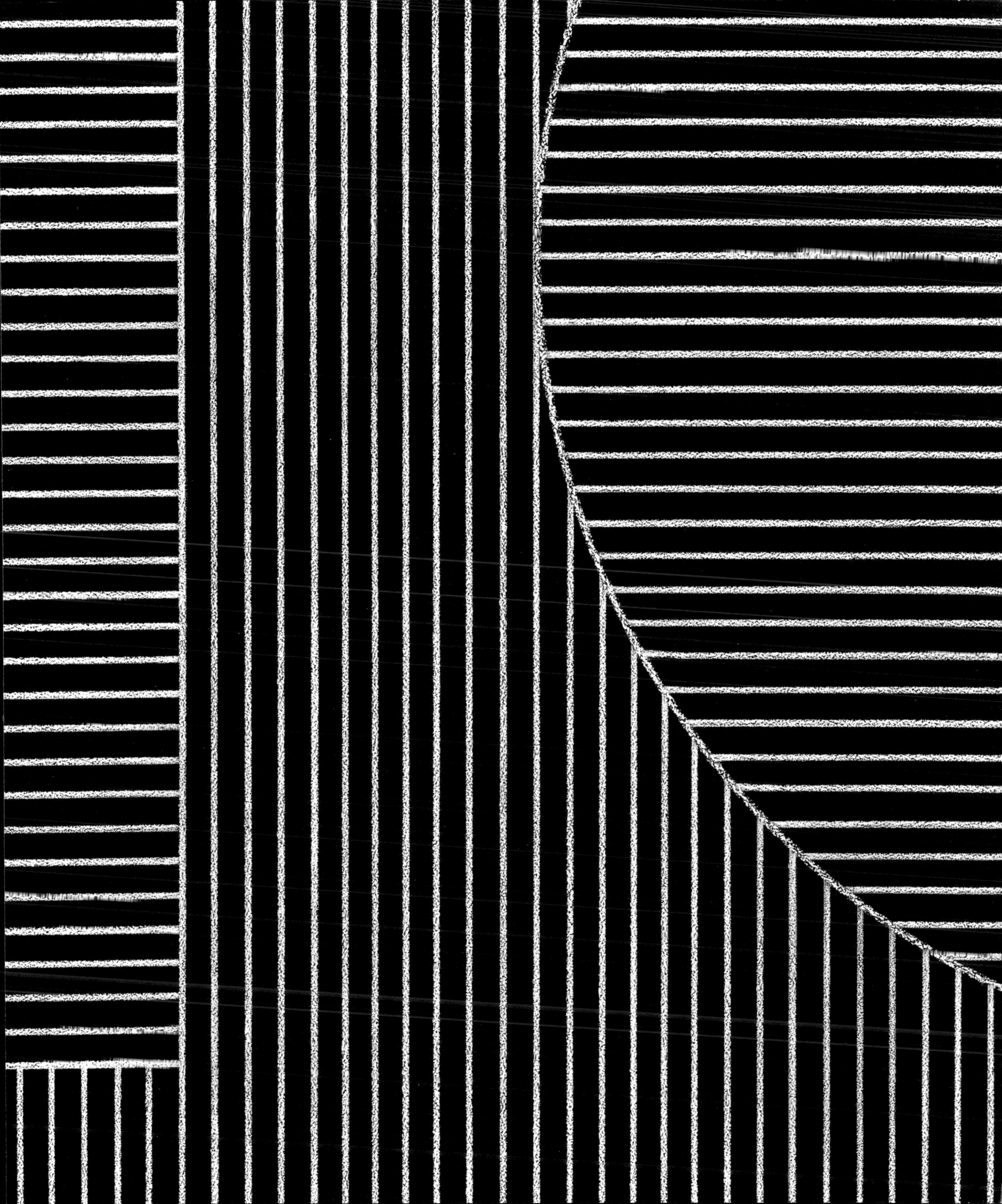

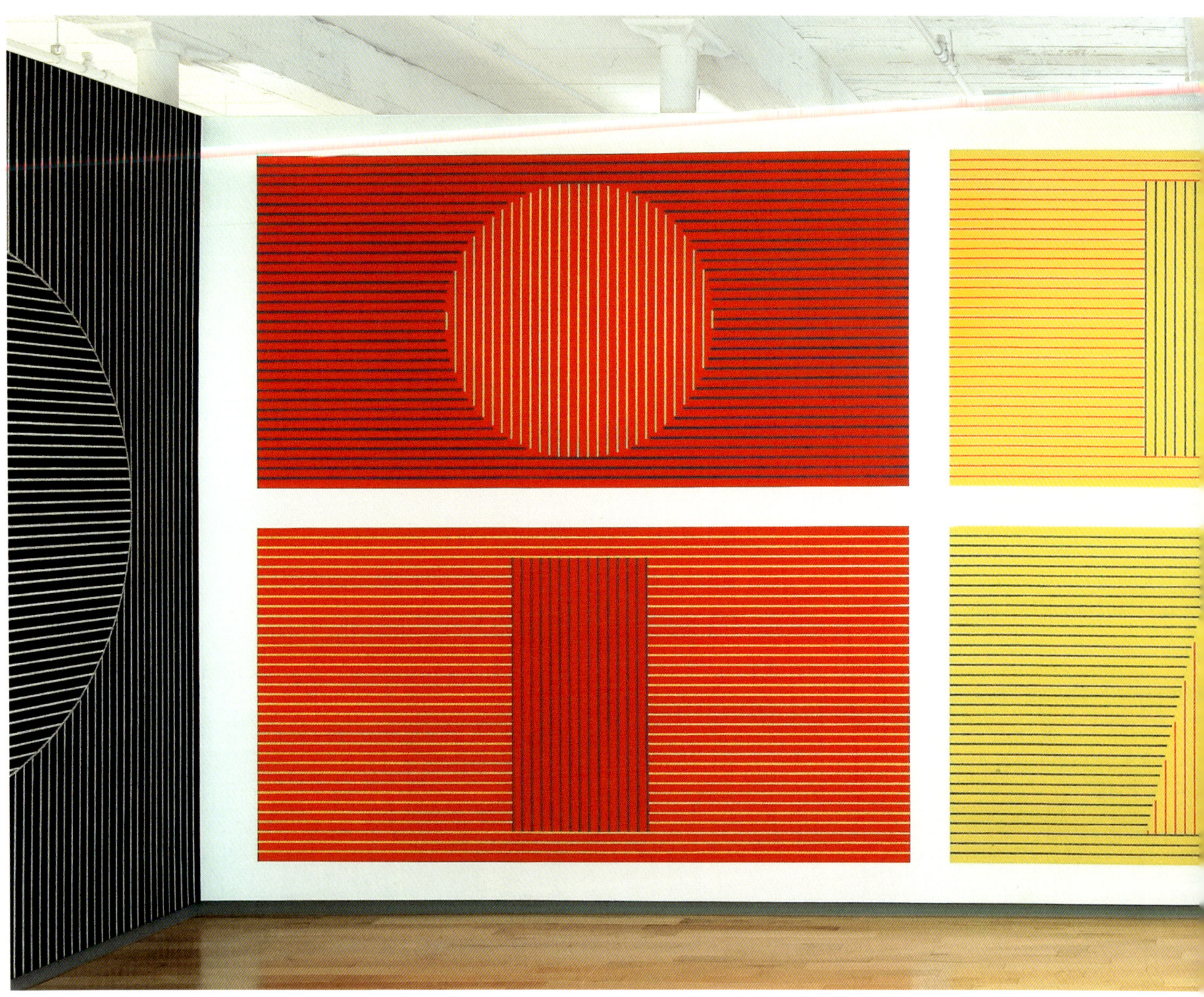

Wall Drawing 340: Six-part drawing. The wall is divided horizontally and vertically into six equal parts. First part: On red, blue horizontal parallel lines, and in the center, a circle within which are yellow vertical parallel lines; second part: On yellow, red horizontal parallel lines, and in the center, a square within which are blue vertical parallel lines; third part: On blue, yellow horizontal parallel lines, and in the center, a triangle within which are red vertical parallel lines; fourth part: On red, yellow horizontal parallel lines, and in the center, a rectangle within which are blue vertical parallel lines; fifth part: On yellow, blue horizontal parallel lines, and in the center, a trapezoid within which are red vertical parallel lines; sixth part: On blue, red horizontal parallel lines, and in the center, a parallelogram within which are yellow vertical parallel lines. The horizontal lines do not enter the figures.   1980

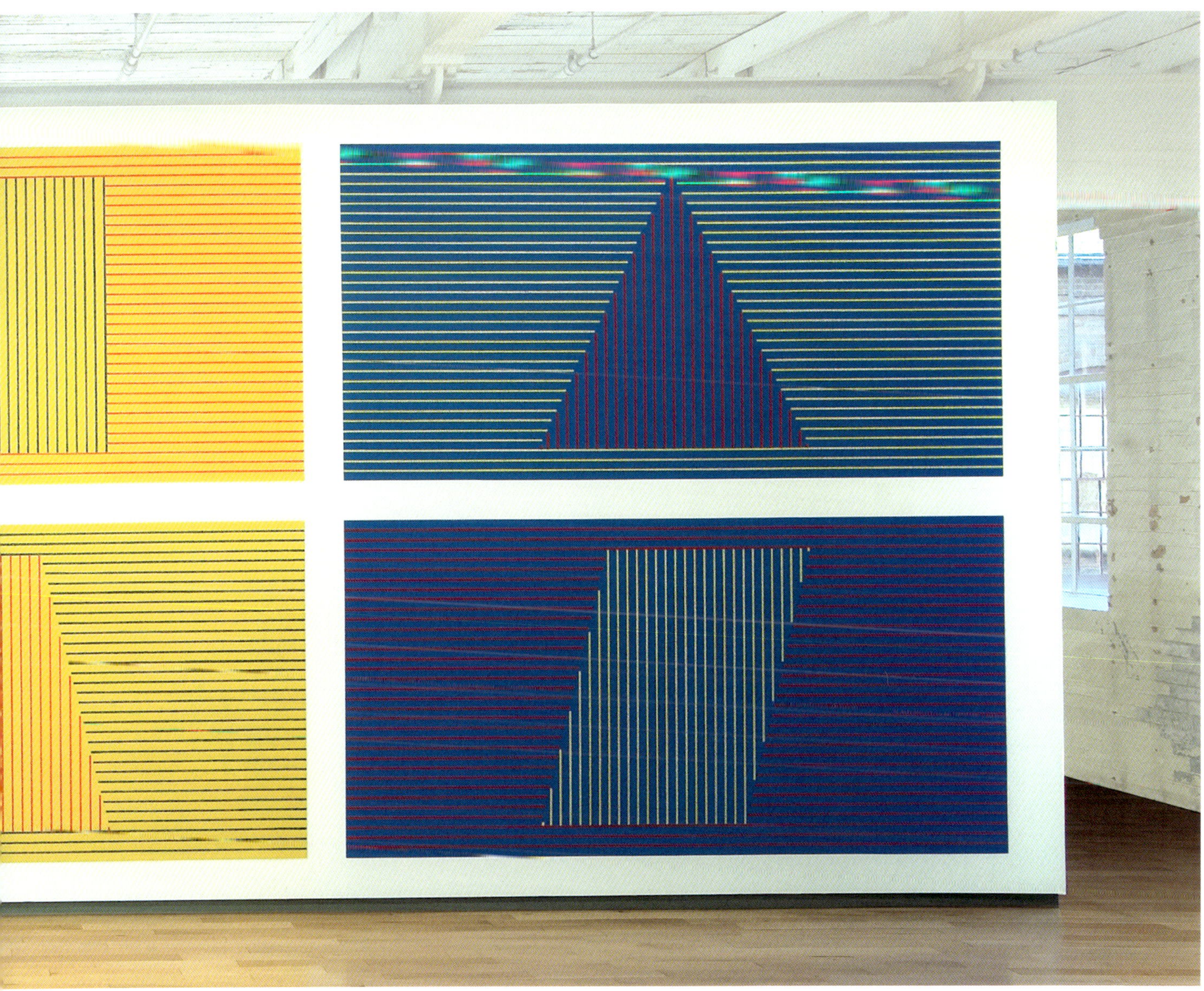

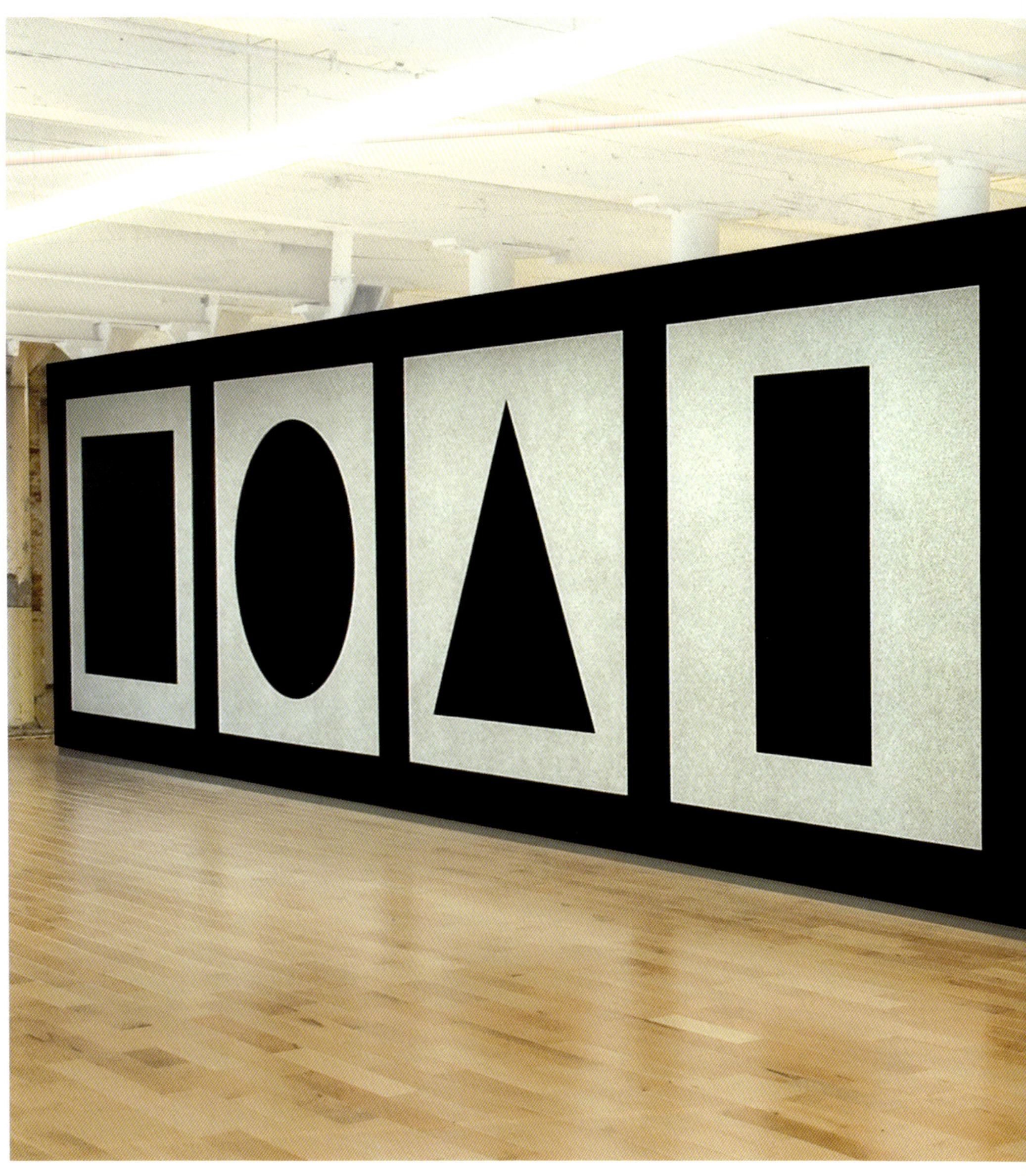

Wall Drawing 343A (Circle); Wall Drawing 343B (Square); Wall Drawing 343C (Triangle);
Wall Drawing 343D (Rectangle); Wall Drawing 343E (Trapezoid); Wall Drawing 343F
(Parallelogram): On a black wall, nine geometric figures (including right triangle, cross, X)
in squares. The backgrounds are filled in solid white.   1980

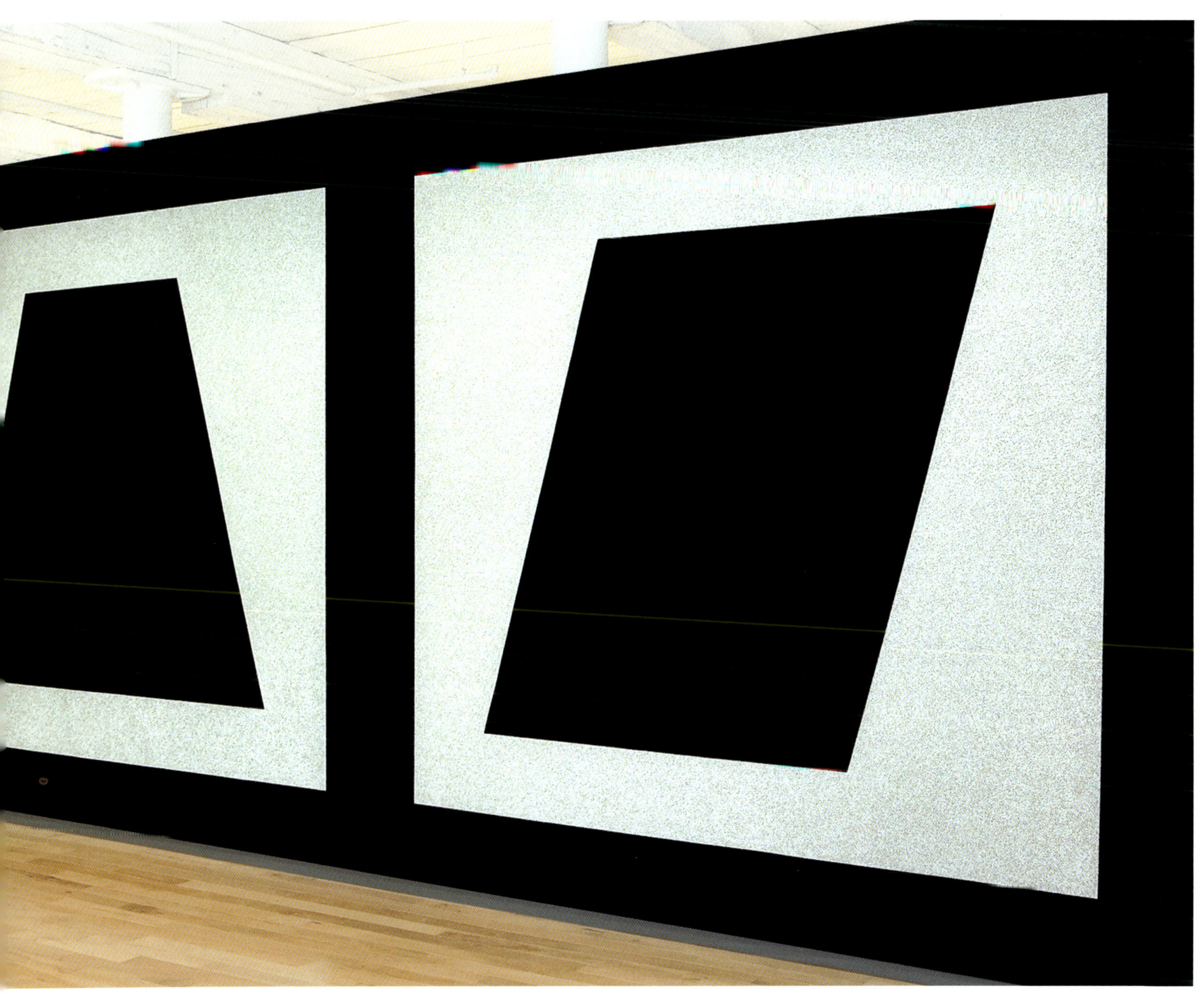

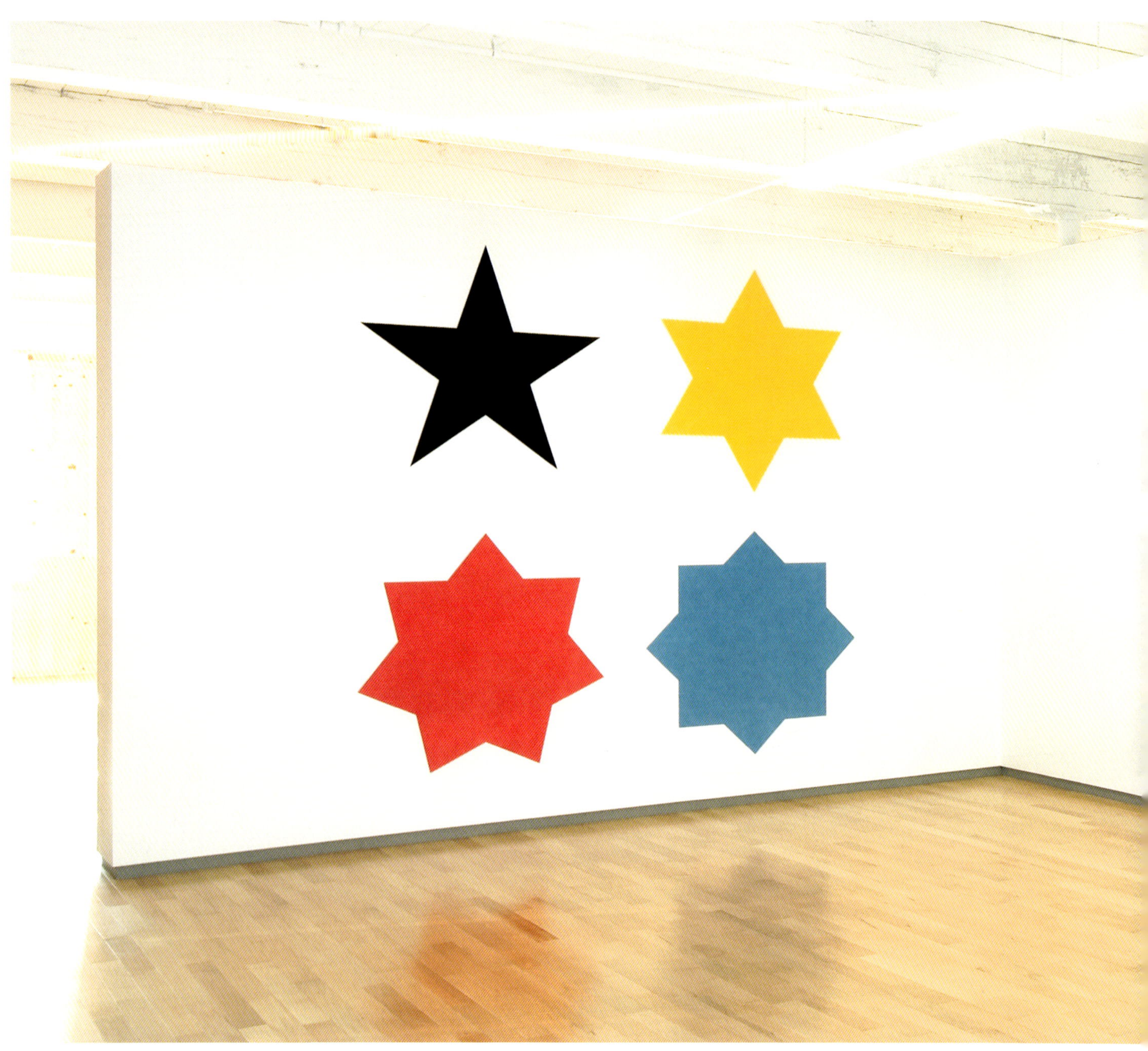

Wall Drawing 396: A black five-pointed star, a yellow six-pointed star, a red seven-pointed star, and a blue eight-pointed star, drawn in color and India ink washes.   1983

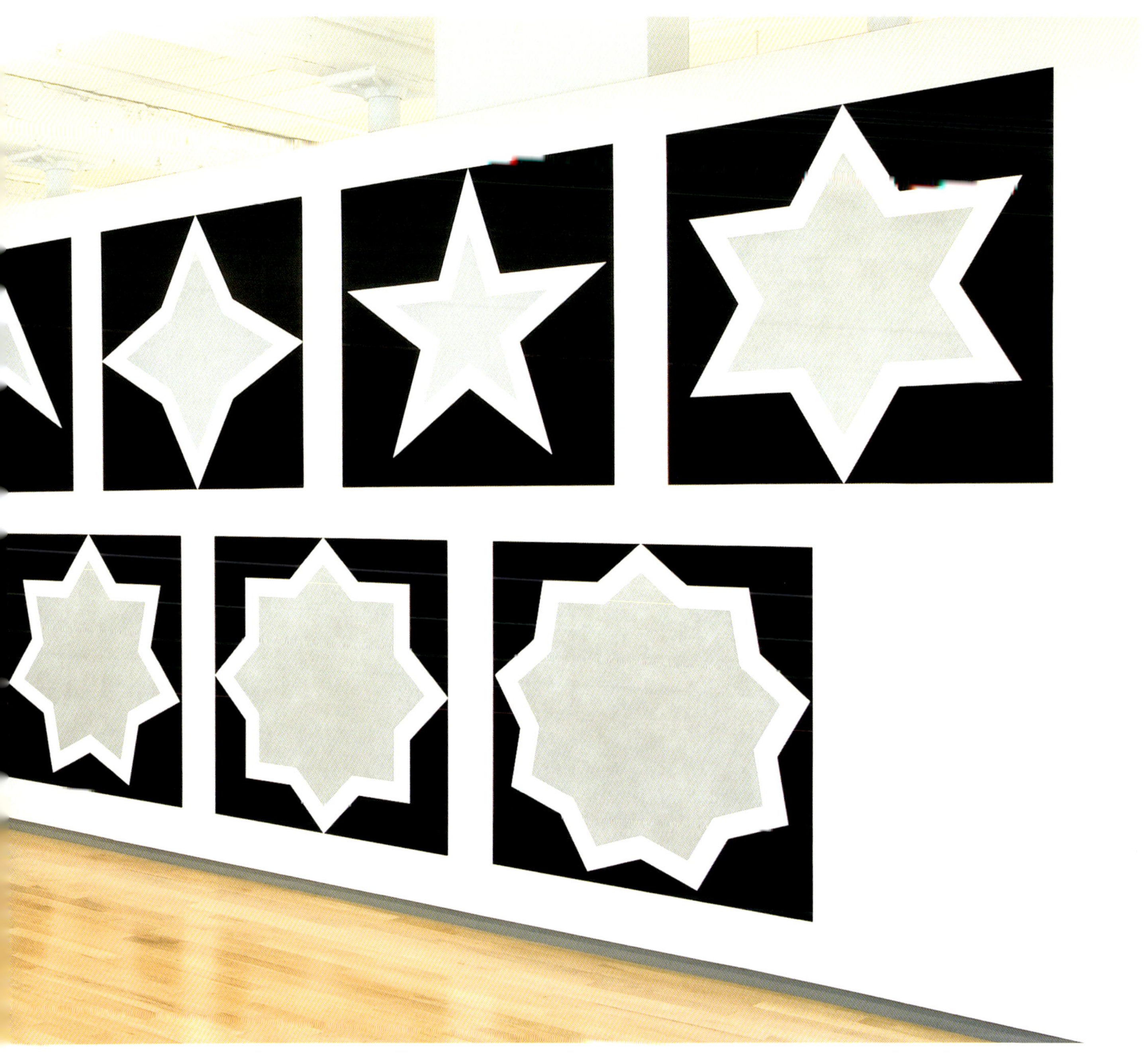

Wall Drawing 386: Stars with three, four, five, six, seven, eight, and nine points, drawn with a light tone India ink wash inside, an India ink wash outside, separated by a 6-inch (15 cm) white band.   1983

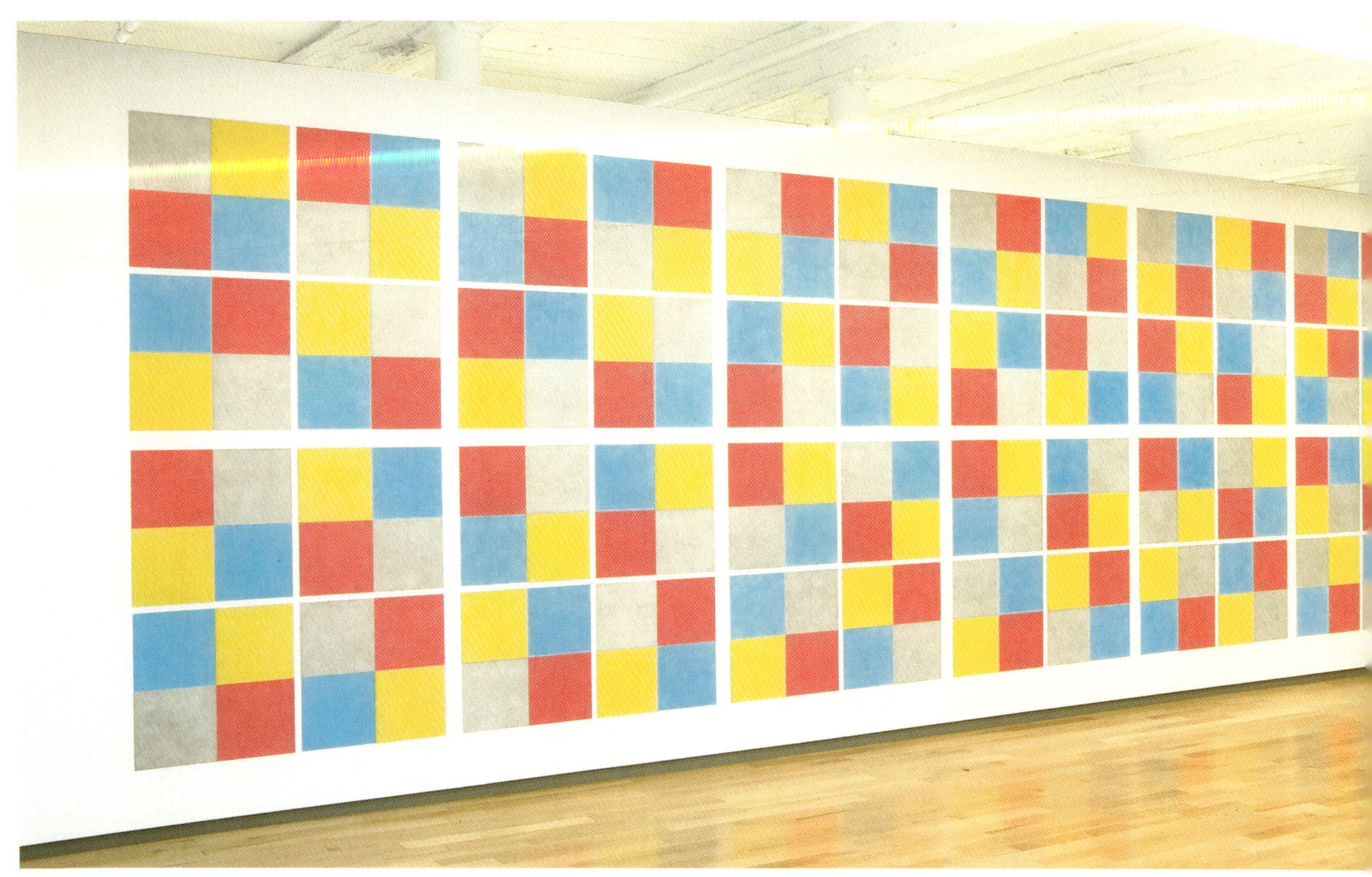

Wall Drawing 413: Drawing Series IV (A) with color ink washes (24 drawings).   1984   (detail opposite)

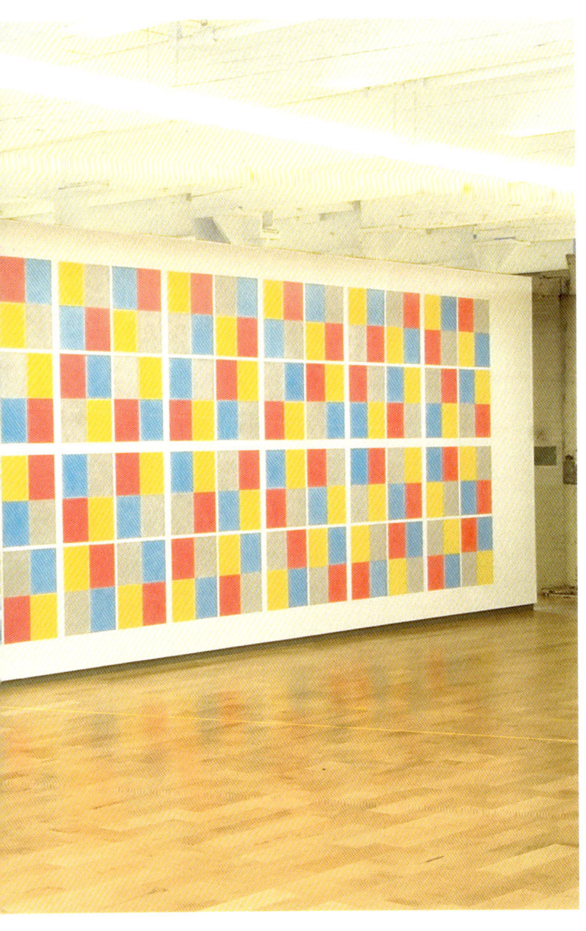

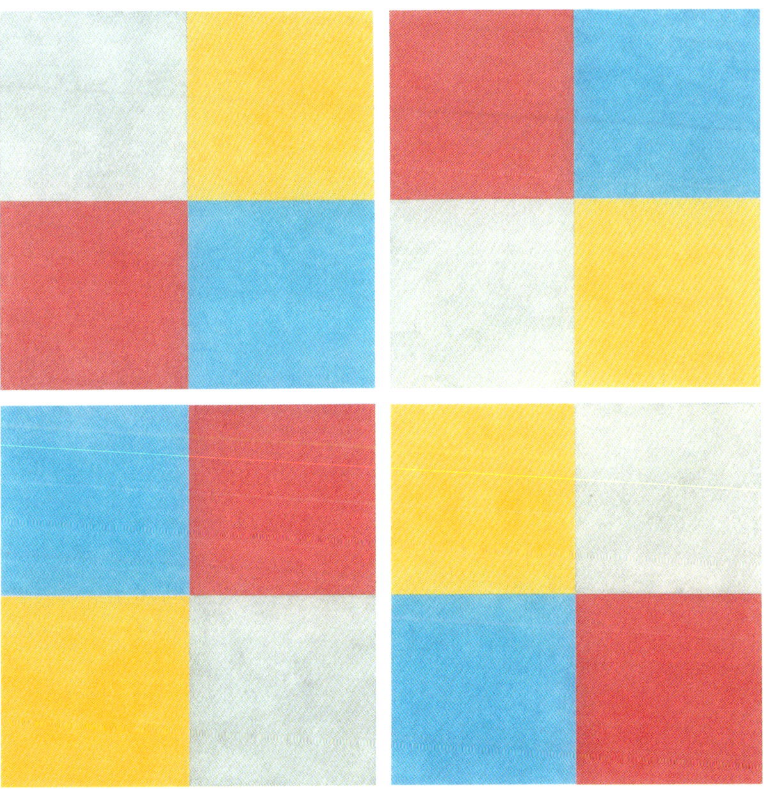

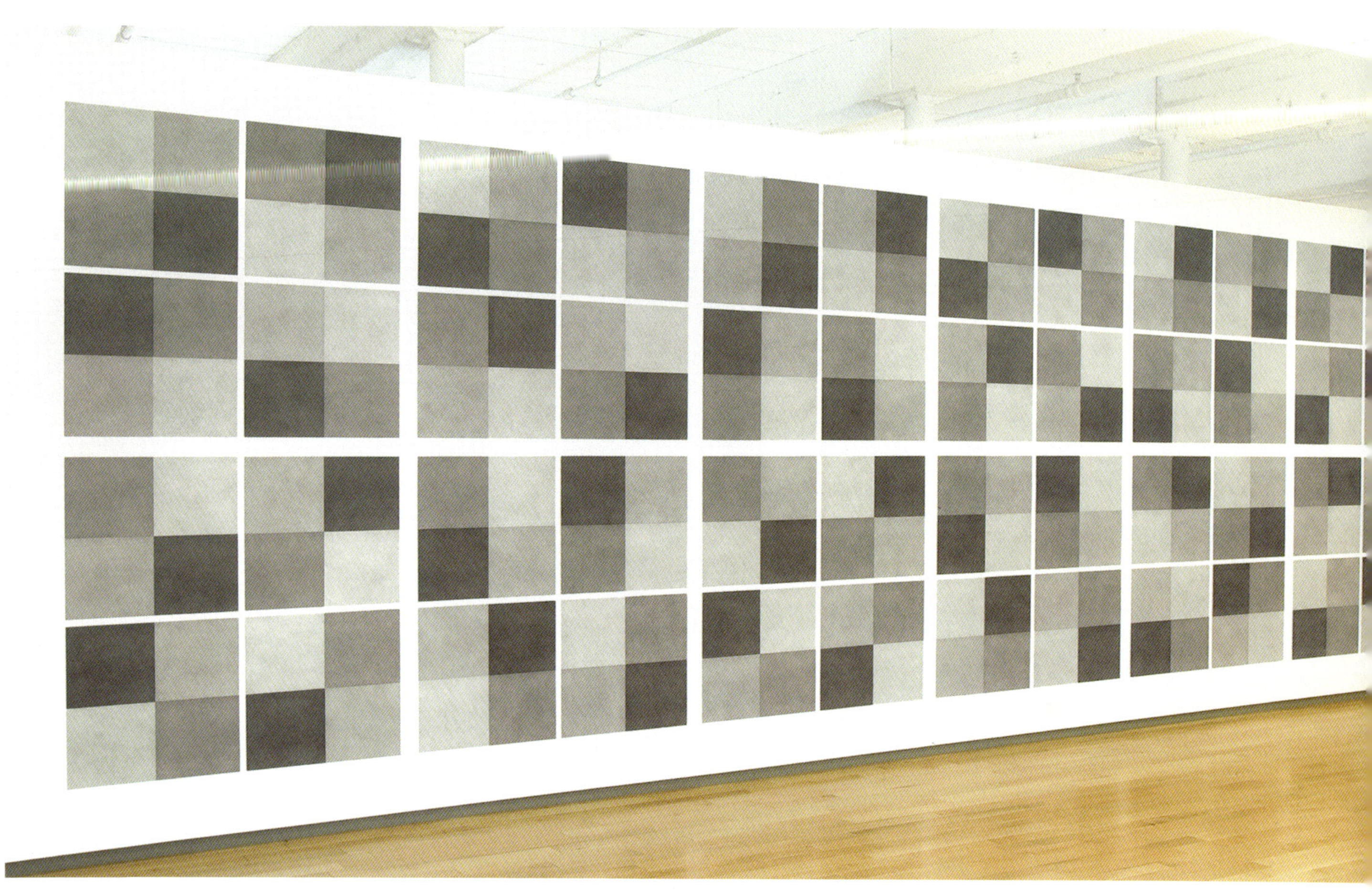

Wall Drawing 414: Drawing Series IV (A) with India ink washes (24 drawings). 1984 (detail opposite)

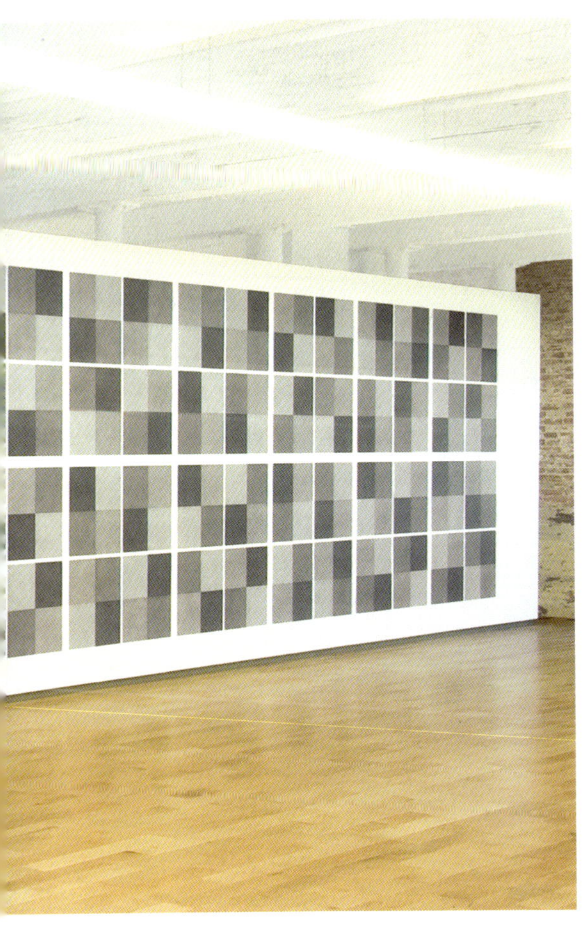

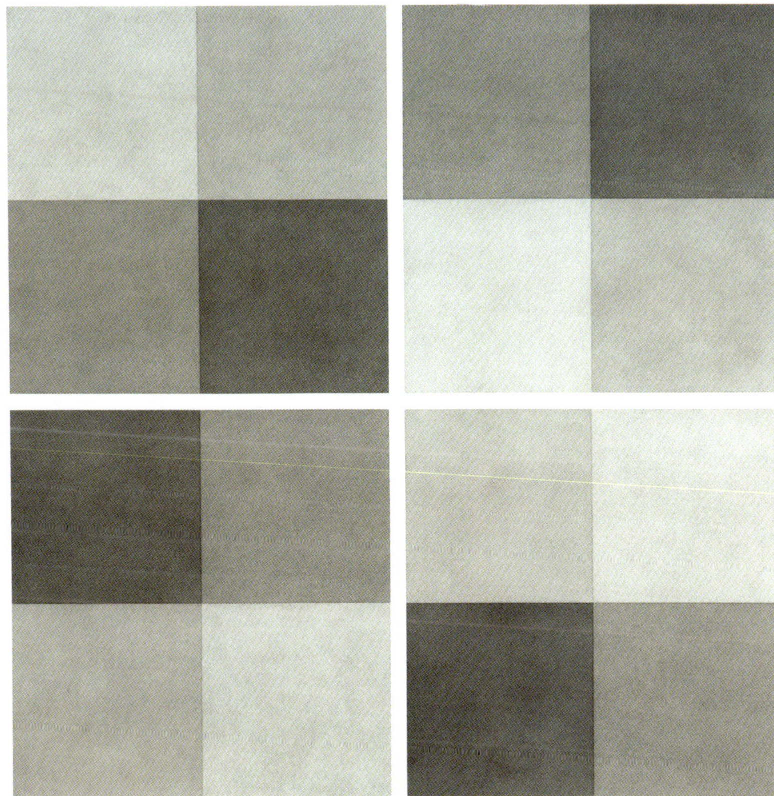

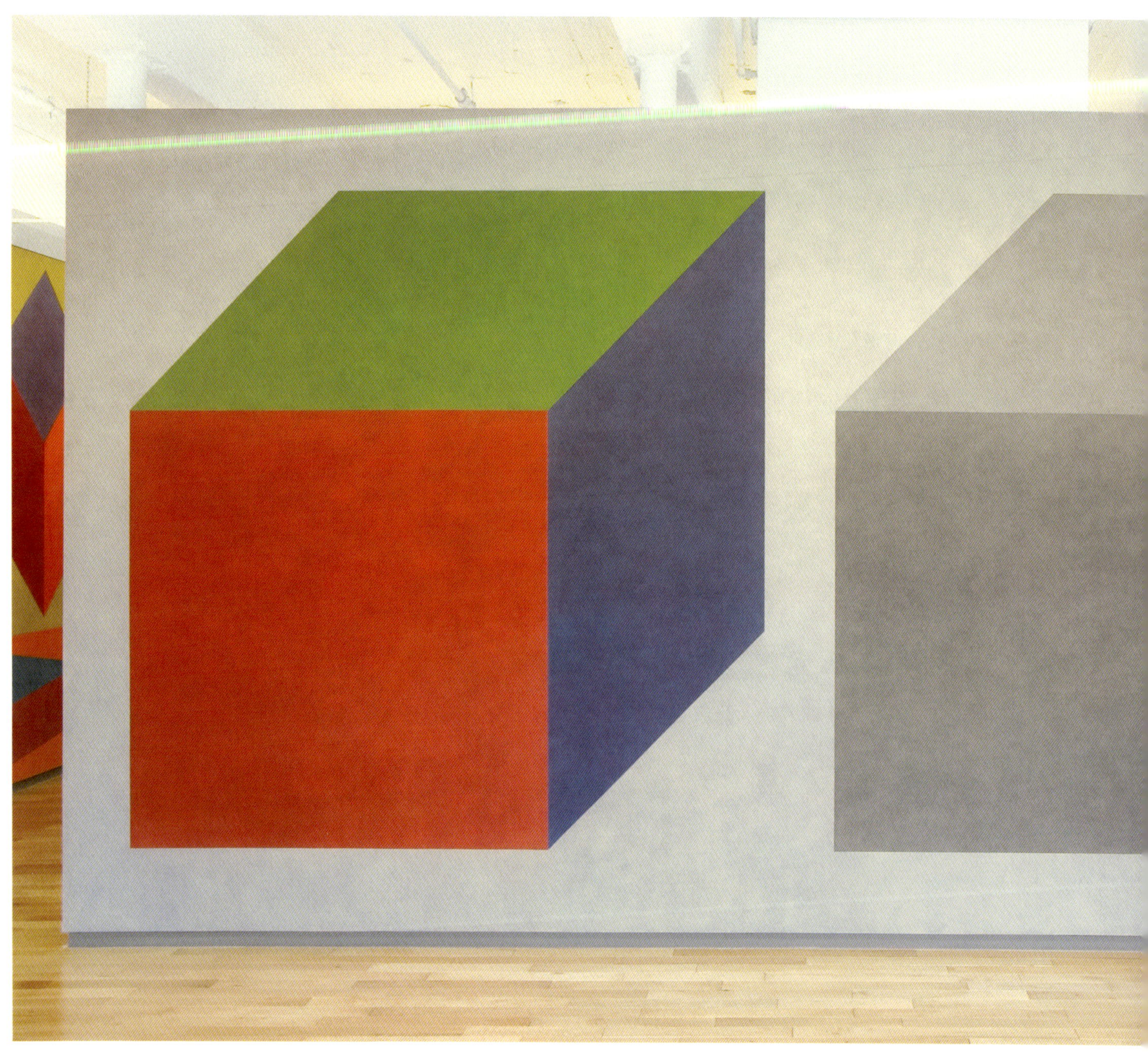

Wall Drawing 415D: Double Drawing. Right: Isometric figure (Cube) with progressively darker gradations of gray on each of three planes; Left: Isometric figure with red, yellow, and blue superimposed progressively on each of the three planes. The background is gray. 1993

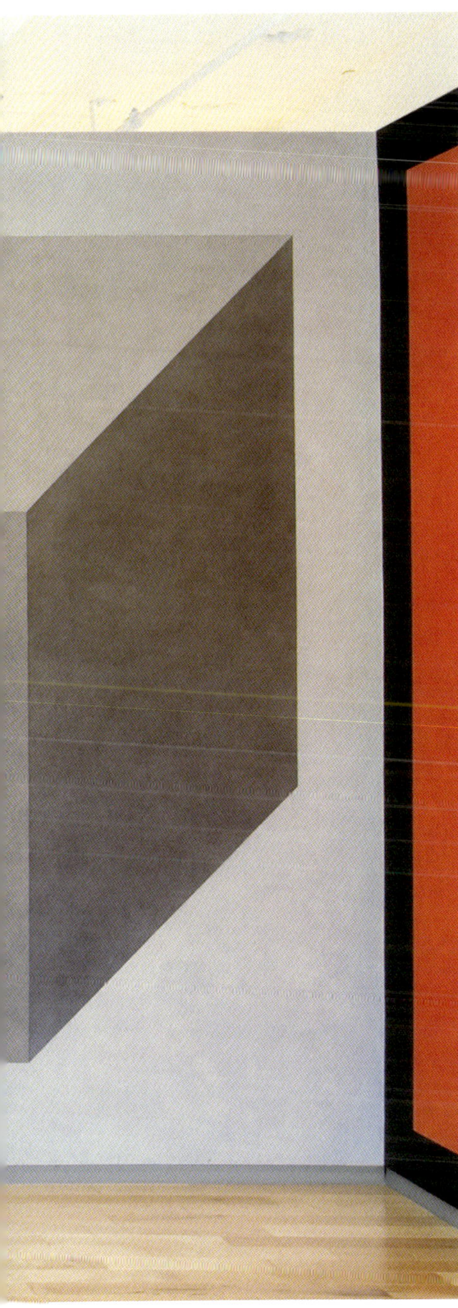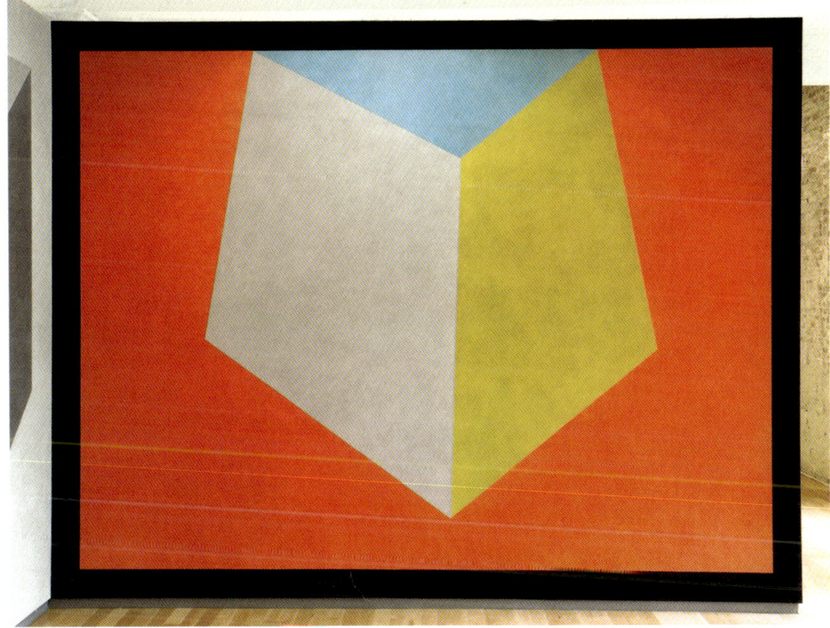

Wall Drawing 552D: Tilted forms with color ink washes superimposed. 1987

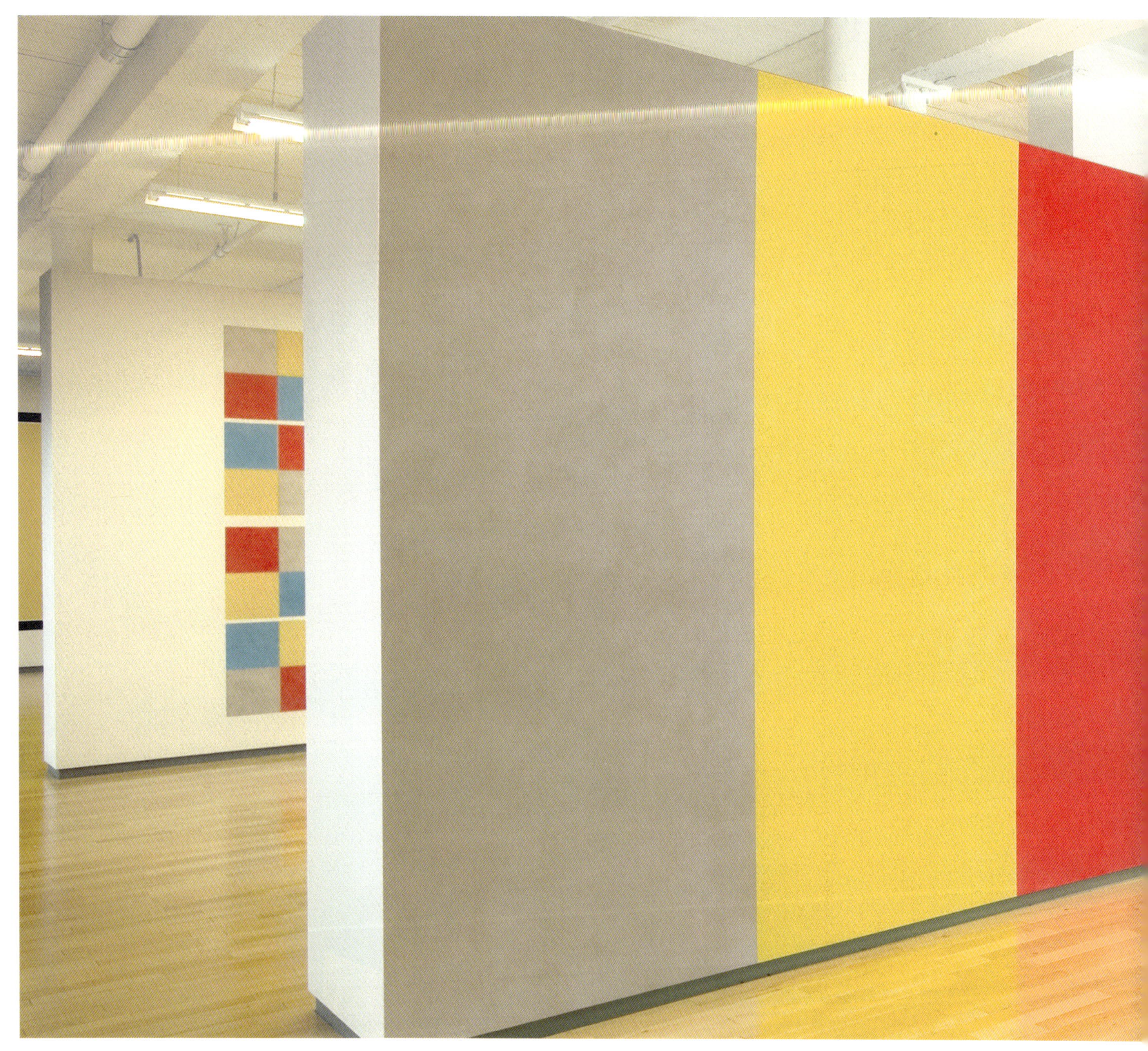

Wall Drawing 422: The room (or wall) is divided vertically into fifteen parts. All one-, two-, three-, and four-part combinations of four colors, using color ink washes. 1984

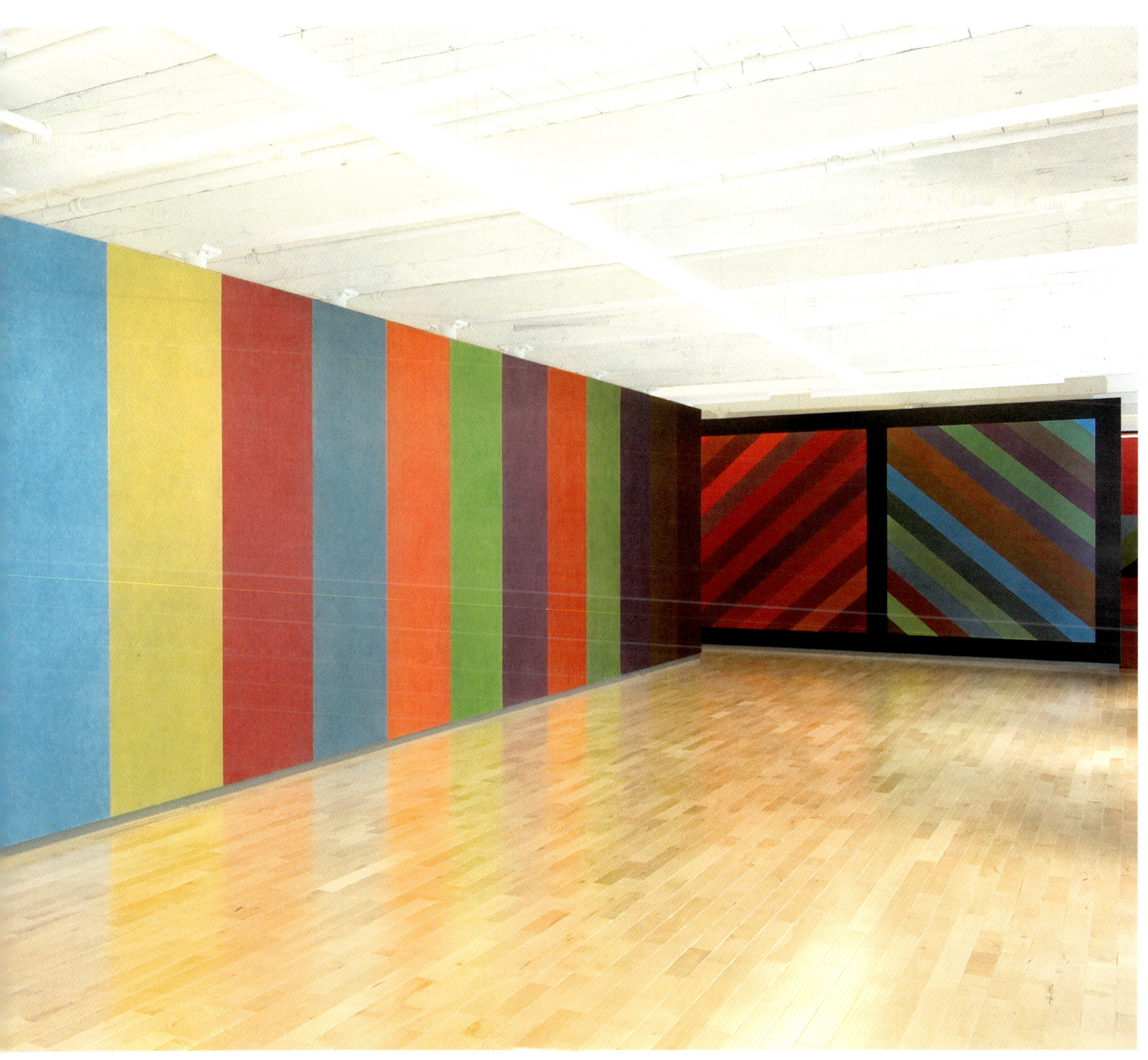

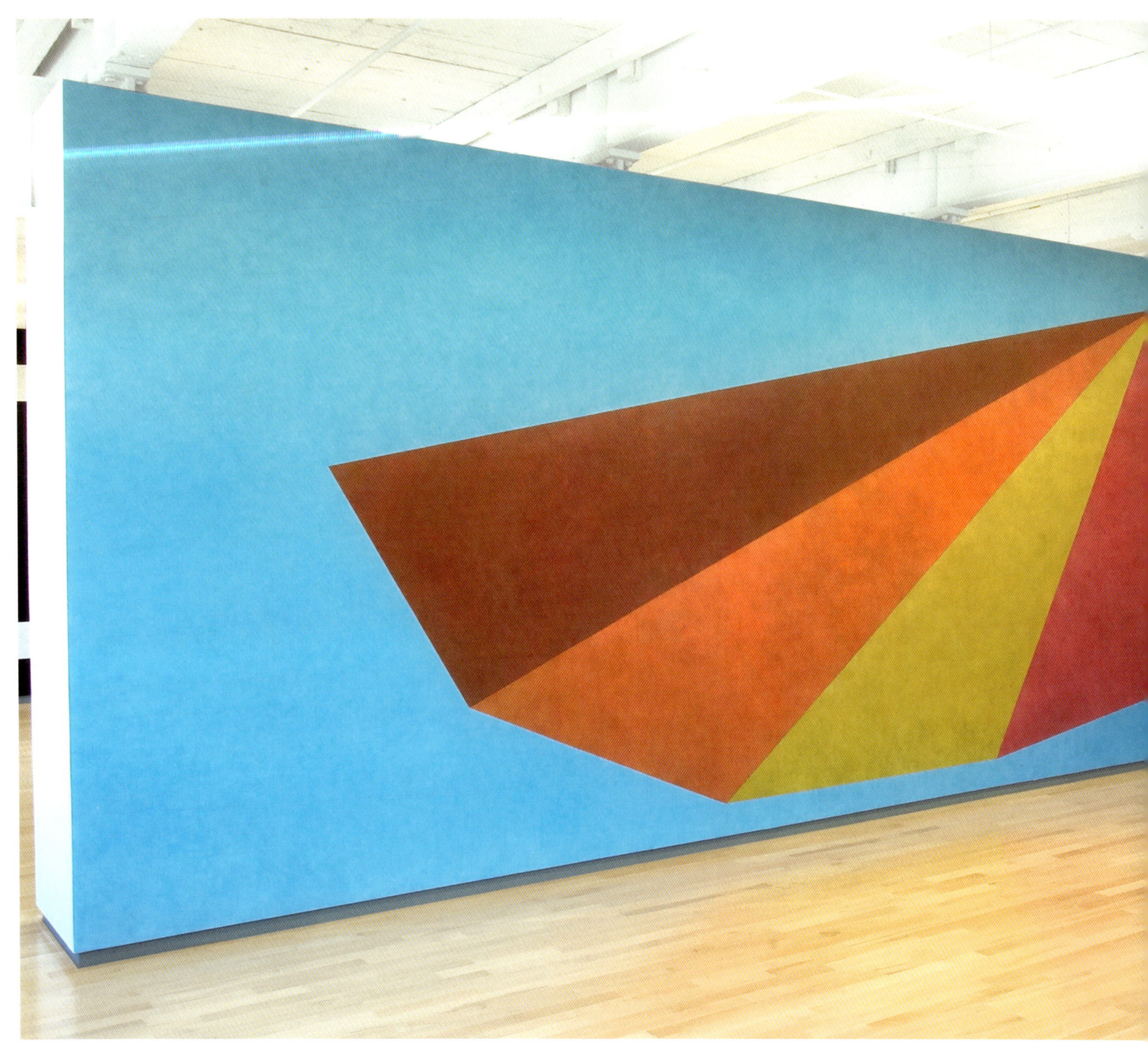

Wall Drawing 439: Asymmetrical pyramid with color ink washes superimposed.   1985

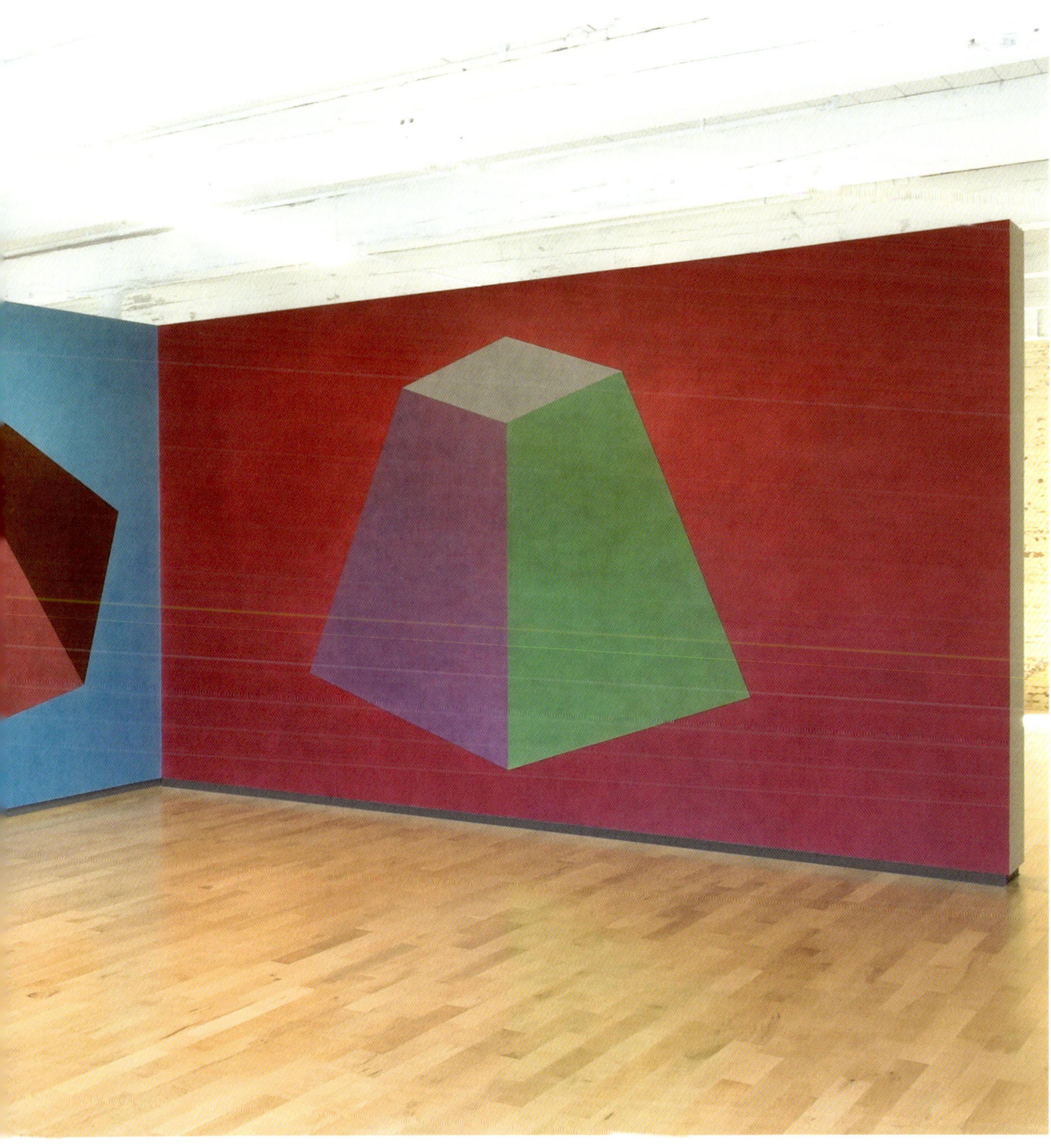

Wall Drawing 527: Two flat-topped pyramids with color ink washes superimposed.   1987

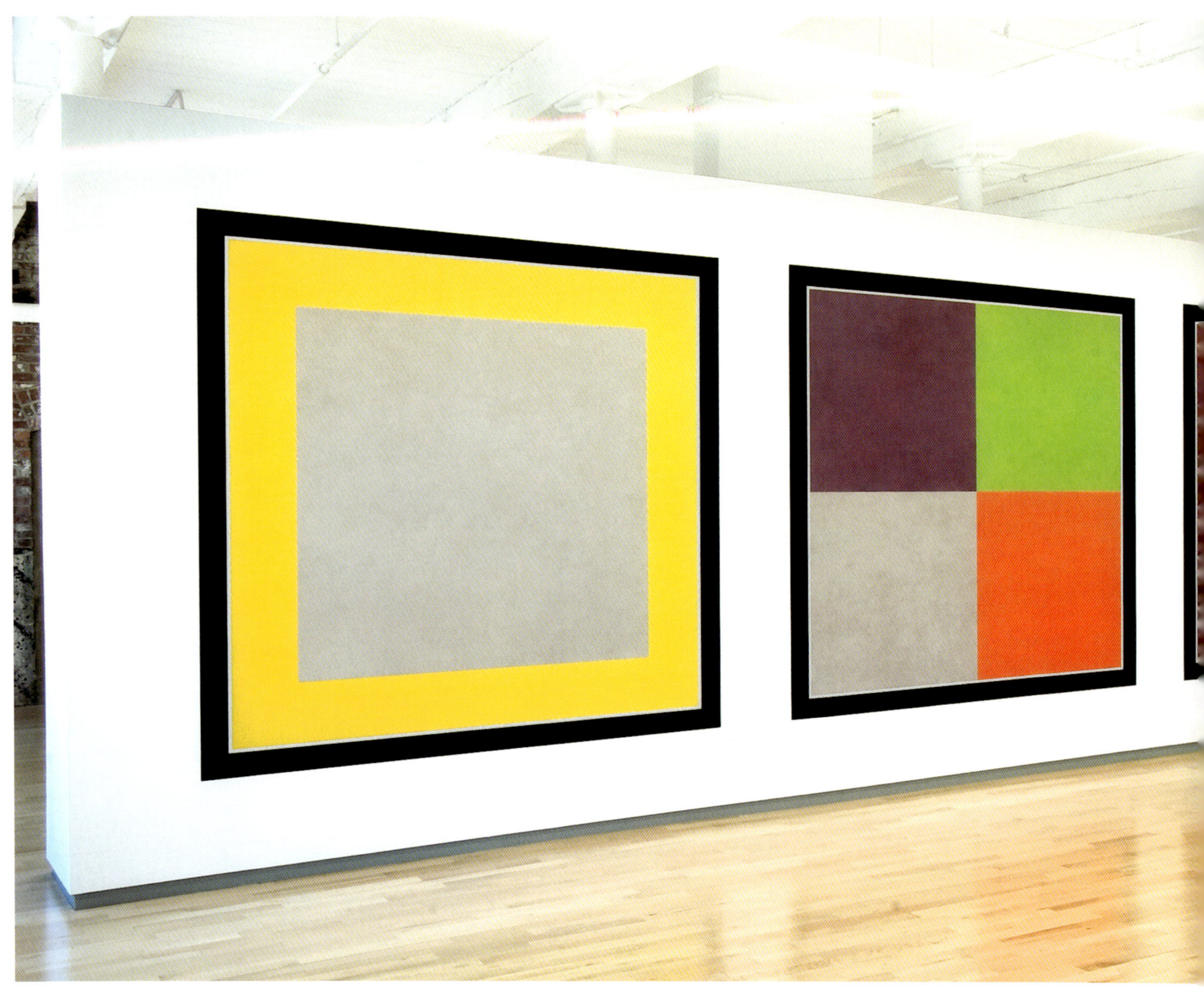

Wall Drawing 583F: Rectangles, with color ink washes superimposed. Each is bordered by a 10-inch (25 cm) band with color ink washes superimposed, a ½-inch (1¼ cm) white band, and a 4-inch (10 cm) black band.   1988

Wall Drawing 584H: Squares, divided horizontally and vertically into four equal parts. Within each part, color ink washes superimposed. The squares are bordered by a ½-inch (1¼ cm) white band and a 4-inch (10 cm) black band.   1989

Wall Drawing 583H: Rectangles, with color ink washes superimposed. Each is bordered by a 10-inch (25 cm) band with color ink washes superimposed, a ½-inch (1¼ cm) white band, and a 4-inch (10 cm) black band.   1988

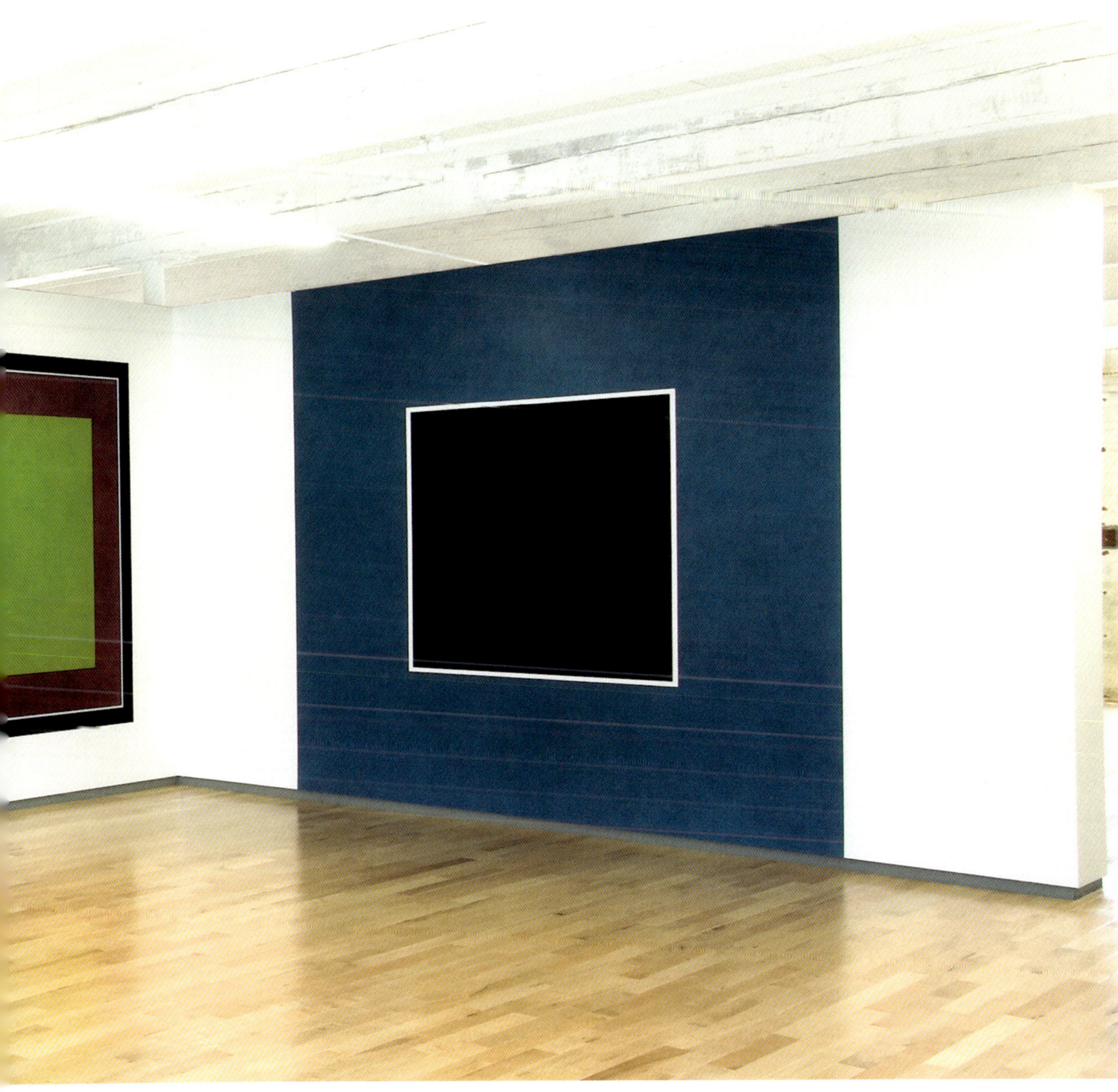

Wall Drawing 725: On a blue wall, a black square within a white border.   1993

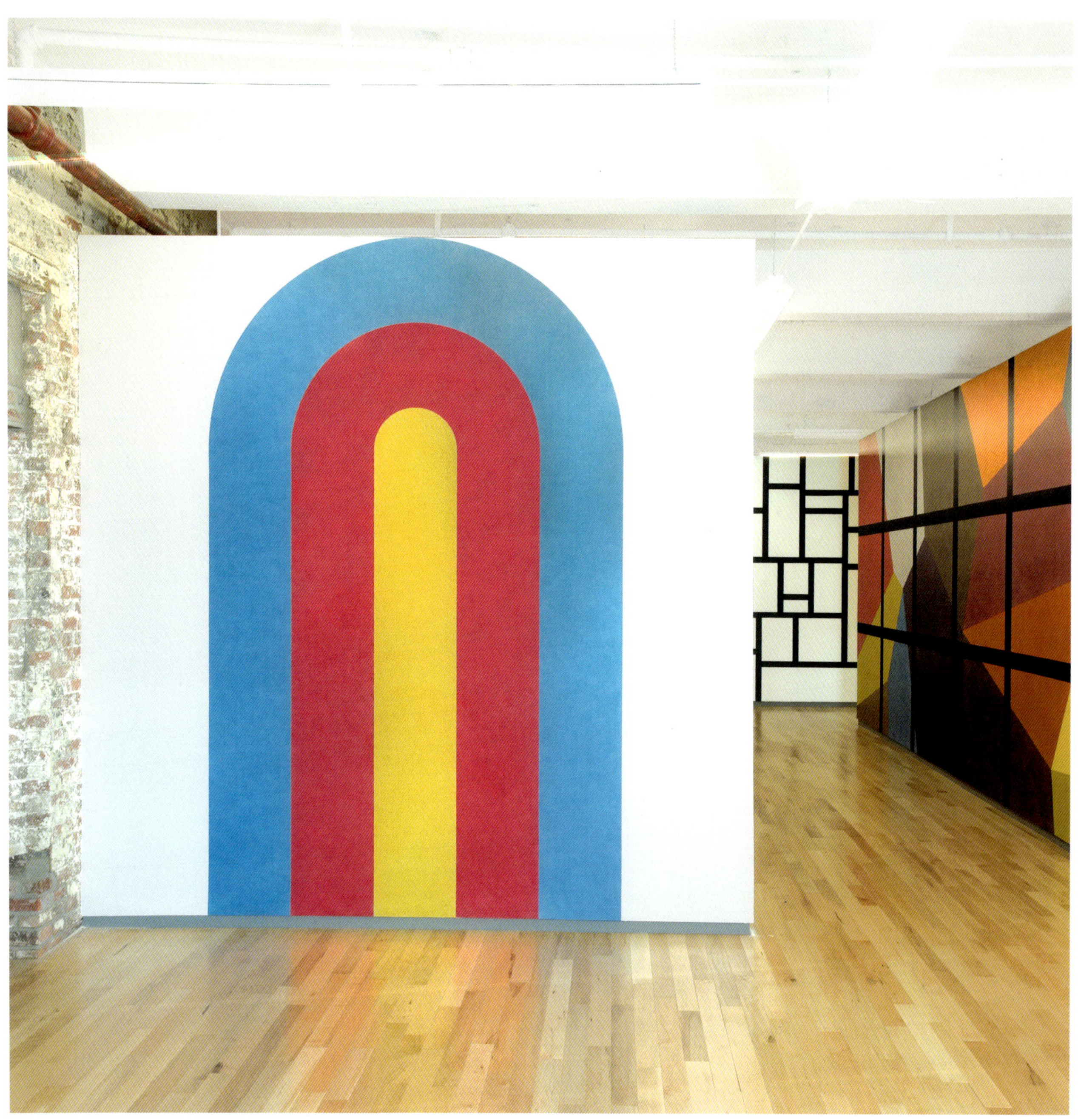

Wall Drawing 579: Three concentric arches. The outside one is blue; the middle red; and the inside one is yellow. 1988

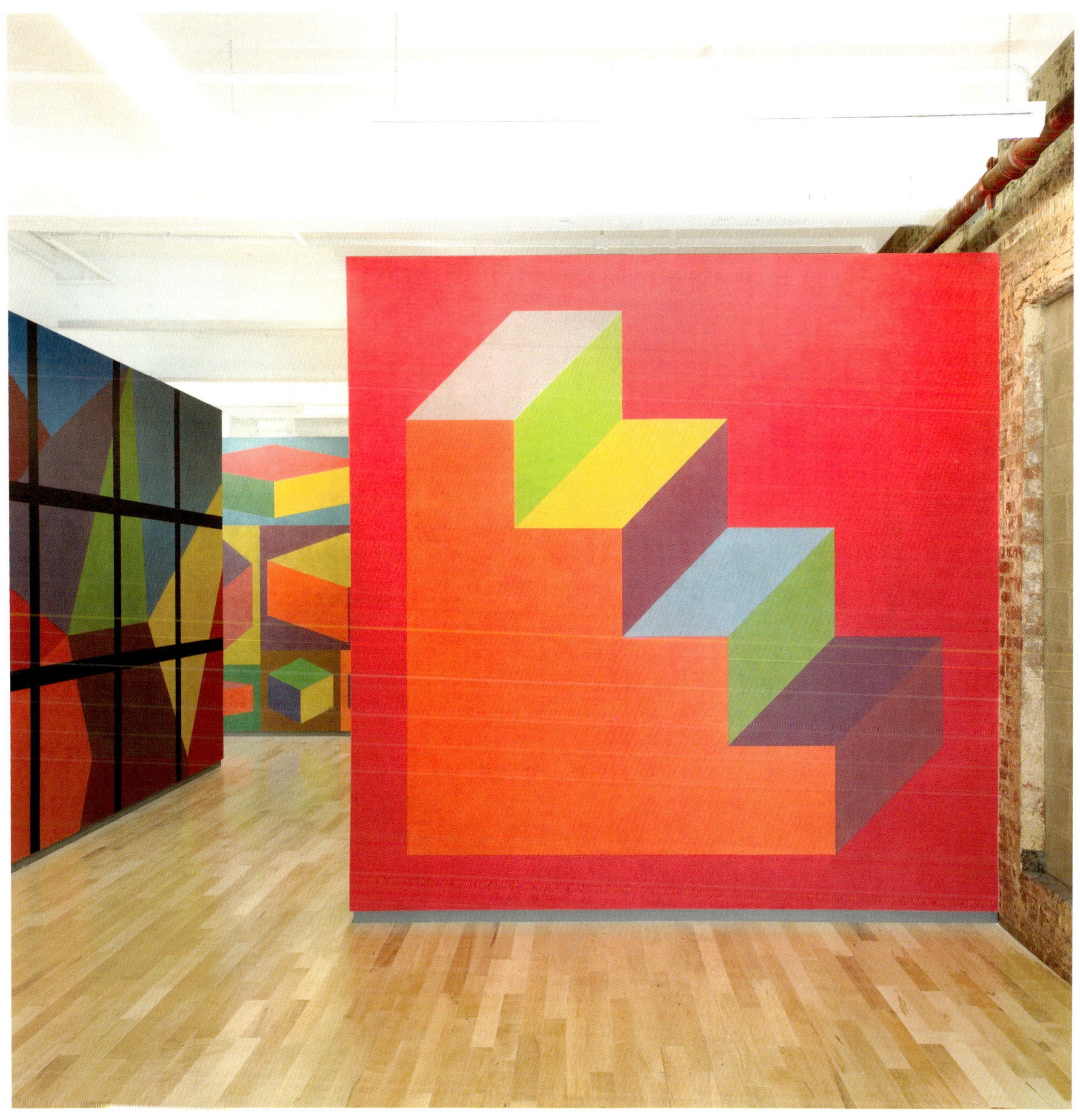

Wall Drawing 610: Isometric figure with color ink washes superimposed. 1989

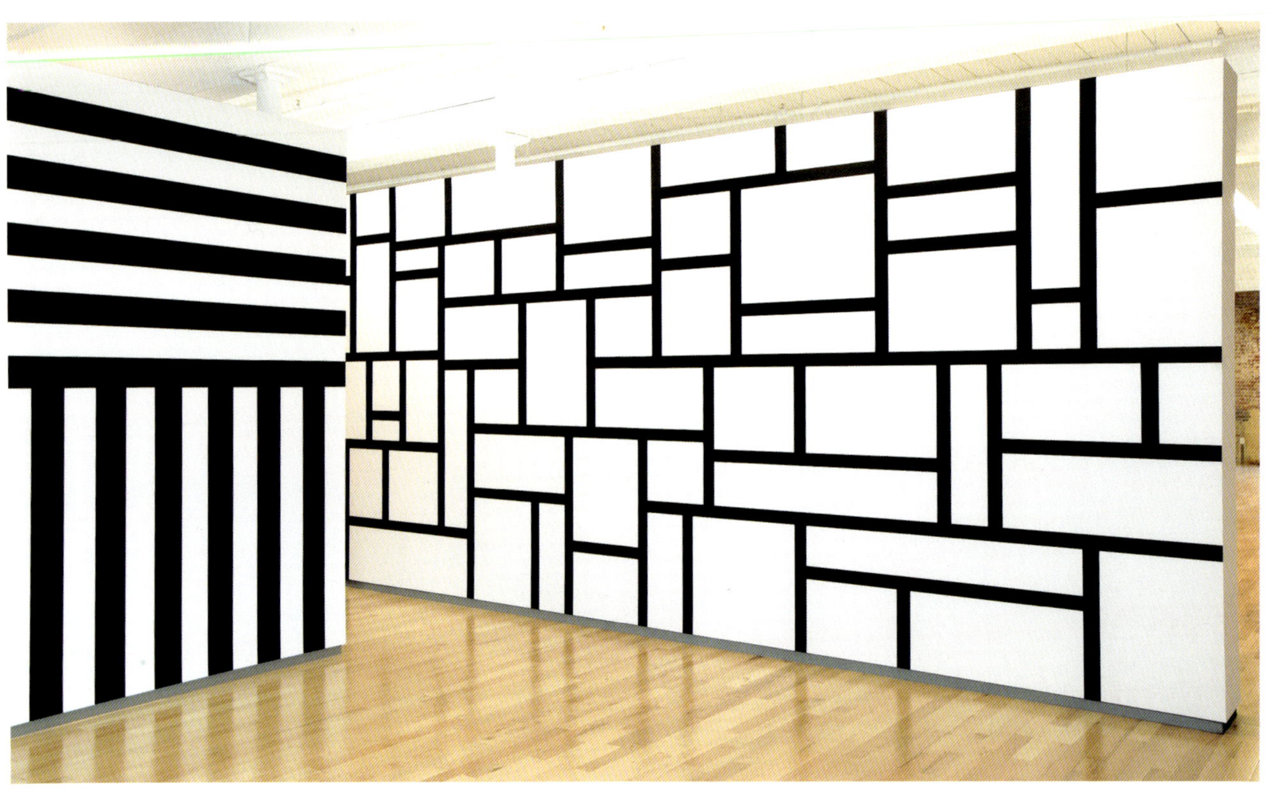

Wall Drawing 614: Rectangles formed by 3-inch (8 cm) wide India ink bands, meeting at right angles. 1989

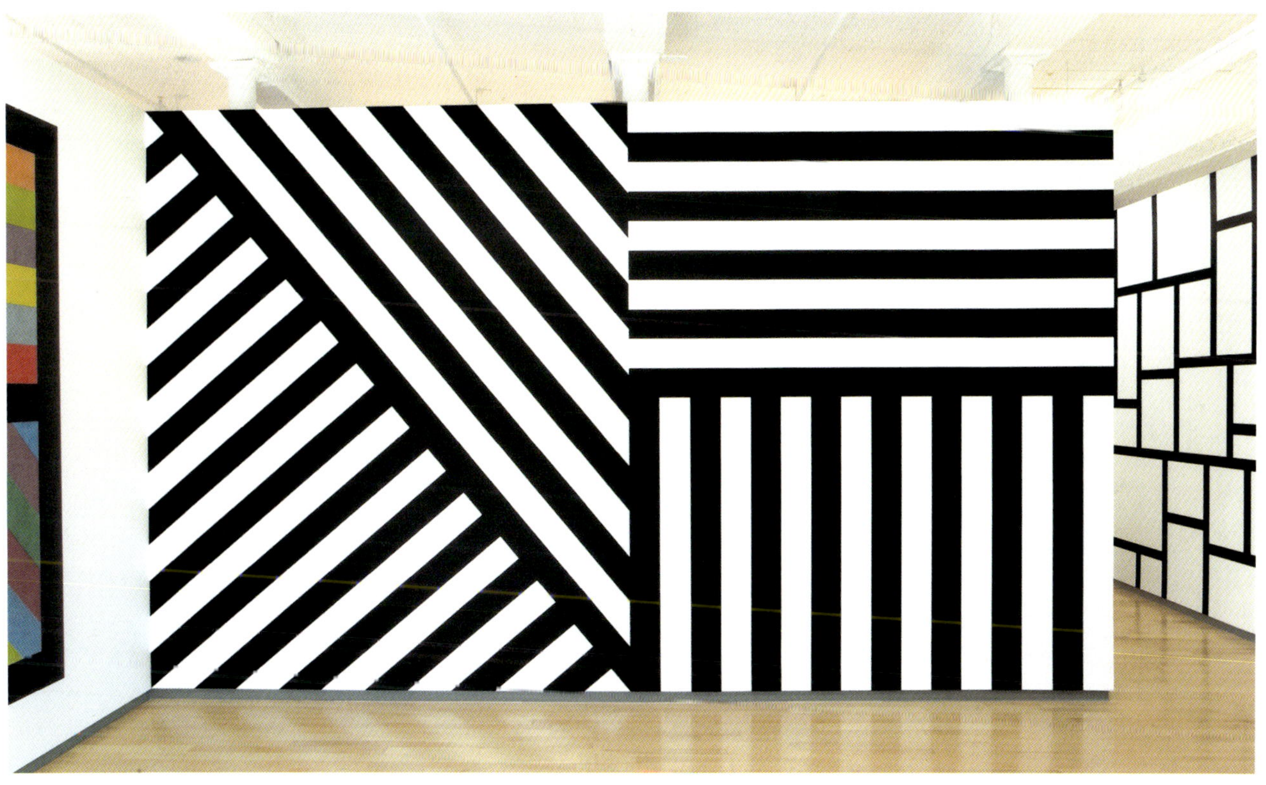

LEFT: *Wall Drawing 631: A wall is divided into two equal parts by a line drawn from corner to corner. Left: alternating diagonal black and white 8-inch (20 cm) bands from the lower left. Right: alternating diagonal black and white 8-inch (20 cm) bands from the upper right.* 1990

RIGHT: *Wall Drawing 630: A wall is divided horizontally into two equal parts. Top: alternating horizontal black and white 8-inch (20 cm) bands. Bottom: alternating vertical black and white 8-inch (20 cm) bands.* 1990

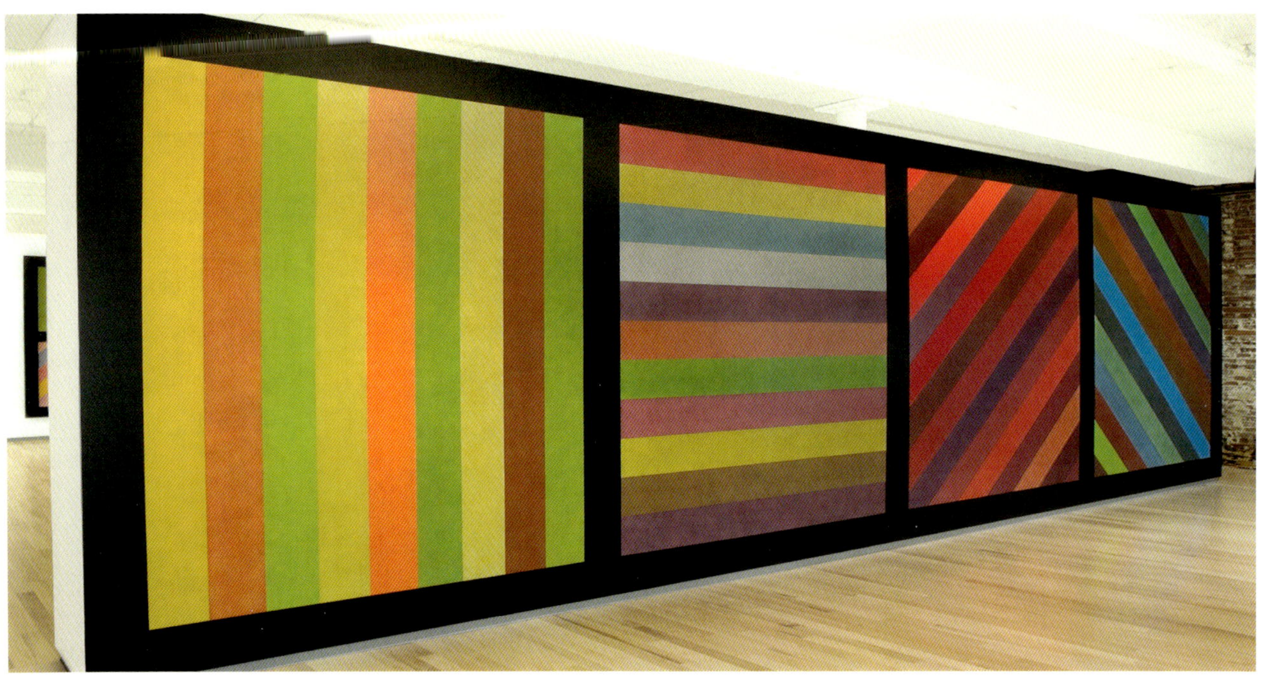

Wall Drawing 681C: A wall divided vertically into four equal squares separated and bordered by black bands.
Within each square, bands in one of four directions, each with color ink washes superimposed.   1993

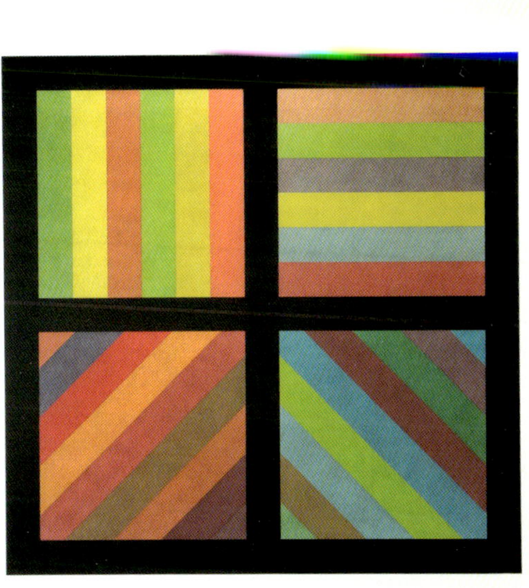

Wall Drawing 684A: Squares bordered and divided horizontally and vertically into four equal squares, each with bands in one of four directions. 1999

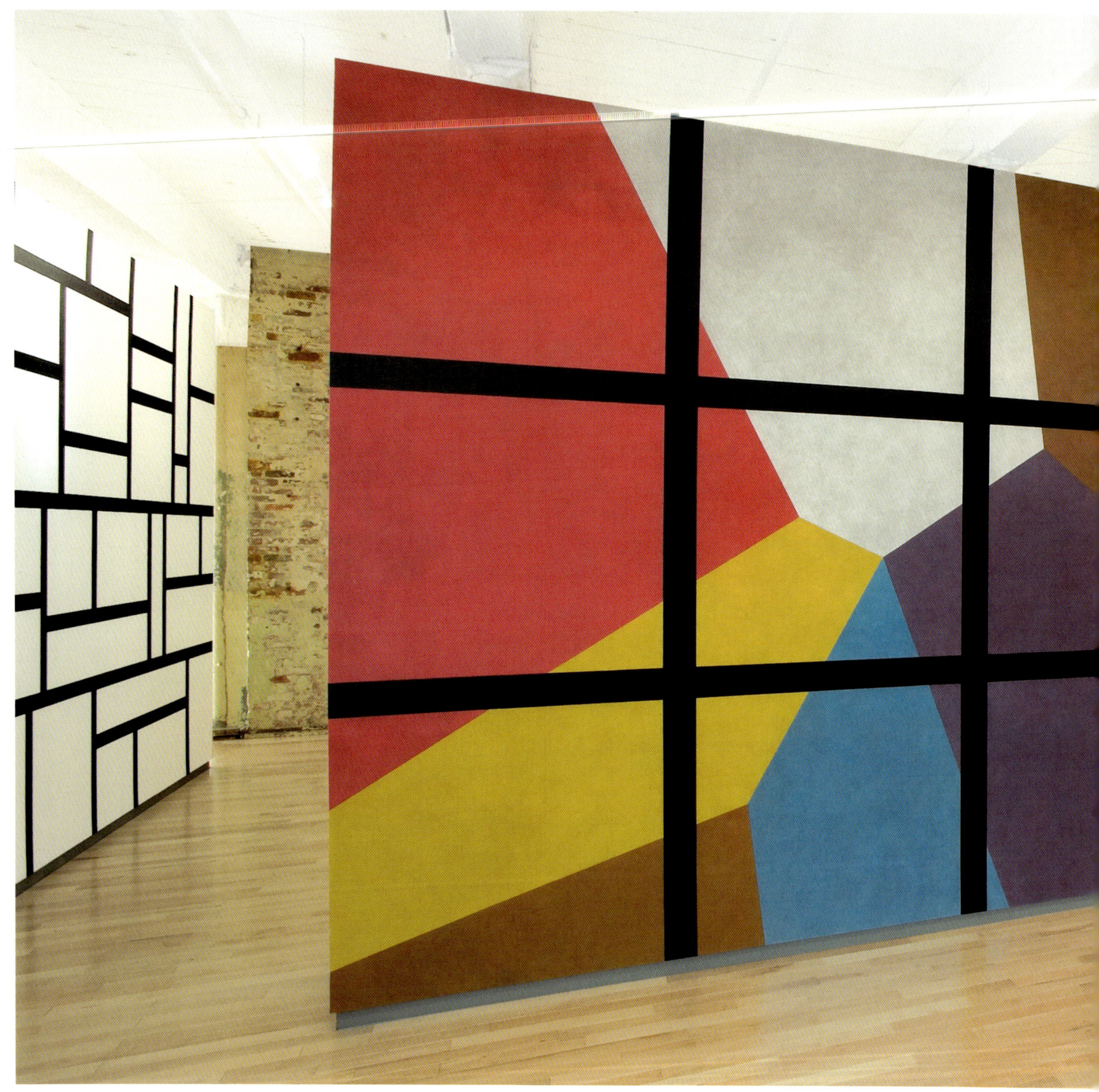

Wall Drawing 692: Continuous forms with color ink washes superimposed.   1991

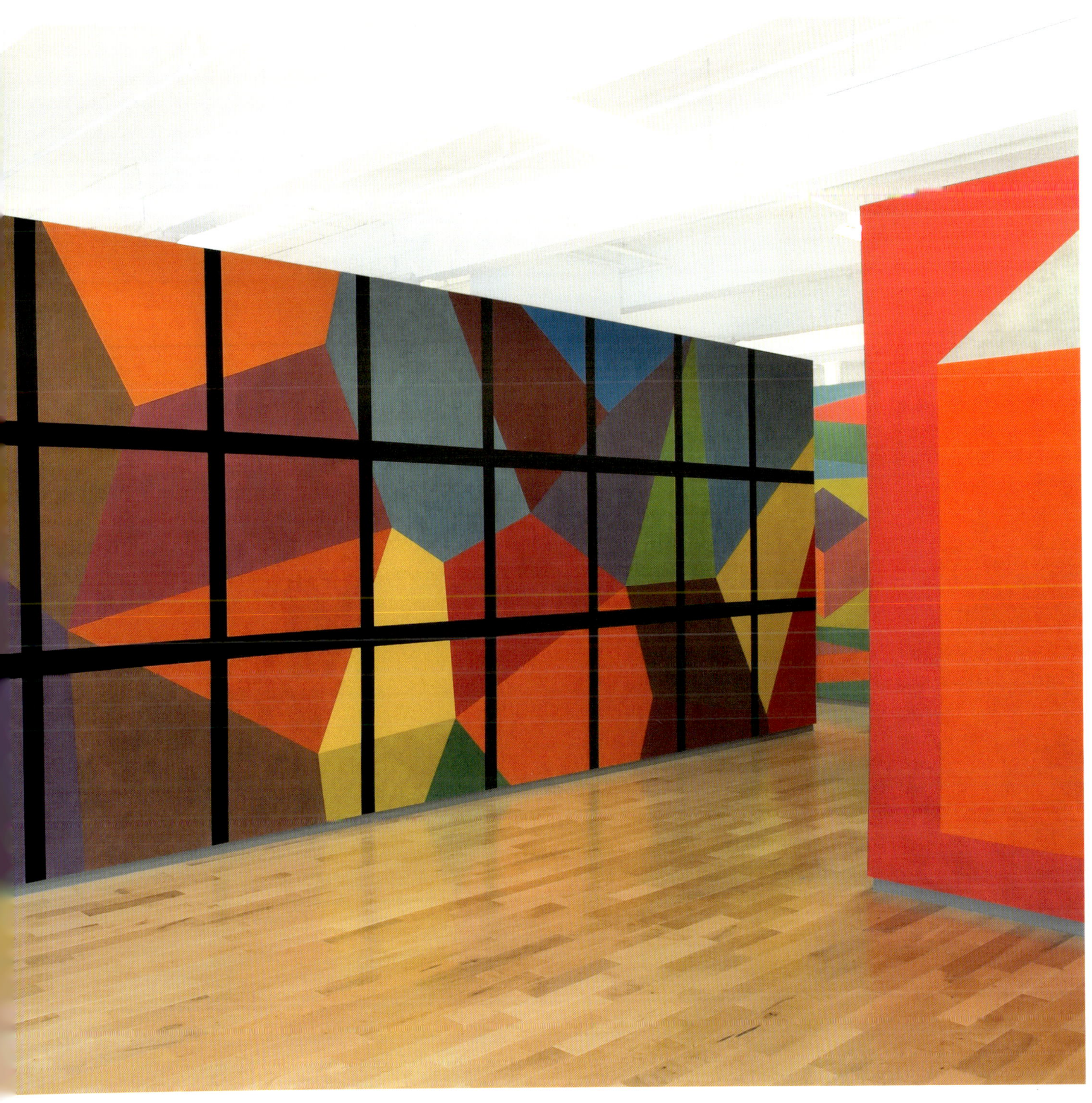

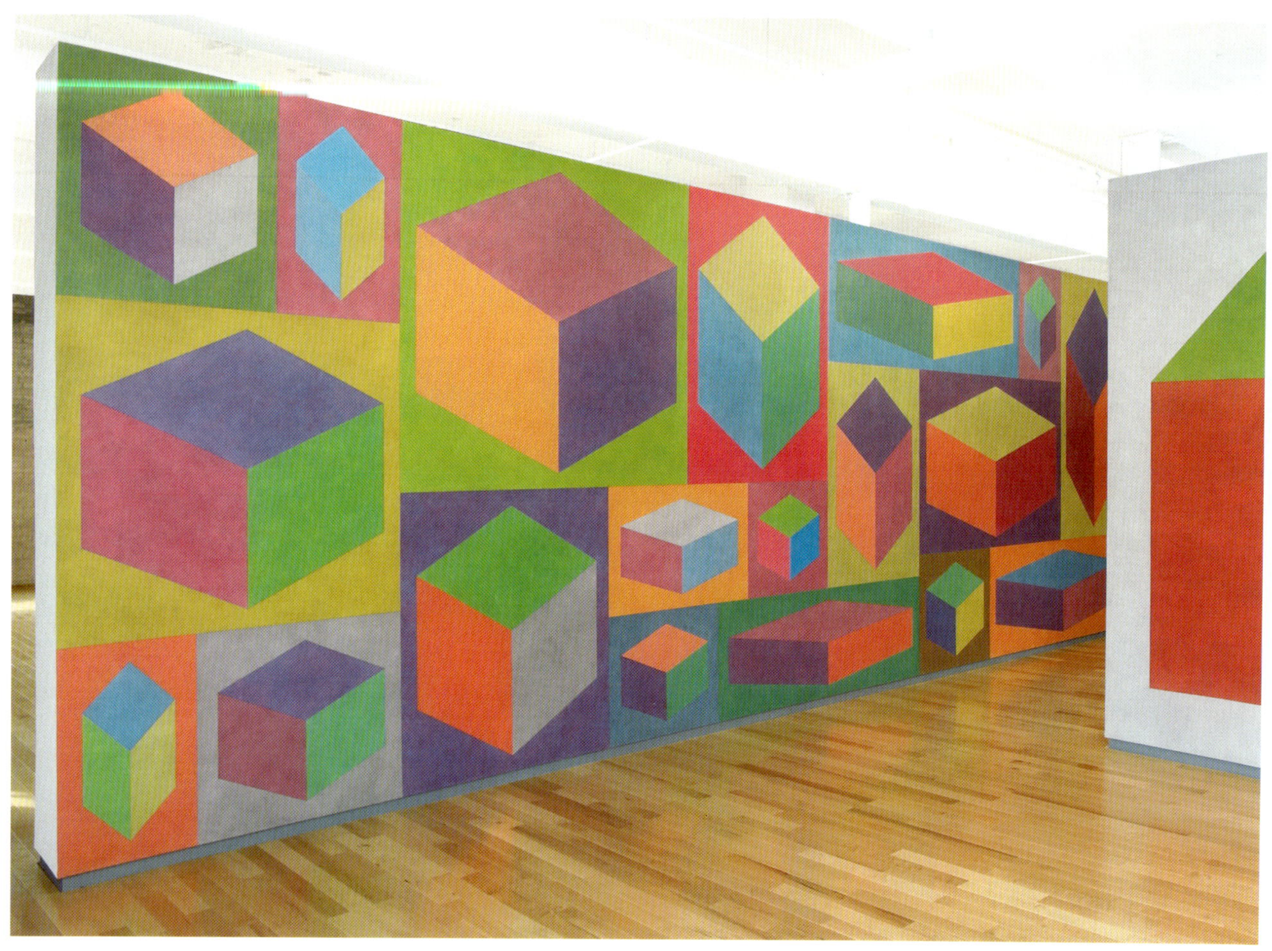

Wall Drawing 766: Twenty-one isometric cubes of varying sizes, each with color ink washes superimposed. 1994 (detail opposite)

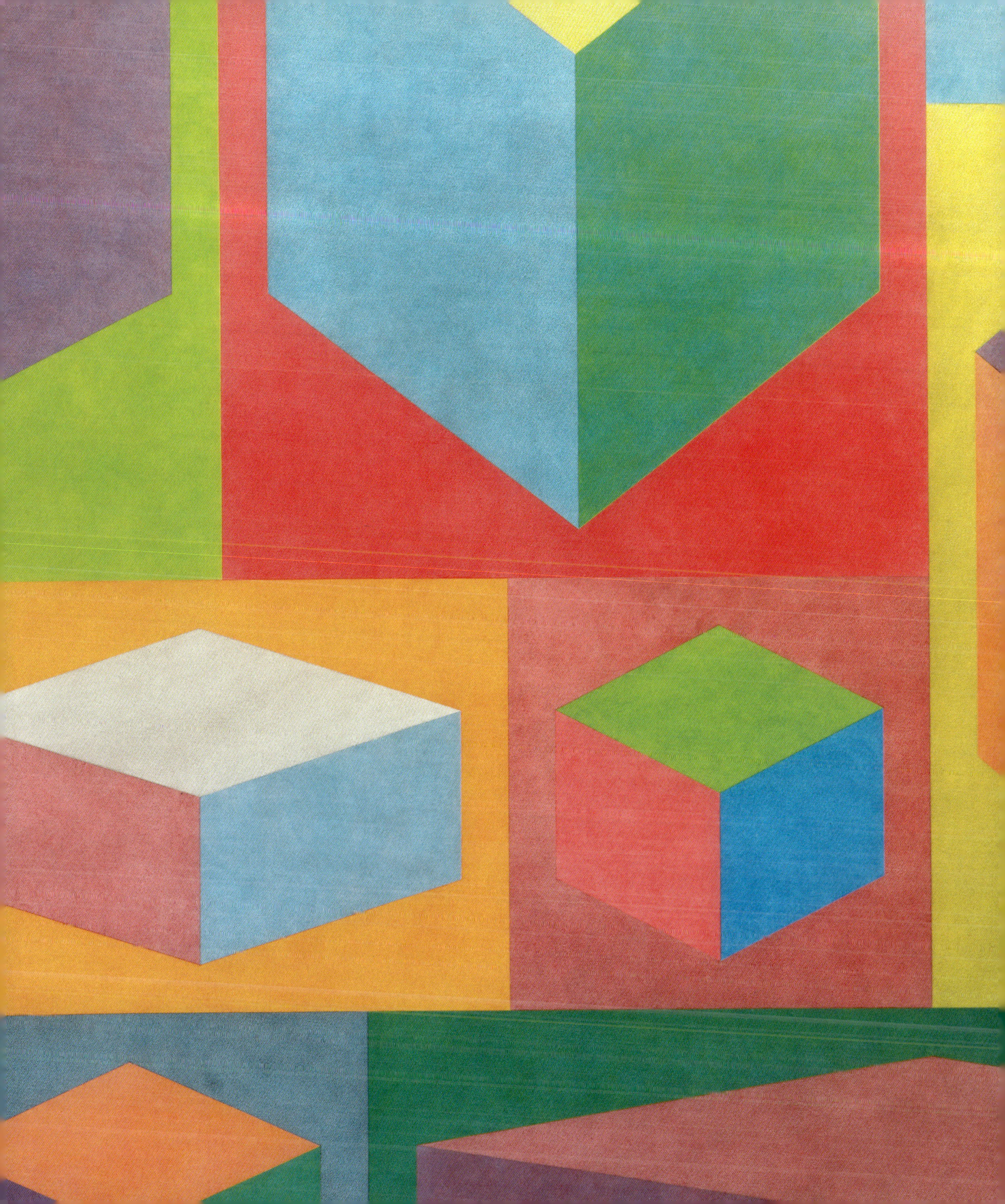

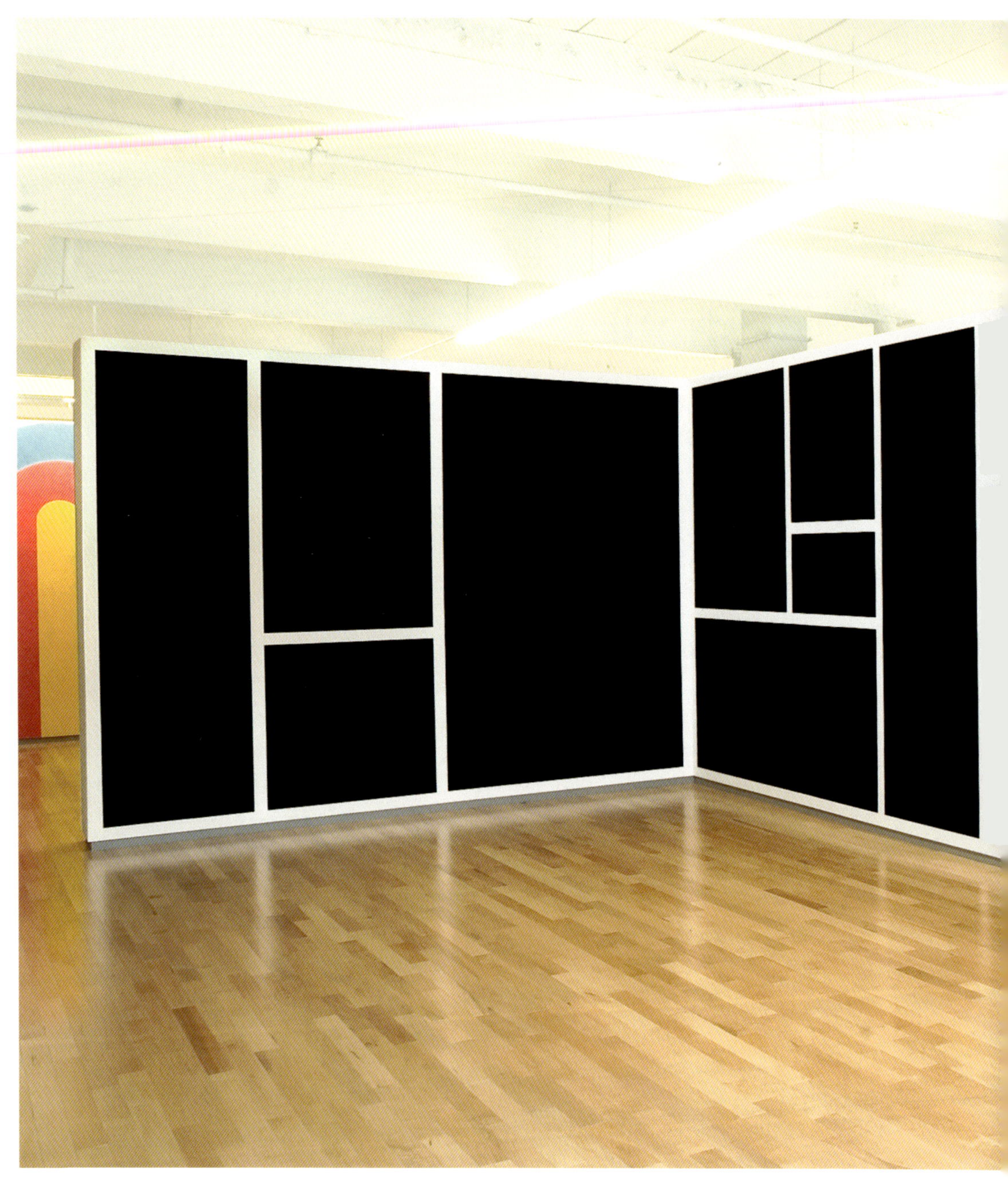

Wall Drawing 792: Black rectangles and squares.   1995

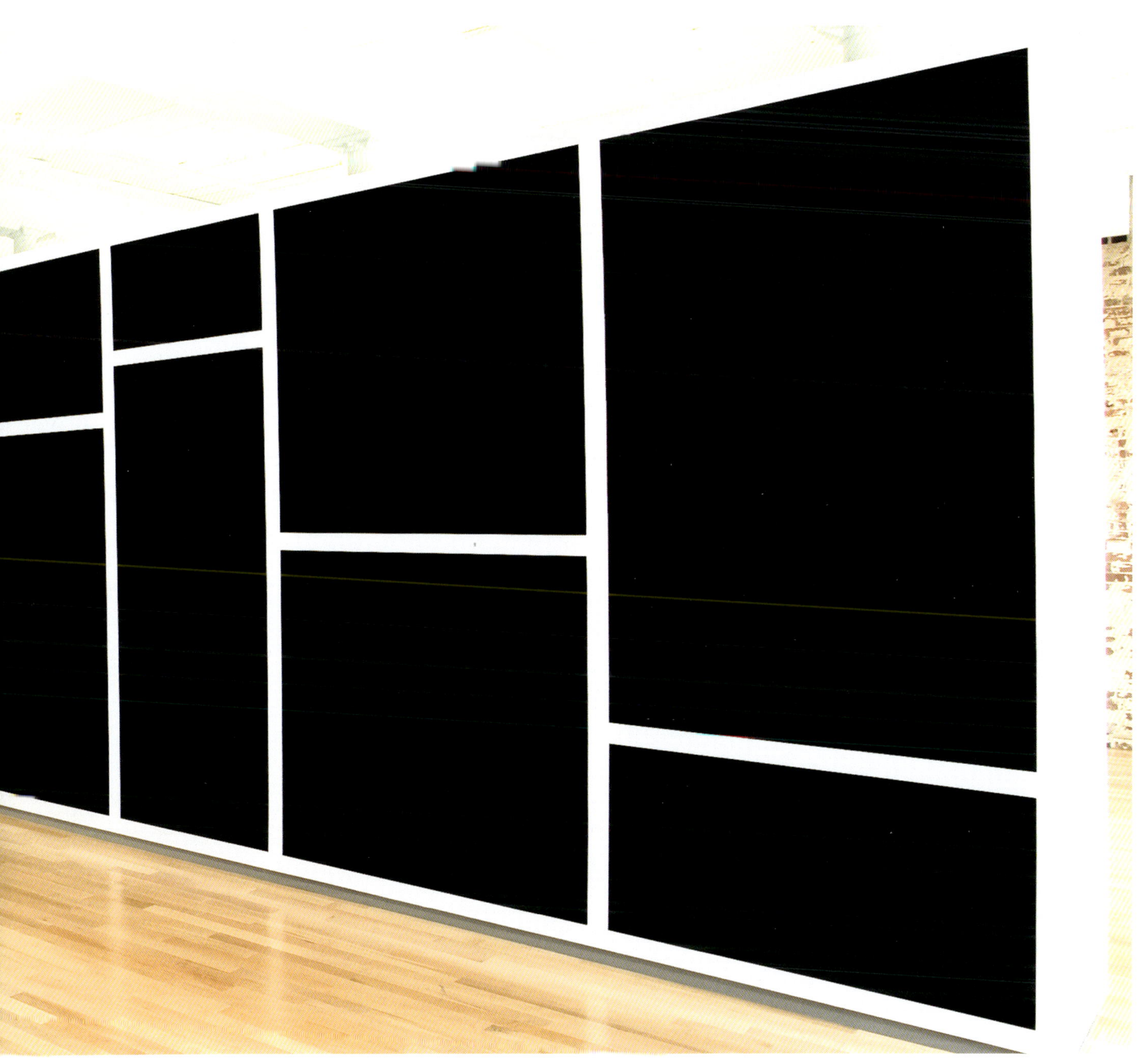

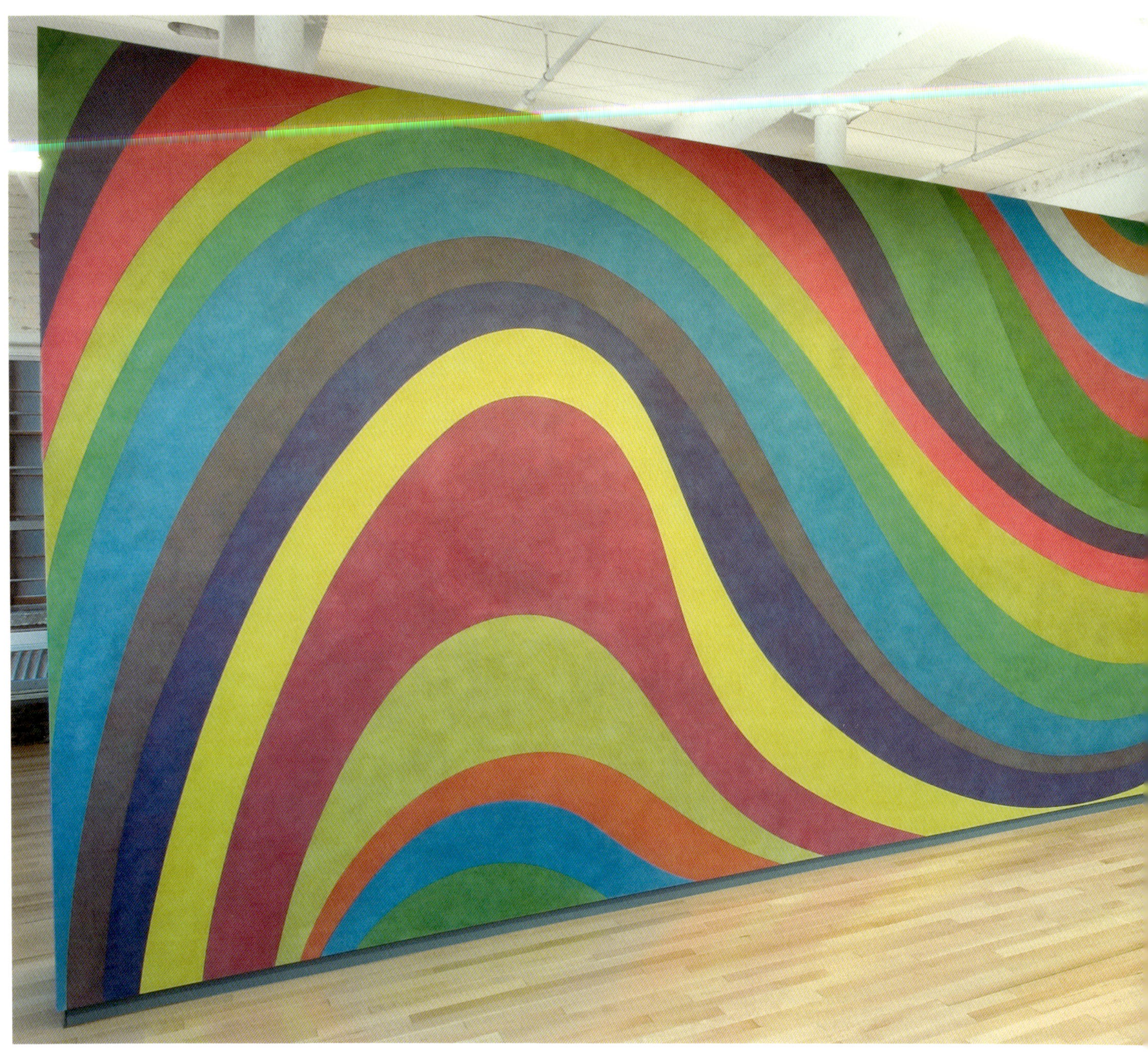

Wall Drawing 793B: Irregular wavy color bands.   1996

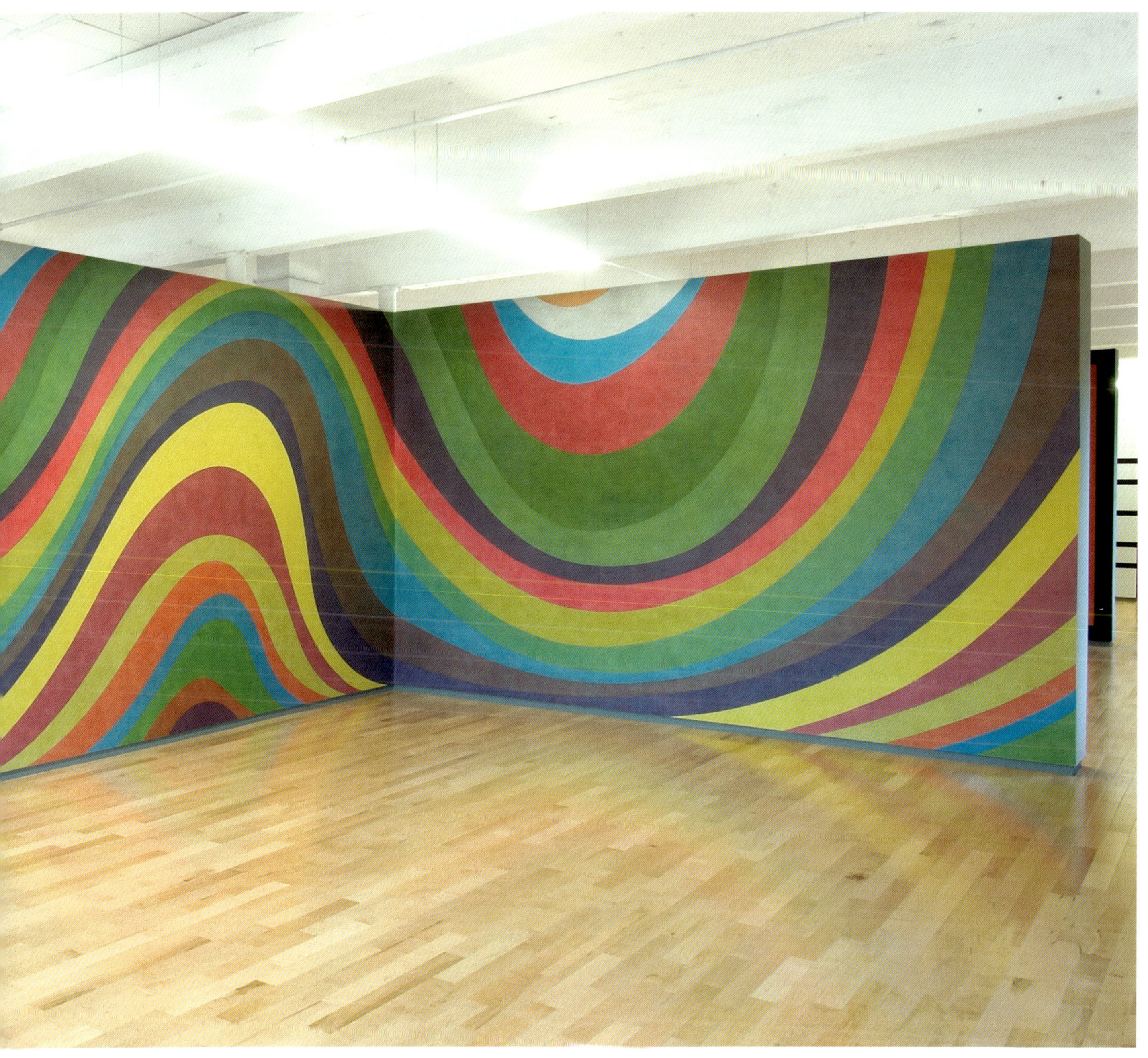

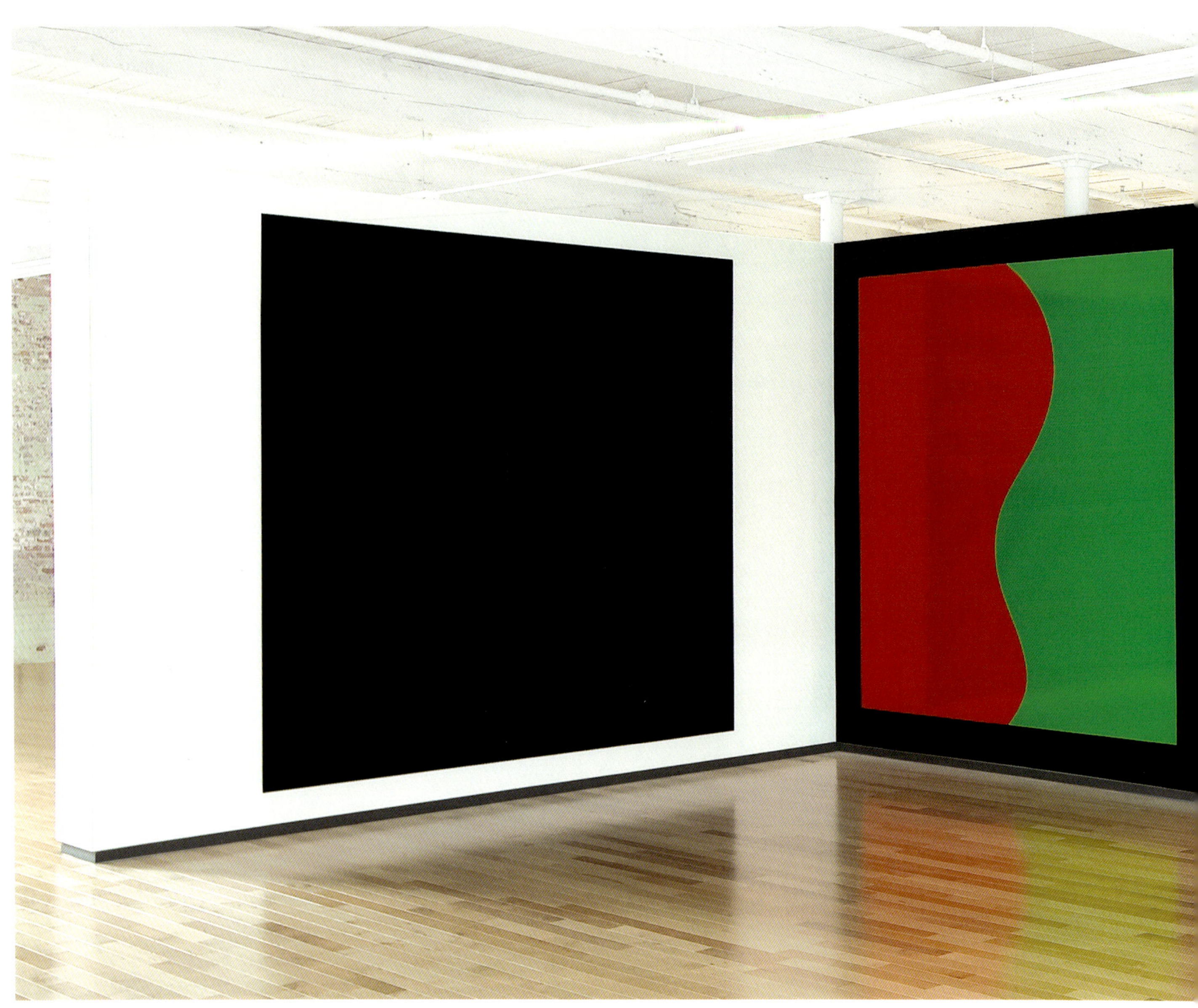

Wall Drawing 821: A black square divided horizontally and vertically into four equal parts, each with a different direction of alternating flat and glossy bands. 1997

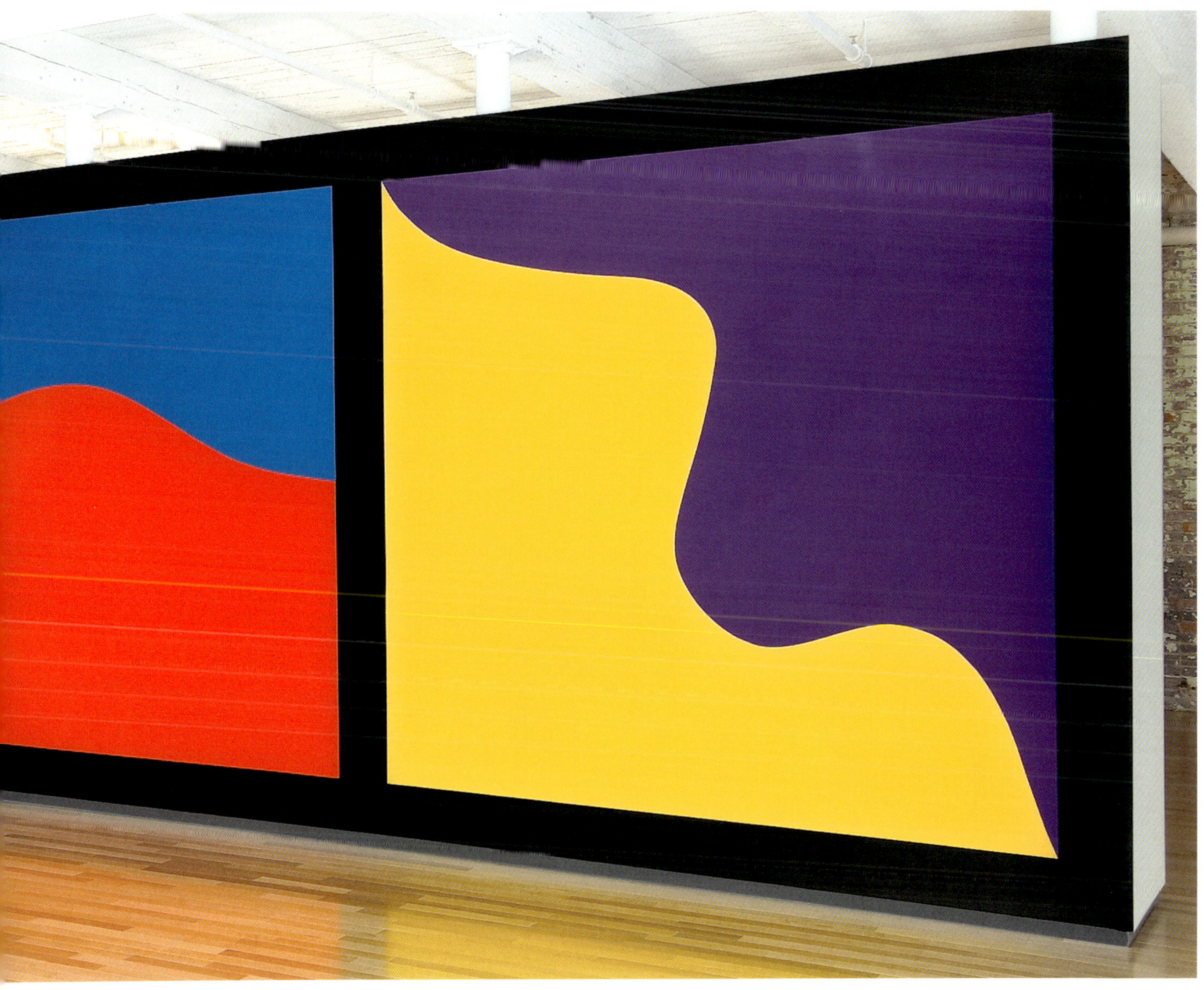

RIGHT WALL, FROM LEFT TO RIGHT:

Wall Drawing 853: A wall bordered and divided vertically into two parts by a flat black band. Left part: a square is divided vertically by a curvy line.
Left: glossy red; right: glossy green; Right part: a square is divided horizontally by a curvy line. Top: glossy blue; bottom: glossy orange.   1998

Wall Drawing 852: A wall divided from the upper left to the lower right by a curvy line; left: glossy yellow; right: glossy purple.   1998

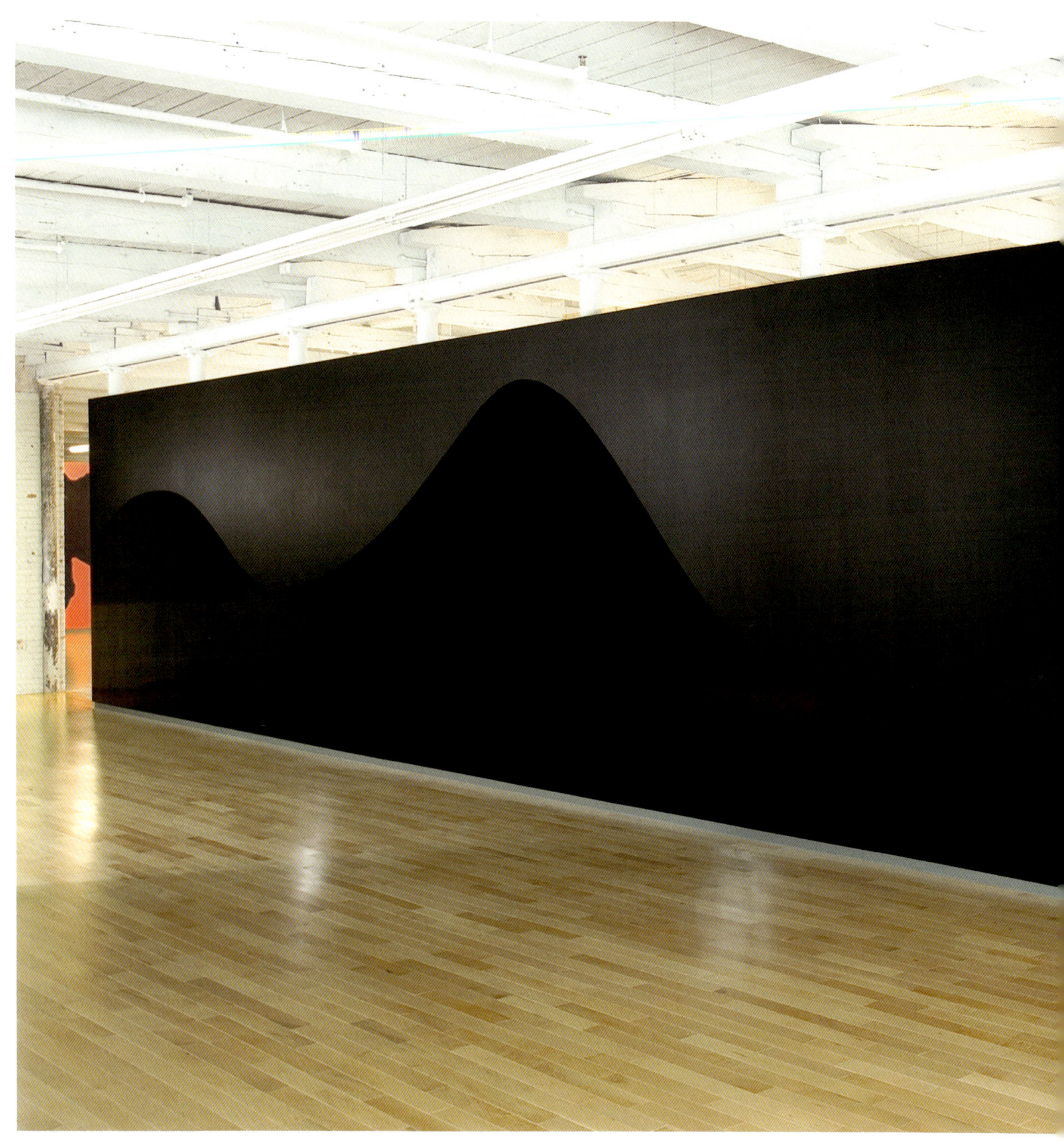

Wall Drawing 822: A wall divided horizontally by a curvy line. The top is flat black; the bottom is glossy black.   1997

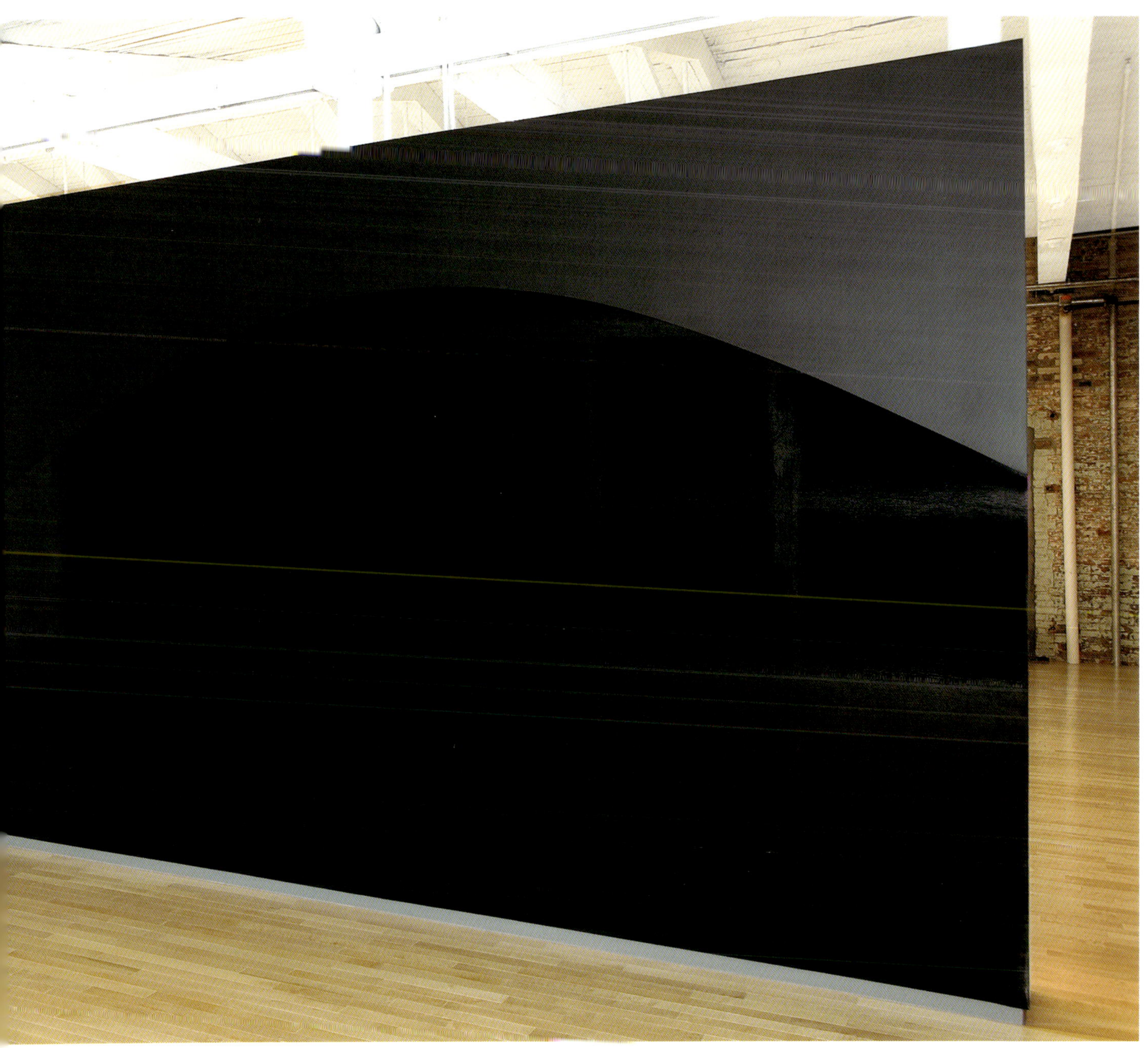

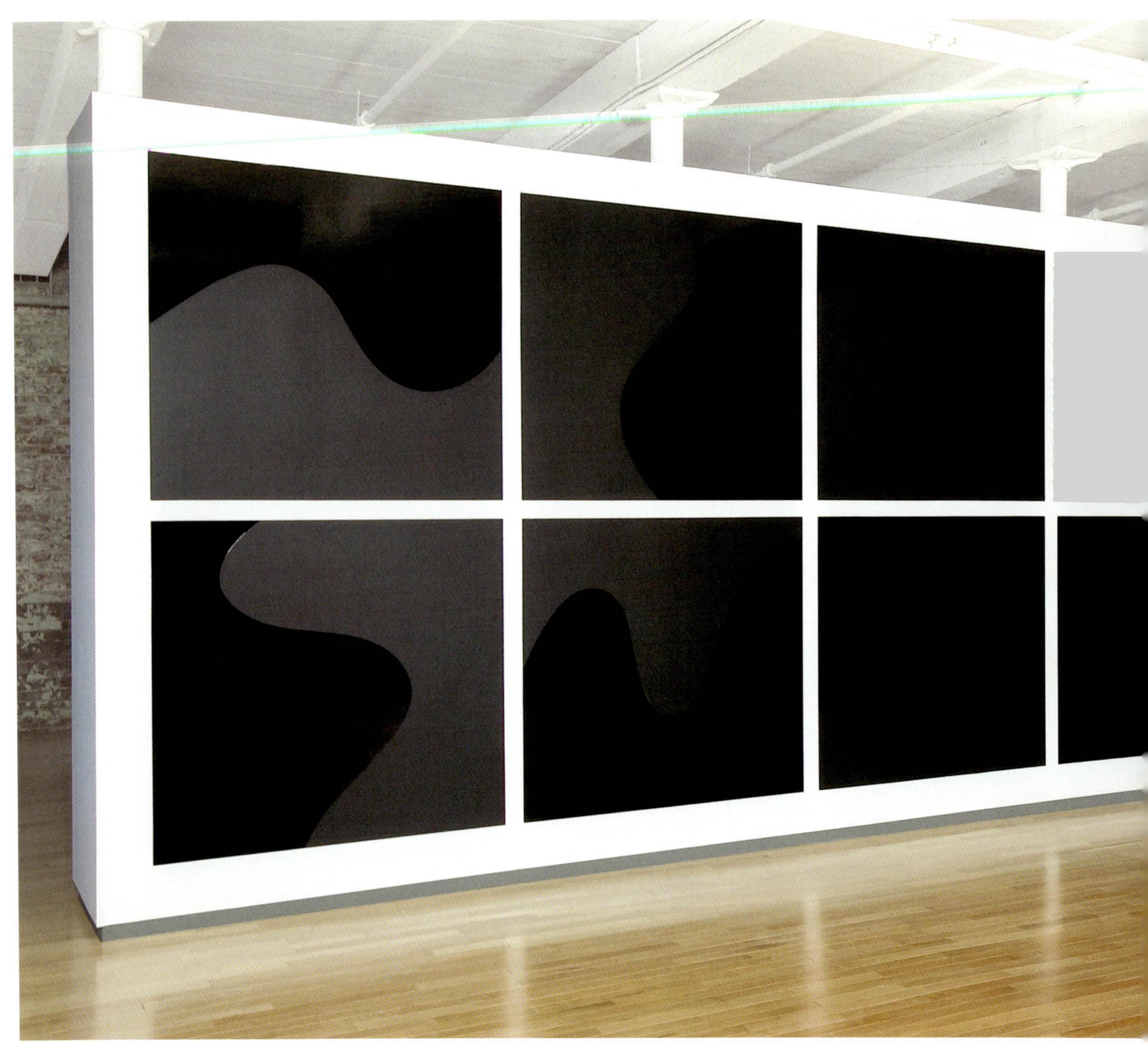

Wall Drawing 824A, 824B, 824C, 824E, 824F, 824G, 824H, 824J, 824K, 824L, 824M, 824N:
A black square divided in two parts by a wavy line. One part flat; one glossy. 1997

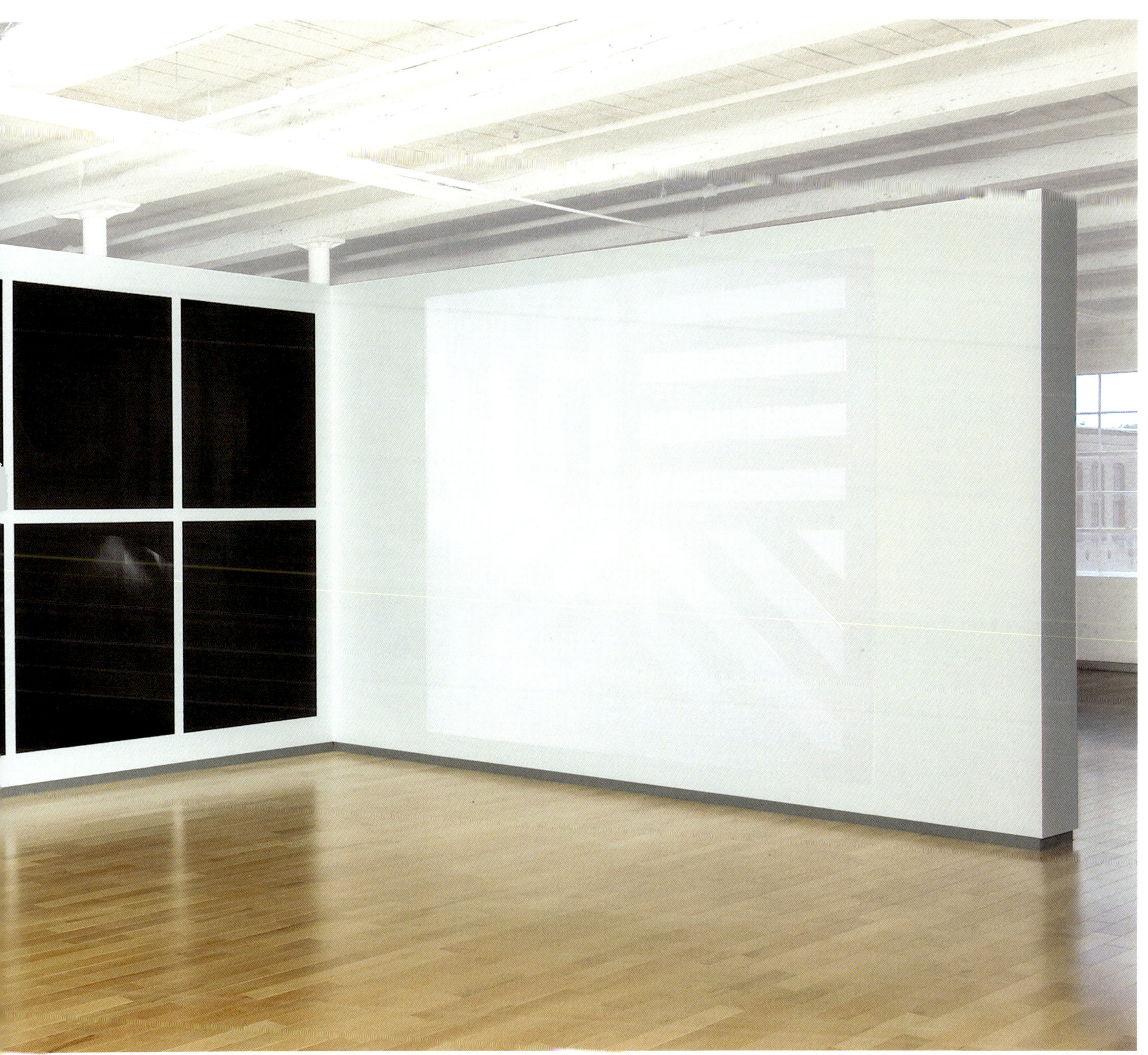

Wall Drawing 821A: A white square divided horizontally and vertically into four equal parts, each with a different direction of alternating flat and glossy bands. 2007

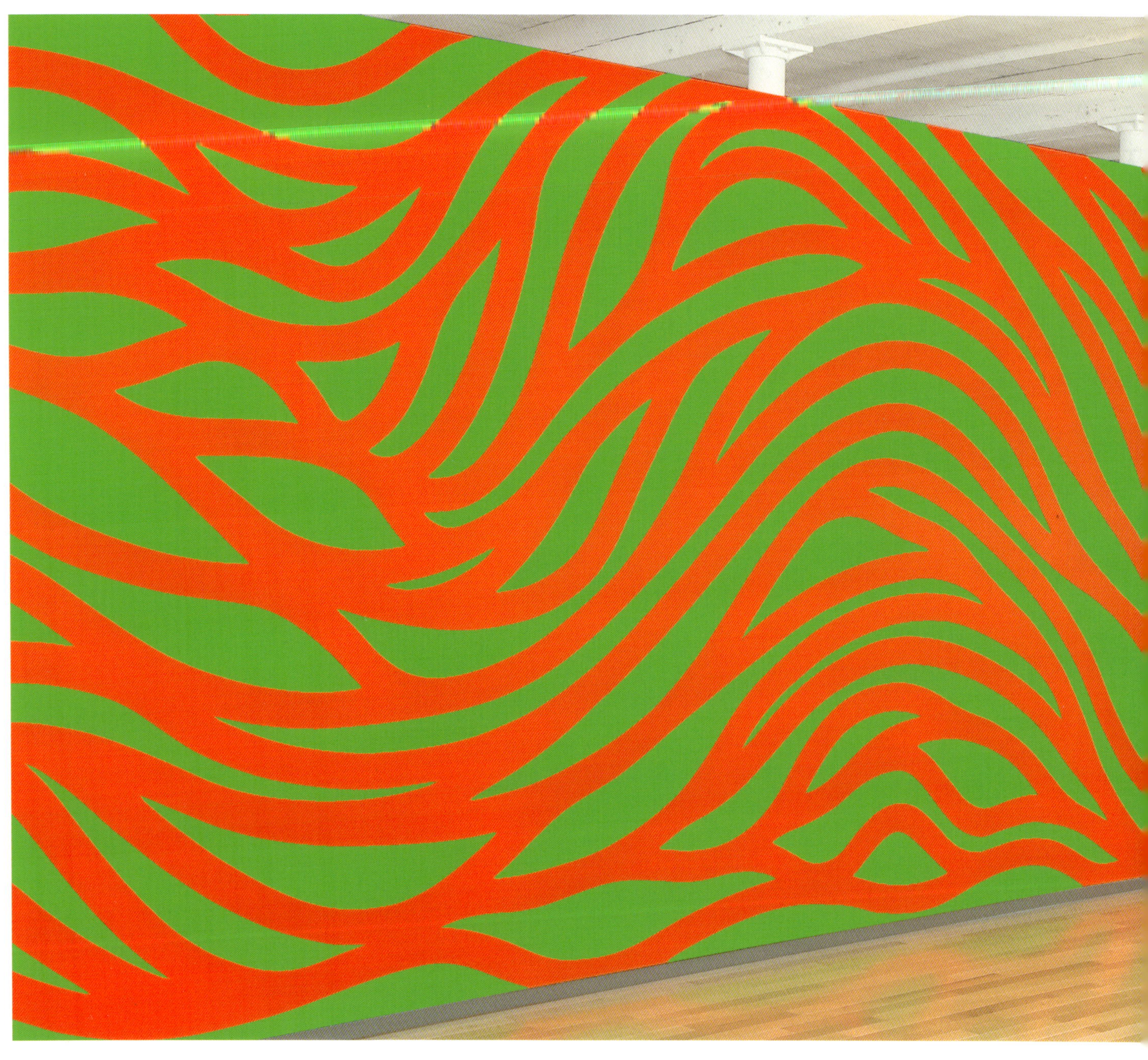

Wall Drawing 880: Loopy Doopy (orange and green).   1998

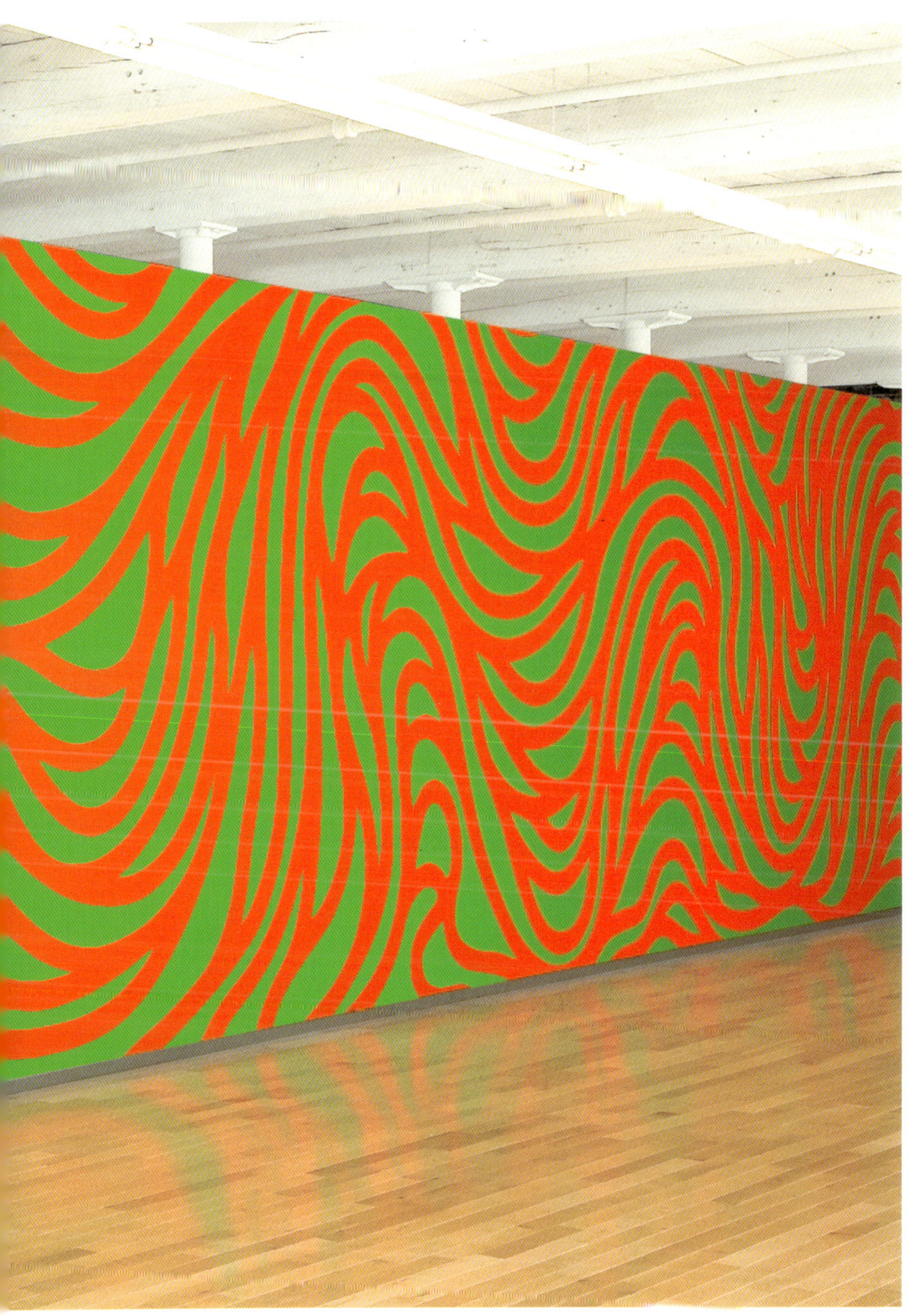

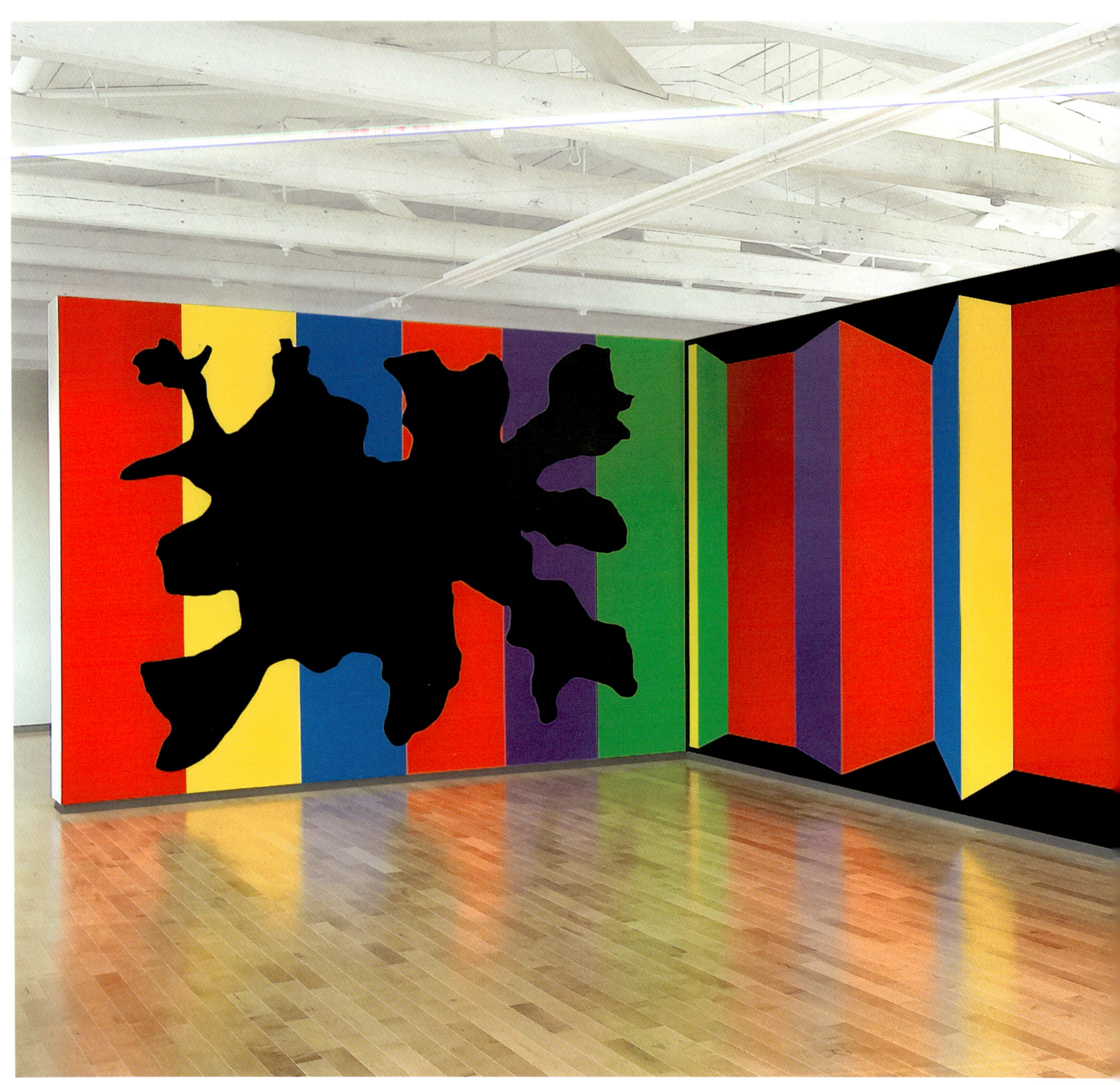

Wall Drawing 901: Color bands and black blob. The wall is divided vertically into six equal bands: red, yellow, blue, orange, purple, green. In the center is a black glossy blob. 1999

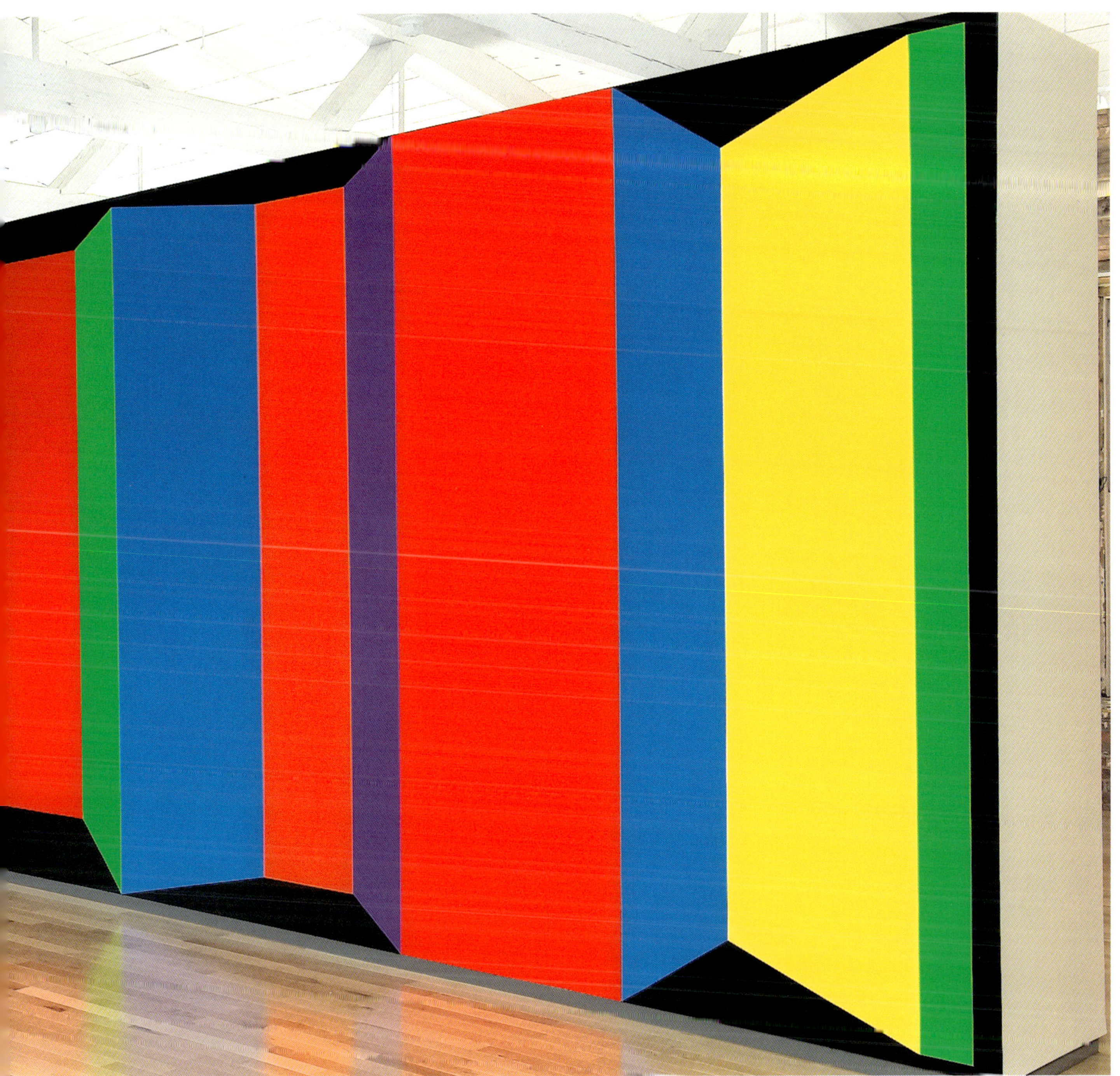

Wall Drawing 1081: Planes of color.   2003

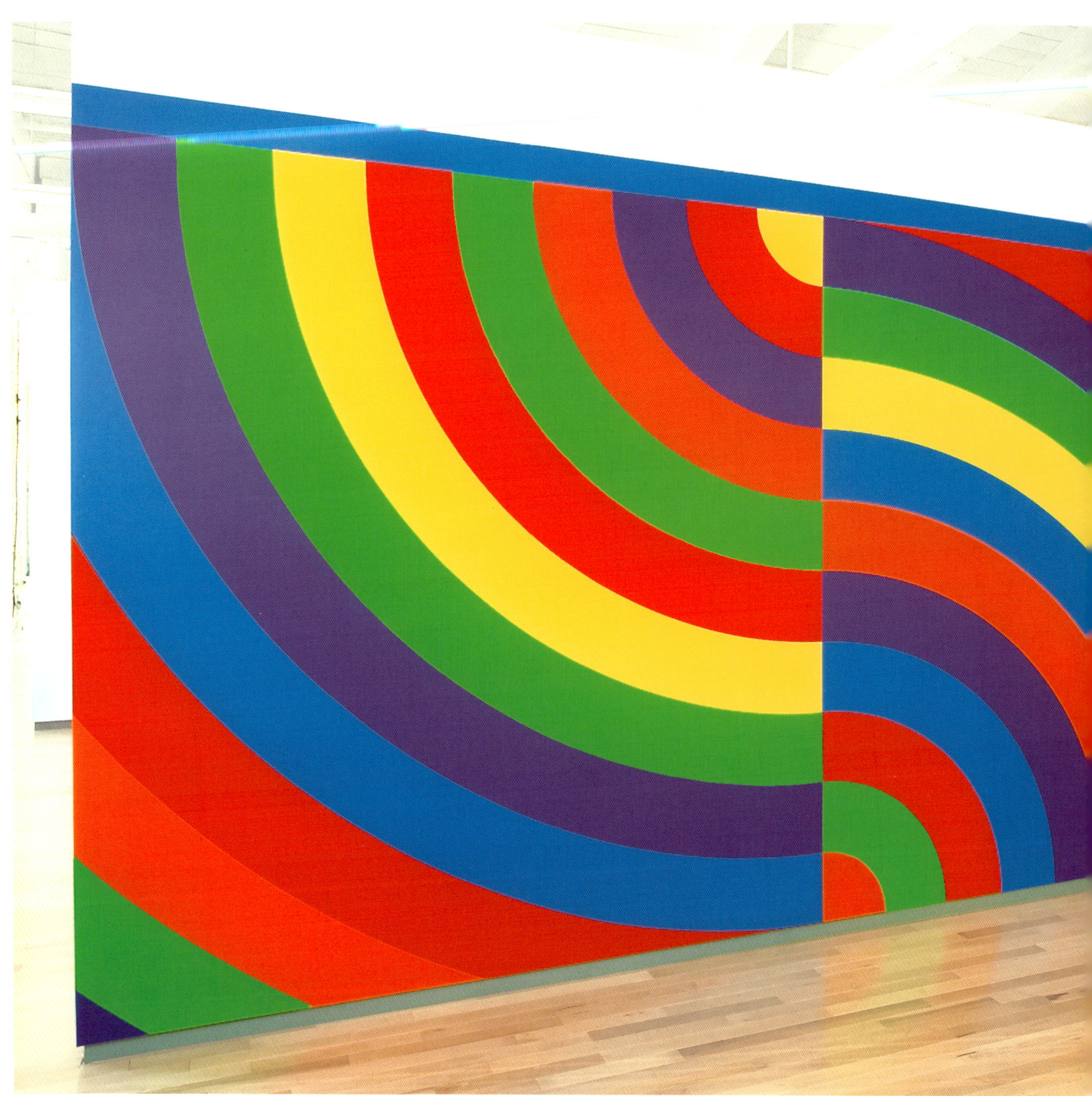

Wall Drawing 915: Arcs, circle, and irregular bands.   1999

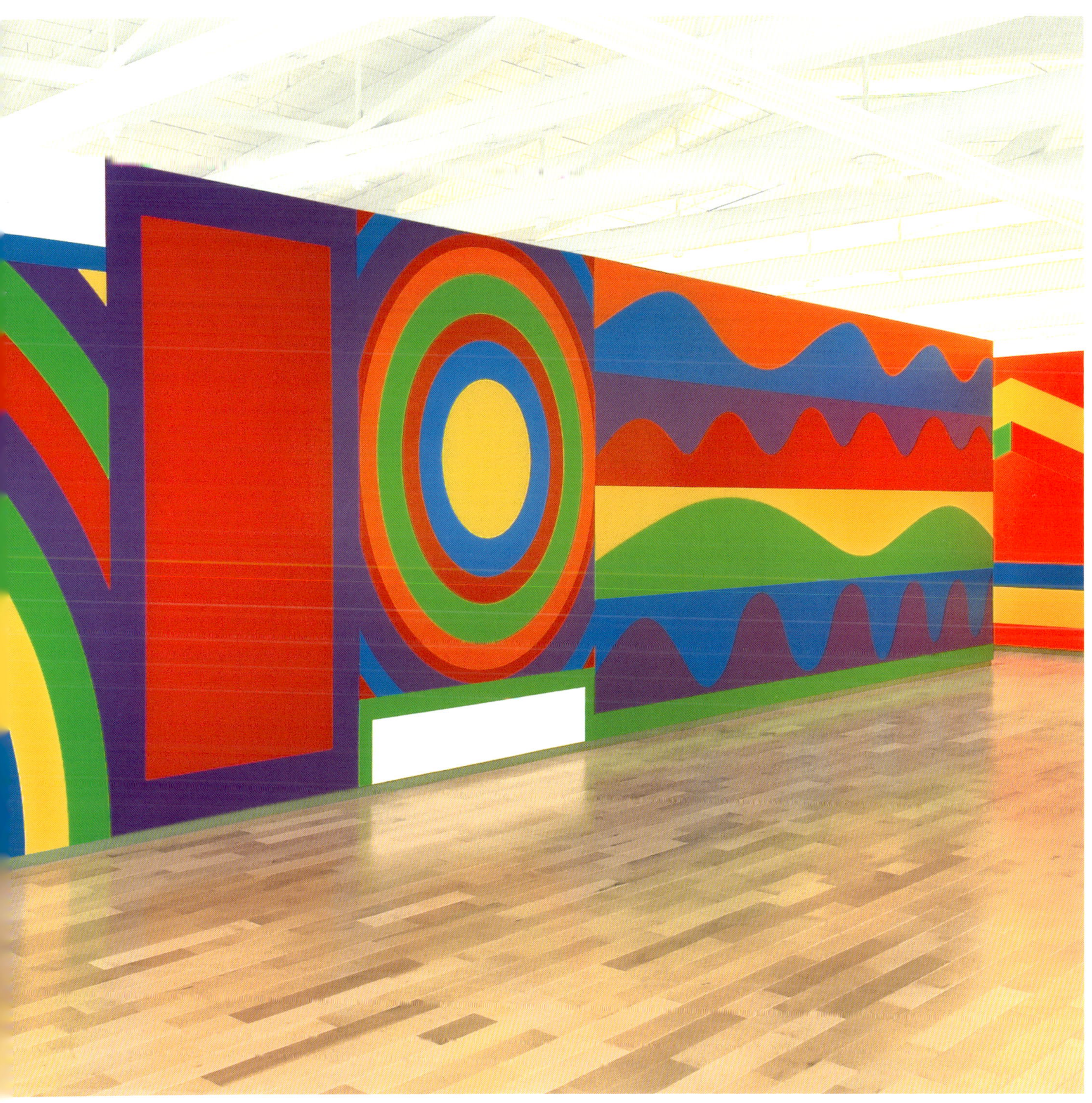

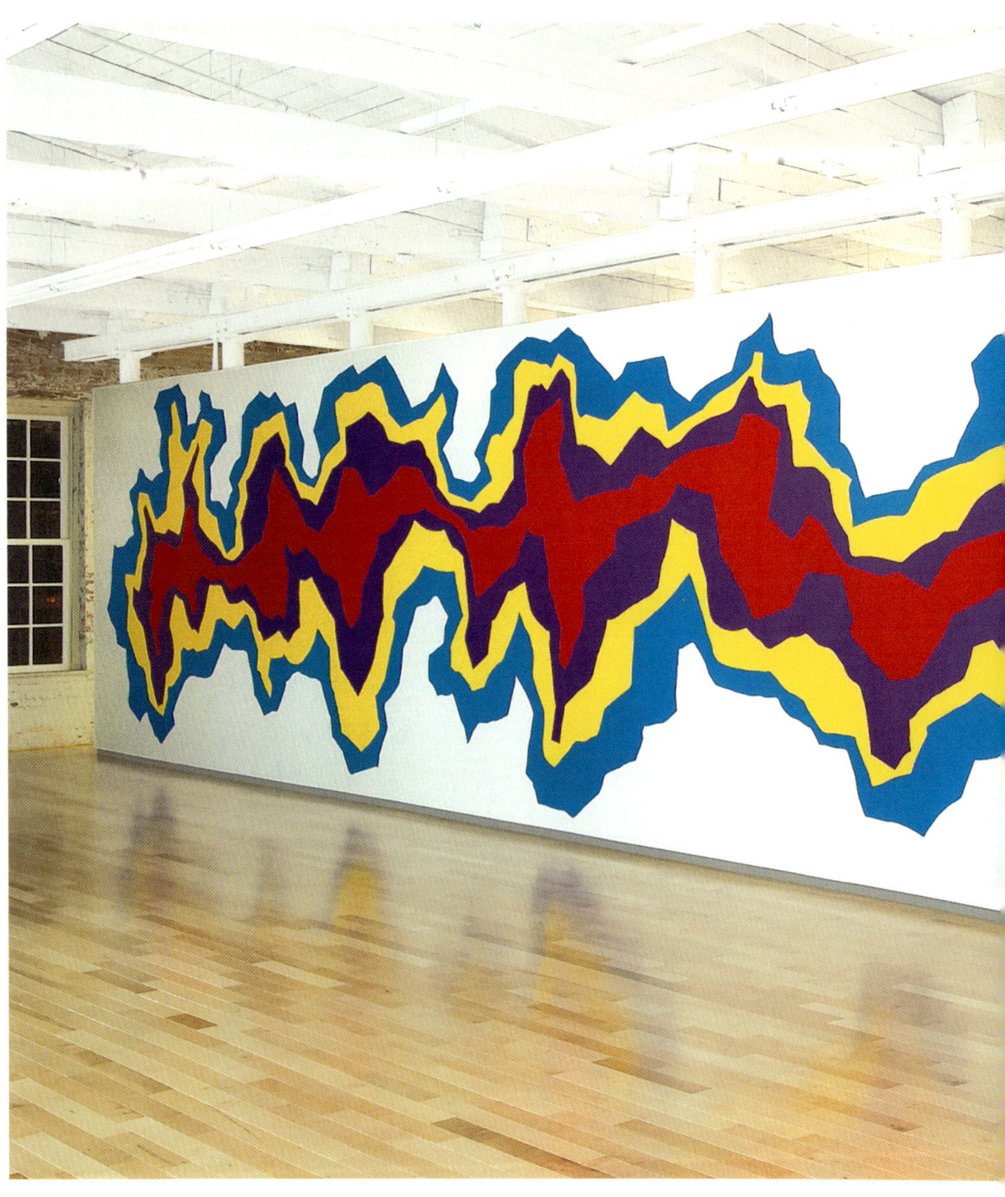

Wall Drawing 958: Splat. 2000

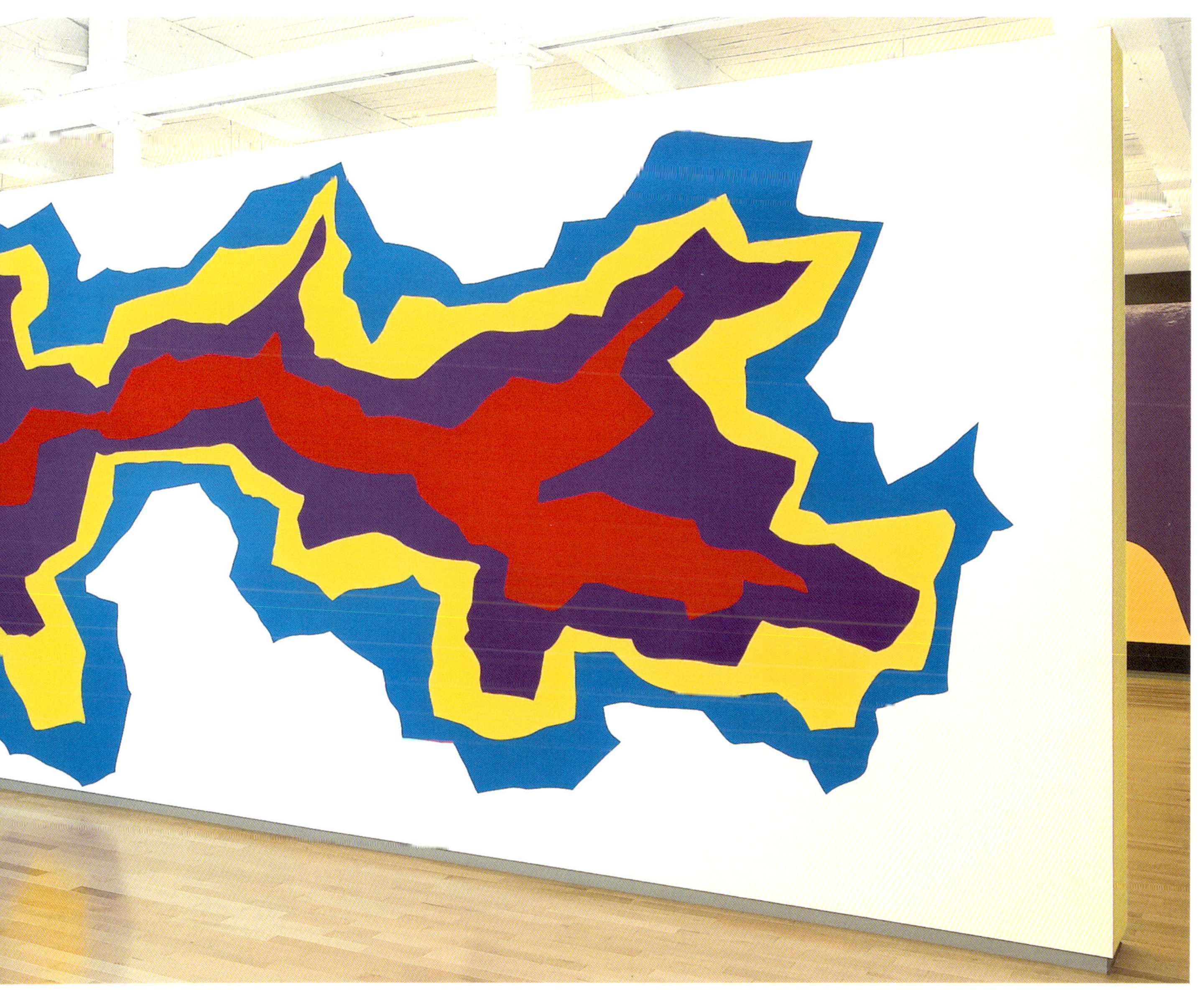

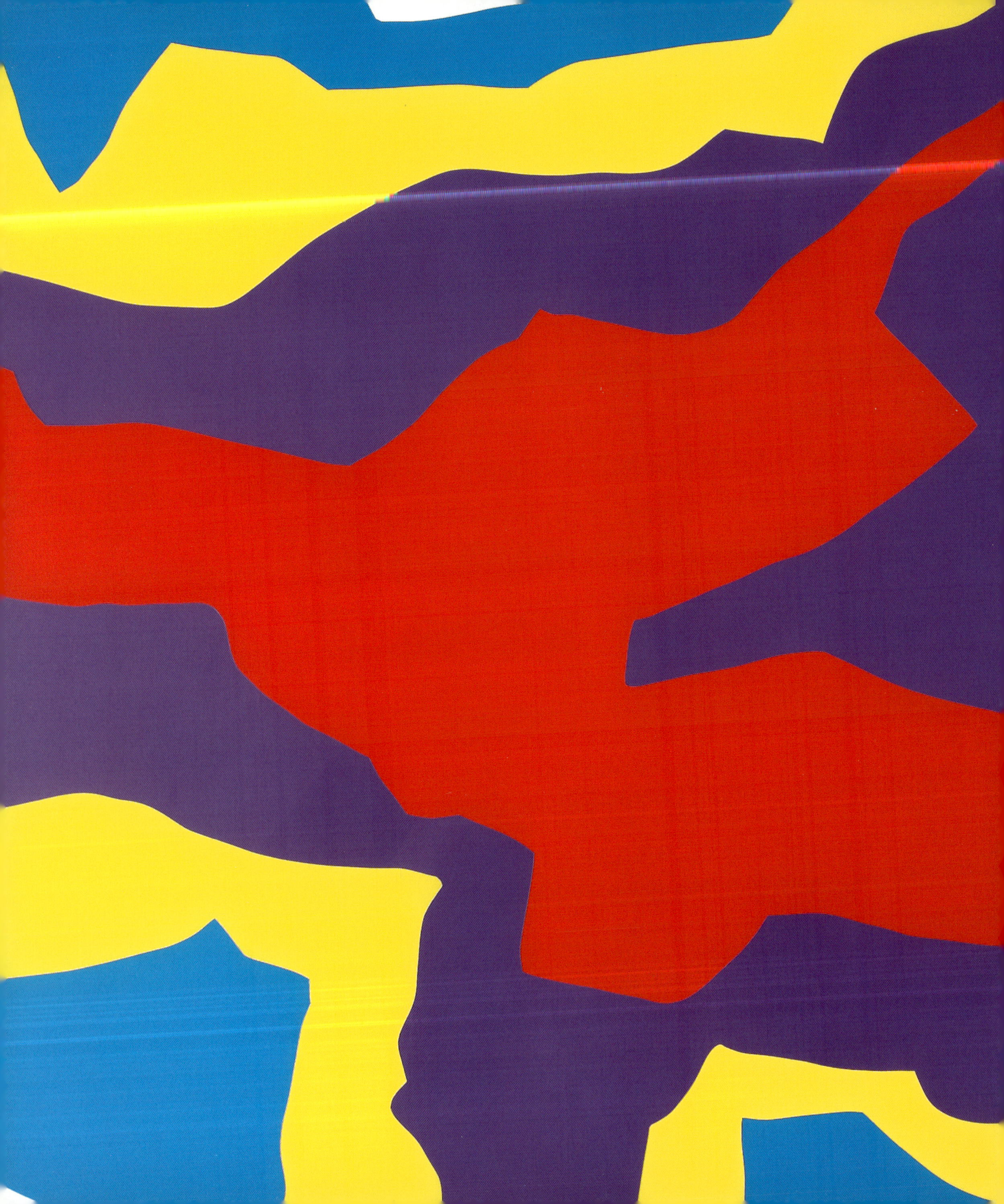

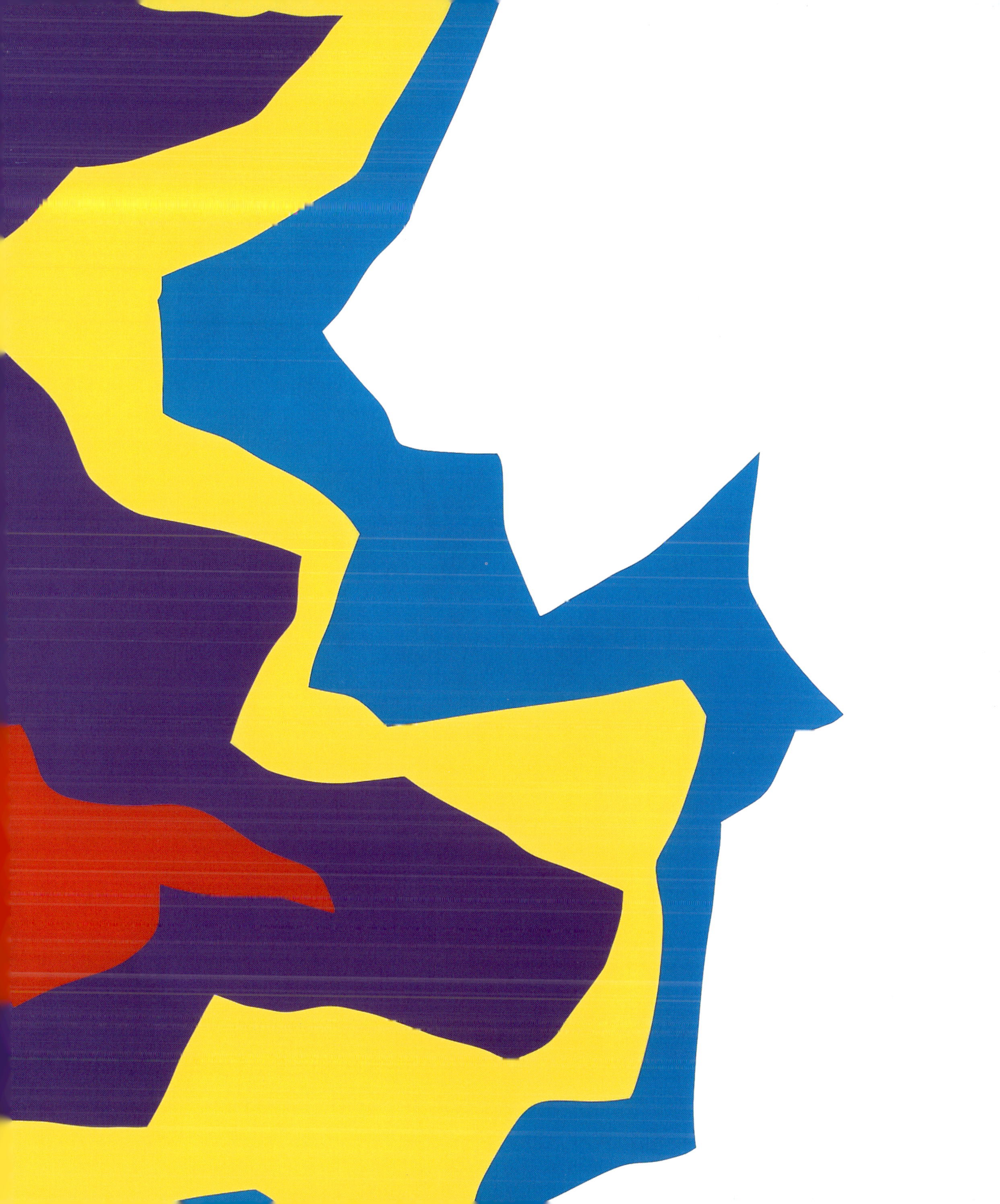

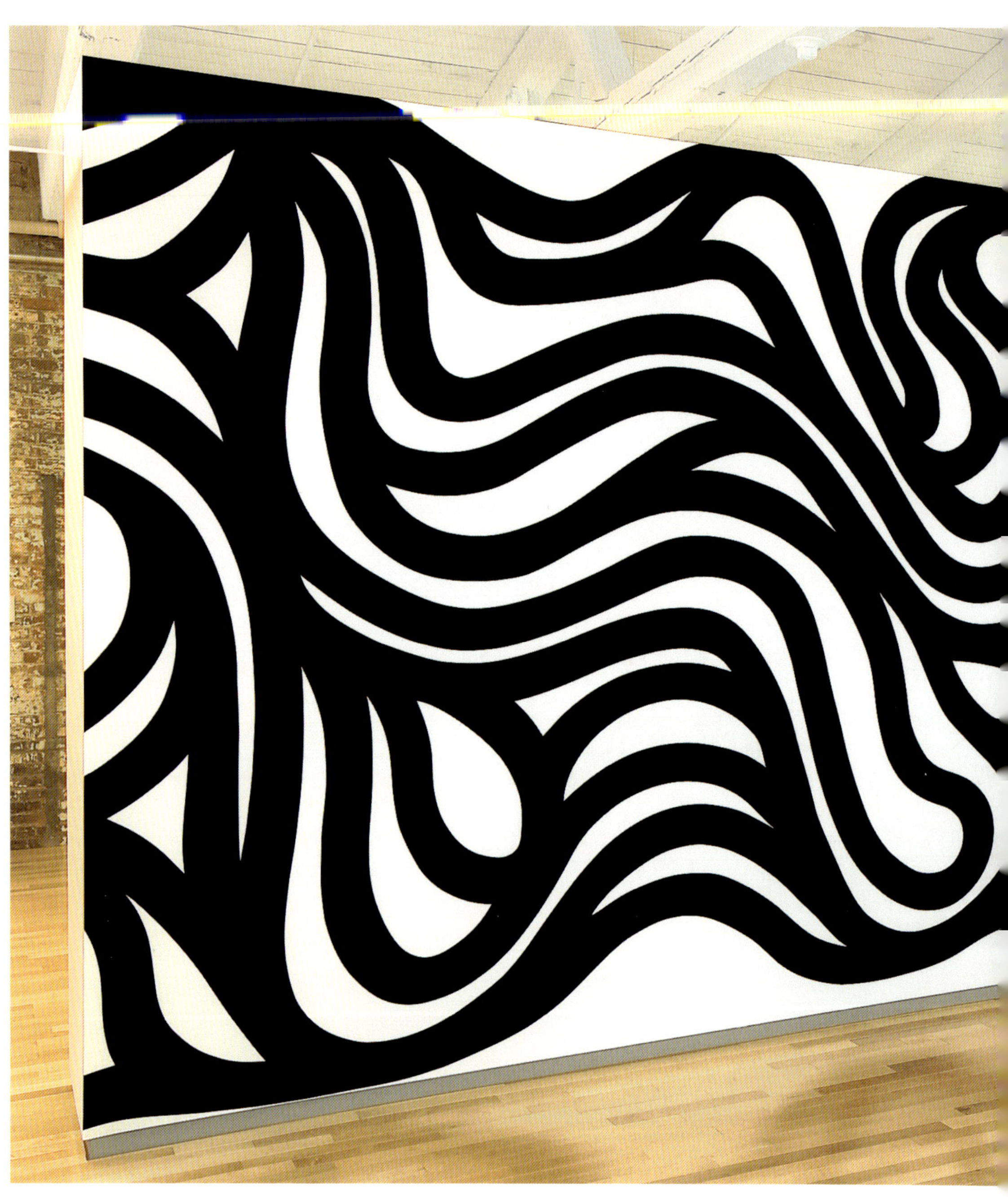

Wall Drawing 999: Parallel curves.   2001

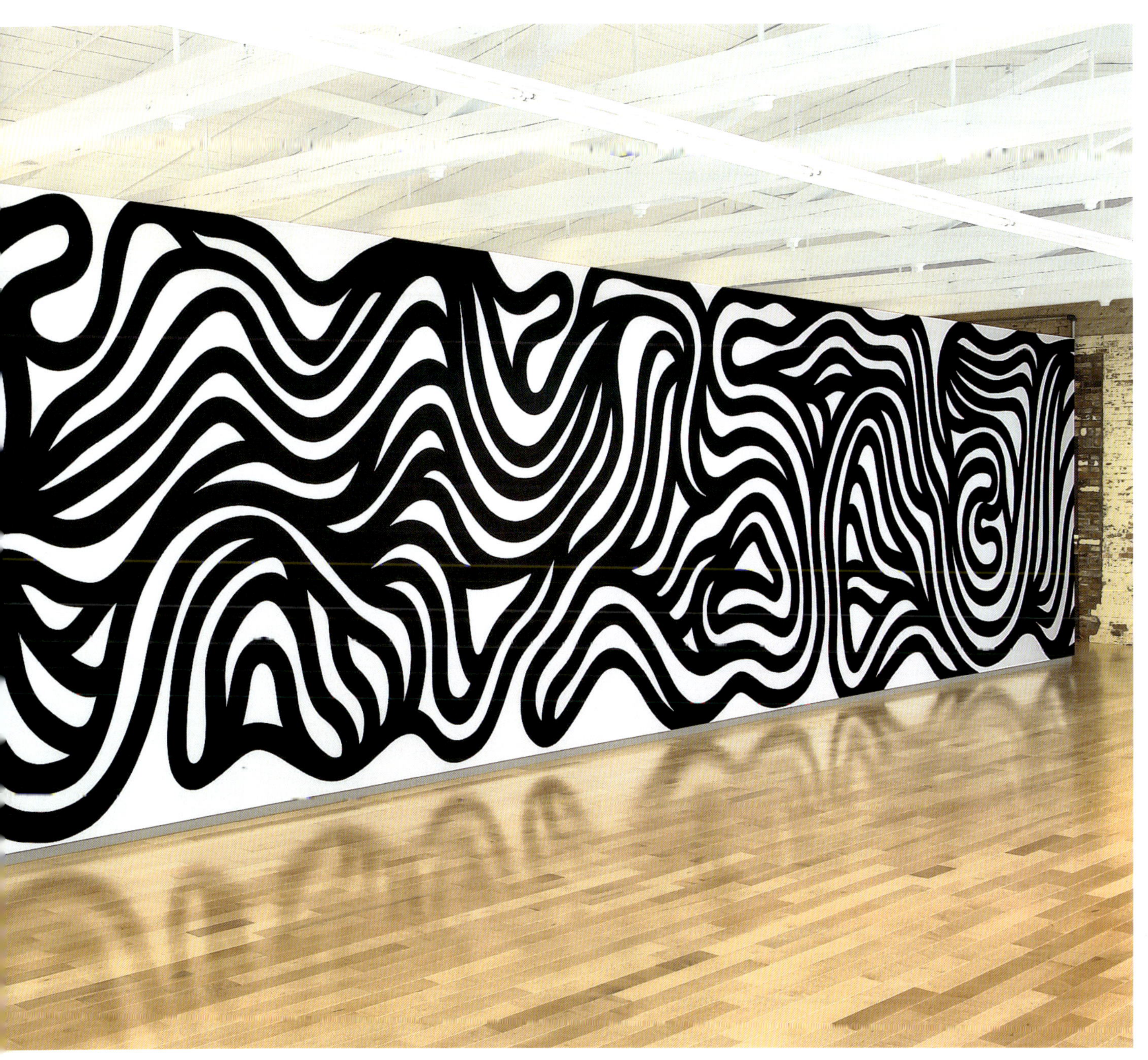

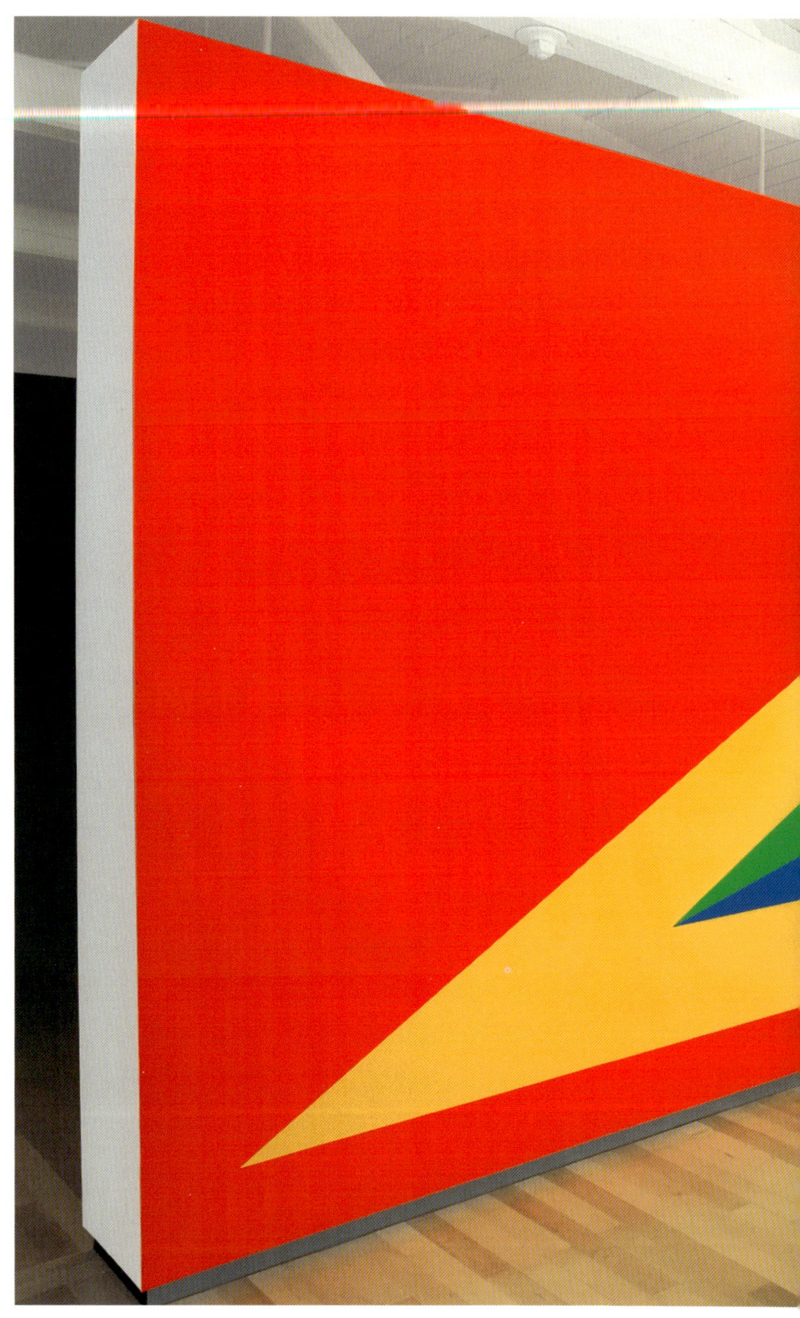

Wall Drawing 1005: Isometric form. 2001

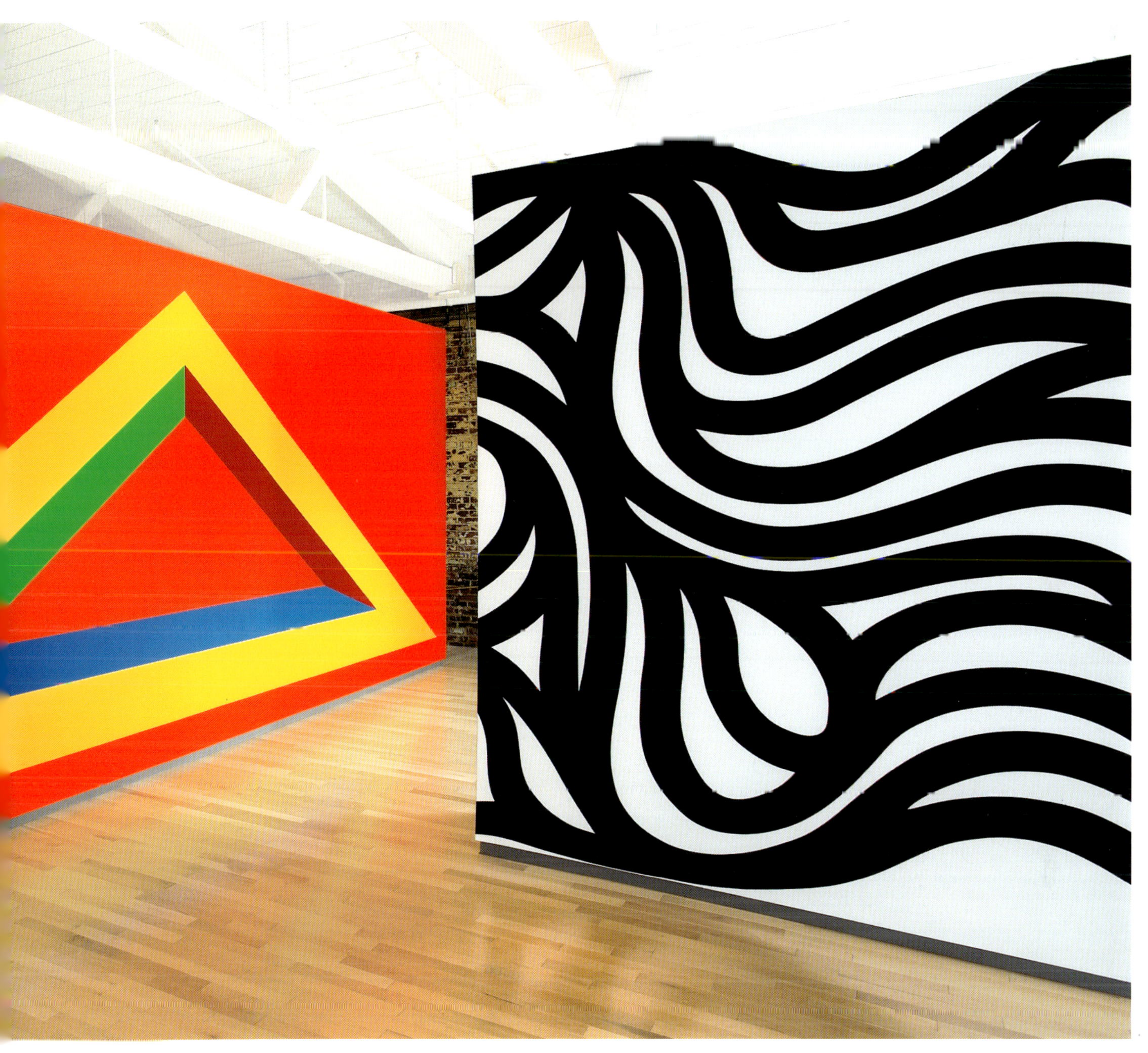

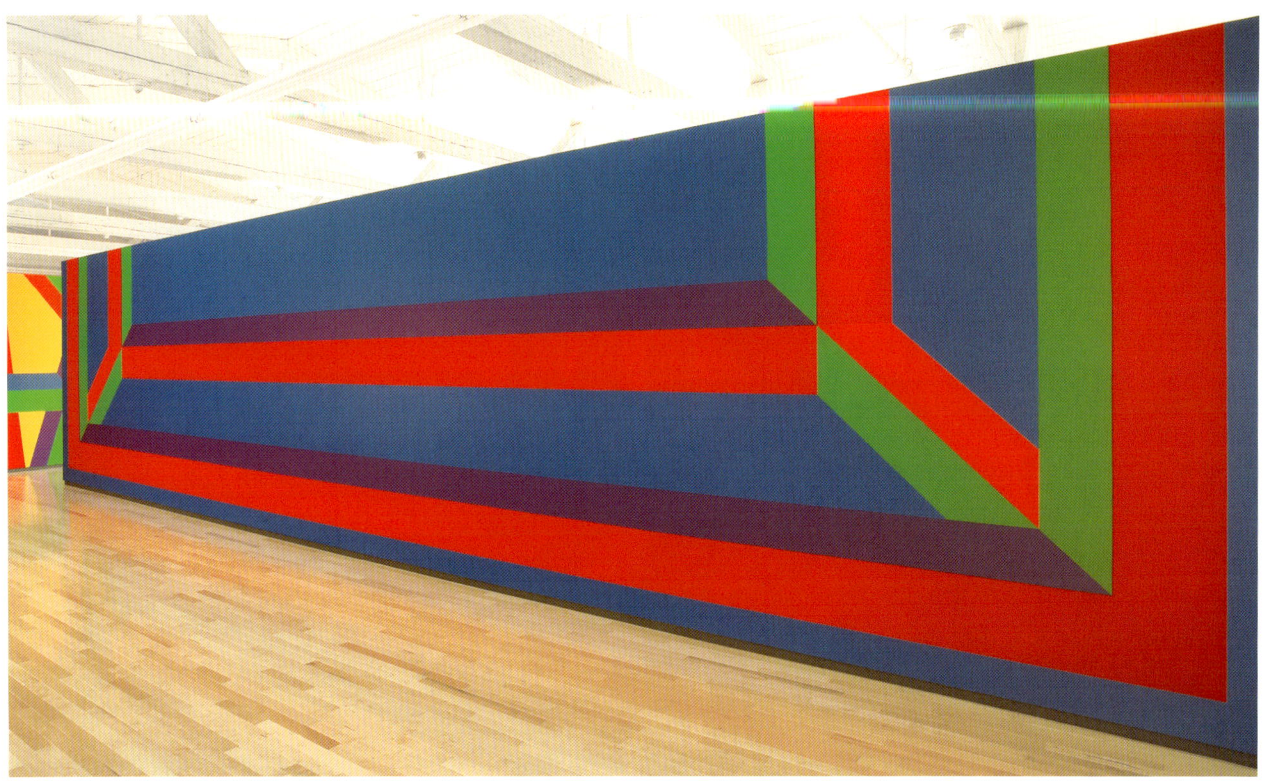

Wall Drawing 1042: Isometric form.   2002

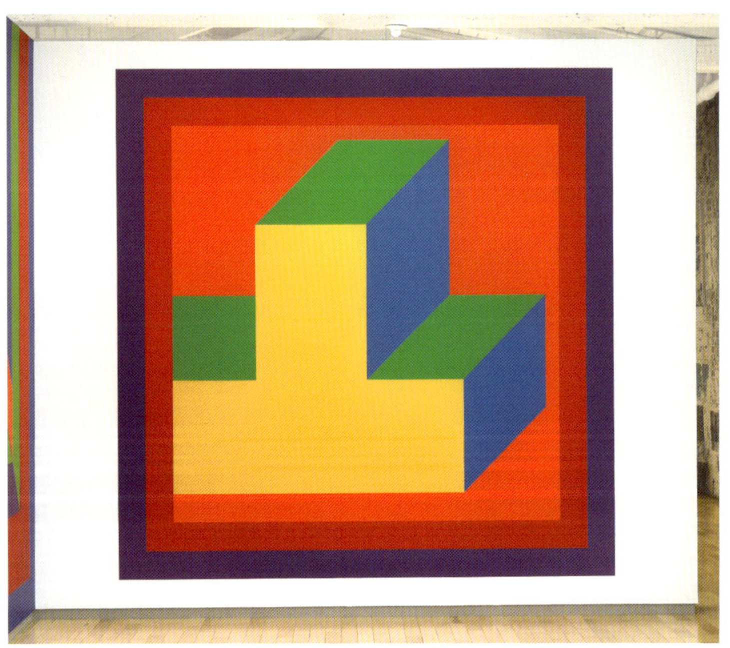

Wall Drawing 1037: Bars of color within a square (#8).   2002

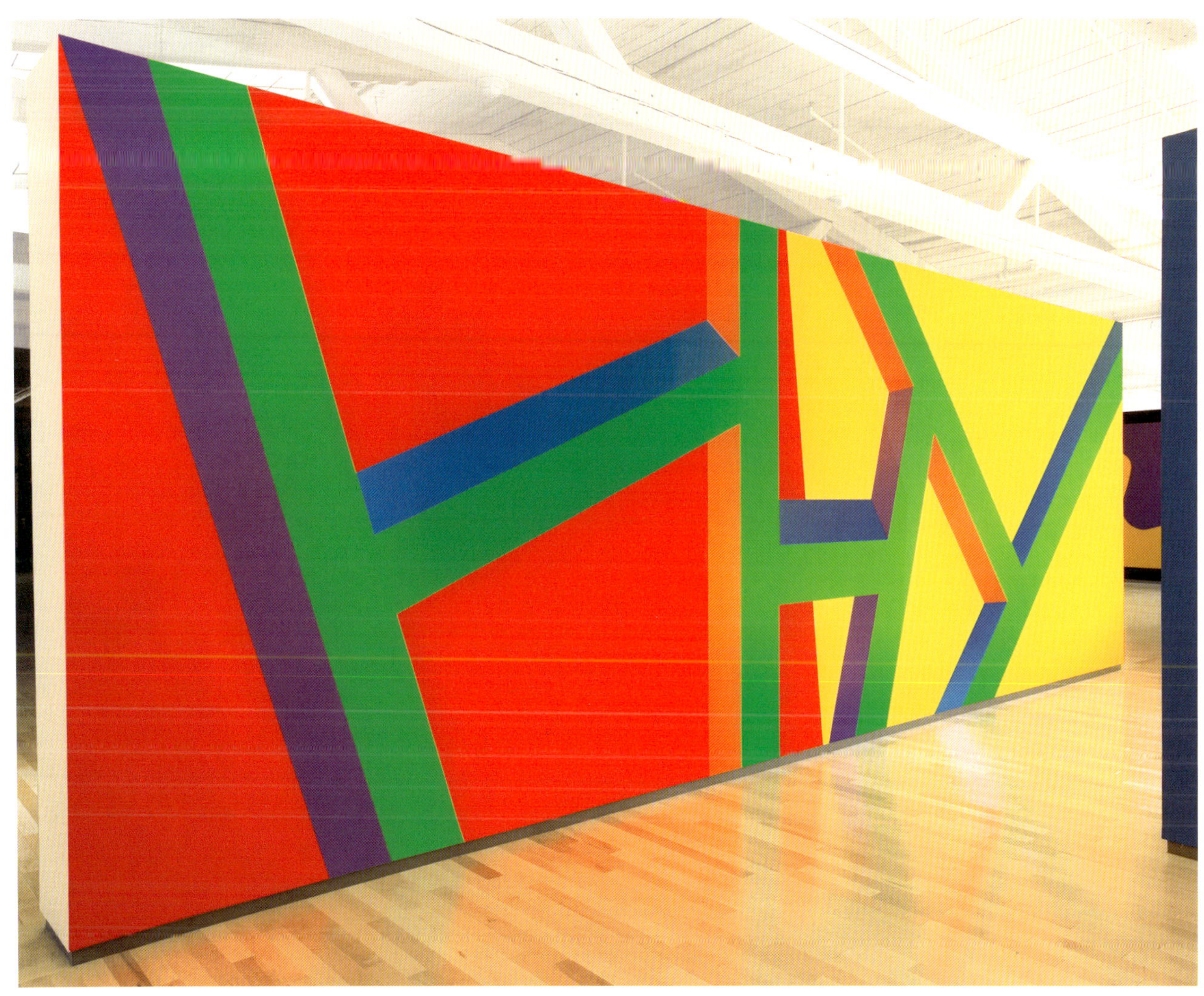

Wall Drawing 1046: Bars of color (La Coruña).   2002

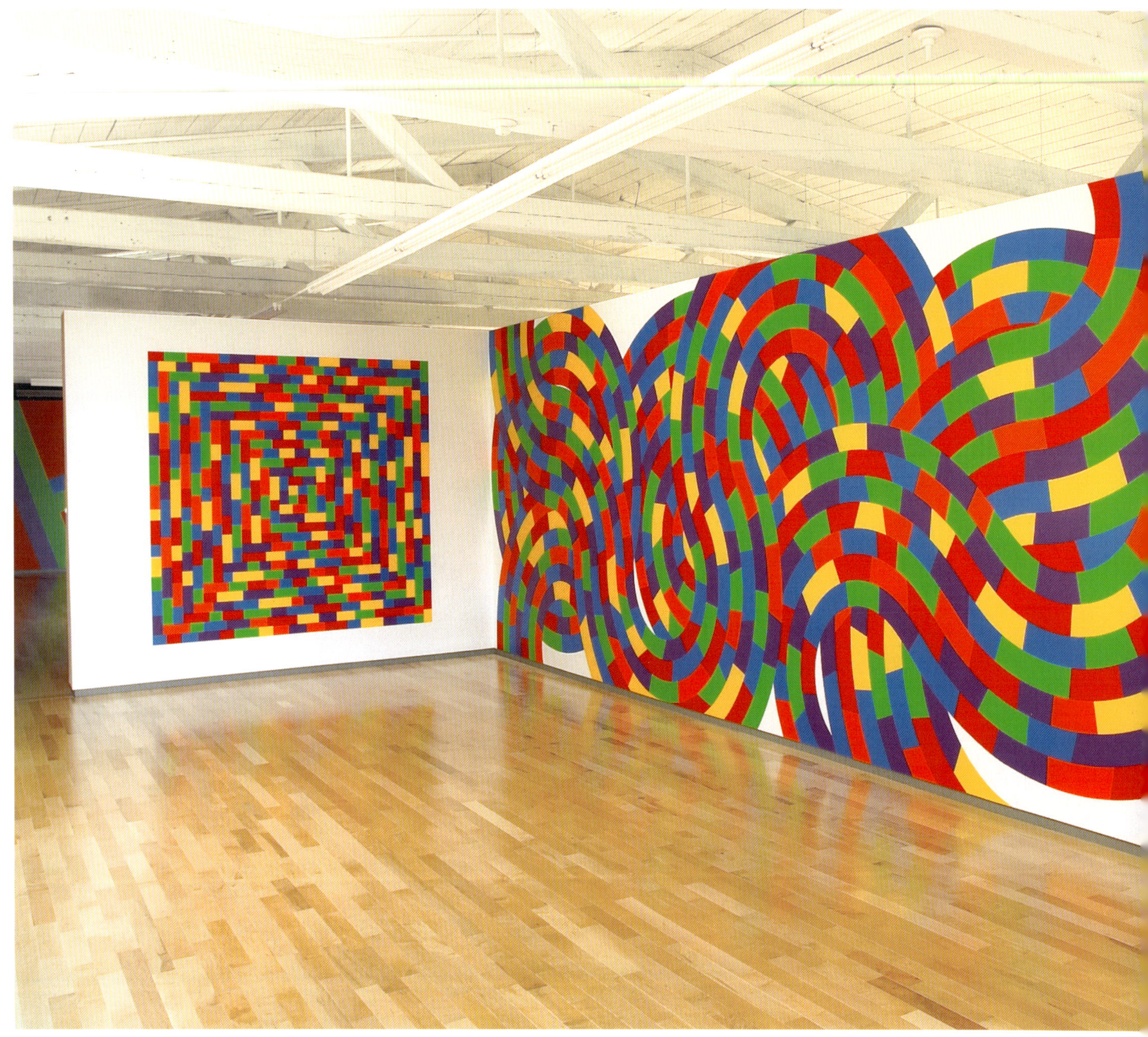

Wall Drawing 1112: Square with broken bands of color.   2003

Wall Drawing 1152: Whirls and twirls (Met).   2005

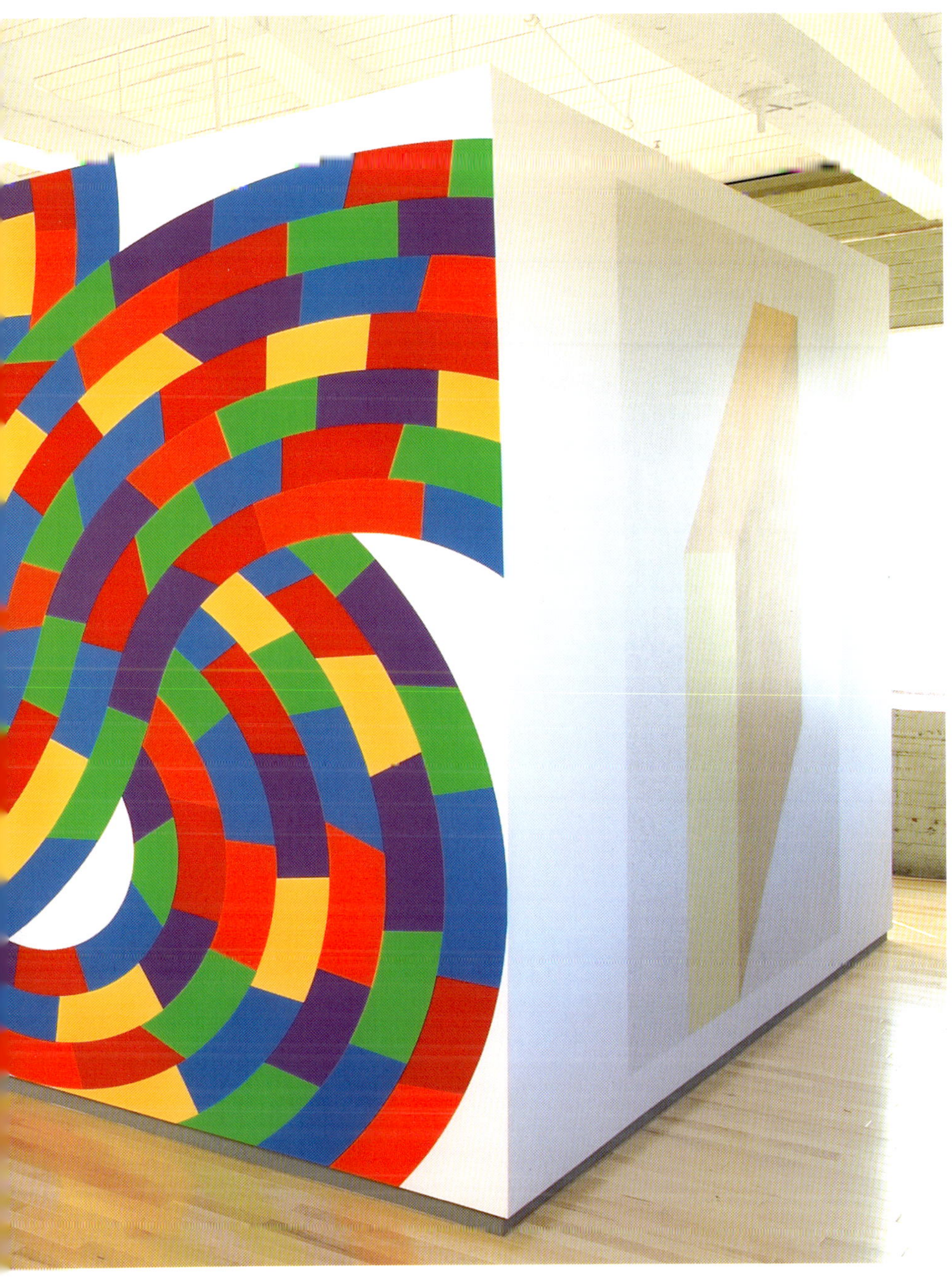

Wall Drawing 1091: Projecting form, 2003

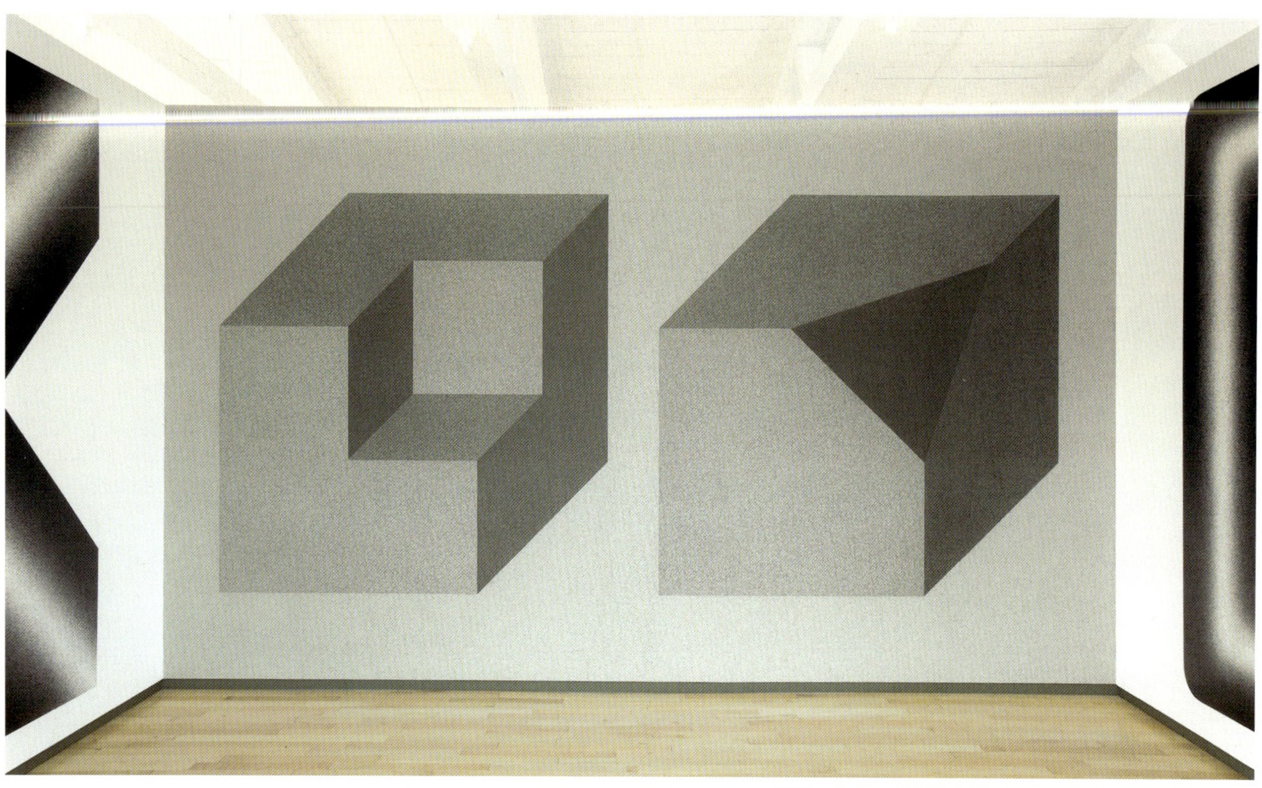

Wall Drawing 1171: Five degrees of scribbles: A cube without a cube; A cube without a corner. 2005

Wall Drawing 1247: Scribbles 7 (PW). 2007 (detail)

Wall Drawing 1185: Scribbles: Inverted curve (horizontal).   2005

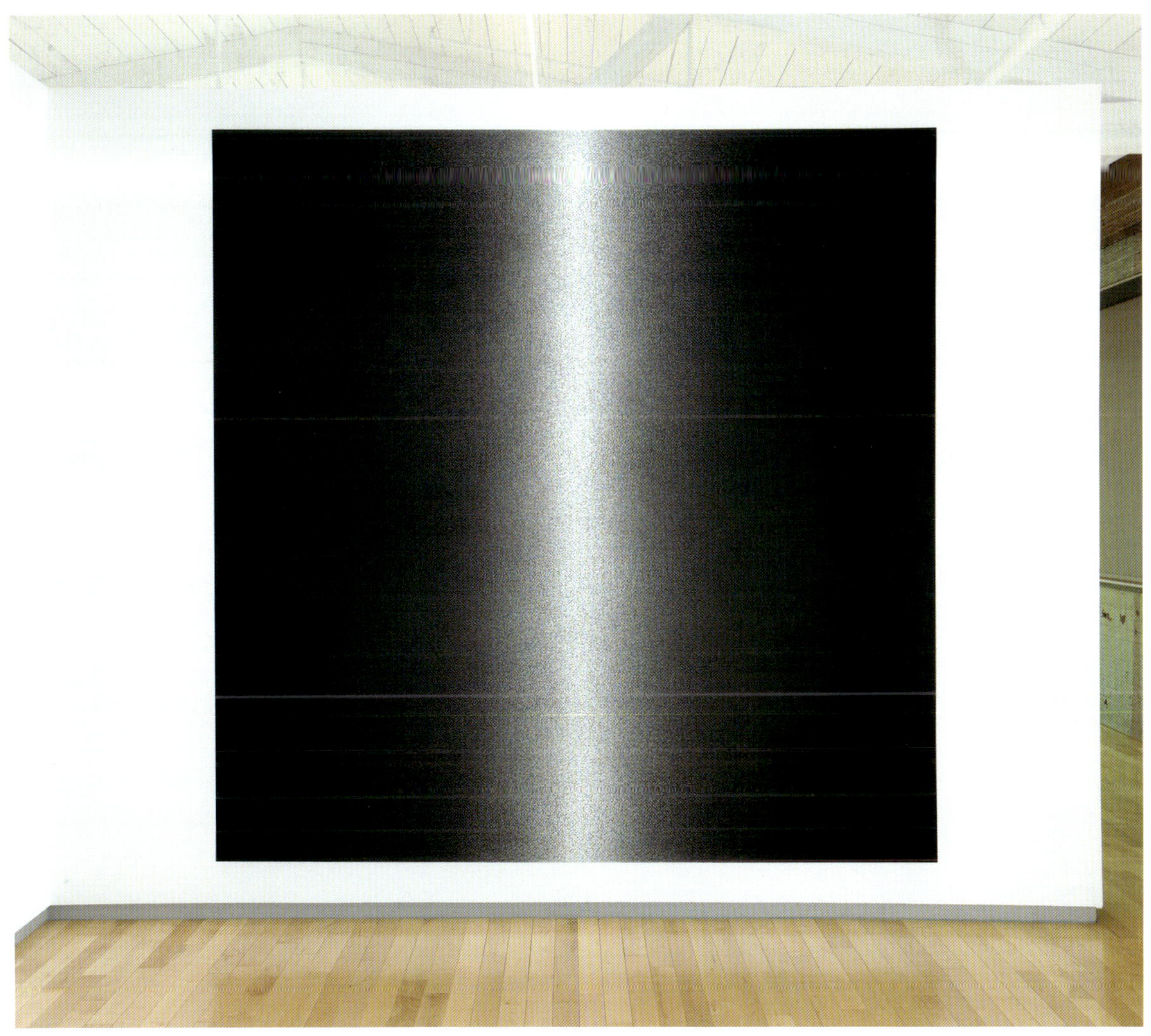

Wall Drawing 1186: Scribbles: Inverted curve (vertical). 2005

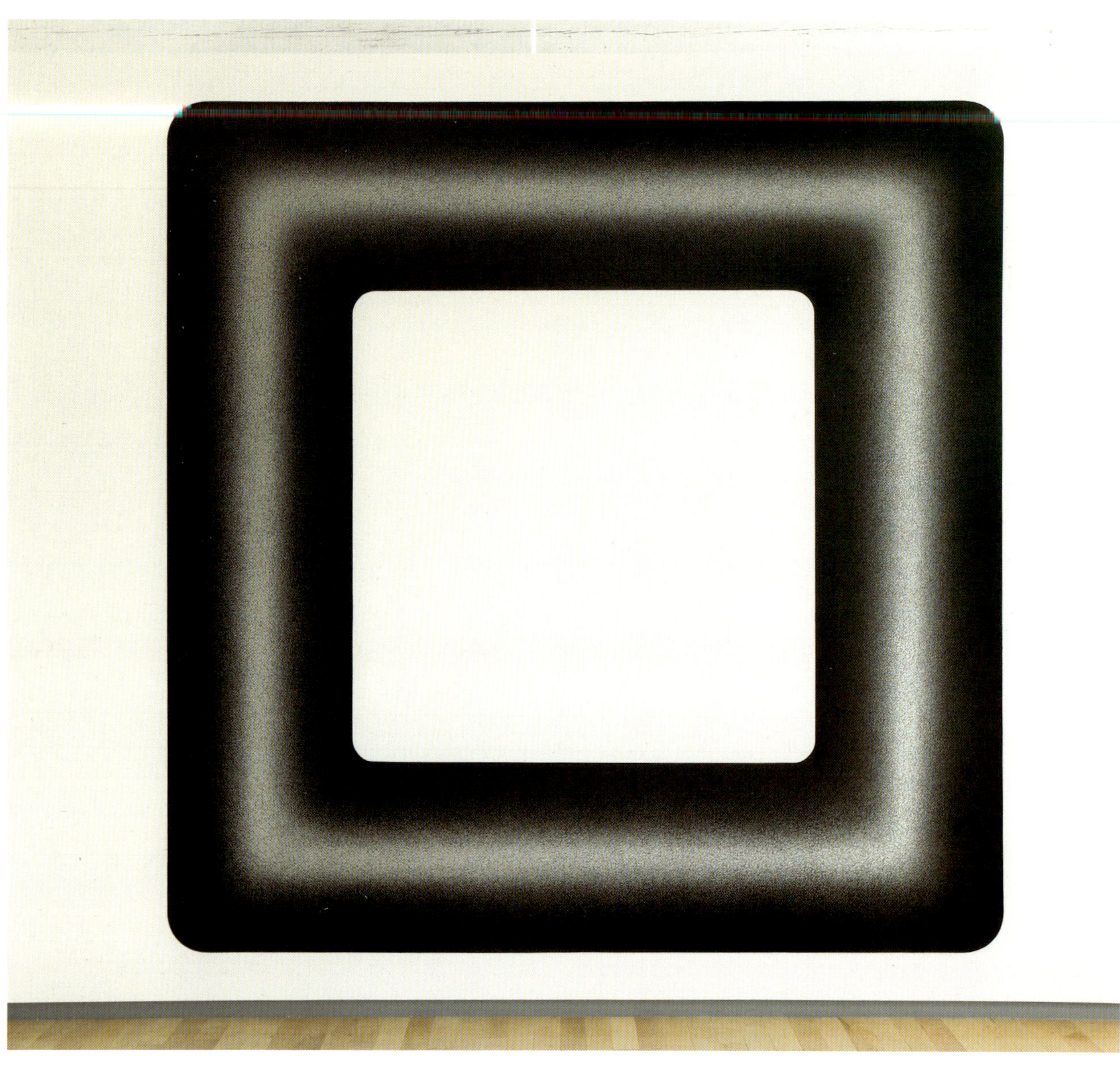

Wall Drawing 1260: Scribble: Square without a square.   2008

Wall Drawing 1261: Scribbles (Yale).   2008   (detail)

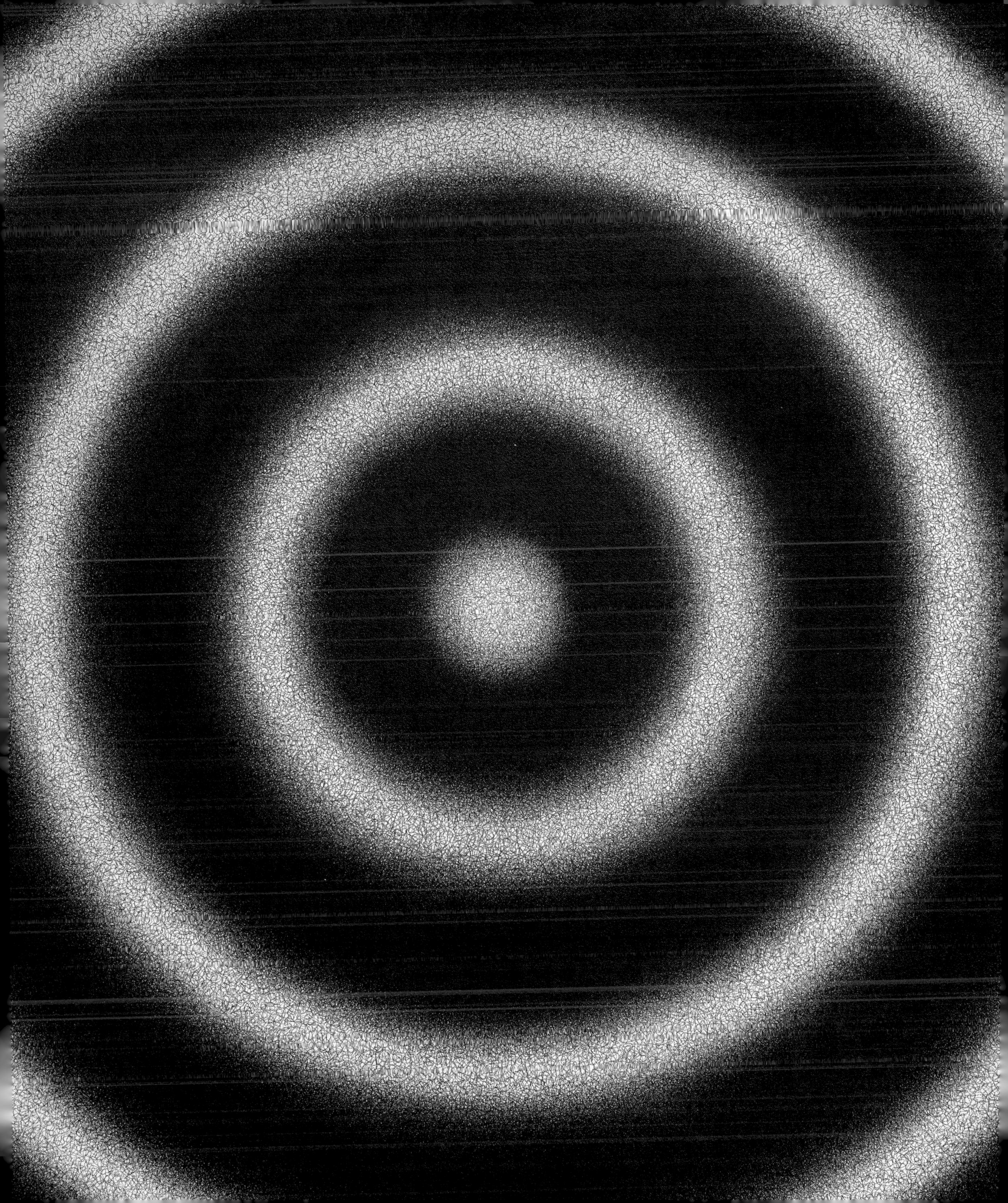

Project History

Conceived by the Yale University Art Gallery in collaboration with Sol LeWitt, and undertaken by Yale, MASS MoCA, and Williams College Museum of Art, *Sol LeWitt: A Wall Drawing Retrospective* opened at MASS MoCA on November 16, 2008. The landmark installation includes forty years of work by one of the most influential contemporary artists of the last half century.

Covering nearly an acre of wall surface, the installation consists of 105 works created from 1968 to 2008. The show will remain on view for twenty-five years in a 27,000-square-foot historic mill building located in the heart of MASS MoCA's campus and renovated specifically for this installation. The drawings were executed over a six-month period by twenty-four assistants, many of whom worked with the artist over many years, and even decades. They were joined by thirty students from Yale University, Williams College, and Massachusetts College of Liberal Arts, as well as by graduate and undergraduate students from other colleges and universities around the country.

The impetus for *Sol LeWitt: A Wall Drawing Retrospective* was a 2004 conversation between Jock Reynolds, the Henry J. Heinz II Director of the Yale University Art Gallery, and LeWitt. Their conversation evolved and resulted in a commitment by the artist to give a substantial number of his wall drawings and his entire wall-drawing archive to the Yale University Art Gallery, which already owned an extensive array of LeWitt's art in a variety of mediums. Yale, in turn, committed to undertake a definitive catalogue raisonné and to hire a curator/archivist to oversee the long-term conservation, research, and general scholarship for LeWitt's installed body of wall drawings around the world. Realizing that the Yale University Art Gallery did not have enough space to install and maintain a large number of the artist's wall drawings at any one time, Reynolds suggested to LeWitt that MASS MoCA, with its vast complex, its reputation for commissioning new projects, and its commitment to training student interns, might be able to realize an extended retrospective of the works.

Reynolds and LeWitt then met with MASS MoCA director Joseph C. Thompson and toured the museum's campus of industrial buildings, where the artist was immediately intrigued by Building 7. The structure, situated at the center of MASS MoCA's multi-building campus and characterized by large banks of windows that open onto two flanking courtyards, appealed to LeWitt as an ideal site for a multi-floor installation of his work. The three-story building was extensively reworked for this exhibition by architects Bruner/Cott & Associates, including a complex sequence of new interior walls designed in close collaboration with LeWitt himself. The partition layouts on the three floors create cloister-like rooms and passages that contain LeWitt's wall drawings, but also long sight lines and large, light-filled spaces, emphasizing the contrast between the new installations and the original brick surfaces of the building's perimeter walls.

Renovation of Building 7 began in early 2007, and although seriously ill at the time, LeWitt lived long enough to know that his wall-drawing retrospective was well under way. As one of the founders of Conceptual art, he was known for saying, "It's hard to bungle a good idea," and with this spirit he enthusiastically embraced this collaborative endeavor. What followed thereafter was indeed quite simple, and the results of a "good idea" are plain to see.

Exhibition Checklist

Wall Drawing 11: A wall divided horizontally and vertically into four equal parts. Within each part, three of the four kinds of lines are superimposed. May 1969. Black pencil. Yale University Art Gallery, New Haven. Gift of Anna Marie and Robert F. Shapiro, B.A. 1956. First drawn by: Jerry Orter, Adrian Piper, Sol LeWitt. First installation: Paula Cooper Gallery, New York.

Wall Drawing 16: Bands of lines 12 inches (30 cm) wide, in three directions (vertical, horizontal, diagonal right) intersecting. September 1969. Black pencil. Collection Michalke. First drawn by: James Walker. First installation: Institute of Contemporary Art, London.

Wall Drawing 17: Four-part drawing with a different line direction in each part. September 1969. Black pencil. Panza Collection. First drawn by: Steven Gwon, Chris Hansen, T. Julia, Al Williams, Sol LeWitt. First installation: Dwan Gallery, New York.

Wall Drawing 19: A wall divided vertically into six equal parts, with two of the four kinds of line directions superimposed in each part. September 1969. Black pencil. Panza Collection. First drawn by: Steven Gwon, Chris Hansen, T. Julia, Al Williams, Sol LeWitt. First installation: Dwan Gallery, New York.

Wall Drawing 38: Tissue paper cut into 1½-inch (4 cm) squares and inserted into holes in the gray pegboard walls. All holes in the walls are filled randomly (detail: three walls of four). April 1970. Colored tissue paper, gray pegboard walls. Panza Collection. First installation: Tokyo Biennial, Tokyo.

Wall Drawing 46: Vertical lines, not straight, not touching, covering the wall evenly. May 1970. Black pencil. LeWitt Collection, Chester, Connecticut. First drawn by: Sol LeWitt. First installation: Yvon Lambert, Paris.

Wall Drawing 47: A wall divided vertically into fifteen equal parts, each with a different line direction, and all combinations. June 1970. Black pencil. Private collection. First drawn by: Kazuko Miyamoto. First installation: Private residence.

Wall Drawing 51: All architectural points connected by straight lines. June 1970. Blue snap lines. LeWitt Collection, Chester, Connecticut. First drawn by: P. Giacchi, A. Giamasco, G. Mosca. First installation: Galleria Sperone, Turin and Museo di Torino, Turin.

Wall Drawing 56: A square is divided horizontally and vertically into four equal parts, each with lines in four directions superimposed progressively. August 1970. Black pencil. LeWitt Collection, Chester, Connecticut. First drawn by: Sol LeWitt. First installation: LeWitt residence, New York.

Wall Drawing 85: A wall is divided into four horizontal parts. In the top row are four equal divisions, each with lines in a different direction. In the second row, six double combinations; in the third row, four triple combinations; in the bottom row, all four combinations superimposed. June 1971. Colored pencil. LeWitt Collection, Chester, Connecticut. First drawn by: Sol LeWitt. First installation: LeWitt residence, New York.

Wall Drawing 86: Ten thousand lines about 10 inches (25 cm) long, covering the wall evenly. June 1971. Black pencil. Private collection. First drawn by: R. Holcomb, Kazuko Miyamoto. First installation: The Rykert Gallery, New York.

Wall Drawing 87: A square divided horizontally and vertically into four equal parts, each with lines and colors in four directions superimposed progressively. June 1971. Colored pencil. LeWitt Collection, Chester, Connecticut. First drawn by: Sol LeWitt. First installation: LeWitt residence, New York.

Wall Drawing 88: A 6-inch (15 cm) grid covering the wall. Within each square, not straight lines in either of four directions. Only one direction in each square but as many as desired, and at least one line in each square. June 1971. Black pencil. Milwaukee Art Museum, Gift of Friends of Art, M2006.1. First drawn by: William Torphy. First installation: The Milwaukee Art Center, Milwaukee.

Wall Drawing 95: On a wall divided vertically into fifteen equal parts, vertical lines, not straight, using four colors in all one-, two-, three-, and four-part combinations. July 1971. Colored pencil. Centre Pompidou, Paris. Musée national d'art moderne/Centre de création industrielle. First drawn by: Sol LeWitt. First installation: Toselli Gallery, Milan.

Wall Drawing 130: Grid and arcs from four corners (ACG 103). March 1972. Black pencil. LeWitt Collection, Chester, Connecticut. First drawn by: S. Kato, Ryo Watanabe. First installation: Paul Toner residence, New York.

Wall Drawing 138: Circles and arcs from the midpoints of four sides (ACG 59). July 1972. Black pencil. Courtesy of the Estate of Sol LeWitt. First drawn by: P. de Jong, Sol LeWitt, F. Spillemackers, L. Verdeeck. First installation: MTL Gallery, Brussels.

Wall Drawing 142: A 10-inch (25 cm) grid covering the wall. An increasing number of vertical not straight lines from the left side and horizontal not straight lines from bottom to top, adding one line per row of the grid. All lines are spaced evenly based on the number of lines, filling the last row of each direction. June 1972. Black pencil. Courtesy of the Estate of Sol LeWitt. First drawn by: Jo Watanabe. First installation: Private residence

Wall Drawing 146A: All two-part combinations of arcs from corners and sides, and straight, not straight, and broken lines within a 36-inch (90 cm) grid. June 2000. White crayon on blue wall. LeWitt Collection, Chester, Connecticut. First drawn by: Mio St. Clair, Ginger Wolfe, James Kendrick. First installation: Museum of Contemporary Art, Chicago.

Wall Drawing 154: A black outlined square with a red horizontal line from the midpoint of the left side toward the middle of the right side. April 1973. Red and black crayon. Courtesy of the Estate of Sol LeWitt (Designated for Yale University Art Gallery). First drawn by: Sol LeWitt, Nicholas Logsdail. First installation: Museum of Modern Art, Oxford, England.

Wall Drawing 159: A black outlined square with a red diagonal line from the lower left corner toward the upper right corner; and another red line from the lower right corner to the upper left. April 1973. Red and black crayon. Private collection, Durham, North Carolina. First drawn by: Sol LeWitt, Nicholas Logsdail. First installation: Museum of Modern Art, Oxford, England.

Wall Drawing 160: A black outlined square with a red diagonal line centered on the axis between the upper left and lower right corners and another red diagonal line centered on the axis between the lower left and upper right corners. April 1973. Red and black crayon. Courtesy of the Estate of Sol LeWitt. First drawn by: Sol LeWitt, Nicholas Logsdail. First installation: Museum of Modern Art, Oxford, England.

Wall Drawing 164: A black outlined square with a red horizontal line centered on the axis between the midpoint of the left side and the midpoint of the right side and a red diagonal line centered on the axis between the lower left and upper right corners. April 1973. Red and black crayon. Courtesy of the Estate of Sol LeWitt. First drawn by: Sol LeWitt, Nicholas Logsdail. First installation: Museum of Modern Art, Oxford, England.

Wall Drawing 237: The location of a trapezoid. June 1974. Black pencil and black crayon. Courtesy of the Estate of Sol LeWitt. First drawn by: Sol LeWitt. First installation: Galleria Sperone, Turin.

Wall Drawing 238: The location of a parallelogram. June 1974. Black pencil and black crayon. LeWitt Collection, Chester, Connecticut. First drawn by: Sol LeWitt. First installation: Galleria Sperone, Turin.

Wall Drawing 274: The location of six geometric figures. (The specific locations are determined by the draftsman.) September 1975. Black pencil and black crayon. The Art Institute of Chicago, through prior gifts of Judith Neisser and Mary and Leigh Block; Norman Waite Harris Purchase Fund, 2006.166. First drawn by: Steingrim Laursen, Sol LeWitt. First installation: Gentofte Kommunes Kunstbibliotek, Copenhagen.

Wall Drawing 289: A 6-inch (15 cm) grid covering each of four black walls. White lines to points on the grids. Fourth wall: twenty-four lines from the center, twelve lines from the midpoint of each of the sides, twelve lines from each corner. (The length of the lines and their placement are determined by the draftsman.) (detail: fourth wall only). July 1976. White crayon lines and black pencil grid on black wall. Whitney Museum of American Art, New York, Purchase, with funds from the Gilman Foundation, Inc. 78.1.1–4. First drawn by: Jo Watanabe. First installation: Detroit Institute of Arts, Detroit. First Installation (fourth wall only): The Museum of Modern Art, New York, January 1978.

Wall Drawing 295: Six white geometric figures (outlines) superimposed on a black wall. October 1976. White crayon on black wall. Los Angeles County Museum of Art, Purchased with matching funds from the National Endowment for the Arts and the Modern and Contemporary Art Council (M.76.103). First drawn by: Chris D'Arcangelo, Sol LeWitt. First installation: Claire Copley Gallery, Los Angeles.

Wall Drawing 305: The location of one hundred random specific points. (The locations are determined by the draftsman.) August 1977. Black pencil and black crayon. Courtesy of the Estate of Sol LeWitt. First drawn by: Jo Watanabe, Sol LeWitt. First installation: Art & Architecture Building, Yale University, New Haven.

Wall Drawing 335: On four black walls, white vertical parallel lines, and in the center of the walls, eight geometric figures (including cross, X) within which are white horizontal parallel lines. The vertical lines do not enter the figures (detail: Square and Circle). May 1980. White crayon on black wall. Tate: Purchased 1980. First drawn by: David Connearn, Jo Watanabe. First installation: Lisson Gallery, London.

Wall Drawing 340: Six-part drawing. The wall is divided horizontally and vertically into six equal parts. First part: On red, blue horizontal parallel lines, and in the center, a circle within which are yellow vertical parallel lines; second part: On yellow, red horizontal parallel lines, and in the center, a square within which are blue vertical parallel lines; third part: On blue, yellow horizontal parallel lines, and in the center, a triangle within which are red vertical parallel lines; fourth part: On red, yellow horizontal parallel lines, and in the center, a rectangle within which are blue vertical parallel lines; fifth part: On yellow, blue horizontal parallel lines, and in the center, a trapezoid within which are red vertical parallel lines; sixth part: On blue, red horizontal parallel lines, and in the center, a parallelogram within which are yellow vertical parallel lines. The horizontal lines do not enter the figures. July 1980. Red, yellow, blue crayon on red, yellow and blue wall. Carnegie Museum of Art, Pittsburgh; Purchase: gift of Carol R. Brown and Family and A.W. Mellon Acquisition Endowment Fund, 84.79.1. First drawn by: Jo Watanabe. First installation: ROSC, Dublin.

Wall Drawing 343A (Circle); Wall Drawing 343B (Square); Wall Drawing 343C (Triangle): On a black wall, nine geometric figures (including right triangle, cross, X) in squares. The backgrounds are filled in solid white. December 1980. White crayon on black wall. Private collection, Switzerland, courtesy BFAS Blondeau Fine Arts Services. First drawn by: Jo Watanabe. First installation: Gagosian Gallery, Venice, California.

Wall Drawing 343D (Rectangle); Wall Drawing 343E (Trapezoid); Wall Drawing 343F (Parallelogram): On a black wall, nine geometric figures (including right triangle, cross, X) in squares. The backgrounds are filled in solid white. December 1980. White crayon on black wall. Courtesy of the Estate of Sol LeWitt. First drawn by: Jo Watanabe. First installation: Gagosian Gallery, Venice, California.

Wall Drawing 365: A square divided horizontally and vertically into four equal parts, each with a progressively darker gradation of gray. February 1984. India ink wash and color ink wash. LeWitt Collection, Chester, Connecticut. First drawn by: David Higginbotham, Anthony Sansotta, and others. First installation: Stedelijk Museum, Amsterdam.

Wall Drawing 381: A square divided horizontally and vertically into four equal parts, one gray, one yellow, one red and one blue, drawn with color and India ink washes. December 1982. India ink wash and color ink wash. LeWitt Collection, Chester, Connecticut. First drawn by: Anthony Sansotta. First installation: John Weber Gallery, New York.

Wall Drawing 386: Stars with three, four, five, six, seven, eight, and nine points, drawn with a light tone India ink wash inside, an India ink wash outside, separated by a 6-inch (15 cm) white band. January 1983. India ink wash. Courtesy of the Estate of Sol LeWitt. First drawn by: Julie Jarvis, Renee Miliken, Anthony Sansotta. First installation: Carol Taylor Art, Dallas.

Wall Drawing 391: Two-part drawing. The two walls are each divided horizontally and vertically into four equal parts. First wall: 12-inch (30 cm) bands of lines in four directions, one direction in each part, drawn in black India ink. Second wall: Same, but with four colors drawn in India ink and color ink washes. April 1983. India ink, India ink wash and color ink wash. Musée d'Art Contemporain de Bordeaux (CAPC). First drawn by: Salah 'Abid, Jean-Luc Arvers, Michel Harismendy, David Higginbotham, Jean Marie Perrier, Francois Robert, Anthony Sansotta. First installation: Musée d'Art Contemporain de Bordeaux, Bordeaux.

Wall Drawing 396: A black five-pointed star, a yellow six-pointed star, a red seven-pointed star, and a blue eight-pointed star, drawn in color and India ink washes. May 1983. India ink wash and color ink wash. LeWitt Collection, Chester, Connecticut. First drawn by: Oriano Baldelli, Alain Bolzan, Luca Constantini, Eduard Winkließer. First installation: Accademia de Belle Arti, Perugia.

Wall Drawing 413: Drawing Series IV (A) with color ink washes (24 drawings). March 1984. Color ink wash. LeWitt Collection, Chester, Connecticut. First drawn by: David Higginbotham, Jo Watanabe. First installation: Moderna Museet, Stockholm.

Wall Drawing 414: Drawing Series IV (A) with India ink washes (24 drawings). March 1984. India ink wash. LeWitt Collection, Chester, Connecticut. First drawn by: David Higginbotham, Jo Watanabe. First installation: Moderna Museet, Stockholm.

Wall Drawing 415D: Double Drawing. Right: Isometric figure (Cube) with progressively darker gradations of gray on each of three planes; Left: Isometric figure with red, yellow, and blue superimposed progressively on each of the three planes. The background is gray. March 1993. Color ink wash. LeWitt Collection, Chester, Connecticut. First drawn by: John Crowley, Christina Hejtmanek, Addison Parks, Anthony Sansotta, Mark Snow, Eric Ziemann. First installation: Addison Gallery of American Art, Phillips Academy, Andover, Massachusetts.

Wall Drawing 419: The wall is bordered and divided horizontally and vertically into four equal parts with a 6-inch (15 cm) black ink band. Each quarter has alternating parallel 6-inch (15 cm) bands of white and color ink bands. Upper left: gray; upper right: yellow; lower left: red; lower right: blue. September 1984. Color ink wash. LeWitt Collection, Chester, Connecticut. First drawn by: Takeshi Arita, David Higginbotham. First installation: Yvon Lambert, Paris.

Wall Drawing 422: The room (or wall) is divided vertically into fifteen parts. All one-, two-, three-, and four-part combinations of four colors, using color ink washes. November 1984. Color ink wash. Courtesy of the Estate of Sol LeWitt. First drawn by: Anthony Sansotta, Marien Schouten, Wim Starkenburg, Willem Wolff. First installation: Stedelijk Museum, Amsterdam.

Wall Drawing 439: Asymmetrical pyramid with color ink washes superimposed. May 1985. Color ink wash. Cuomo Collection. First drawn by: David Higginbotham, Jo Watanabe. First installation: Sala de Exposiciones de la Fundación, Caja de Pensiones, Madrid.

Wall Drawing 462: On four walls, one room, arcs 4 inches (10 cm) wide, from the midpoints of four sides, drawn with alternating bands of gray and black ink wash (detail: three walls). January 1986. India ink wash. LeWitt Collection, Chester, Connecticut. First drawn by: Sergio Cavazzini, Mauro Pittaccolo, Anthony Sansotta, Sergio Sarra. First installation: Galleria Studio G7, Bologna.

Wall Drawing 527: Two flat-topped pyramids with color ink washes superimposed (detail: one of two pyramids). April 1987. Color ink wash. Courtesy of the Estate of Sol LeWitt. First drawn by: Fransje Killaars, Ton van der Laaken, Roy Villevoye. First installation: Bonnefantenmuseum, Maastricht, The Netherlands.

Wall Drawing 552D: Tilted forms with color ink washes superimposed. December 1987. Color ink wash. Courtesy of the Estate of Sol LeWitt. First drawn by: David Higginbotham, Linda Taylor, Jo Watanabe. First installation: Royal Scottish Academy, Edinburgh.

Wall Drawing 579: Three concentric arches. The outside one is blue; the middle red; and the inside one is yellow. November 1988. Color ink wash. Private collection, New York. First drawn by: Andrea Marescalchi. First installation: Sala 1, Rome.

Wall Drawing 583F: Rectangles, with color ink washes superimposed. Each is bordered by a 10-inch (25 cm) band with color ink washes superimposed, a ½-inch (1¼ cm) white band, and a 4-inch (10 cm) black band. December 1988. Color ink wash. Courtesy of the Estate of Sol LeWitt (designated for Yale University Art Gallery). First drawn by: Connie Butler, Douglas Geiger, Paul Mankins, Tory Pomeroy, Anthony Sansotta, Rebecca Schwab, Janice Shotwell, Michael Willoughby. First installation: Des Moines Art Center, Des Moines.

Wall Drawing 583H: Rectangles, with color ink washes superimposed. Each is bordered by a 10-inch (25 cm) band with color ink washes superimposed, a ½-inch (1¼ cm) white band, and a 4-inch (10 cm) black band. December 1988. Color ink wash. Courtesy of the Estate of Sol LeWitt. First drawn by: Connie Butler, Douglas Geiger, Paul Mankins, Tory Pomeroy, Anthony Sansotta, Rebecca Schwab, Janice Shotwell, Michael Willoughby. First installation: Des Moines Art Center, Des Moines.

Wall Drawing 584H: Squares, divided horizontally and vertically into four equal parts. Within each part, color ink washes superimposed. The squares are bordered by a ½-inch (1¼ cm) white band and a 4-inch (10 cm) black band. January 1989. Color ink wash. Courtesy of the Estate of Sol LeWitt. First drawn by: Babette Berger, Vincent Chablais, David Higginbotham, Marianne Kohler, Maria Lichsteiner, Michael Lüscher, Andrea Marescalchi, Axel Morgenthaler, Anthony Sansotta, Martin Schnidrig, Rebecca Schwab, Claude Spiess, Lucia Stäuble, Sigi Stucki. First Installation: Kunsthalle Bern, Bern.

Wall Drawing 610: Isometric figure with color ink washes superimposed. June 1989. Color ink wash. Courtesy of the Estate of Sol LeWitt. First drawn by: David Higginbotham, Elizabeth Sacre. First installation: Fundacio Joan Miró, Barcelona.

Wall Drawing 614: Rectangles formed by 3-inch (8 cm) wide India ink bands, meeting at right angles. July 1989. India ink. Yale University Art Gallery, Gift of the artist. First drawn by: David Higginbotham, Liam Longman, Philip Riley, Jim Rogers, Elizabeth Sacre. First installation: Lisson Gallery, London.

Wall Drawing 630: A wall is divided horizontally into two equal parts. Top: alternating horizontal black and white 8-inch (20 cm) bands. Bottom: alternating vertical black and white 8-inch (20 cm) bands. January 1990. India ink. Collection of Frances Dittmer. First drawn by: Paul Kleijne, Milco Onrust, Marien Schouten. First installation: Galerie Onrust, Amsterdam.

Wall Drawing 631: A wall is divided into two equal parts by a line drawn from corner to corner. Left: alternating diagonal black and white 8-inch (20 cm) bands from the lower left. Right: alternating diagonal black and white 8-inch (20 cm) bands from the upper right. January 1990. India ink. Collection of Frances Dittmer. First drawn by: Paul Kleijne, Milco Onrust, Marien Schouten. First installation: Galerie Onrust, Amsterdam.

Wall Drawing 681C: A wall divided vertically into four equal squares separated and bordered by black bands. Within each square, bands in one of four directions, each with color ink washes superimposed. August 1993. Color ink wash. National Gallery of Art, Washington, D.C. Dorothy and Herbert Vogel Collection, 1993. First drawn by: Sachiko Cho, Kei Tsujimura. First installation: National Gallery of Art, Washington, D.C.

Wall Drawing 684A: Squares bordered and divided horizontally and vertically into four equal squares, each with bands in one of four directions. June 1999. Color ink wash. Courtesy of the Estate of Sol LeWitt. First drawn by: Fransje Killaars, Roy Villevoye. First installation: Galerie Franck + Schulte, Berlin.

Wall Drawing 692: Continuous forms with color ink washes superimposed. October 1991. Color ink wash. Collection of Martin E. Zimmerman/LFC. First drawn by: Rebecca Schwab. First installation: LINC Group, Chicago.

Wall Drawing 725: On a blue wall, a black square within a white border. April 1993. India ink, color ink wash, gouache. Yale University Art Gallery, Katharine Ordway Fund. First drawn by: Sachiko Cho, Leslie Maloney, Shawn Perry, Anthony Sansotta, Philip Sirois. First installation: Addison Gallery of American Art, Phillips Academy, Andover, Massachusetts.

Wall Drawing 766: Twenty-one isometric cubes of varying sizes, each with color ink washes superimposed. September 1994. Color ink wash. San Francisco Museum of Modern Art, Accessions Committee Fund, gift of Barbara and Gerson Bakar, Emily Carroll and Thomas Weisel, Jean and James E. Douglas, Jr., Evelyn D. Haas, the Modern Art Council, Phyllis and Stuart G. Moldaw, Robin Wright Moll, Norah and Norman Stone, Danielle and Brooks Walker Jr., and Judy and John Webb. First drawn by: Isabelle Beaumont, Antoine Bonhomme, Flavien Damarigny, Anthony Sansotta. First installation: Renn Espace, Paris.

Wall Drawing 792: Black rectangles and squares. June 1995. Dispersion paint. Courtesy of the Estate of Sol LeWitt. First drawn by: Alge Algermissen, Sabine Griesingen, Paul James Haworth, Hartmt Hengerer, Anthony Sansotta, Jeroen van der Velden, Miriam Wawrzihek, Jogi Wegrzyn. First installation: Ludwigsburger Schlossfestspiele, Ludwigsburg.

Wall Drawing 793B: Irregular wavy color bands. January 1996. Color ink wash. Courtesy of the Estate of Sol LeWitt. First drawn by: Sachiko Cho, Jo Watanabe. First installation: Sala de las Alhajas, Madrid.

Wall Drawing 797: The first drafter has a black marker and makes an irregular horizontal line near the top of the wall. Then the second drafter tries to copy it (without touching it) using a red marker. The third drafter does the same, using a yellow marker. The fourth drafter does the same, using a blue marker. Then the second drafter, followed by the third and fourth, copies the last line drawn until the bottom of the wall is reached. October 1995. Black, red, yellow, blue marker. Courtesy of the Estate of Sol LeWitt (Designated for Yale University Art Gallery). First drawn by: Jeffrey Howington, Andrea Latvis, Peggy Soung, Lisa Yurwit. First installation: Mead Art Museum, Amherst College, Amherst, Massachusetts.

Wall Drawing 821: A black square divided horizontally and vertically into four equal parts, each with a different direction of alternating flat and glossy bands. April 1997. Acrylic paint. The Art Institute of Chicago, through prior gifts of Judith Neisser and Mary and Leigh Block; Norman Waite Harris Purchase Fund, 2006.168. First drawn by: Sachiko Cho, Artistides Dé Leon, Derek Edwards, Naomi Fox, Henry Levine, Sunhee Lim, Jason Livingston, Emil Memon, Travis Molkenbur, Caroline Rothwell. First installation: Ace Gallery, New York.

Wall Drawing 821A: A white square divided horizontally and vertically into four equal parts, each with a different direction of alternating flat and glossy bands. March 2007. Acrylic paint. LeWitt Collection, Chester, Connecticut. First drawn by: John Hogan. First installation: Sean Kelly Gallery, New York.

Wall Drawing 822: A wall divided horizontally by a curvy line. The top is flat black; the bottom is glossy black. April 1997. Acrylic paint. Courtesy of the Estate of Sol LeWitt. First drawn by: Artistides Dé Leon, Sachiko Cho, Derek Edwards, Naomi Fox, Henry Levine, Sunhee Lim, Jason Livingston, Emil Memon, Travis Molkenbur, Caroline Rothwell. First installation: Ace Gallery, New York.

Wall Drawing 824A, 824B, 824C, 824E, 824F: A black square divided in two parts by a wavy line. One part flat; one glossy. April 1997. Acrylic paint. All courtesy of the Estate of Sol LeWitt (Designated for Yale University Art Gallery). First drawn by: Artistides Dé Leon, Sachiko Cho, Derek Edwards, Naomi Fox, Henry Levine, Sunhee Lim, Jason Livingston, Emil Memon, Travis Molkenbur, Caroline Rothwell. First installation: Ace Gallery, New York.

Wall Drawing 824G: A black square divided in two parts by a wavy line. One part flat; one glossy. April 1997. Acrylic paint. Lent by Alan Gibbs. First drawn by: Artistides Dé Leon, Sachiko Cho, Derek Edwards, Naomi Fox, Henry Levine, Sunhee Lim, Jason Livingston, Emil Memon, Travis Molkenbur, Caroline Rothwell. First installation: Ace Gallery, New York.

Wall Drawing 824H, 824J, 824K, 824L, 824M, 824N: A black square divided in two parts by a wavy line. One part flat; one glossy. April 1997. Acrylic paint. All courtesy of the Estate of Sol LeWitt (Designated for Yale University Art Gallery). First drawn by: Artistides Dé Leon, Sachiko Cho, Derek Edwards, Naomi Fox, Henry Levine, Sunhee Lim, Jason Livingston, Emil Memon, Travis Molkenbur, Caroline Rothwell. First installation: Ace Gallery, New York.

Wall Drawing 852: A wall divided from the upper left to the lower right by a curvy line; left: glossy yellow; right: glossy purple. June 1998. Acrylic paint. Courtesy of the Estate of Sol LeWitt. First drawn by: Cristina Caterinangeli, Anthony Sansotta. First installation: Galleria d'Arte Moderna e Contemporanea Palazzo Forti, Verona.

Wall Drawing 853: A wall bordered and divided vertically into two parts by a flat black band. Left part: a square is divided vertically by a curvy line. Left: glossy red; right: glossy green; Right part: a square is divided horizontally by a curvy line. Top: glossy blue; bottom: glossy orange. June 1998. Acrylic paint. Courtesy of the Estate of Sol LeWitt. First drawn by: Cristina Caterinangeli, Anthony Sansotta. First installation: Galleria d'Arte Moderna e Contemporanea Palazzo Forti, Verona.

Wall Drawing 880: Loopy Doopy (orange and green). September 1998. Acrylic paint. Addison Gallery of American Art, Andover, Massachusetts; partial gift of the artist and partial museum purchase with funds from Mimi Won Techentin and anonymous donor. First drawn by: Elizabeth Alderman, Sachiko Cho, Edy Ferguson, Anders Felix Paux Hedberg, Choichi Nishikawa, Jim Prez, Emily Ripley, Mio Takashima. First installation: PaceWildenstein, New York.

Wall Drawing 901: Color bands and black blob. The wall is divided vertically into six equal bands: red, yellow, blue, orange, purple, green. In the center is a black glossy blob. May 1999. Acrylic paint. Courtesy of the Estate of Sol LeWitt (Designated for Yale University Art Gallery). First drawn by: Elyce Abrams, David Dempewolf, Joy Feasley, Meghan Ganser, John Gibbons, Michael Gibbons, Chris Hensel, John Hogan, Beth Leatherman, Tristin Lowe, Stephen Malmed, Sarah McEneaney, Matthew Pruden, Scott Rigby, Paul Swenbeck, Clint Takeda. First installation: Institute of Contemporary Art, Philadelphia.

Wall Drawing 915: Arcs, circle, and irregular bands. September 1999. Acrylic paint. Courtesy of the Estate of Sol LeWitt. First drawn by: Dana Carlson, Christina Hejtmanek, Emily Ripley, James Sheehen. First installation: Paula Cooper Gallery, New York.

Wall Drawing 957: Form derived from a cube. November 2000. Black pencil. Collection of Deborah Ronnen. First drawn by: Mio St. Clair. First installation: Whitney Museum of American Art, New York.

Wall Drawing 958: Splat. November 2000. Acrylic paint. LeWitt Collection, Chester, Connecticut. First drawn by: Takeshi Arita, Cristina Caterinangeli, Sachiko Cho, Kevin Oster. First installation: PaceWildenstein, New York.

Wall Drawing 999: Parallel curves (detail: one of two walls). August 2001. Acrylic paint. Collection of Thomas Weisel. First drawn by: Paolo Arao, Nicole Awai, Ian Dapot, Megan Dyer, Sarah Heinemann, John Hogan, Eric Hongisto, Tomas Ramberg. First installation: Lever House, New York.

Wall Drawing 1005: Isometric form. December 2001. Acrylic paint. Courtesy of the Estate of Sol LeWitt. First drawn by: Ignacio Amespil, Cecilia de Arriba, Veronica del Toro, Tomas Fraccia, Francisco Gomez, Bruno Grisanti, Favio Guadagna, Walter Mantegazza, Erik Martinut, Barbara Mendez de Leo, Lola Quiroz, Anthony Sansotta, Santiago Solda. First installation: Fundación PROA, Buenos Aires.

Wall Drawing 1037: Bars of color within a square (#8). April 2002. Acrylic paint. Courtesy of the Estate of Sol LeWitt. First drawn by: Sachiko Cho, Pia Frade Dodriguez, Aurora Ortega, Rafael Aragon Romero. First installation: Galleria Juana de Aizpuru, Madrid.

Wall Drawing 1042: Isometric form. May 2002. Acrylic paint. Courtesy of the Estate of Sol LeWitt. First drawn by: Anthony Elms, John Hogan, Colleen Kelsey. First installation: Donald Young Gallery, Chicago.

Wall Drawing 1046: Bars of color (La Coruña). May 2002. Acrylic paint. Courtesy of the Estate of Sol LeWitt. First drawn by: German Tajes Camiño, Sachiko Cho, Jose Ramon Fraga, Manuel Gracia Solana, Jose Carlos Soliño, Constantino Diaz Vazquez, Jose Luis Vazquez, Jo Watanabe. First installation: Fundación Pedro Barrié de la Maza, La Coruña.

Wall Drawing 1081. Planes of color. March 2003. Acrylic paint. Courtesy of the Estate of Sol LeWitt (Designated for Yale University Art Gallery). First drawn by: José Augusto, Michael Aurich, Proa Daniel, Megan Dyer, Jan Kummer, Frank Maibier, Hilmar Messenbrink, Erik Neukirchner, Tomas Ramberg, Ralph [illegible]. Kunstammlungen Chemnitz, Chemnitz.

Wall Drawing 1094: Projecting form. May 2003. Colored pencil (scribbles). Collezione La Gaia, Busca, Italy. First drawn by: Anthony Sansotta, Angelo Volpe. First installation: Alfonso Artiaco, Pozzuoli, Italy.

Wall Drawing 1094A: Projecting form. July 2003. Colored pencil. Courtesy of the Estate of Sol LeWitt. First drawn by: Jason Rulnick, Anthony Sansotta. First installation: PaceWildenstein, New York.

Wall Drawing 1112: Square with broken bands of color. December 2003. Acrylic paint. LeWitt Collection, Chester, Connecticut. First drawn by: Juozas Cernius, Vincent Como, Sandra Dillon, John Hogan, Josh Mills. First installation: Rhona Hoffman Gallery, Chicago.

Wall Drawing 1152: Whirls and twirls (Met). April 2005. Acrylic paint. LeWitt Collection, Chester, Connecticut. First drawn by: Takeshi Arita, Sarah Heinemann, Gabriel Hurier, Chie Shimizu. First installation: Iris and B. Gerald Cantor Roof Garden, Metropolitan Museum of Art, New York.

Wall Drawing 1171: Five degrees of scribbles: A cube without a cube; A cube without a corner. August 2005. Black pencil. Collection of Arne and Milly Glimcher. First drawn by: Anthony Sansotta, Roland Lusk. First installation: Glimcher residence, East Hampton, New York.

Wall Drawing 1185: Scribbles: Inverted curve (horizontal). October 2005. Graphite. Courtesy of the Estate of Sol LeWitt. First drawn by: Rachela Abbate, Asmir Ademagic, Marco Bertozzi, Elisa Cancucci, Alessandra Frisan, Elena Latini, Luca Lolli, Viviana Longo, Benny Mangone, Juri Marsigli, Anthony Sansotta, Maria Lucrezia Schiavarelli, Francesca Simeone, Alessio Tugnoli, Simone Vagnetti. First installation: Galleria Studio G7, Bologna.

Wall Drawing 1186: Scribbles: Inverted curve (vertical). October 2005. Graphite. Collection of Alessandro Maccaferri. First drawn by: Rachela Abbate, Asmir Ademagic, Marco Bertozzi, Elisa Cancucci, Alessandra Frisan, Elena Latini, Luca Lolli, Viviana Longo, Benny Mangone, Juri Marsigli, Anthony Sansotta, Maria Lucrezia Schiavarelli, Francesca Simeone, Alessio Tugnoli, Simone Vagnetti. First installation: Galleria Studio G7, Bologna.

Wall Drawing 1211: Drawing Series—Part I–IV, #1–24, A+B (192 drawings). August 2006. Colored pencil. Courtesy of the Estate of Sol LeWitt. First drawn by: Lacey Fekishazy, Mary Gagne, Nick Kozak, Roland Lusk, Tanya Merrill, Darin Roberts, Anthony Sansotta. First installation: Dia:Beacon, Beacon, New York.

Wall Drawing 1247: Scribbles 7 (PW). August 2007. Graphite. Collection of Mr. and Mrs. Donald Fisher, San Francisco. First drawn by: Charles Allen, Takeshi Arita, Andrew Colbert, Sarah Heinemann, John Hogan, Gabriel Hurier, Sara Krugman, Roland Lusk, Anthony Sansotta, Michael Benjamin Vedder. First installation: PaceWildenstein, New York.

Wall Drawing 1260: Scribble: Square without a square. July 2008. Graphite. LeWitt Collection, Chester, Connecticut. First drawn by: Takeshi Arita, Jennifer Chian, Aran Jones, Michael Benjamin Vedder. First Installation: MASS MoCA, North Adams, Massachusetts.

Wall Drawing 1261: Scribbles (Yale). July 2008. Graphite. Courtesy of the Estate of Sol LeWitt (Designated for Yale University Art Gallery). First drawn by: Takeshi Arita, Jennifer Chian, Aran Jones, Michael Benjamin Vedder. First installation: MASS MoCA, North Adams, Massachusetts.

Selected Exhibition History
(Solo Exhibitions)

Please also see Gary Garrels, ed. *Sol LeWitt: A Retrospective*, Exh. Cat., New Haven and London: Yale University Press, 2000 and Alicia Legg, ed. *Sol LeWitt*, Exh. Cat., New York: The Museum of Modern Art, 1978.

1965
John Daniels Gallery, New York

1966
Dwan Gallery, New York

1967
Dwan Gallery, Los Angeles

1968
Galerie Konrad Fischer, Düsseldorf

Dwan Gallery, New York

Galerie Bischofberger, Zürich

Galerie Heiner Friederich, Munich

Ace Gallery, Los Angeles
(Catalogue)

1969
Galerie Konrad Fischer, Düsseldorf

Galleria L'Attico, Rome

Galerie Ernst, Hannover

Wall Drawings, Dwan
Gallery, New York

*Sol LeWitt: Sculptures and
Wall Drawings*, Museum
Haus Lange, Krefeld

Galerie Bischofberger, Zürich

1970
Art & Project, Amsterdam

Yvon Lambert, Paris

Wall Drawings, Galleria
Sperone, Turin

Dwan Gallery, New York

Lisson Gallery, London

Gemeentemuseum, The
Hague (Catalogue)

Galerie Heiner Friederich, Munich

Pasadena Art Museum, Pasadena,
California (Brochure)

1971
Wall Drawings, Protetch-Rivkin
Gallery, Washington, D.C.

Prints and Drawings,
Dwan Gallery, New York

Lisson Gallery, London

Galerie Stampa, Basel

Galleria Toselli, Milan

Informations-Raum 3, Basel

Galerie Konrad Fischer, Düsseldorf

Art & Project, Amsterdam

Structures and Wall Drawings,
John Weber Gallery, New York

Dunkelman Gallery, Toronto

1972
Wall Drawings, *Sculpture*, Hayden
Gallery, Massachusetts Institute
of Technology, Cambridge

Harkus-Krakow Gallery, Boston

Dayton Art Institute, Dayton

Kunsthalle Bern, Bern (Catalogue)

Gallery A-402, California
Institute of the Arts, Valencia

Anna Leonowens Gallery,
Nova Scotia College of
Art & Design, Halifax

Galerie MTL, Brussels

Galerie Konrad Fischer, Düsseldorf

Art & Project, Amsterdam

1973
Cercles & lignes: Sol LeWitt,
Yvon Lambert, Paris (Catalogue)

John Weber Gallery, New York

Rosa Esman Gallery, New York

Lisson Gallery, London

Museum of Modern Art,
Oxford, England

Galleria L'Attico, Rome

Galerie Toselli, Milan

Galleria Marilena Bonomo,
Bari (Catalogue)

Wall Drawings, Portland
Center for the Visual Arts,
Portland, Oregon (Catalogue)

Six Wall Drawings, Cusack
Gallery, Houston (Catalogue)

A Wall Drawing, Vehicule
Art, Inc., Montréal

Art & Project, Amsterdam/
Galerie MTL, Brussels

1974
Incomplete Open Cubes,
Yvon Lambert, Paris

Lisson Gallery, London

*The Location of Eight
Points*, Max Protetch Gallery,
Washington, D.C. (Catalogue)

*Location of Three Geometric
Figures*, Palais des Beaux
Arts, Brussels

Rijksmuseum Kröller Muller,
Otterlo, The Netherlands

Incomplete Open Cubes,
John Weber Gallery, New
York (Catalogue)

Galerie December,
Münster, Germany

Ace Gallery, Venice, California

Daniel Weinberg Gallery,
San Francisco

Galleria Sperone, Turin

Galleria Scipione, Macerata, Italy

Galerie Vega, Liège

Prints, Stedelijk Museum,
Amsterdam

Gian Enzo Sperone, New York

Fifty Drawings 1964–1974, New York Cultural Center, New York. Traveled to: Vancouver Art Gallery, Vancouver; Everson Museum of Art, Syracuse; High Museum of Art, Atlanta; San Francisco Museum of Modern Art, San Francisco; Mint Museum of Art, Charlotte; Tyler Museum of Art, Tyler, Texas; Arkansas Arts Center, Little Rock; University Galleries, Illinois State University, Normal, Illinois; The Winnipeg Art Gallery, Winnipeg; Herbert F. Johnson Museum of Art, Cornell University, Ithaca

1975

Sol LeWitt, The Location of a Rectangle: Matrix 3, Wadsworth Atheneum Museum of Art, Hartford

Wall Drawings, Israel Museum, Jerusalem (Catalogue)

Incomplete Open Cubes, Art & Project, Amsterdam

Incomplete Open Cubes and Wall Drawings, Scottish National Gallery of Modern Art, Edinburgh

Incomplete Open Cubes, Galleria Sperone, Turin

Graphik: 1970–1975, Kunsthalle Basel, Basel (Catalogue)

Incomplete Open Cubes, Kunsthalle Basel, Basel

Claire Copley Gallery, Los Angeles

Printmakers' Workshop, Edinburgh

Wall Drawings, Drawings, and Incomplete Open Cubes, Daniel Weinberg Gallery, San Francisco

Galerie Konrad Fischer, Düsseldorf

Saman Gallery, Genoa

Galleria Peccolo, Livorno, Italy

Lines and Color, Annemarie Verna Galerie, Zürich Traveled to: Rolf Preisig Gallery, Basel

Galeria Marilena Bonomo, Bari

1976

Visual Arts Museum, New York

Dag Hammarskjöld Plaza Sculpture Garden, New York

Incomplete Open Cubes, Cologneischer Kunstverein, Cologne

Gian Enzo Sperone, Rome

Drawings, Prints, and Cubes, B.R. Kornblatt Gallery, Baltimore

Wall Drawings, Structures, and Prints, Fine Arts Gallery, University of Colorado, Boulder

Wall Drawings, Claire Copley Gallery, Los Angeles

Incomplete Open Cubes, Centre d'Art Contemporain, Geneva

Geometric Figures, Galerie MTL, Brussels

Wall Drawings, Matrix Gallery, Wadsworth Atheneum Museum of Art, Hartford

Galerie T.H. Keller, Kempfenhausen, Germany

Incomplete Open Cubes, Stedelijk van Abbemuseum, Eindhoven

1977

Geometric Figures within Geometric Figures, Utah Museum of Fine Arts, Salt Lake City

Structures, John Weber Gallery, New York

Lisson Gallery, London

Geometric Figures, Galerie Konrad Fischer, Düsseldorf

The Art Gallery of New South Wales, Sydney (Catalogue)

Torre Vecchio, Spoleto; Galleria Marilena Bonomo, Bari

University of North Dakota Art Gallery, University of North Dakota, Grand Forks

Incomplete Open Cubes, Museum of Modern Art, Oxford, England

Saman Gallery, Genoa

Art & Architecture Gallery, Yale University, New Haven

Incomplete Open Cubes, Prints, and Wall Drawings, Fine Arts Center, University of Massachusetts, Amherst

1978

Graphics, 1970–1975, Brooklyn Museum of Art, New York

Geometric Figures, Rolf Preisig Gallery, Basel

Prints and Drawings, John Weber Gallery, New York

Protetch MacIntosh Gallery, Washington, D.C.

Drawings, Michael Berger Gallery, Pittsburgh

Galleria Marilena Bonomo, Bari

Hallen für Internationalle Neue Kunst, Zürich

Sol LeWitt, Museum of Modern Art, New York. Traveled to: Museum of Contemporary Art, Montréal; Krannert Museum of Art, University of Illinois, Champaign; Museum of Contemporary Art, Chicago; La Jolla Museum of Contemporary Art, La Jolla, California (Catalogue)

1979

Geometric Structures, Lisson Gallery, London

Konrad Fischer Gallery, Düsseldorf

Sol LeWitt: New Structures and Photogrids, Young Hoffman Gallery, Chicago

Yvon Lambert, Paris

Margo Leavin Gallery, Los Angeles

Rosa Esman Gallery, New York

The Graphics of Sol LeWitt, New Britain Museum of American Art, New Britain, Connecticut

1980

John Weber Gallery, New York

All Four-Part Combinations of Six Geometric Figures, Galerie Watari, Tokyo (Catalogue)

Galleria Marilena Bonomo, Bari

Grids & Color, Rudiger Schottle, Munich

Photogrids, Protetch MacIntosh Gallery, Washington, D.C.

Sol LeWitt: New Structures, Wall Drawings, Drawings, Young Hoffman Gallery, Chicago

Galleria Ugo Ferranti, Rome

Statues (A Melodrama), John Weber Gallery, New York

Sol LeWitt: Structures and Wall Drawings, Texas Gallery, Houston

Six Geometric Figures and All Their Double Combinations, Yvon Lambert, Paris (Catalogue)

1981

Mercer Union Art Gallery, Toronto

Saman Gallery, Genoa

Miami-Dade Community College Art Gallery, Miami-Dade Community College, Miami

Gagosian Gallery, Los Angeles

Sol LeWitt: New Structures; Works on Paper, David Bellman Gallery, Toronto

Project: Wall Drawings, Geometric Figures, Max Protetch Gallery, New York

Sol LeWitt: Strukturen 1978–80, Annemarie Verna Galerie, Zürich

Konrad Fischer Gallery, Düsseldorf

Palace of Culture, Warsaw

Sol LeWitt Wall Drawings: 1968–1981, Wadsworth Atheneum Museum of Art, Hartford

Sol LeWitt: Six Geometric Figures, Real Art Ways, Hartford

Paula Cooper Gallery, New York

Graphics 1 and 2, Boston

Wall Drawings and Drawings, Daniel Weinberg Gallery, San Francisco

Photogrids, Brick Wall, Autobiography, On the Walls of the Lower East Side, University Art Gallery, New Mexico State University, Las Cruces, New Mexico

Wall Drawings and Drawings, Graeme Murray Gallery, Edinburgh

Van Krimpen Gallery, Amsterdam

1982

Drawings, David Bellman Gallery, Toronto

Sol LeWitt Wall Drawings, The Kemper Room Art Gallery, Illinois Institute of Technology, Chicago

Sol LeWitt: Structures, Galleria Ugo Ferranti, Rome

Sol LeWitt: Wall Drawings, Galleria Marilena Bonomo, Bari

William Aronowitsch Gallery, Stockholm

Wall Drawings: Sol LeWitt, Rudiger Schöttle Gallery, Munich

Banco Gallery, Milan and Brescia

Young Hoffman Gallery, Chicago

Isometric Drawings, Paula Cooper Gallery, New York (Catalogue)

Barbara Toll Fine Arts, New York

1983

Wall Drawings, Aquatints, Woodcuts, Screenprints, Galeriet, Lund

Wall Drawings, Galleria Ugo Ferranti, Rome

CAPC Musée d'Art Contemporain de Bordeaux, Bordeaux

Accademia delle Belle
Arti, Perugia

Centre d'Art Contemporain,
Geneva

*Sol LeWitt: Drawings,
Watercolors and Prints,*
Lisson Gallery, London

Sol LeWitt: Three Portfolios, Brooke
Alexander Gallery, New York

Sol LeWitt: Star Prints,
Matrix Gallery, University
of California, Berkeley

Locus Solus, Genoa

Piramide, Galleria Mario
Pieroni, Rome

1984
*Sol LeWitt Wall Drawings
1968–1984,* Stedelijk Museum,
Amsterdam. Travelled to the
Stedelijk Museum, Amsterdam; van
Abbemuseum, Eindohoven; and
the Wadsworth Atheneum Museum
of Art, Hartford (Catalogue)

Structures, Stedelijk Van
Abbemuseum, Eindhoven

Books: 1968–1983, Gallery
A, Amsterdam

Wall Drawings, Gewad, Ghent

Wall Drawings, Raum
für Kunst, Hamburg

Wall Drawings and Drawings,
Annemarie Verna Galerie, Zürich

Wall Drawings, Au Fond de la
Cour À Droite, Chagny, France

Sol LeWitt Sculptures: 1964–1974,
Galerie Daniel Templon, Paris

Skulpturen von Sol LeWitt, Konrad
Fischer Gallery, Düsseldorf

Drawings, Yvon Lambert, Paris

Wall Drawings, Lisson
Gallery, London

Galleria Marilena Bonomo, Bari

1985
Light Gallery, New York

Sculture di Sol LeWitt a Tecnopolis,
Galleria Marilena Bonomo, Bari

*Wall Drawings and
Structures,* Daniel Weinberg
Gallery, Los Angeles

*Pyramid: A Wall Drawing
by Sol LeWitt,* Brooklyn
Museum of Art, New York

Diciannove Poliedre in Legno,
Fausto Scaramucci, Spoleto

New Works: Sol LeWitt,
Harvard University Art
Museums, Harvard University,
Cambridge, Massachusetts

The Saatchi Gallery, London

1986
Studio G7 di Ginevra
Grigolo, Bologna

Galerie Peter Pakesch, Vienna

*Sol LeWitt: Works on Paper
from the RSM Collection,*
The Contemporary Arts
Center, Cincinnati

Marco Noire, Turin

Intervento Su Parete, Spazio
immagine, Foligno, Italy

New Wall Drawings, Rhona
Hoffman Gallery, Chicago

Pyramids, John Weber
Gallery, New York

*Sol LeWitt: Wall Drawings,
Dessins, et Aquarelles,*
Galerie Vega, Liège

New Structures, Donald
Young Gallery, Chicago

Galleria Mario Pieroni, Rome

Wall Drawings, Magasin, Centre
National d'Art Contemporain
de Grenoble, Grenoble

*Pyramides Aquarelles Sur
Papier,* Yvon Lambert, Paris

*Inaugural Exhibition: Wall
Drawings by Sol LeWitt,* The
Drawing Center, New York,

Sol LeWitt: Prints 1970–1986,
The Tate Gallery, London
(Catalogue)

Sol LeWitt: Wall Drawings,
Institute for Contemporary
Art, London

Foggia Sculpture, Cassa di
Risparmio di Puglia, Bari/
Galleria Marilena Bonomo, Bari

Structures: 1978–1986, Annemarie
Verna Galerie, Zürich

1987
Open Structures, New Prints,
Galleria Marilena Bonomo, Bari

Wall Drawings, Musée d'Art
Moderne de la Ville de Paris, Paris

Double Pyramids, John
Weber Gallery, New York

Structure: 3 × 3 × l, Doris
Freedman Plaza, New York

Sol LeWitt Wall Drawings, The
Cleveland Museum of Art, Cleveland

Sol LeWitt: Wall Drawings,
Galleria Ugo Ferranti, Rome

*Sol LeWitt Tilted Forms/
Wall Drawings,* Westfälischer
Kunstverein, Münster,
Germany (Catalogue)

Sol LeWitt Wall Drawings, Konrad
Fischer Gallery, Düsseldorf

Sol LeWitt Wall Drawings, Galleria
Alessandra Bonomo, Rome

Sol LeWitt Wall Drawings,
Yvon Lambert, Paris

Sol LeWitt Wall Drawings,
Galerie Ressle, Stockholm

Works: Sol LeWitt, Hirshhorn
Museum and Sculpture Garden,
Washington, D.C. (Brochure)

Sol LeWitt Wall Drawings, Graeme
Murray Gallery, Edinburgh

*Pick Up the Book, Turn the Page,
and Enter the System: Books by
Sol LeWitt,* Minnesota Center for
Book Arts, Minneapolis (Catalogue)

Drawing Now: Sol LeWitt,
The Baltimore Museum
of Art, Baltimore

*Sol LeWitt: Gravures, Gouaches,
Dessins,* Galerie Vega, Liège

1988
*Sol LeWitt Wall Drawings
and Works on Paper,* Donald
Young Gallery, Chicago

Sol LeWitt Prints, Walker
Art Center, Minneapolis

Wallworks, Williams College
Museum of Art, Williams College,
Williamstown, Massachusetts

Sol LeWitt: New Structures,
John Weber Gallery, New York

Sol LeWitt: Structures, Galerie
Peter Pakesch, Vienna

*Sol LeWitt: Wall Drawings:
Continuous Forms with Color and
Gouache Superimposed,* Wiener
Secession, Vienna (Catalogue)

Sol LeWitt Wall Drawings,
Annemarie Verna Galerie, Zürich

*Sol LeWitt: 12 Recent Works on
Paper,* Lisson Gallery, London

*Sol LeWitt: Forme di Righe
in Bianco e Nero,* Salone
dei Camuccini, Museo Di
Capodimonte, Naples, Italy

Sol LeWitt: Wall Drawings,
Kestner-Gesellschaft,
Hannover (Catalogue)

Sol LeWitt: Wall Drawings,
Le Case d'Arte, Milan

Sol LeWitt: Cube, John
Weber Gallery, New York

Sol LeWitt: Structures,
Massimo Minini, Brescia

*Sol LeWitt: Installation and
Sculpture,* B.R. Kornblatt
Gallery, Washington, D.C.

Sol LeWitt: Wall Drawings, Des
Moines Art Center, Des Moines

Lawrence Oliver Gallery,
Philadelphia

1989
*Sol LeWitt Prints: 1970–
1986,* New Britain Museum of
American Art, New Britain,
Connecticut; Ezra & Cecile Zilka
Gallery, Wesleyan University,
Middletown, Connecticut

Sol LeWitt: 3 recente zeefdrukken,
Galerie de Expeditie, Amsterdam

Sol LeWitt: Incomplete Open Cubes,
Galerie Le Gall Peyroulet, Paris

*Sol LeWitt Wall Drawings
1984–1988,* Kunsthalle
Bern, Bern (Catalogue)

Galerie Tanit, Munich (Catalogue)

Sol LeWitt: Recent Drawings,
Daniel Weinberg Gallery, Los
Angeles (with Alan Saret)

Sol LeWitt Wall Drawings,
Galleria Ugo Ferranti, Rome

Alfonso Artiaco, Naples, Italy

*Sol LeWitt: Wall Drawings/
Works on Paper,* Thomas
Segal Gallery, Boston

*Sol LeWitt: Sculture e gouaches
recenti,* Galleria Marilena
Bonomo, Bari

Sol LeWitt: Complex Form #8,
Camera di Commercio di Bari, Bari

Gibbes Museum of Art,
Charleston (Catalogue)

*Sol LeWitt: A Wall Drawing
Exhibition,* Lisson Gallery, London

*Sol LeWitt: Prints and Related
Works,* Brooke Alexander
Editions, New York

Sol LeWitt: Works on Paper,
Shea & Beker, New York

Sol LeWitt: Wall Drawings, Galeria 57, Madrid

Sol LeWitt: Wall Drawings y Gouaches, Galeria Juana de Aizpuru, Madrid

Sol LeWitt: Serigraphies et dessins, Gilbert Brownstone et Cie., Paris

Sol LeWitt: Sculpture and Drawings, Daniel Weinberg Gallery, Los Angeles

Sol LeWitt: Sculture/ Acquarelli, Studio G7 di Ginevra Grigolo, Bologna

1990
Sol LeWitt: New Wall Drawings, John Weber Gallery, New York

Sol LeWitt: Recent Prints, Lawrence Oliver Gallery, Philadelphia

Spazio d'Arte, Naples, Italy

American Academy, Rome

Sol LeWitt: Papiers Déchirés de 1975, Galerie de Poche, Paris

Sol LeWitt: Structures, Galerie Vega, Liège

Sol LeWitt: New Structures, Rhona Hoffman Gallery, Chicago

Sol LeWitt: Wall Drawings and Gouaches, Donald Young Gallery, Chicago

Sol LeWitt: Recent Works, Touko Museum of Contemporary Art, Tokyo (Catalogue)

Sol LeWitt: Opere recenti, pyramids, complex forms, e folding screens, Palazzo Rosari-Spada, Spoleto (Catalogue)

Sol LeWitt: Four Wall Drawings, Zonder Titel, Amsterdam

New Structures and Gouaches, Galerie Pierre Huber, Geneva

Sol LeWitt: Wall Drawings, Galleria Persano, Turin

Sol LeWitt: Prints and Related Works, Tomoko Liguori Gallery, New York

Sol LeWitt: Books 1966–1990, Portikus, Frankfurt (Catalogue)

Sol LeWitt: Complex Forms, Wall Drawings, Gerichtsgeäude E, Frankfurt (Catalogue)

Sol LeWitt: Structures & Prints, Galleria Juana de Aizpuru, Seville

Sol LeWitt: Prints, Susan Sheehan Gallery, New York

Sol LeWitt: Large Scale Concrete Block Sculpture, Max Protetch Gallery, New York

Sol LeWitt: Wall Drawings, Galeria Benet Costa, Barcelona

1991
Sol LeWitt: New Structures, Lisson Gallery, London

Sol LeWitt: Wall Drawings, John Weber Gallery, New York

Sol LeWitt: Wall Drawings, Structures & Gouaches, John Stoller & Co., Minneapolis

Donald Young Gallery, Chicago

Sol LeWitt: Wall Drawings, Barbara Krakow Gallery, Boston

Sol LeWitt: Structures, Thomas Segal Gallery, Boston

Galleria Alessandra Bonomo, Rome

Sol LeWitt: Complex Forms, Annemarie Verna Galerie, Zürich

Galleria Marilena Bonomo, Bari

Original Copies: International Faxed Art, Lazelle Gallery, Auckland

Sol LeWitt: Wall Drawings and Gouaches, Galerie Ressle, Stockholm

Sol LeWitt: Wall Drawings #44, 45, 46, 1970, Yvon Lambert, Paris

Gallery Cellar, Nagoya, Japan

Konrad Fischer Galerie, Düsseldorf

Sol LeWitt: Wall Drawing, Bündner Kunstmuseum, Chur

Sol LeWitt: Five Geometric Structures and their Combinations, Graeme Murray Gallery, Edinburgh

Sol LeWitt: Black Gouaches, Julian Pretto Gallery, New York

Sol LeWitt: Sculptures et gouaches, Galerie Patrick Roy, Lausanne

Sol LeWitt: New Structures, Donald Young Gallery, Seattle

Galerie 1900–2000, Paris

1992
John Weber Gallery, New York

Sol LeWitt: New Aquatints, The Aldrich Museum, Ridgefield, Connecticut

Complex Forms: Structures and Prints, Akus Gallery, Eastern Connecticut State University, Willimantic, Connecticut

Sol LeWitt: Recente Gouaches, Galerie Onrust, Amsterdam

Sol LeWitt: Wall Drawings, Butler Gallery, Kilkenny

Sol LeWitt: Black Gouaches, Galerie Natkin Berta, Paris

Sol LeWitt: New Wall Drawings, Quint Krichman Projects, La Jolla, California/Quint Contemporary Art, San Diego

Sol LeWitt: Una Struttura per Esterno, Massimo Minini, Brescia

Sol LeWitt Drawings 1958–1992, Gemeentemuseum, The Hague. Traveled to: Museum of Modern Art, Oxford, England; Westfälisches Landesmuseum, Münster, Germany; Leeds City Art Gallery, Leeds; Kunstmuseum Winterthur, Winterthur; Centre Georges Pompidou, Paris/Musée de Picardie, Amiens; Fundació Tapiès, Barcelona; Museum of Fine Arts, Boston; The Baltimore Museum of Art, Baltimore (Catalogue)

1993
Sol LeWitt: Recent Work, New Britain Museum of American Art, New Britain, Connecticut

Sol LeWitt: 1975–1993, Galerie Natkin-Berta, Paris

Sol LeWitt: Twenty-Five Years of Wall Drawings, 1968–1993, Addison Gallery of American Art, Phillips Academy, Andover, Massachusetts (Catalogue)

Styrofoam Wall Installation (Room), Ace Gallery, Los Angeles

Galleria Klemens Gasser, Bolzano

Galeria Tovar y Tovar, Bogotá

Styrofoam Wall Installation (Room), Julian Pretto, New York

Styrofoam Wall Installation, Yvon Lambert, Paris

Sol LeWitt: Wall Drawings from the Collection of Robert and Sana Risman, Francis Colburn Gallery, University of Vermont, Burlington

New Wall Pieces, Galerie Konrad Fischer, Düsseldorf

Sol LeWitt: œuvres sur papier, Galerie Vega, Liège

Sol LeWitt Structures 1962–1993, Museum of Modern Art, Oxford, England. Traveled to: Villa Stuck, Munich; Leeds City Art Gallery, Leeds; Fruitmarket Gallery, Edinburgh; Neues Museum Weserburg, Bremen (Catalogue)

1994
John Weber Gallery, New York

Sol LeWitt Wall Drawings, PaceWildenstein, New York

Testwall, TZ'Art & Co, New York

Sol LeWitt: Brushstrokes in Different Colors in Two Directions, Quartet Editions, New York

Sol LeWitt: Recent Works on Paper, Annemarie Verna Galerie, Zürich

Sol LeWitt 1975–1993, Galerie Natkin-Berta, Paris

Sol LeWitt Wall Drawings, Art & Public, Geneva

Sol LeWitt Wall Drawings, Zerynthia, Contrada Cervinara di Paliano, Paliano, Italy

Sol LeWitt Wall Work: White Styrofoam on Black & Related Works on Paper, Barbara Krakow Gallery, Boston

Galeria Juana de Aizpuru, Madrid

Sol LeWitt Working Drawings, Thomas Segal Gallery, Boston

Sol LeWitt Wall Drawings 25 Years of Wall Drawings, 1969–1994, RENN Espace d'Art Contemporain, Paris

1995
Lisson Gallery, London

Sol LeWitt: Working Drawings, John Weber Gallery, New York. Traveled to: Rhona Hoffman Gallery, Chicago (Catalogue)

Sol LeWitt: Wall Drawings 1970–1971, Lawrence Markey, New York

Sol LeWitt: Cinderblock Structures, Ace Gallery, New York

Sol LeWitt: Wall Drawings, Kukje Gallery, Seoul

Sol LeWitt: Obra gràfica, Edicions T Galeria d'Art, Barcelona

Sol LeWitt: New Wall Works, Joseloff Gallery, West Hartford, Connecticut

Sol LeWitt: Complex Form #7, Harn Museum of Art, University of Florida, Gainesville

Sol LeWitt: Styrofoam Wall Pieces, Kunstverein Ludwigsburg, Ludwigsburg/ Villa Franck, Ludwigsburg

Sol LeWitt: Wall Drawings, Ludwigsburger Schlossfestspiele, Ludwigsburg

Sol LeWitt: Complex Form #3, Williams College Museum of Art, Williams College, Williamstown, Massachusetts

Sol LeWitt: Structures, Galerie Pietro Spartà, Chagny, France

Sol LeWitt: Gouaches, Daniel Weinberg Gallery, San Francisco

Sol LeWitt: Very Large Gouaches, Gagosian Gallery, New York

Sol LeWitt: 25 Small Gouache Drawings, Gallery 128, New York

Sol LeWitt: 26 Gouaches, Chester Gallery, Chester, Connecticut

Sol LeWitt: New Gouaches, PaceWildenstein, Los Angeles

1996
Sol LeWitt Prints: 1970–1995, Museum of Modern Art, New York. Traveled to Blaffer Gallery, University of Houston, Houston; The Cleveland Museum of Art, Cleveland; The Detroit Institute of Arts, Detroit (Catalogue)

Sol LeWitt: Wall Drawing Installation and Styrofoam Installation, St. Marks Position, New York

Sol LeWitt: Dibujos Murales, Wall Drawings, Sala de Las Alhajas, Madrid (Catalogue)

Sol LeWitt Drawings, Colby College Museum of Art, Colby College, Waterville

Sol LeWitt Walls, Galerie Franck + Schulte, Berlin

Sol LeWitt: New Work, Skoto Gallery, New York

Sol LeWitt: New Wall Drawings, The Pier Arts Centre, Stromness, Scotland

Sol LeWitt: Drawings and Sculptures, Barbara Krakow Gallery, Boston

Sol LeWitt: Stars, Betsy Senior Gallery, New York

Sobre o sol e as estrelas: Desenhos de parede de Sol LeWitt/of Sun and Stars: Sol LeWitt Wall Drawings, XXIII Bienal Internacional de São Paulo, São Paulo (Catalogue)

Sol LeWitt Gouches, Dan Galeria, São Paulo

Sol LeWitt: Large Scale Monoprints, Pace Prints, New York

Works on Paper, Philadelphia

Galerie Konrad Fischer, Düsseldorf

Two Works by Sol LeWitt, Stedelijk Van Abbemuseum, Eindhoven

1997
Sol LeWitt, Artist of the Year, Art/ Place, Southport, Connecticut

Sol LeWitt: Stars, Hiram Butler Gallery, Houston

Sol LeWitt: New Work; Wall Drawing and Sculpture, Rice University Art Gallery, Rice University, Houston

Sol LeWitt: 100 Cubes, Kunsthaus, Aarau, Aarau. Traveled to Karoter Landesgalerie; Galerie de la Ville de Prague, Czech Republic; Kunsthalle Baden-Baden, Baden-Baden

Sol LeWitt: New Works, Galerie Nächt St. Stephan, Vienna

Piece Unique, Paris

Sol LeWitt: Drawings and Structures, Montserrat College of Art Gallery, Montserrat College, Beverly, Massachusetts

Sol LeWitt: Wall Drawings and Prints, Cummings Art Center, Connecticut College, New London

New Work, Rhona Hoffman Gallery, Chicago

Wall Paintings, Ace Gallery, New York

Wall Drawings, Donald Young Gallery, Seattle

Sol LeWitt: Tables (1981–1997) & Related Work, A/D, New York

New Wall Drawing, TZ'Art & Co., New York

Paula Cooper Gallery, New York

Sol LeWitt: Sculpture and Works on Paper, Jan Weiner Gallery, Kansas City, Missouri

Sol LeWitt: Cinque quadri, Galleria Ugo Ferranti, Rome

Sol LeWitt: Works of the 60s and 70s, Ubu Gallery, New York

Sol LeWitt: Recent Works, Annemarie Verna Galerie, Zürich

Roland Dahinden/Sol LeWitt: Collaboration—Sound Sculpture/ Wall Drawing, Kuppelsaal, Landesmuseum Joanneum, Graz

1998
Sol LeWitt: Wall Drawings and Photographs 1969–1998, Fraenkel Gallery, San Francisco

Liliana Tovar, Stockholm

Sol LeWitt: Wall Pieces (Drawings 1972–1998 and Maquettes for Large Scale Structures), Lisson Gallery, London

Sol LeWitt: Recent Gouaches, PaceWildenstein, Los Angeles

Sol LeWitt: Flat and Glossy Colors, PaceWildenstein, Los Angeles

Sol LeWitt: Large Gouaches, Alfonso Artiaco, Naples, Italy

Galleria d'Arte Moderna e Contemporanea Palazzo Forti, Verona (Catalogue)

Sol LeWitt: Works on Paper, San Jose Institute of Contemporary Art, San Jose

Sol LeWitt in Italia, Rocca Paolina, Perugia (Catalogue)

Sol LeWitt: New Wall Pieces, Museum of Contemporary Art, Sydney (Catalogue)

Sol LeWitt: New Wall Drawings, PaceWildenstein, New York

Sol LeWittt: Bands of Lies: A Wall Drawing, Birmingham Bloomfield Art Center, Birmingham, Michigan

Galleria Continua, San Gimignano, Italy

Sol LeWitt: Wall Works, Alyce de Roulet Wiliamson Gallery, Art Center College of Design, Pasadena, California

Museum Moderner Kunst Landkreis Studio A—Sammlung Konkreter Kunst, Cuxhaven (Catalogue)

1999
Sol LeWitt: New Work, Galerie Meert Rihoux, Brussels

Sol LeWitt: New Work (Black and Colors), Institute of Contemporary Art, University of Pennsylvania, Philadelphia

Sol LeWitt: Irregular Forms, Galerie Franck + Schulte, Berlin

Sol LeWitt: Neue Gouachen, Galerie Daniel Blau, Munich

Sol LeWitt, Volume!, Rome

Sol LeWitt: New Work, Paula Cooper Gallery, New York (Brochure)

Sol LeWitt: Circles Arcs and Bands, Rhona Hoffman Gallery, Chicago

Decades and Dialogues: Perspectives on the MCA Collection, Museum of Contemporary Art, Chicago

Sol LeWitt: Indoors: Drawings and Models: Outdoors: Concrete Block, P.S. 1 Contemporary Art Center, New York

Sol LeWitt: New Wall Drawings, Galerie Pietro Sparta, Chagny, France

2000
Sol LeWitt: Sculptures and Gouaches, Barbara Krakow Gallery, Boston

Sol LeWitt 1971–1999: Etchings, Screenprints, Woodcuts, Crown Point Press, San Francisco/ Refusalon, San Francisco/ Helene Fried Associate Galleries, San Francisco

Wall to Wall: A Decade of Prints by Sol LeWitt, Alva Gallery, New London

Black Cubes, Konrad Fischer Galerie, Düsseldorf

Juliana Gallery, Seoul

Donald Young Gallery, Chicago

Sol LeWitt: Works on Paper; Structures, Rhona Hoffman Gallery, Chicago

Riverhouse Editions 1990–1999, The van Straaten Gallery, Chicago

Sol LeWitt: New Structures, Galerie Tschudi, Glarus

Palazzo delle Esposizioni, Rome

Alfonso Artiaco, Naples, Italy

Sol LeWitt: A Retrospective, San Francisco Museum of Modern Art, San Francisco. Travelled to Museum of Contemporary Art, Chicago; Whitney Museum of American Art, New York (Catalogue)

Stars by Sol LeWitt, University of Michigan Museum of Art, University of Michigan, Ann Arbor

Sol LeWitt New Work: Structure, Wall Drawing, and Gouaches, PaceWildenstein, New York

Sol LeWitt: Sculpture, Paula Cooper Gallery, New York

2001
Celebrating 75 Years: A Wall Drawing by Sol LeWitt, Williams College Museum of Art, Williams College, Williamstown, Massachusetts

Sol LeWitt: Wall Drawings and Prints, Chestnut Hill Academy, Philadelphia

Sol LeWitt, Wall Drawings, Structure, Gouaches, Annemarie Verna Galerie, Zürich

Sol LeWitt: New Gouaches, Art and Public Gallery, Geneva

Sol LeWitt: New Wall Drawings, Galerie Thomas Schulte, Berlin

Sol LeWitt: Works on Paper, Galerie Meert Rihoux, Brussels

Atelier del Bosco di Villa Medici, Rome

Sol LeWitt: Wall Drawings, Artspace, New Haven

Sol LeWitt: Wall Drawings, Yvon Lambert, Paris

Sol LeWitt: New Work, Margo Leavin Gallery and Regen Projects, Los Angeles

Sol LeWitt New Editions: Distorted Cubes, Pace Prints, New York

Sol LeWitt: Incomplete Open Cubes, Wadsworth Atheneum Museum of Art, Hartford. Traveled to: Colby College Museum of Art, Colby College, Waterville; The Cleveland Museum of Art, Cleveland; Scottsdale Museum of Contemporary Art, Scottsdale (Catalogue)

Sol LeWitt: New Wall Drawings, Irish Museum of Modern Art, Dublin

Sol LeWitt: Wall Drawings y gouaches, Fundación Proa, Buenos Aires (Catalogue)

2002
Sol LeWitt: Recent Prints, Augen Gallery, Portland, Oregon

Sol LeWitt: Wall Drawing—New Gouaches, Galerie Sfeir Semler, Hamburg

Sol LeWitt: Wall Drawing, Philip Alan Gallery, New York

Juliana Gallery, Seoul

Sol LeWitt: Wall Drawings y Gouaches, Galeria Juana de Aizpuru, Madrid

Alfonso Artiaco, Naples, Italy

Sol LeWitt, Fundación Pedro Barrié de la Maza, La Coruña (Catalogue)

Sol LeWitt: L'image de la pensée, Château de Villeneuve, Vence, France (Catalogue)

Sol LeWitt Drawings, Prints and Books 1968–1988, National Gallery of Australia, Canberra

Sol LeWitt: Copied Lines, CCNOA, Brussels

Sol LeWitt: New Wall Drawings, PaceWildenstein, New York

Sol LeWitt: New Editions, Pace Prints, New York

Sol LeWitt Prints: 1982–2001, Saint Joseph College Art Gallery, West Hartford, Connecticut

Sol LeWitt: Gouches, Paula Cooper Gallery, New York

Sol LeWitt, The Nordic Watercolor Museum, Skärham, Sweden

2003
Sol LeWitt: Recent Acquisitions, Addison Gallery of American Art, Phillips Academy, Andover, Massachusetts

Sol LeWitt: Wall Drawings, Gouaches, Galleria Alessandra Bonomo, Rome

Sol LeWitt: Wall Drawing, Kunstammlungen Chemnitz, Chemnitz

Sol LeWitt: Models for Proposed Dome Structures and Recent Gouaches, Barbara Krakow Gallery, Boston

Sol LeWitt: Fotografia, Fundación ICO, Madrid. Traveled to: Tecla Sala, Barcelona; Camera Austria, Kunsthaus Graz, Graz; Collection Lambert, Avignon; Gemeentemuseum, The Hague (Catalogue)

Sol LeWitt: New Drawings, Margo Leavin Gallery, Los Angeles

LeWitt's LeWitt and Selections from the Collection of Sol and Carol LeWitt, New Britain Museum of American Art, New Britain, Connecticut

Sol LeWitt: Wall Drawing for 192 Books, Paula Cooper Gallery, New York

Sol LeWitt: New Gouaches, Paula Cooper Gallery, New York

Sol LeWitt: Wall Drawing, Prints, Works on Paper, Galerie Nächst Stephan, Vienna

Sol LeWitt: Brick and Block Outdoor Sculpture, Max Protetch: Sculpture Beacon, Beacon, New York

Sol LeWitt: Horizontal Brushstrokes, Livingstone Gallery, The Hague

Sol LeWitt: Maquettes 1979–2003, Maiden Land Exhibition Space, New York

Sol LeWitt: New Work, Galerie Konrad Fischer, Düsseldorf

Sol LeWitt New Wall Drawings and Gouaches, Rhona Hoffman Gallery, Chicago

2004
Sol LeWitt: Recent Works, Katonah Museum of Art, New York (Catalogue)

Sol LeWitt: Wall Drawing, Structure, Gouaches, Annemarie Verna Galerie, Zürich

Sol LeWitt: Structures 1962–2003, PaceWildenstein, New York (Catalogue)

Sol LeWitt: Recent Acquisitions, The RISD Museum, Rhode Island School of Design, Providence

Sol LeWitt: Wall, Kunsthaus Graz am Landesmuseum Joanneum, Graz (Catalogue)

Sol LeWitt: New Wall Drawings and Photographs, Fraenkel Gallery, San Francisco

Sol LeWitt: New Work, Lisson Gallery, London

XXIV Andamenti: Sol LeWitt— Mimmo Paladino, Galleria Nazionale d'Arte Moderna, Rome, Italy; Santa Maria Capua Vetere (Ce) Museo Archeologico dell'Antica Capua, Capua

Sol Lewitt Wall Drawing: Whirls and Twirls Reggio Emilia: No. 1126, Sala di lettura, Biblioteca Panizzi, Reggio Emilia, Italy (Catalogue)

Sol LeWitt: Wall Drawing 1123: [illegible], The Aldrich Contemporary Art Museum, Ridgefield, Connecticut

Sol LeWitt: Indoor/Outdoor Exhibition, Laumeier Sculpture Park, St. Louis

Sol LeWitt: Zürich Project, Haus Konstruktiv, Zürich

2005
Sol LeWitt and Alvin Lucier: A Collaboration, Ezra and Cecile Zilkha Gallery, Wesleyan University, Middletown, Connecticut

Sol LeWitt: Drawings for Projects, Donald Young Gallery, Chicago

Sol LeWitt: Wall Drawing 801, Bonnefanten Museum, Maastricht

Sol LeWitt: New Work, Galerie Meert Rihoux, Brussels

Disegni a Matita Sul Muro: Sol LeWitt Al Bportico d'Ottavia, Valentina Bonomo Arte Contemporanea, Rome

Sol LeWitt: Recent Work, Lyman Allyn Museum of Art, Connecticut College, New London

Sol LeWitt: Photographic Works, Gemeentemuseum, Den Haag, The Hague

Lost Voices, Synagogue Stommeln, Pulheim, Germany

Minimal LeWitt, Alva Gallery, New London

Galleria Massimo Minini, Brescia

Sol LeWitt on the Roof: Splotches, Whirls and Twirls, Iris and B. Gerald Cantor Roof Garden, The Metropolitan Museum of Art, New York

Sol LeWitt in Madison Square Park, Madison Square Park, New York

Sol LeWitt: Complex Form No. 7, Everson Museum of Art, Syracuse University, Syracuse

Sol LeWitt: New Wall Drawings, Alfonso Artiaco, Naples, Italy

Sol LeWitt 123: All Three-Part Variation on Three Different Kinds of Cubes, 1967/2003, Riggio Galleries, Dia: Beacon, Beacon, New York

Sol LeWitt: New Wall Drawings, PaceWildenstein, New York

Sol LeWitt: Wall Drawing 1176 Seven Basic Colors and All Their Combinations in a Square Within a Square, Josef Albers Museum, Bottrop (Catalogue)

Sol LeWitt, Gouaches, Paula Cooper Gallery, New York

Variations on a Theme by Sol LeWitt and Paula Robison, Isabella Stewart Gardner Museum, Boston

Sol LeWitt Gouaches, Yvon Lambert, Paris

Sol LeWitt: Splotches and Gouaches, Margo Leavin Gallery, Los Angeles

2006
Sol LeWitt: Portfolios—Sets 1971–1983, Barbara Krakow Gallery, Boston

Sol LeWitt: Wall Drawings and Gouaches, Studio G7 di Ginevra Grigolo, Bologna (Catalogue)

Al Galeria, Budapest

Sol LeWitt: Table, Dorfman Projects, New York

Sol LeWitt Monoprints, Pace Prints, New York

Replication: The Books of Sol LeWitt, The New York Art Book Fair, New York

Sol LeWitt: Wall Drawing and Early Works, Le Case d'Arte, Milan

Sol LeWitt: Wall Drawings 1973, Lisson Gallery, London

Sol LeWitt Drawing Series…, Dia: Beacon, Beacon, New York (Brochure)

LeWitt × 2: Structure and Line/Selections from the LeWitt Collection, Madison Museum of Contemporary Art, Madison; Miami Art Museum, Miami; Weatherspoon Art Museum, The University of North Carolina, Greensboro; Austin Museum of Art, Austin (Catalogue)

2007
Sol LeWitt at the AMAM, Allen Memorial Art Museum, Oberlin College, Oberlin, Ohio

Sol LeWitt: Gouaches, Muller Muller Gallery, Knokke-Heist, Belgium

Sol LeWitt in Memoriam, Museum of Contemporary Art, Chicago

Paula Cooper Gallery, New York

Sol LeWitt: Scribble Wall Drawings, PaceWildenstein, New York (Catalogue)

2008
Sol LeWitt: Prints, Annemarie Verna Galerie, Zürich

Barbara Krakow Gallery, Boston

Sol LeWitt: Wall Drawing 139, Smith College Museum of Art, Smith College, Northampton, Massachusetts

Sol LeWitt: Color and Line, Reproduced, Smart Museum of Art, University of Chicago, Chicago

Sol LeWitt, Storm King Art Center, Mountainville, New York

Sol LeWitt: Early Works, Bjorn Ressle Gallery, New York

The ABCDs of Sol LeWitt, Williams College Museum of Art, Williams College, Williamstown, Massachusetts

Focus: Sol LeWitt, The Museum of Modern Art, New York

Selected Exhibition History
(Group Exhibitions)

1966

Multiplicity, Institute of Contemporary Arts, Boston

Primary Structures: Younger American and British Sculptors, The Jewish Museum, New York (Catalogue)

1966

10, Dwan Gallery, New York and Los Angeles

Working Drawings and Other Visible Things On Paper Not Necessarily Meant to be Viewed as Works of Art, School of Visual Arts, New York

1967

American Sculpture of the Sixties, Los Angeles County Museum of Art, Los Angeles. Traveled to: Philadelphia Museum of Art, Philadelphia (Catalogue)

1968

Cool Art—1967, The Aldrich Museum of Contemporary Art, Ridgefield, Connecticut

Documenta IV, Kassel (Catalogue)

Prospect 68, Kunsthalle Düsseldorf, Düsseldorf

Benefit for Student Mobilization Committee to End the War in Vietnam, Paula Cooper Gallery, New York

Minimal Art, Gemeentemuseum, The Hague. Traveled to: Kunsthalle Düsseldorf; Akademie der Kunst, Berlin; Neue Pinakothek, Munich; Kunstverein, Hamburg; Neue Nationalgalerie, Berlin; Kunsthalle Bern, Bern (Catalogue)

The Art of the Real, Museum of Modern Art, New York. Traveled to: Grand Palais, Paris; Kunsthaus, Zürich; Tate Gallery, London (Catalogue)

1969

When Attitudes Become Form, Kunsthalle Bern, Bern. Traveled to: Institute of Contemporary Art, London and Museum Haus Lange, Krefeld

Art of the Real, Tate Gallery, London

Konzeption/Conception, Stadtisch Museum, Schloss Morsbroich, Leverkusen (Catalogue)

1970

10th Tokyo Biennale, Metropolitan Museum of Art, Tokyo

Conceptual Art, Arte Povera Land Art, Galleria Civica d'Arte Moderna, Turin (Catalogue)

Information, Museum of Modern Art, New York (Catalogue)

Walls, The Jewish Museum, New York

1971

Sonsbeek '71, Arnhem

1972

Grids, Institute of Contemporary Art, University of Pennsylvania, Philadelphia (Catalogue)

Documenta V, Kassel (Catalogue)

1974

Some Recent American Art, organized by the International Council of Museum of Modern Art, New York. Traveled to: The National Gallery of Victoria, Melbourne; Art Gallery of New South Wales, Sydney; Art Gallery of South Australia, Adelaide; West Australian Art Gallery, Perth; City of Auckland Art Gallery, Auckland (Catalogue)

Kunst-Über Kunst: Werke und Theorie eine Ausstellung in drei Teilen, Coldgneischer Kunstverein, Cologne (Catalogue)

Art Now 74: A Celebration of the American Arts, John F. Kennedy Center for the Performing Arts, Washington, D.C. (Catalogue)

1975

34th Biennial of Contemporary American Painting, Corcoran Gallery of Art, Washington, D.C.

Painting, Drawing, & Sculpture of the '60s and the '70s from the Dorothy and Herbert Vogel Collection, Institute of Contemporary Art, University of Pennsylvania, Philadelphia. Traveled to: Contemporary Arts Center, Cincinnati

Color as Language, organized by Museum of Modern Art, New York. Traveled to: Museo de Arte Moderno, Bogotá; Museu de Arte Assis Chauteaubriand, São Paulo; Museu de Arte Moderna, Rio de Janeiro; Museo de Bellas Artes, Caracas; Museo de Arte Moderno, Mexico City

American Art Since 1945, organized by Museum of Modern Art, New York. Traveled to: Worcester Art Museum, Worcester; Toledo Museum of Art, Toledo; Denver Art Museum, Denver; Fine Arts Gallery of San Diego, San Diego; Dallas Museum of Fine Arts, Dallas; Joslyn Art Museum, Omaha; Greenville County Museum, Greenville, South Carolina; Virginia Museum of Fine Arts, Richmond; Bronx Museum of the Arts, New York (Catalogue)

1976

Drawing Now, The Museum of Modern Art, New York (Catalogue)

200 Years of American Sculpture, Whitney Museum of American Art, New York

Three Decades of American Art, organized by Whitney Museum of American Art, New York. Traveled to: Seibu Department Store Art Gallery, Tokyo

The 37th Venice Biennial, Venice (Catalogue)

1977
10 Alumni, Visual Arts Museum, School of Visual Arts, New York

Documenta VI, Kassel

Drawing Now, Tel Aviv Museum, Tel Aviv

The Word as Image, Museum of Contemporary Art, Chicago

Works from the Collection of Dorothy & Herbert Vogel, University of Michigan Museum of Art, University of Michigan, Ann Arbor

1978
Between Sculpture and Painting, Worcester Art Museum, Worcester

Artists' Books USA, organized by ICI, New York. Traveled to: Dalhousie Art Gallery, Dalhousie University, Halifax; The University Art Gallery, University of California, Irvine; Allen Memorial Art Museum, Oberlin College, Oberlin, Ohio; Gallery 209, University of Wisconsin-Stout, Menomonie, Wisconsin; The Joseloff Gallery, Hartford Art School, Hartford

Numerals: Mathematical Concepts in Contemporary Art, Leo Castelli Gallery, New York. Traveled to: Yale University Art Gallery, Yale University, New Haven; Dartmouth College Gallery, Dartmouth College, Hanover, New Hampshire; University Art Gallery, University of North Dakota, Grand Forks; The University Art Gallery, University of California, Irvine; Art Museum of South Texas, Corpus Christi, Texas; University Art Galleries, Illinois State University, Normal; Martin Art Gallery, Muhlenberg College, Allentown; New Gallery of Contemporary Art, Cleveland; MCAD Gallery, Minneapolis College of Art and Design, Minneapolis

1979
Prospectus: The Seventies, The Aldrich Museum of Contemporary Art, Ridgefield, Connecticut

Drawings About Drawings: New Directions (1968–1978), Ackland Art Center, University of North Carolina, Chapel Hill

1979 Whitney Biennial, Whitney Museum of American Art, New York

The Reductive Object: A Survey of the Minimal Aesthetic in the 1960's, Institute of Contemporary Art, Boston

Patterns +, Dayton Art Institute, Dayton

The Minimal Tradition, The Aldrich Museum of Contemporary Art, Ridgefield, Connecticut (Catalogue)

Exchanges 1, Henry Street Settlement, New York

The Decade In Review, Whitney Museum of American Art, New York

1980
The 39th Venice Biennial, Venice

Perceiving Modern Sculpture: Selections for the Sighted and Non-Sighted, Grey Art Gallery, New York University, New York

International Sculpture Exhibition, Basel

1981
Artists' Gardens and Parks: Plans, Drawings and Photographs, Hayden Corridor Gallery, Massachusetts Institute of Technology, Cambridge. Traveled to: Museum of Contemporary Art, Chicago

Mapped Art: Charts, Routes, Regions, UMC Art Gallery, University of Colorado, Boulder

1982
A Century of Modern Drawing, Museum of Modern Art, New York. Traveled to: The British Museum, London

Documenta VII, Kassel

Prints by Contemporary Sculptors, Yale University Art Gallery, Yale University, New Haven

Minimalism × 4: Carl Andre, Donald Judd, Sol LeWitt, Robert Morris, Whitney Museum of American Art, New York

20th Anniversary Exhibition of the Vogel Collection, Brainerd Art Gallery, SUNY Potsdam, Potsdam, New York

1983
Big Pictures by Contemporary Photographers, Museum of Modern Art, New York

17th Bienniale of Sculpture, Antwerp

Artists' Use of Language, Part I, Franklin Furnace, New York

Sol LeWitt, Cy Twombly: New Works, Ugo Ferranti Gallery, Rome

1984
Flyktpunkter: Vanishing Points: Mel Bochner, Tom Doyle, Dan Graham, Eva Hesse, Sol LeWitt, Robert Smithson, Ruth Vollmer, Moderna Museet, Stockholm

Olympian Gestures, Los Angeles County Museum of Art, Los Angeles

1985
Art Minimal 1: Carl Andre, Donald Judd, Sol LeWitt, Robert Mangold, Robert Morris, CAPC Musée d'Art Contemporain de Bordeaux, Bordeaux

Process and Konstruction, Kunstwerksstatton, Munich

Carnegie International, Carnegie Museum of Art, Pittsburgh

Contrasts of Form: Geometric Abstract Art 1910–1980, Museum of Modern Art, New York

1986
Political Geometries: Daniel Buren, Peter Halley, Sherrie Levine, Sol LeWitt, Blinky Palermo, Robert Ryman, Hunter College Art Gallery, Hunter College, New York

Forty Years of Modern Art: 1945–1985, Tate Gallery, London

Chambre Des Amis, Museum van Heddandaagse Kunst, Ghent

Individuals: A Selected History of Contemporary Art, 1945–1986, Museum of Contemporary Art, Los Angeles

Art Minimal II, CAPC Musée d'Art Contemporain de Bordeaux, Bordeaux

1987
1987 Whitney Biennial, Whitney Museum of American Art, New York

Skulptur Projekte Münster, Münster, Germany

Drawing Now 1: Sol LeWitt and Robert Mangold, The Baltimore Museum of Art, Baltimore (Brochure)

Edinburgh International: Reason & Emotion in Contemporary Art, Royal Scottish Academy, Edinburgh

Coleccion Sonnabend, Centro de Arte Reina Sofia, Madrid

Daniel Buren/Sol LeWitt, Centre National d'Art Contemporain, Grenoble (Catalogue)

1988
Rot, Gelb, Blau, Kunstmuseum St. Gallen, St. Gallen, Switzerland. Traveled to: Museum Fridericianum, Kassel

Collection Sonnabend, CAPC Musée d'Art Contemporain de Bordeaux, Bordeaux

Zeitlos, Hamburger Bahnhof, Berlin (Catalogue)

The 43rd Venice Biennial, Venice

The Turning Point: Art & Politics in 1968; Twentieth Anniversary Exhibition, The Cleveland Center for Contemporary Art, Cleveland. Traveled to: Lehman College Art Gallery, The City University of New York, New York (Catalogue)

24 Cubes, Fine Arts Center, University of Massachusetts, Amherst, Massachusetts

From the Collection of Dorothy and Herbert Vogel, Arnot Art Museum, Elmira. Traveled to: Grand Rapids Art Museum, Grand Rapids; Terra Museum of American Art, Chicago; Laumeier Sculpture Park, St. Louis; Art Museum at Florida International University, Miami

1989
Abstraction, Museum of Modern Art, New York

Minimalism, Tate Gallery, Liverpool

200 Years of American Painting from the Collection of the Wadsworth Atheneum, Galleries Lafayette, Paris

Second Annual Istanbul Biennial, Istanbul

L'Art Conceptuel, Une Perspective, Musée d'Art Moderne de la Ville de Paris, Paris. Traveled to: Sala de Exposiciones de la Fundacion Caja de Pensiones, Madrid; Deichtorhallen, Hamburg; Le Musée d'Art Contemporain de Montréal, Montréal

The Presence of Absence: New Installations, organized by ICI, New York. Traveled to: Gallery 400, University of Illinois, Chicago

1990

Collection du Musée: Boltanski, Buren, Gilbert & George, Kounellis, LeWitt, Long, Merz, CAPC Musée d'Art Contemporain de Bordeaux, Bordeaux

[illegible] la Collection Panza, Musée d'Art Moderne de la Ville de Paris

Minimalist Vision: Buren, LeWitt, Mangold, Cleveland Center for Contemporary Art, Cleveland

Contemporary Illustrated Books: Word and Image 1967–1988, organized by ICI, New York and Franklin Furnace Archive, Inc., New York. Traveled to: The Nelson-Atkins Museum of Art, Kansas City, Missouri, and The University of Iowa Museum of Art, University of Iowa, Iowa City

Minimalism and Post-Minimalism: Drawing Distinctions, Hood Museum of Art, Dartmouth College, Hanover, New Hampshire. Traveled to: Parrish Art Museum, Southampton, New York

1991

The Political Arm, Washington University Gallery of Art, Washington University, St. Louis

Collection du capcMusée: Jannis Kounellis, Sol LeWitt, Richard Long, Mario Merz, CAPC Musée d'Art Contemporain de Bordeaux, Bordeaux

American Abstraction at the Addison, The Addison Gallery of American Art, Phillips Academy, Andover, Massachusetts

Reprise: The Vera G. List Collection, A Twentieth Anniversary Exhibition, David Winton Bell Gallery, Brown University, Providence (Catalogue)

Motion and Document Sequence and Time: Eadweard Muybridge and Contemporary American Photography, National Museum of American Art, Washington, D.C. (Catalogue)

1992

Allegories of Modernism: Contemporary Drawing, Museum of Modern Art, New York

TransForm: BildObjektSkulptur im 20. Jahrhundert, Kunsthalle Basel, Basel

Series and Sequences: Contemporary Drawings and Prints from the Permanent Collection, National Gallery of Art, Washington, D.C.

1993

The [illegible] Tradition in American Art 1930–1990, Whitney Museum of American Art, New York

PREFAB! Reconsidering the Legacy of the Sixties, Rose Art Museum, Brandeis University, Waltham, Massachusetts

Rolywholyover: A Circus, Museum of Contemporary Art, Los Angeles. Traveled to: Menil Collection, Houston; Solomon R. Guggenheim Museum, New York; Art Tower Museum, Mito, Japan; Philadelphia Museum of Art, Philadelphia

Construction in Process IV: My Home is Your Home, The Artists Museum, Lodz

1994

The Art of Memory: Holocaust Memorials in History, The Jewish Museum, New York (Catalogue)

Minimal Art: Andre, Flavin, Judd, LeWitt, Morris, Mangold, Ryman, Weiner: a new condensed exhibition presenting early and new works, which questions the common label 'Minimal Art,' Hallen für Neue Kunst, Schaffhausen

For 25 Years: Brooke Alexander Editions, Museum of Modern Art, New York

Contemporary Abstract American Prints, Addison Gallery of American Art, Phillips Academy, Andover, Massachusetts

Wall to Wall: Robert Barry, Daniel Buren, Sol LeWitt, Simon Patterson, Julie Roberts, Lily van der Stokker, Southampton City Art Gallery, Southampton, England

From Minimal to Conceptual Art: Works from the Dorothy and Herbert Vogel Collection, National Gallery of Art, Washington, D.C.

Même si c'est la nuit, CAPC Musée d'Art Contemporain de Bordeaux, Bordeaux

Drawing Rooms: Jonathan Borofsky, Sol LeWitt, Richard Serra, Modern Art Museum, Fort Worth

A Century of Artists Books, Museum of Modern Art, New York

1995

Drawn on the Museum, The Aldrich Museum of Contemporary Art, Ridgefield, Connecticut

RAW Space, Real Art Ways, Hartford

Carl Andre, Hanne Darboven, Sol LeWitt, Lawrence Weiner: Drawings, Structures, Relations, Susan Inglett Gallery, New York

45° Nord & Longitude: Oeuvres de la Collection du CAPC Musée de la Collection du Frac Aquitaine et de Collections privées, CAPC Musée d'Art Contemporain de Bordeaux, Bordeaux

Printmaking in America: Collaborative Prints and Presses 1960–1990, The Jane Voorhees Zimmerli Art Museum, Rutgers University, New Brunswick, New Jersey. Traveled to: Mary and Leigh Block Gallery, Northwestern University, Evanston; The Museum of Fine Arts, Houston; National Museum of American Art, Washington, D.C.

In Two Worlds: The Graphic Work of Modern Sculptors, Mead Art Museum, Amherst College, Amherst, Massachusetts

Revolution in Contemporary Art: The Art of the Sixties, Museum of Contemporary Art, Tokyo

1965–1975: Reconsidering the Object of Art, The Museum of Contemporary Art, Los Angeles (Catalogue)

1996

Main Stations: Newman, Pollock, Beuys, Broodthaers, Klein, Warhol, LeWitt, Johns, Stella, Ryman, Kounellis, Nauman, Weiner, Casino Luxembourg—Forum D'Art Contemporain, Luxembourg

Passions Privées, Musée d'Art Moderne de la ville de Paris, Paris

The 23rd International Bienal of São Paulo, São Paulo

Thinking Print: Books to Billboards 1980–1995, Museum of Modern Art, New York

1997

Skulptur Projekte, Münster, Germany

The 47th Venice Biennial, Venice

In Visible Light: Photography and Classification in Art, Science and the Everyday, Museum of Modern Art, Oxford, England

7 × 6: Bochner, Hunt, LeWitt, Mazur, Morris, Plimack Mangold, Fine Arts Center, University of Massachusetts, Amherst, Massachusetts

The Serial Attitude: Paintings, [illegible] and Works on Paper, Addison Gallery of American Art, Phillips Academy, Andover, Massachusetts

Thirty-Five Years at Crown Point Press: Making Prints, Doing Art, National Gallery of Art, Washington, D.C.; Fine Arts Museums of San Francisco, San Francisco

Drawing is Another Kind of Language: Recent American Drawings from a New York Private Collection, Arthur M. Sackler Museum, Harvard University, Cambridge, Massachusetts. Traveled to: Graphische Sammlung Albertina, Vienna; Kunstmuseum, Winterthur; Kunst-Museum, Ahlen, Germany; Akademie der Kunste, Berlin; The Parrish Art Museum, Southampton, New York

1998

The Edge of Awareness, Art for the World, Geneva. Traveled to: Siège des Nations Unies à New York, New York; P.S. 1 Contemporary Art Center, New York; SESC Pompeia, São Paulo; National Academy of Art, New Delhi

Then and Now: Art Since 1945 at Yale, Yale University Art Gallery, Yale University, New Haven

100 Years of Sculpture: From the Pedestal to the Pixel, Walker Art Center, Minneapolis

PAPER + works on Dieu Donné paper, The Gallery at Dieu Donné Papermill, New York

Artist/Author: Contemporary Artists' Books, Museum of Contemporary Art, Chicago. Organized by the American Federation of Arts. Traveled to: Lowe Art Museum, Coral Gables; The Western Gallery, Bellingham; Fine Arts Center, University of Massachusetts, Amherst

Een keuze uit de eigen collectie: A Choice from the Collection, Van Abbemuseum, Eindhoven

1999

Afterimage: Drawing Through Process, The Museum of Contemporary Art, Los Angeles. Traveled to: Contemporary Arts Museum, Houston, and Henry Art Gallery, Seattle

Primarily Structural: Minimalist and Post-Minimalist Works on Paper, P.S. 1 Contemporary Art Center, New York

Art at Work: Forty Years of The Chase Manhattan Collection, Museum of Fine Arts, Houston, and the Contemporary Arts Museum, Houston. Traveled to: The Queens Museum of Art, New York

Global Conceptualism: Points of Origin, 1950s–1980s, The Queens Museum of Art, New York. Traveled to: MIT List Visual Arts Center, Massachusetts Institute of Technology, Cambridge

Sculpture in Context, Addison Gallery of American Art, Phillips Academy, Andover, Massachusetts

Multiple Configurations, Presenting the Contemporary Portfolio, Busch-Reisinger Museums, Harvard University, Cambridge, Massachusetts

Contemporary American Masters: The 1960s, The Nassau County Museum of Art, Roslyn Harbor, New York

Correspondence: Harry Roseman: Sol LeWitt and Italian Goddess from 2 B.C., College Center Gallery, Vassar College, Poughkeepsie

Art in our Time: 1950 to the Present, Walker Art Center, Minneapolis

Alfred Stieglitz and the Equivalent: Reinventing the Nature of Photography, Yale University Art Gallery, Yale University, New Haven

2000

Celebrating 75 Years—Permanent Change: Contemporary Works from the Williams College Museum of Art, Williams College Museum of Art, Williams College, Williamstown, Massachusetts

(E COSÍ VIA) (AND SO ON), 99 *artisti della Collezione Marzona*, Galleria Comunale d'Arte Moderna e Contemporanea, Rome

Stephan Anotonakos: Time Boxes 2000, with Richard Artschwager, Daniel Buren, Sol LeWitt, and Robert Ryman, Rose Art Museum, Brandeis University, Waltham, Massachusetts

Many Colored Objects Placed Side By Side To Form A Row of Many Colored Objects: Works from the Collection of Annick and Anton Herbert, Casino Luxembourg—Forum D'Art Contemporain, Luxembourg

Hard Pressed—600 Years of Prints and Process, Axa Gallery, New York; Boise Art Museum, Boise; Museum of Santa Fe, Santa Fe

Minimalism Then and Now, University Art Museum, University of California, Berkeley

Changing Perceptions: The Panza Collection at the Guggenheim, Guggenheim Museum, Bilbao

Under Pressure: Prints from Two Palms, Lyman Allyn Museum of Art, Connecticut College, New London. Traveled to: Schick Art Gallery, Skidmore College, Saratoga Springs; Meadows Museum, Southern Methodist University, Dallas; Fine Arts Center, University of Massachusetts, Amherst; Kent State University Art Gallery, Kent State University, Kent, Ohio; Arthur A. Houghton Jr. Gallery, Cooper Union, New York; Sonoma Museum of Visual Art, Santa Rosa, California (Catalogue)

2001

Objective Color, Yale University Art Gallery, Yale University, New Haven

An Added Dimension: Sculptors as Printmakers, Cincinnati Art Museum, Cincinnati

Sammlung Marzona—Kunst am 1968, Kunsthalle Bielefeld, Bielefeld

Conceptions. Conceptual Documents 1968–1972, Norwich Gallery, Norwich, England. Traveled to: Morris and Helen Belkin Art Gallery, University of British Columbia Vancouver, Vancouver

Watercolor: In the Abstract, The Hyde Collection Art Museum, Glens Falls, New York. Traveled to: Michael C. Rockefeller Arts Center Gallery, SUNY Fredonia, Fredonia, New York; Butler Institute of American Art, Youngstown; Ben Shawn Gallery, William Patterson University, Wayne, New Jersey; Sarah Moody Gallery of Art, University of Alabama, Tuscaloosa

A Century of Drawing: Works on Paper from Degas to LeWitt, National Gallery of Art, Washington, D.C.

Noncomposition: Fifteen Case Studies, Wadsworth Atheneum Museum of Art, Hartford

2002

Trisha Brown: Dance and Art in Dialogue, 1961–2001, Addison Gallery of American Art, Philips Academy, Andover, Massachusetts. Traveled to: The Tang Teaching Museum and Art Gallery, Skidmore College, Saratoga Springs; Contemporary Arts Museum, Houston; New Museum of Contemporary Art, New York; Henry Art Gallery, University of Washington, Seattle (Catalogue)

Defying Distinction: Works from the Addison Collection, Addison Gallery of American Art, Phillips Academy, Andover, Massachusetts

In Between, Museum für Moderne Kunst, Frankfurt

Conceptual Art (1965–1975) from Dutch and Belgian Collections, Stedelijk Museum, Amsterdam

Extra-Ball: Martin Barré, Simon Hantaï, Sol Lewitt, François Morellet, Fonds régional d'Art Contemporain Poitou-Charentes, Hôtel St Simon, Angoulême, France

Jim, Jonathan, Kenny, Frances and Sol, Stedelijk Museum Bureau, Amsterdam

Some Chromes, Fogg Art Museum, Harvard University, Cambridge, Massachusetts

Assembly/Line: Works by Twentieth Century Sculptors, Mead Art Museum, Amherst College, Amherst, Massachusetts

2003

Beter één vogel:, A Bird in the hand..., Gemeentemuseum, The Hague

Treasures of Modern Art: The Legacy of Phyllis Wattis at SFMOMA, San Francisco Museum of Modern Art, San Francisco

Kingston Sculpture Biennial 5, Kingston, New York

Ramen Windows, EdamsMuseum, Edam

Dessins de la Collection Paul Maenz, Frac Picardie, Amiens

The Last Picture Show: Artists Using Photography, 1960–1982, Walker Art Center, Minneapolis. Traveled to: UCLA Hammer Museum, Los Angeles; MARCO, Vigo, Spain; Fotomuseum Winterthur, Winterthur; Miami Art Museum, Miami (Catalogue)

Work Ethic, Baltimore Museum of Art, Baltimore. Traveled to: Des Moines Art Center, Des Moines

Primary Matters: The Minimalist Sensibility 1959 to the Present, San Francisco Museum of Modern Art, San Francisco

Temporal Values—From Minimal to Video, ZKM Museum für Neue Kunst, Karlsruhe

2004

Singular Forms (Sometimes Repeated): Art from 1951 to the Present, Solomon R. Guggenheim Museum, New York

A Minimal Future? Art As Object 1958–1968, Museum of Contemporary Art, Los Angeles (Catalogue)

Beyond Geometry: Experiments in Form, Los Angeles County Museum of Art, Los Angeles

Le Opere e i Giorni tre, Certosa di San Lorenzo, Padua

Art and Utopia. Action Restricted, Museu d'Art Contemporani de Barcelona, Barcelona

Intra-muros, Musée d'Art Moderne et d'Art Contemporain, Nice (Catalogue)

Traces, National Museum of Modern Art, Kyoto

An American Odyssey 1945/1980, Circulo de Bellas Artes, Madrid. Traveled to: Domus Artium 2002, Salamanca, Spain; Kiosco Alfonso, La Coruña; QCC Art Gallery, Queensborough Community College, New York

Beyond Geometry: Experiment in Form, 1940s–70s, Los Angeles County Museum of Art, Los Angeles. Traveled to: Miami Art Museum, Miami (Catalogue)

Design Is Not Art: Functional Objects From Donald Judd to Rachel Whiteread, National Design Museum, New York. Traveled to: Aspen Art Museum, Aspen

Specific Objects: The Minimalist Influence, Museum of Contemporary Art, San Diego

Contemporary Art: Floor to Ceiling, Wall to Wall, Wadsworth Atheneum Museum of Art, Hartford

Small: The Object in Film, Video, and Slide Installation, Whitney Museum of American Art, New York

2005

Conceptual Artists Books from the Van Abbemuseum Collection, Van Abbemuseum, Eindhoven

Sets, Series, and Suites: Contemporary Prints, Museum of Fine Arts, Boston

Open Systems: Rethinking Art c. 1970, The Tate Gallery, London (Catalogue)

Extreme Abstraction: An Exhibition, Albright-Knox Gallery, Buffalo (Catalogue)

The Plain of Heaven, Creative Time, New York (Catalogue)

Elemental, Walker Art Center, Minneapolis

Sol LeWitt–Robert Mangold: Drawing into Print, Senior & Shopmaker Gallery, New York

2006

Public Space / Two Audiences: Works and Documents from the Herbert Collection, Museu d'Art Contemporani de Barcelona, Barcelona

Crisis of Modernism: The Post-Minimal Rebellion, Milwaukee Art Museum, Milwaukee

I Will Not Make Any More Boring Art: Lithographs, Publications & Ephemera from the Nova Scotia College of Art & Design, Printed Matter, New York

Full House: Views of the Whitney's Collection at 75, Whitney Museum of American Art, New York

Le Noir est Une Couleur: Hommage Vivant à Aimé Maeght, Fondation Marguerite et Aimé Maeght, Saint-Paul, France

Plane/Figure: Amerikanische Kunst aus Schweizer Privatsammlungen und aus dem Kunstmuseum Winterthur, Kunstmuseum Winterthur, Winterthur

Ideal City—Invisible Cities, Öffentlicher Raum, Potsdam

Faster, Bigger, Better, ZKM Museum für Neue Kunst, Karlsruhe

Second Lodz Biennial, Lodz Art Center, Lodz

Sol LeWitt/Mario Merz, Fondazione Merz, Turin

Twice Drawn, The Frances Young Tang Teaching Museum, Skidmore College, Saratoga Springs

Out of Line: Drawings from the Collection of Sherry and Joel Mallin, Herbert F. Johnson Museum of Art, Cornell University, Ithaca

Le Mouvement des Image, Centre Pompidou, Musée National d'Art Moderne—Centre de Creation Industrielle, Paris (Catalogue)

Form and Function: Mathematics and Beyond in Contemporary Art, Noyes Museum of Art, Oceanville, New Jersey

Wrestle, Hessel Museum of Art/ CCS Bard Galleries, Bard College, Annandale-on-Hudson, New York

Responding to Kahn: A Sculptural Conversation, Yale University Art Gallery, Yale University, New Haven

2007

REALLIFE 1979–1990, Artists Space, New York

L'aura della serialita, Centro de Arte Moderna e Contemporanea della Spezia, La Spezia, Italy

Calzolari—Degottex—LeWitt, L'Or du Temps, Paris

Konceptualna umetnost, Muzej Savremene Umetnosti Vojvodine, Novi Sad, Serbia

Orthodoxe/Heterodoxe: Choisir sa Ligne, Le 10 Neuf, Centre Regional d'Art Contemporain, Montbelliard, France

O Debuxo nas Colleccion Publicas de Santiago, Centro Galego de Arte Contemporánea, Santiago de Compostela, Spain

Artisti, parole, immagini dal 1960 al 1968, Fondazione Sandretto Re Rebaudengo, Cirie, Italy

Black Square: Hommage à Malevich, Hamburger Kunsthalle, Hamburg

Feedback, Laboral—Centro de Arte y Creacion Industrial, Gijon

Connecticut Contemporary, The Wadsworth Atheneum Museum of Art, Hartford

The Happiness of Objects, Sculpture Center, New York

Dump—Postmodern Sculpture in the Dissolved Field, The National Museum for Art, Architecture and Design, Oslo

The 52nd Venice Biennial, Venice

Works from the Collection of Societe Generale Paris, National Museum of Contemporary Art, Bucharest

Repeat Performances: Seriality and Systems Art Since 1960, Allen Memorial Art Museum, Oberlin College, Oberlin, Ohio

The Panza Collection: An Experience of Color and Light, Albright-Knox Art Gallery, Buffalo

2008

How Artists Draw: Toward the Menil Drawing Institute and Study Center, The Menil Collection, Houston

Based on Paper: The Marzona Collection, Middlesbrough Institute of Modern Art, Middlesbrough

Exact + Different: Art and Mathematics from Dürer to Sol LeWitt, Museum Moderner Kunst Stiftung Ludwig Wien, MuseumsQuartier, Vienna

Color Chart: Reinventing Color, 1950 to Today, The Museum of Modern Art, New York (Catalogue)

Styrofoam, RISD Museum of Art, Rhode Island School of Design, Providence (Brochure)

To Infinity and Beyond: Mathematics in Contemporary Art, The Heckscher Museum of Art, Huntington, New York

21: Contemporary Art at the Brooklyn Museum, Brooklyn Museum, New York

XXth Century, Gemeentemuseum, The Hague

U S A, Galerie Lindner, Vienna

Selected Bibliography

Please also see Gary Garrels, ed. *Sol LeWitt: A Retrospective*, Exh. Cat., New Haven and London: Yale University Press, 2000 and Alicia Legg, ed. *Sol LeWitt*, Exh. Cat., New York: The Museum of Modern Art, 1978.

Artist Writings

LeWitt, Sol. Letter to Eva Hesse, April 14, 1965, reprinted in *Art on Paper* 9 no. 6 (July–August 2005), 54–55. Artist Correspondence.

————————. "Serial Project No. 1." *Aspen Magazine*, nos. 5 and 6, 1966, unpaginated

————————. "Ziggurats." *Arts Magazine 41*, no. 1 (November 1966), 24–25.

————————. "Paragraphs on Conceptual Art." *Artforum 5*, no. 10 (June 1967), 79–83.

————————. ["The Cube"] in Lippard, Lucy R. et al. "Homage to the Square." *Art in America* 54, no. 4 (July–August 1967), 54.

————————. "Sentences on Conceptual Art." *Art-Language* 1, no. 1 (May 1969), 11–13.

————————. "Wall Drawings." *Arts Magazine* 44, no. 6 (February 1970), 39–44.

————————. "Doing Wall Drawings." *Art Now: New York* 3, no. 2 (June 1971), unpaginated.

————————. "Comments on an Advertisement Published in Flash Art, April 1973." *Flash Art*, no. 41 (June 1973), 2.

Artist Books and Projects

LeWitt, Sol. *Drawing Series, Set IIA, 1–24*. Exh. Cat. Los Angeles: Ace Gallery, 1968.

————————. *49 three-part variations using three different kinds of cubes*. Zurich: Bruno Bischofberger, 1969.

————————. *Four Basic Kinds of Straight Lines*. London: Studio International, 1969.

————————. *Four Basic Kinds of Lines & Colours*. London: Lisson Gallery & Studio, 1971.

————————. "Ten Thousand Lines/Six Thousand Two Hundred and Fifty-Five Lines." *Art & Project*, no. 32 (1971).

————————. *Arcs, Circles & Grids*. Exh. Cat. Bern: Kunsthalle Bern & Paul Bianchini, 1972.

————————. *Cercles & Lignes*. Exh. Cat. Paris: Galerie Yvon Lambert, 1973.

————————. *Sol LeWitt*. Exh. Cat. Bari: Galleria Marilena Bonomo, 1973.

————————. *Wall Drawings: Seventeen Squares of Eight Feet with Sixteen Lines and One Arc*. Exh. Cat. Portland, Oregon: Portland Center for the Visual Arts, 1973.

————————. *Six Wall Drawings: Arcs with Straight Lines, Not-Straight Lines and Broken Lines*. Exh. Cat. Houston: Cusack Gallery, 1973.

————————. *Grids, Using Straight Lines, Not-Straight Lines & Broken Lines in All Their Possible Combinations*. New York: Parasol Press, 1973.

————————. *The Location of Eight Points*. Exh. Cat. Washington, D.C.: Max Protetch Gallery, 1974.

————————. *Incomplete Open Cubes*. Exh. Cat. New York: John Weber Gallery, 1974.

————————. *Wall Drawings and Structures: The Location of Six Geometric Figures/Variations of Incomplete Open Cubes*. New York: John Weber Gallery, 1974.

————————. *The Location of Three Geometric Figures*. Turin: Galleria Sperone, 1974.

————————. *Drawing Series I, II, III, IIII, A+B*. Turin: Galleria Sperone and Düsseldorf Galerie Konrad Fischer, 1979.

————————. *The Location of Lines*. London: Lisson Publications, 1974.

————————. *Red, Blue and Yellow Lines from Sides, Corners and the Center of the Page to Points on a Grid*. Exh. Cat. Jerusalem: Israel Museum, 1975.

————————. *Graphik 1970–1975*. Exh. Cat. Bern: Kunsthalle Basel & Verlag Kornfeld und Cie., 1975.

————————. *Modular Drawings*. Geneva: Adelina von Furstenberg, 1976.

————————. *The Location of Straight, Not-Straight, and Broken Lines and All Their Combinations*. New York: John Weber Gallery, 1976.

————————. *Four Basic Kinds of Lines and Colour*. London and New York: Lisson Gallery, Studio International, and Paul David Press, 1977.

————————. *Geometric Figures & Color*. New York: Harry N. Abrams, Inc., 1979.

————————. *All Four-Part Combinations of Six Geometric Figures*. Exh. Cat. Tokyo: Galerie Watari, 1980.

————————. *Six Geometric Figures and All Their Double Combinations*. Exh. Cat. Paris,: Yvon Lambert, 1980.

————————. *Autobiography*. New York and Boston: Multiples, Inc./Lois and Michael K. Torf, 1980.

————————. "Words." *Art Journal* vol. 42 no. 2 (Summer 1982): 99–100.

————————. *Isometric Drawings*. New York: Paula Cooper Gallery, 1982.

——————. *Lignes en quatre dimensions et toutes leurs combinations*. Bordeaux: CAPC Musée d'art contemporain, 1983.

——————. *Sol LeWitt: Chagny*. Exh. Cat. Chagny, France: Fond de la Cour a Droits, 1984.

——————. *Four Colors and All Their Combinations*. Musée d'art moderne da la ville de Paris, 1987.

——————. *Four Colors and All Their Combinations*. Rome: Fabrizio Pozzilli Editore, 1987.

——————. *Lines & Formes*. Paris: Yvon Lambert, 1989.

——————. *Lines in two directions and in five colors with all their combinations*. Exh. Cat. Minneapolis: Walker Art Center, 1988.

——————. *Cube: A Cube Photographed by Carol Huebner Using Nine Light Sources and All Their Combinations*. Cologne: Walther König, 1990.

——————. *Black Gouaches*. Paris: Nouvelles éditions Séguier, 1992.

——————. *100 Cubes*. Cristina Bechtler and Charlotte von Koerber eds. Ostfildern, Germany: Cantz, 1996.

——————. Black Squares. Paris: Artists Books International, 1996.

——————. *Flat and Glossy Squares*. Ghent: Imschoot, 1998.

——————. *Bands of Color*. Chicago: Museum of Contemporary Art, 1999.

——————. "Scribbles." Artforum vol. 45, no. 9 (May 2007): 342–349.

Siegelaub, Seth and John Wendler eds.. *[Xerox Book]*. New York: Siegelaub/Wendler, 1968.

Solo Exhibition Catalogues and Monographs

Accame, Giovanni Maria et al. *Sol LeWitt: Wall Drawings, allo Studio G7*. Exh. Cat. Bologna: Damiani Editore, 2006.

Amanshauser, Hildegund et al. *Sol LeWitt: Wall Drawings: Continuous Forms with Color and Gouache Superimposed*. Exh. Cat. Vienna. Wiener Secession, 1988.

Baume, Nicholas. *Sol LeWitt: Incomplete Open Cubes*. Exh. Cat. Hartford: The Wadsworth Atheneum Museum of Art, 2001.

——————. *Sol LeWitt Wall Pieces*: John Kaldor Art Project. Sydney: Museum of Contemporary Art, 1998.

Braun, Emily. *Sol LeWitt: Recent Works*. Exh. Cat. Katonah, New York: Katonah Museum of Art, 2004.

Brenson, Michael and Susanna Singer. *Sol LeWitt: Concrete Block Structures*. Milan: Alberico Cetti Serbelloni, 2002.

Bright, Betty. *Pick Up the Book, Turn the Page, and Enter the System: Books by Sol LeWitt*. Exh. Cat. Minneapolis: Minnesota Center for Book Arts, 1987.

Chandler, John N. et al. *Sol LeWitt*. Exh. Cat. The Hague: Gemeentemuseum/Dijkmans, 1970.

Corà, Bruno. *Sol Lewitt Wall Drawing: Whirls and Twirls Reggio Emilia: No. 1126*. Exh. Cat. Pistoia: Gli Ori, 2004.

Corà, Bruno and Zia Mirabdolbaghi. *Sol LeWitt: l'image de la pensée*. Exh. Cat. Vence, France: Château de Villeneuve, 2002.

Corà, Bruno et al. *Sol LeWitt in Italia*. Exh. Cat. Perugia: Rocca Paolina, 1998.

Cortenova, Giorgio et al. *Sol LeWitt*. Exh. Cat. Verona: Galleria d'arte Moderna e Contemporanea Palazzo Forti, 1998.

Daniel Buren/Sol LeWitt. Exh. Cat. Grenoble, France: Magasin/Centre national d'art contemporain, 1987.

de Corral, Lorena M. et al. *Sol LeWitt: Dibujos Murales, Wall Drawings*. Exh. Cat. Madrid: Sala de las Alhajas, 1996.

Friedman, Martin and Dean Swanson eds. *LeWitt × 2*. Exh. Cat. Madison: Madison Museum of Contemporary Art, 2006.

Garrels, Gary ed. *Sol LeWitt: A Retrospective*. Exh. Cat. New Haven and London: Yale University Press, 2000.

Haenlein, Carl. *Sol LeWitt Wall Drawings*. Exh. Cat. Hannover: Kestner-Gesellschaft, 1988.

Harvey, Michael. *Notes of the wall drawings of Sol LeWitt*. Geneva: Adelina von Furstenberg, 1977.

Hickey, Dave. *Sol LeWitt: Structures 1962–2003*. Exh. Cat. New York: PaceWildenstein, 2004.

Iles, Chrissie ed. *Sol LeWitt: Structures 1962–1993*. Exh. Cat. Oxford, England: Museum of Modern Art, 1993.

Legg, Alicia ed. *Sol LeWitt*. Exh. Cat. New York: The Museum of Modern Art, 1978.

Lewison, Jeremy. *Sol LeWitt: Prints 1970–1986*. Exh. Cat. London: Tate Gallery, 1986.

Liesbrock, Heinz. *Sol LeWitt: Wall Drawing 1176 Seven Basic Colors and All Their Combinations in a Square Within a Square*. Exh. Cat. Düsseldorf: Richter Verlag, 2006.

Miller-Keller, Andrea. *Sol LeWitt*. Exh. Cat. Charleston: Gibbes Art Gallery, 1989.

Miller-Keller, Andrea et al. *Sobre o sol e as estrelas: Desenhos de parede de Sol LeWitt/Of Sun and Stars: Sol LeWitt Wall Drawings*. Exh. Cat. São Paolo: XXIII Bienal Internacional de São Paolo, 1996.

Mössinger, Ingrid. *Sol LeWitt: Complex Forms, Wall Drawings*. Exh. Cat. Frankfurt Am Main: Gerichtsgeäude E, 1990.

Nordal, Bera and Sol LeWitt. *Sol LeWitt*. Exh. Cat. Skärhamn, Sweden: Nordiska Akverellmusett, 2002.

Oliva, Achille Bonito et al. *Sol LeWitt: Opere recenti, pyramids, complex forms, e folding screens*. Exh. Cat. Spoleto: Palazzo Rosari-Spada, 1990.

Pakesch, Peter and Katrin Bucher. *Sol LeWitt: Wall*. Exh. Cat. Graz, Austria: Kunsthaus Graz am Landesmuseum Joanneum/Walther König, 2004.

Princenthal, Nancy. *Wall Drawings*. Exh. Cat. New York: Paula Cooper Gallery, 2004.

Rein, Ingrid. *Sol LeWitt*. Exh. Cat. Munich: Galerie Tanit, 1989.

Reynolds, Jock and Andrea Miller-Keller. *Sol LeWitt: 25 Years of Wall Drawings, 1968–1993*. Exh. Cat. Andover, Massachusetts: Addison Gallery of American Art, 1993.

Rosenzweig, Phyllis. *Sol LeWitt Works—Interview with Sol LeWitt*. Exh. Brochure. Washington, D.C.: Hirshhorn Museum and Sculpture Garden, 1987.

Schike, Ulrike. *Sol LeWitt*. Exh. Cat. Cuxhaven, Germany: Museum Moderner Kunst Landkreis Studio A—Sammlung Konkreter Kunst, 1998.

Schraenen, Guy. *Sol LeWitt's Systeme in Buchform*. Bremen: Neues Museum Weserburg, 1994.

Singer, Susanna et al. *Sol LeWitt Wall Drawings 1968–1984*. Exh. Cat. Amsterdam: Stedelijk Museum; Eindhoven: Van Abbemuseum; Hartford: Wadsworth Atheneum, 1984.

Singer, Susanna et al. *Sol LeWitt Wall Drawings 1984–1988*. Exh. Cat. Bern: Kunsthalle Bern, 1989.

Singer, Susanna, ed. *Sol LeWitt Wall Drawings 1984–1992*. Exh. Cat. Bern: Kunsthalle Bern, 1992.

Singer, Susanna, et al. *Sol LeWitt Drawings 1958–1992*. Exh. Cat. The Hague: Haags Gemeentemuseum, 1992.

Singer, Susanna et al. *Sol LeWitt: Working Drawings*. Exh. Cat. New York: John Weber Gallery, 1995.

Sol LeWitt. Exh. Brochure. Pasadena, California: Pasadena Art Museum, 1970.

Sol LeWitt: Books 1966–1990. Exh. Cat. Cologne: Walther König, 1990.

Sol LeWitt: Recent Works. Exh. Cat. Tokyo: Touko Museum of Contemporary Art, 1990.

Stockebrand, Marianne. *Sol LeWitt Tilted Forms/Wall Drawings*. Exh. Cat. Münster, Germany: Westfälischer Kunstverein, 1987.

Stolz, George. *Sol LeWitt: Fotografía*. Exh. Cat. Madrid: La Fábrica/Fundación ICO, 2009.

Stolz, George and Francis X. Timoney. *Sol LeWitt: catálogo exposición junio–septiembre 2002.* Exh. Cat. La Coruña: Fundación Pedro Barrié de la Maza, 2002.

Storr, Robert. *Sol LeWitt Scribble Wall Drawings.* Exh. Cat. New York: PaceWildenstein, 2007.

Wall Drawings in Australia. Exh. Cat. Sydney: The Art Gallery of New South Wales/John Kaldor, 1977.

Weitman, Wendy. *Sol LeWitt Prints 1970–1995.* Exh. Brochure. New York: The Museum of Modern Art, 1996.

Zevi, Adachiara. *Sol LeWitt: Wall Drawings y gouaches en Fundación Proa.* Exh. Cat. Buenos Aires: Fundación Proa, 2001.

Zevi, Adachiara, ed. *Sol LeWitt: Critical Texts.* Rome: I Libri di AEIUO, 1996.

Articles and Reviews

Alloway, Lawrence. "Sol LeWitt: Modules, Walls, Books." *Artforum* 13, no. 8 (April 1975), 38–45.

Amy, Michael. "Sol LeWitt at PaceWildenstein and Paula Cooper." *Art in America* 96, no. 2 (February 2008), 138.

Armstrong, Richard. "Sol LeWitt." *Artforum* 21, no. 7 (March 1983), 70–71.

Ayers, Robert. "Sol LeWitt." *Artnews* 104, no. 9 (October 2005), 162.

Barry, Robert. "Sol LeWitt, June 12, 1969." in Barry, Robert et al. *Recording Conceptual Art.* Berkeley: University of California Press, 2001.

Beatty, Frances. "Sol LeWitt at MoMA." *Art/World* (February 1978), 4.

Bochner, Mel. "Serial art systems: solipsism." *Arts Magazine* 41 (Summer 1967), 39–43.

—————. "Sol LeWitt." *Arts Magazine* 40, no. 9 (September–October 1966), 61.

—————. "The Serial Attitude." *Artforum* 6, no. 4 (December 1967), 28–33.

Bochner, Mel and John Baldessari. "Outside the box: Mel Bochner and John Baldessari on Sol LeWitt." *Artforum* 45, no. 10 (Summer 2007), 101–102.

Bois, Yve-Alain. "Sum and the Parts." *Artforum* 38, no. 6 (February 2000), 92–97.

Brenson, Michael. "High Concept." *New York Magazine* (December 25, 2000), 84–86.

—————. "Sol LeWitt Drawing at Brooklyn Museum." *New York Times*, June 28, 1985, C23.

Brown, Susan Rand. "The LeWitt Riddle." *Hartford Courant Magazine*, October 23, 1981.

Calame, Ingrid. "Sol LeWitt at Margo Leavin and Regen Projects." *Art issues* no. 70 (November–December 2001), 48.

Carson, Juli. "Five Paragraphs on Sol LeWitt." *artUS* no. 8 (May–June 2005), 29–37.

Carson, Juli and Nicholas Baume. "Sol LeWitt: Incomplete Open Cubes." *Art Journal* 61, no. 4 (2002), 105.

Celant, Germano. "LeWitt." *Casabella* no. 367 (July 1972), 38–42.

—————. "Venice Sleep and Sparks." *Domus* no. 608 (July–August 1980), 48–56.

Christofori, Ralf. "Sol LeWitt." trans. by Nicholas Grindell. *Frieze* no. 84 (June–August 2004), 143–144.

Coen, Ester. "Sol LeWitt idée al cubo." *La Republica*, July 10, 1994.

Cotter, Holland. "El Anatsui and Sol LeWitt." *New York Times*, July 5, 1996, 24.

—————. "Sol LeWitt." *New York Times*, January 24, 1992, 18.

Danto, Arthur C. "A Taste for Desert Landscapes? (Sol LeWitt's Art)." *The Nation* 272, no. 5 (February 5, 2001), 34–37.

Dickel, Hans. "Sol LeWitt (1928–2007)." *Texte zur Kunst*, 17, no. 66 (June 2007), 86–87.

Ebony, David. "Sol LeWitt Six Walls: ghost of Tilted Arc?" *Art in America* 93, no. 1 (January 2005), 158.

Frankel, David. "Sol LeWitt: A Retrospective." *Artforum* 38, no. 5 (January 2000), 33.

Garrels, Gary and Sol LeWitt. "Sol LeWitt (Interview)." *New Art Examiner* 28, no. 4 (December–January 1985), 13–15.

Gibson, Eric. "Sol LeWitt Thought Inside the Cube." *Wall Street Journal*, April 21, 2007, 16.

Gintz, Claude. "Sol LeWitt's Irrational Logic." *Art Press* no. 195 (October 1994), 24–31.

Glueck, Grace. "Sol LeWitt Making Waves and Sending a Message." *New York Times*, August 15, 1997, 24.

Graham, Dan. "Models and Monuments: The Plague of Architecture." *Arts Magazine* 41, no. 5 (March 1967), 32–35.

Haldane, John. "Sol LeWitt." *Modern Painters* 13, no. 4 (Winter 2000), 100.

Hawkins, Margaret. "Sol LeWitt: A Retrospective." *Chicago Sun Times*, August 1, 2000, 34.

Hudson, Suzanne. "Sol LeWitt: Metropolitan Museum of Art/ Madison Square Park/ PaceWildenstein." *Artforum* 44, no. 3 (November 2005), 250–251.

Johnson, Ken. "Sol LeWitt— Paula Cooper Gallery." *New York Times*, October 22, 1999, E2.

—————. "Sol LeWitt, 78: expanded perception of art through concepts." *Boston Globe*, April 10, 2007, A13.

Joselit, David. "For Minimalists, the Art is the Object." *Boston Ledger* (March 1979), 23–30.

Kalina, Richard. "Means and Ends—A traveling retrospective tracks Sol LeWitt's formal concerns from conceptual projects to vibrant wall drawings." *Art in America* vol. 88 no. 11 (November 2000), 113.

—————. "Sol LeWitt at Ace." *Art in America* 85, no. 11 (November 1997), 122.

Kent, Sarah. "Sol LeWitt." *Modern Painters* 19, no. 6 (July–August 2007), 66–71.

Kimmelman, Michael. "Conceptualism by the Gallon Covers the Walls." *New York Times*, December 8, 2000, E37–E42.

—————. "Sol LeWitt, Postwar Artistic Innovator and Master of Conceptualism, Dies at 78." *New York Times*, April 9, 2007, A15.

Knight, Christopher. "LeWitt Turns the Logical into the Spiritual." *Los Angeles Times* (March 8, 2000): F1, F14.

—————. "Sol LeWitt, 78, sculptor and muralist changed art." *Los Angeles Times*, April 10, 2007, B9.

Krauss, Rosalind. "LeWitt's Ark." *October* no. 121 (Summer 2007), 111–114.

—————. "LeWitt in Progress." *The Originality of the Avant-Garde and Other Modernist Myths.* Cambridge, Massachusetts: MIT Press, 1985: 244–258.

—————. "Sol LeWitt: Dwan Gallery." *Artforum* 6, no. 8 (April 1968), 57–58.

Kuspit, Donald B. "Sol LeWitt." *Artforum* 32, no. 2 (October 1993), 97.

—————. "Sol LeWitt: The Drawing Center." *Artforum* 25, no. 5 (January 1987), 108.

—————. "Sol LeWitt: The Look of Thought." *Art in America* 63, no. 5 (September–October 1975), 42–49.

Last, Nina. "Systematic Inexhaustion." *Art Journal* 64, no. 4 (Winter 2005), 110–121.

Lawrence, James. "James Turrell and Sol LeWitt." *Burlington Magazine* 147, no. 1231 (October 2005), 707–708.

Leffingwell, Edward. "Sol LeWitt at PaceWildenstein." *Art in America* 90, no. 12 (December 2002), 106.

Levin, Kim. *"Sol LeWitt."* *Artnews* 100, no. 2 (February 2001), 153.

Lippard, Lucy R. "Back to Square One: Remembering Sol LeWitt (1928–2007)." *Art in America* 95, no. 6 (June–July 2007), 47.

———. "Sol LeWitt: Non–Visual Structure." *Artforum* 5, no. 8 (April 1967), 42–46.

———. "The Third Stream: Painted Structures and Structured Paintings." *Art Voices* 4, no. 4 (Spring 1965), 44–49.

Lippard, Lucy R. and John Chandler. "The Dematerialization of Art." *Art International* 12, no. 2 (February, 1968), 31–36.

MacAdam, Barbara. "Sol LeWitt: A Tale of Two Squares." *Artnews* 95, no. 5 (June 1996), 102.

———. "Sol LeWitt: Ace, Lawrence Markey, John Weber." *Artnews* 94, no. 9 (November 1995), 241.

Maine, Stephen. "Sol LeWitt at the Metropolitan Museum, Madison Square Park, and PaceWildenstein." *Art in America* 93, no. 9 (October 2005), 167–169.

Marcadé, Bernard. "Sol LeWitt." *Artstudio* no. 1 (Summer 1986), 80–93.

Masheck, Joseph. "Kuspit's LeWitt: Has He Got Style?" *Art in America* 64, no. 6 (November–December, 1976), 107–111.

———. "Hard-Core Painting." *Artforum* 16, no. 8 (April 1978), 46–55.

McQuaid, Cate. "Minimalist Exhibit Showcases Classic LeWitt." *Boston Globe*, February 24, 2000, F6.

———. "Nearing 75, Artist Shapes New Path." *Boston Globe*, June 13, 2003, C17.

Meltzer, Eve. "The dream of the information world." *Oxford Art Journal* 29, no. 1 (March 2006), 115–135, 163.

Meyer, James. "LeWitt at the Dwan Gallery. displacement into conceptualism." *Minimalism: Art and Polemics in the Sixties*. New Haven: Yale University Press, 2004, 200–208.

Miller-Keller, Andrea. "Le Musée comme oeuvre et artifact." *Les Cahiers du musée national d'art moderne* (Spring 1989), 67–68.

Morgan, R.C. "A Leap into the Unknown: A Conversation with Sol LeWitt." *Sculpture* 25, no. 3 (2006), 22–27.

Opie, Julian. "Remembering Sol LeWitt." *Art Newspaper* 16 (May 2007), 49.

Ostrow, Saul. "Sol LeWitt (Interview)." *BOMB Magazine* no. 85 (Fall 2003), 22–29.

Persing, Stephen. "Climbing the walls for art." *Art in America* 93, no. 9 (October 2005), 146–151.

Pillow, Kirk. "Did Goodman's Distinction Survive LeWitt?" *The Journal of Aesthetics and Art Criticism* 61, no. 4 (Fall 2003), 365–380.

Pohlen, Annelie. "Ausstellungen— Sol LeWitt, Synagogue Stommeln." *Kunstforum International* no. 176 (2005), 326.

Reise, Barbara. "Sol LeWitt Drawings, 1968–1969." *Studio International* 178, no. 917 (December 1969), 222–225.

Robins, Corinne. "Object, Structure, or Sculpture: Where Are We?" *Arts Magazine* 40, no. 9 (September–October 1966), 33–37.

Rorimer, Anne. "Recollecting LeWitt." *Art Monthly* 307 (June 1, 2007), 18.

Rothkopf, Scott. "Sol LeWitt incomplete open cubes: Wadsworth Atheneum, Hartford." *Artforum* 39, no. 10 (Summer 2001), 177.

Sausset, Damien. "Fenêtres sur cour de Sol LeWitt." *Connaissance des arts* no. 627 (May 2005), 38.

Schjeldahl, Peter. "Less is Beautiful." *The New Yorker* (March 13, 2000), 98–99.

Smith, Roberta. "An In-Depth Look at Some Writing on the Wall." *New York Times*, May 23, 1993, 35.

———. "Gridlock." *Village Voice* (July 1981),15–21.

———. "Parting Thoughts from a Master of the Ephemeral." *New York Times*, April 21, 2007, 7.

———. "Sol LeWitt." *Artforum* 13, no. 5 (January 1975), 60–62.

———. "Touring the Outer Limits of the LeWitt Sensibility." *New York Times*, April 7, 1995, 35.

"Sol LeWitt." *The Times* (London), April 17, 2007, 65.

Storr, Robert. "View from the bridge—Lead by Example— Sol LeWitt's exemplary approach to art and life." *Frieze* no. 11 (2007),19.

Sweet, Matthew. "Art: It's the chapel of his eye." *The Independent* (London), August 22, 1999, 4.

Tillyard, Virginia. "Sol LeWitt: New York." *Burlington Magazine* 43, no. 1177 (April 2001), 244–246.

Weinberg, Adam D. "Backstage Stars." *Culture + Travel* (October–November 2007), 34.

Weiner, Lawrence. "Sol LeWitt (1970)." in *Having Been Said: Writings & Interviews of Lawrence Weiner 1968–2003*. Gerti Fietzek and Gregor Stemmrich eds. Ostfildern, Germany: Hatje Cantz Verlag, 2004, 38.

Wilson, Andrew. "Sol LeWitt Interviewed." *Art Monthly* no. 164 (March 1993), 3–9.

Wooster, Ann-Sargent. "Sol LeWitt's Expanding Grid." *Art in America* 68, no. 5 (May 1980), 143–147.

Zevi, Adachiara. "Sol LeWitt: Un Concettuale informa l'architettura." *L'Architettura* 35, no. 4 (April 1989), 292–298.

The drawings for *Sol LeWitt: A Wall Drawing Retrospective* were executed from April 1 through September 30, 2008, by:

Beverly Acha
Chip Allen
Aaron Andrews
Emily Arauz
Takeshi Arita
Cameron Arnold
Sylvia Birns-Swindlehurst
Alexandra Bouwsma
Matthew Capezzuto
Kim Carlino
Jennifer Chain
Sachiko Cho
Elizabeth Christ
Chris Cobb
Andrew Colbert
Emily Colman
Megan Dyer
Lacey Fekishazy
Miriam Foster
Alison Gaby
Corin Godfrey
Alexander West Guerrero
Sarah Heinemann
Karli Hendrickson
John Hogan
Gabriel Hurier
Julia Isenberg
Aran Jones
Rebecca Kane
David Kant

Noa Kaplan-Sears
Clinton King
Nicholas Kozak
Sophia LaCava-Bohanan
Georgia Lassner
Robert Liles
Roland Lusk
Samuel McCune
Diana Mellon
Kristina Mooney
Susan Morrow
Nancy Nichols
Hidemi Nomura
Anna Pickens
Tomas Ramberg
Amy Rathbone
Jessica Robinson
Anna Robinson-Sweet
Alexandra Rose
Anthony Sansotta
Benjamin Schweizer
Mio St. Clair
Wim Starkenburg
Jordan Starr-Bochiccho
Laura Staugaitis
Nobuto Suga
Michael Benjamin Vedder
Julia Wagner
Jo Watanabe
Zach Whitehurst

Installation photos of *Sol LeWitt: A Wall Drawing Retrospective* at MASS MoCA. 2008. Photos by Chris Cobb (pages 265–268) and Will Reynolds (page 269)

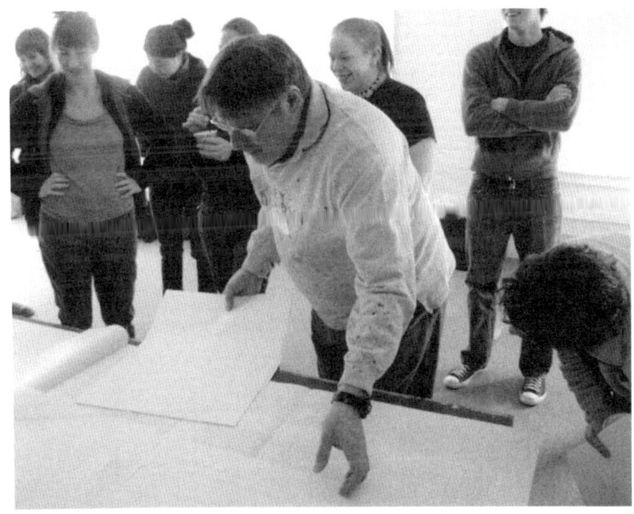
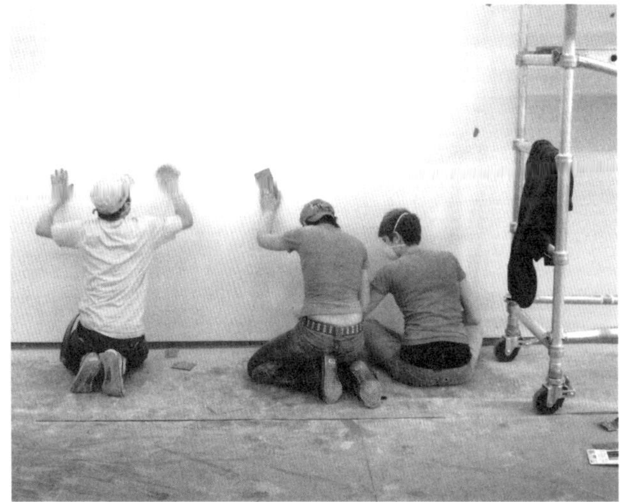
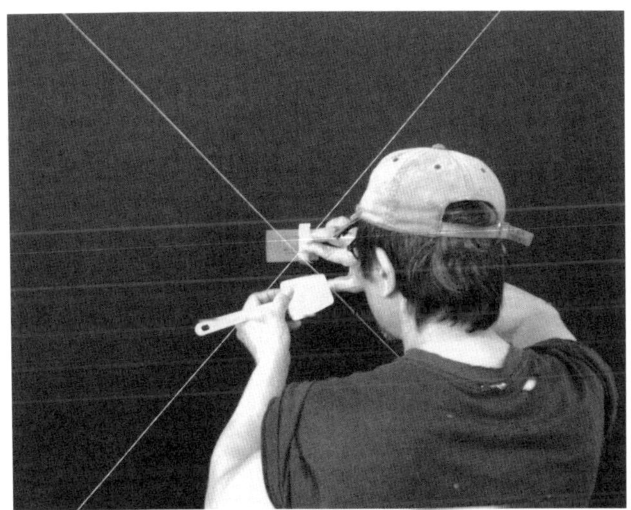
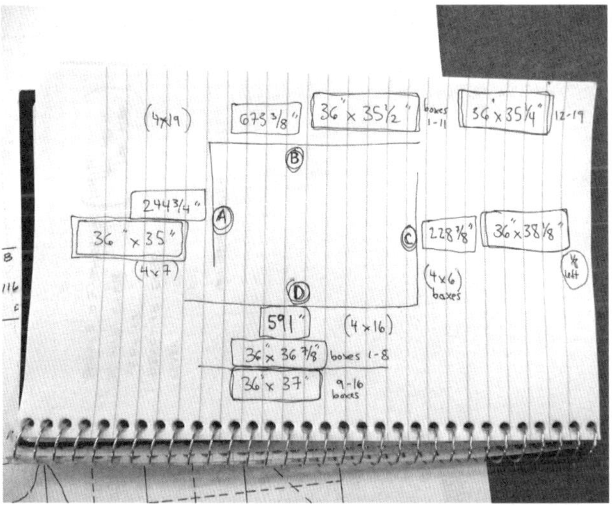

(4x19)
675 3/8"
36" x 35 1/2"
boxes 1-11
36" x 35 1/4"
12-19
B
244 3/4"
A
36" x 35"
(4x7)
C
228 3/8"
36" x 38 1/8"
(4x6) boxes
1/2 left
D
591"
(4 x 16)
36" x 36 7/8"
boxes 1-8
36" x 37"
9-16 boxes

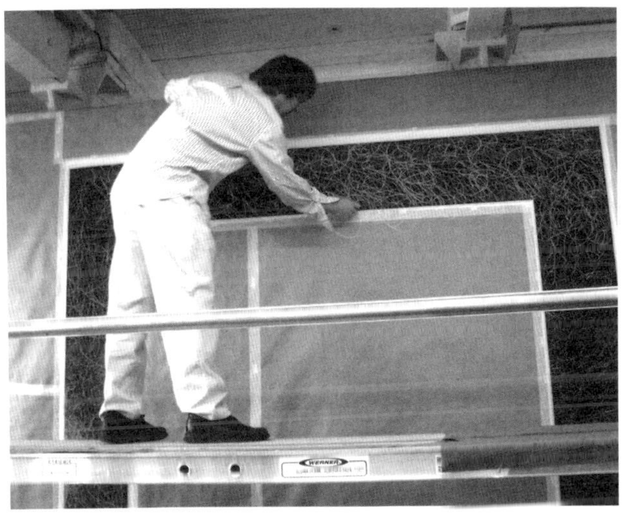
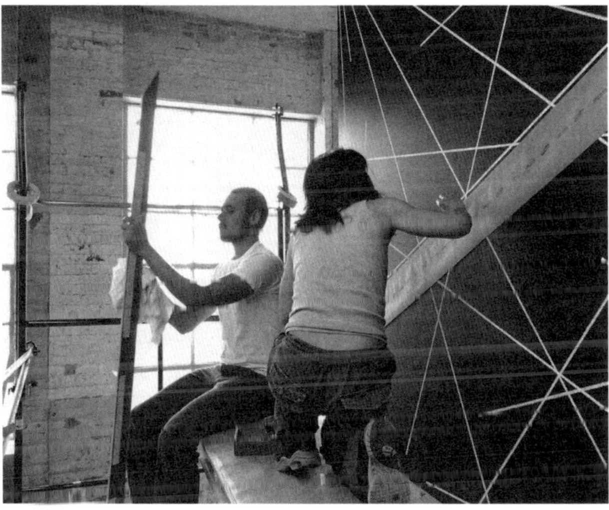

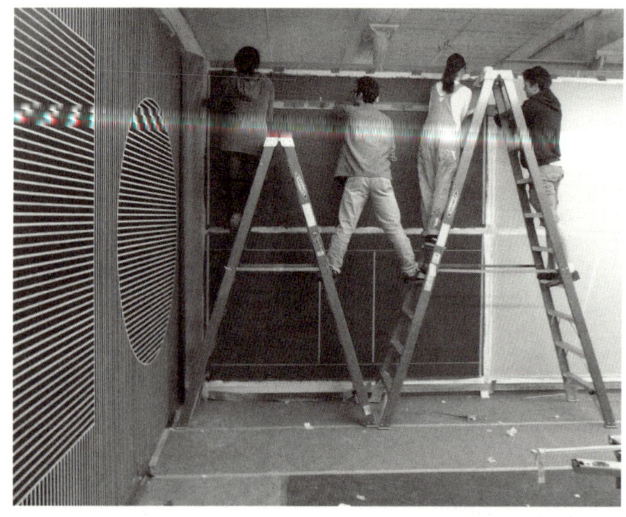
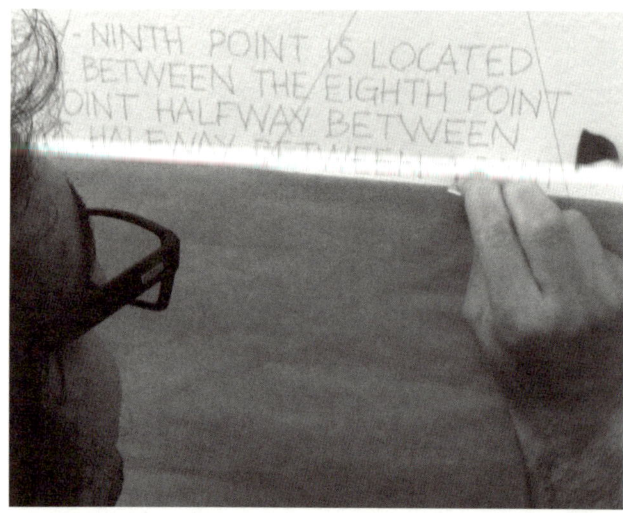
-NINTH POINT IS LOCATED
BETWEEN THE EIGHTH POINT
OINT HALFWAY BETWEEN
HALFWAY BETWEEN
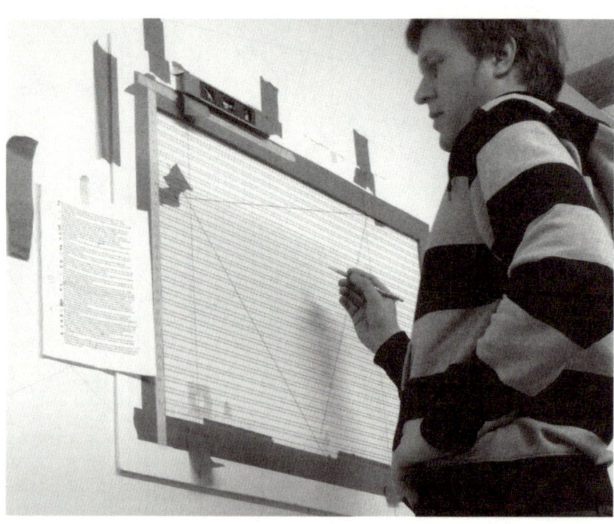
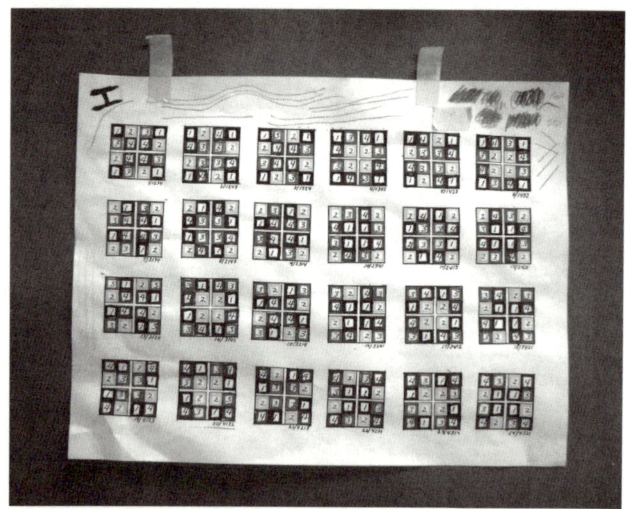
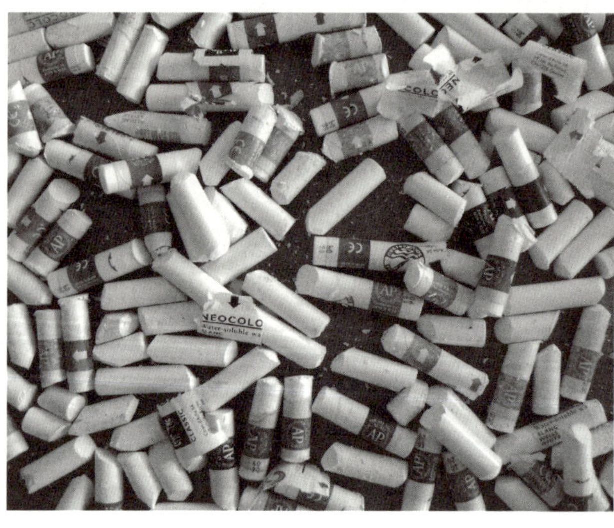
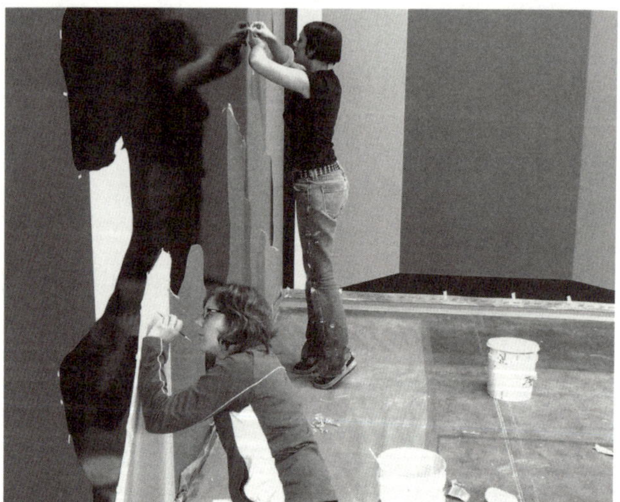

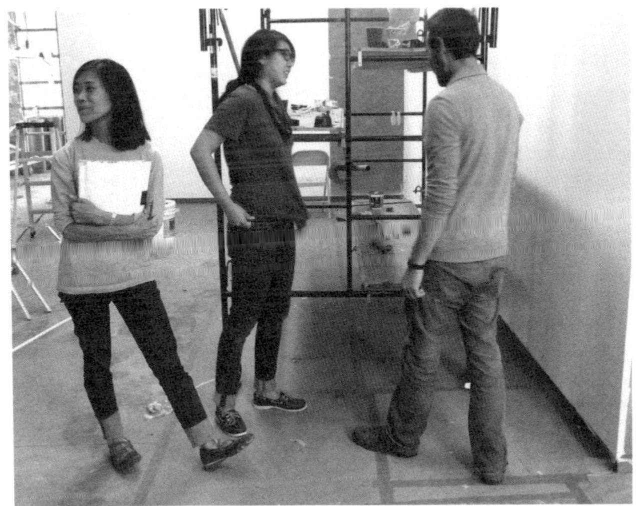
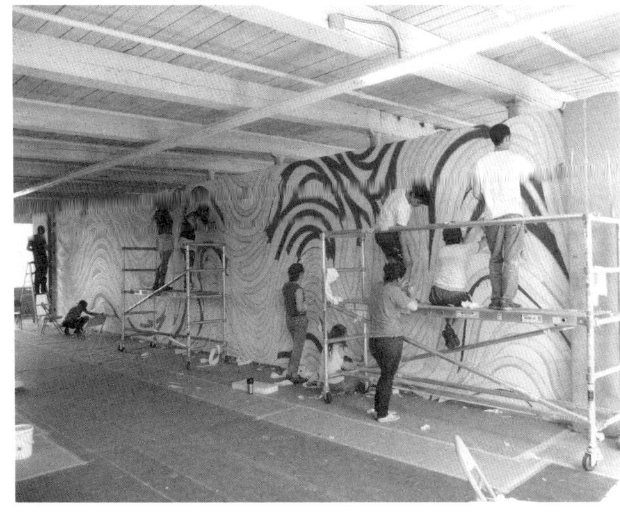
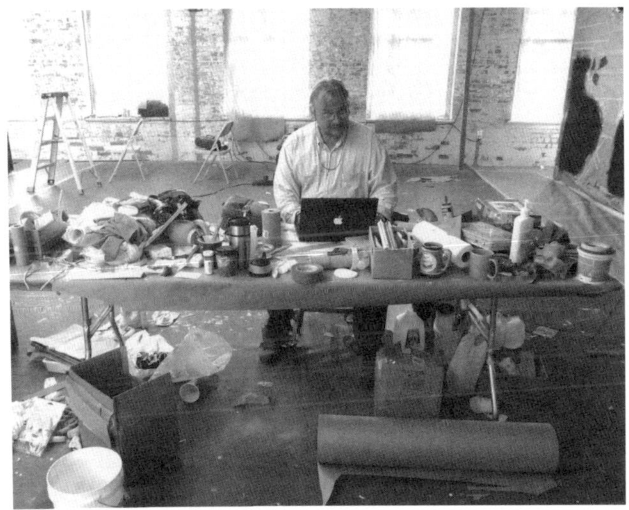
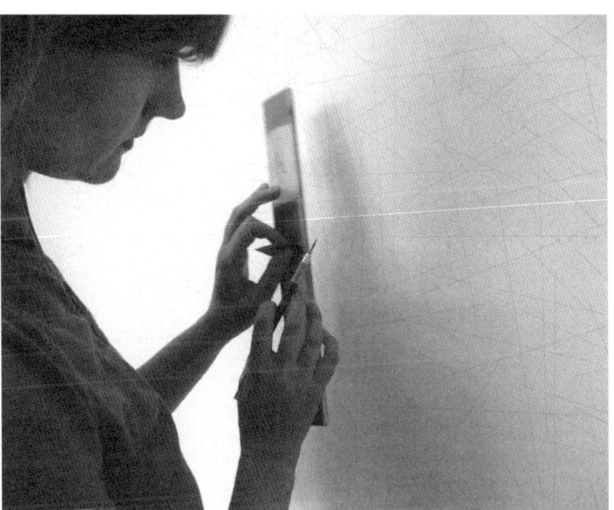
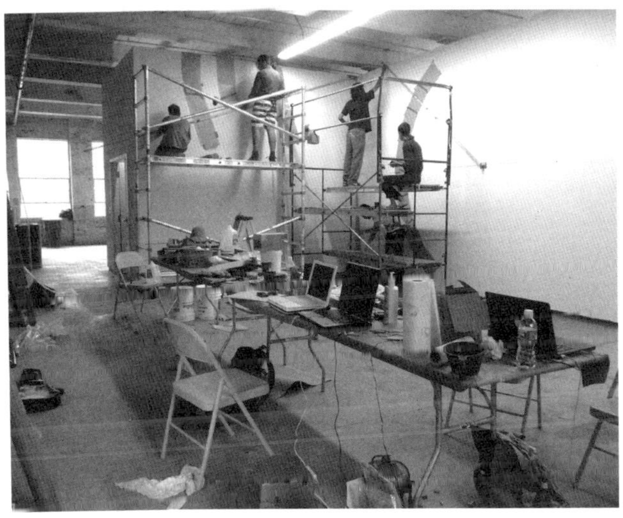
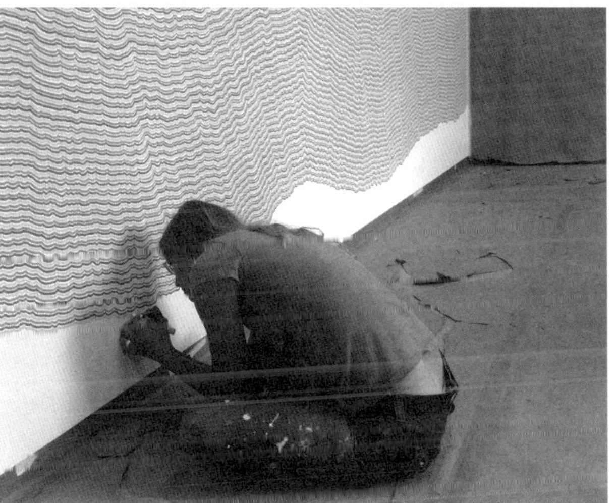

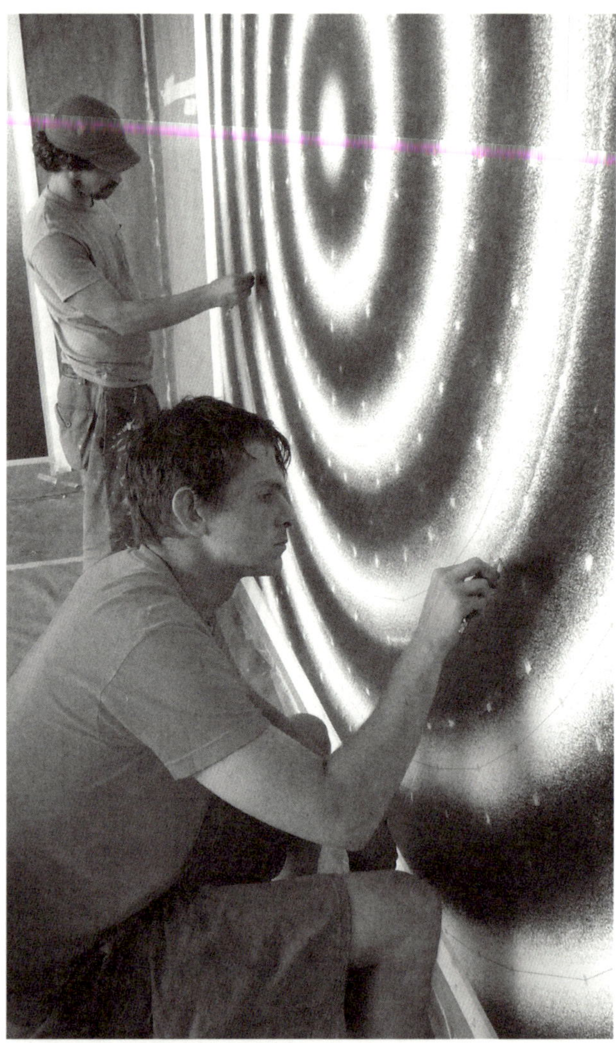

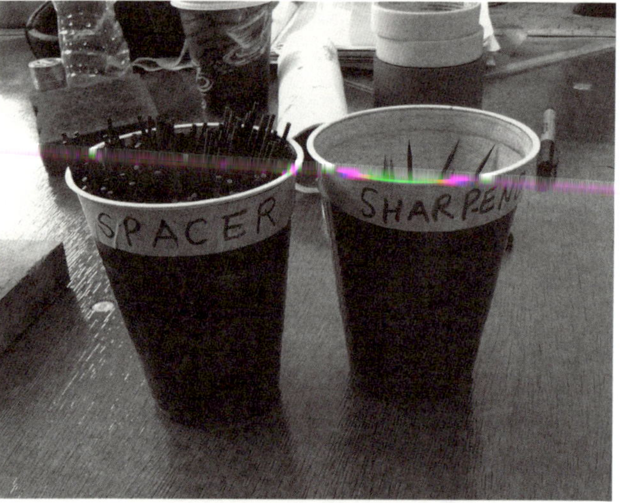
SPACER
SHARPEN

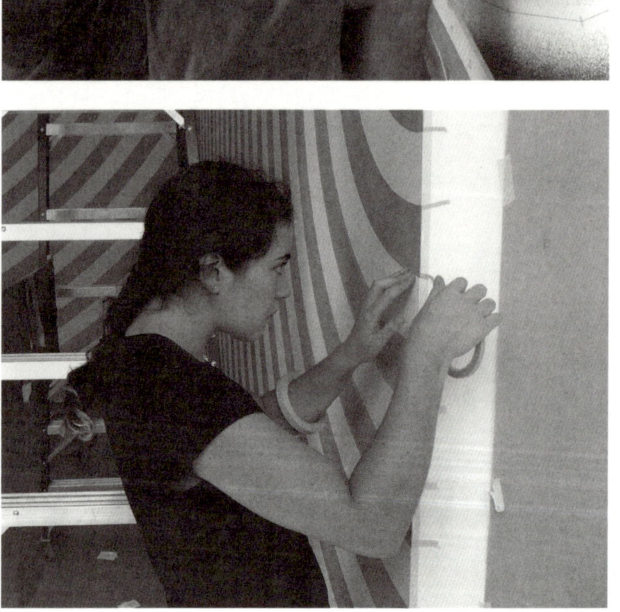

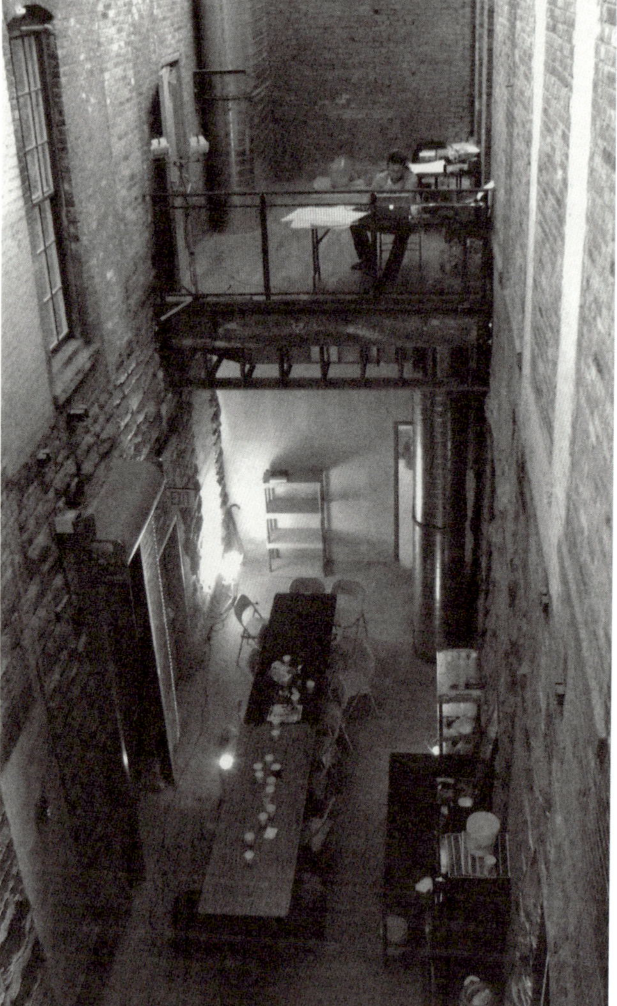

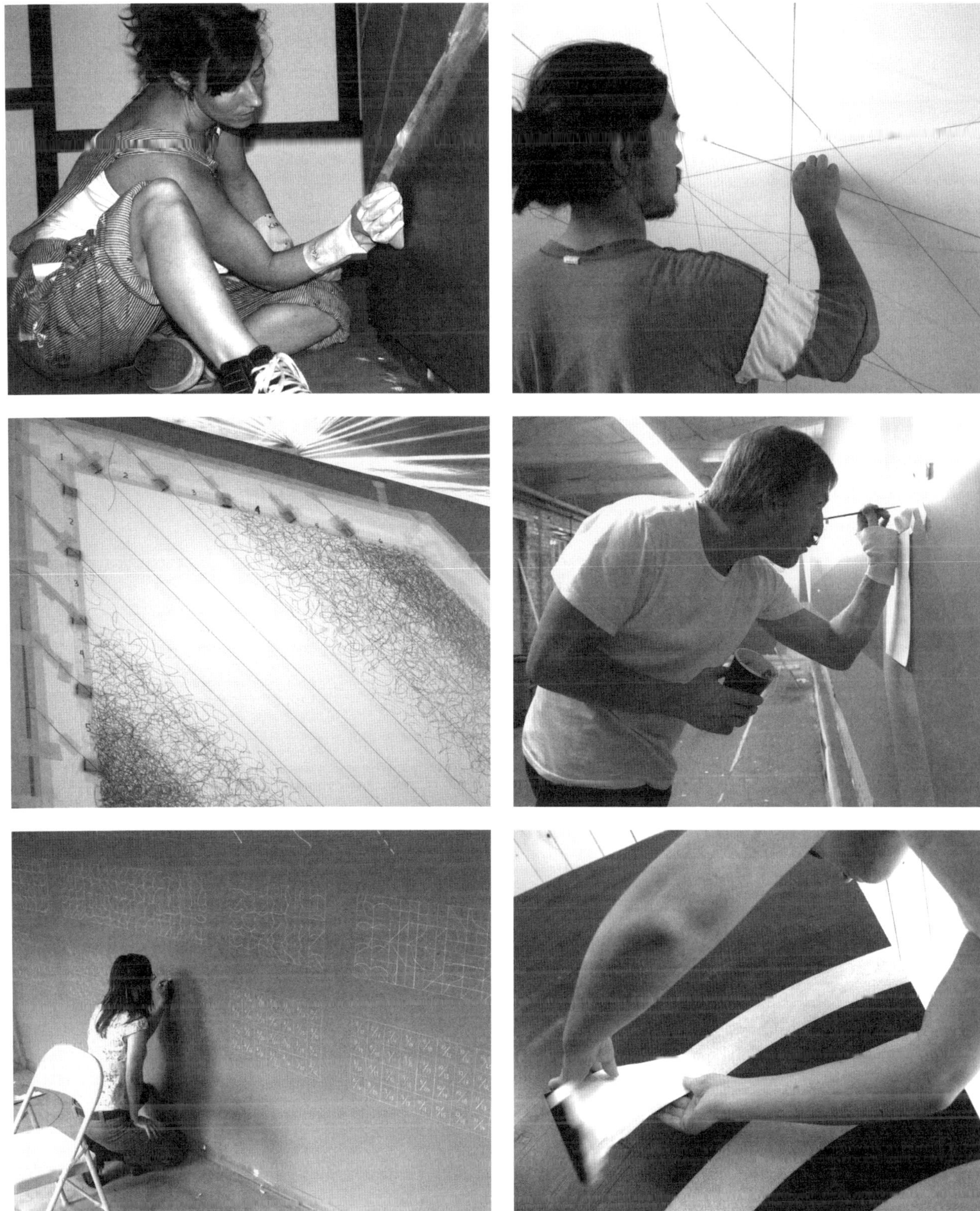

Sol LeWitt: A Wall Drawing Retrospective and related scholarly programs are
a collaboration of Yale University Art Gallery, Williams College Museum of Art,
and MASS MoCA, with additional support from:

Irwin & Mary Ackerman
Marjorie Ackerman
George W. Ahl III
Anne & Gregory Avis
Elizabeth Ballantine
Irving & Esther Bashevkin
Robert & Barbara Bashevkin
JoAnn Belson
Andrew & Nicole Bernheimer
Ellen J. Bernstein
Joyce S. Bernstein & Lawrence M. Rosenthal
Peder Bonnier
Steven & Ellen Bowman
Susan & Duncan Brown
Cartin Family
Julia Childs & Harrison H. Augur
Neil & Kathleen Chrisman
Chuck Close & Leslie Rose Close
Eric & Stacy Cochran
Eileen & Michael Cohen
Paula Cooper Gallery
Lisa Corrin & Peter Erickson
George David
The Dobbins Foundation
Adrian & Liz Ann Doherty
Bob & Happy Doran
Virginia Dwan
Katharine Haklisch Earnhardt
Jane Eckert
Robert A. Feldman, Esq., Julia Mangold &
 Hannah R. Mangold
Jose & Barbara Fichmann
Nancy Fitzpatrick & Lincoln Russell
Paul E. Francis
Maxine & Stuart Frankel Foundation
Allan & Judy Fulkerson
Timur Galen & Linda Genereux

Robert L. Gold & Amy Barrett
Susan W. Gold
Horace W. Goldsmith Foundation
Leslie Gould & Simeon Bruner
Francis Greenburger & Isabelle Autones
Greenhill Family Foundation
Nina M. Griggs
Carolyn H. Grinstein & Gerald Grinstein
Agnes Gund & Daniel Shapiro
Ann & Graham Gund
Mimi and Peter Haas Fund
Melinda Hackett
Andrew & Christine Hall
Ann Hatch & Paul Discoe
James Hedges
Betsy & John Hellman
Steve Henry & Philip Shneidman
Irene Hunter
James M. & Joan Hunter
James Jacobs
The Jerome Family
Kristen Johanson
Alvin & Barbara Krakow
Richard & Pamela Kramlich
Peter & Jill Kraus
Michelle & Lawrence Lasser
Lorie Peters Lauthier
Marc & Debra Levy
Carol LeWitt
Dorothy Lichtenstein
Robert Lipp & Martha Berman
Will & Helen Little
Henry Luce Foundation
Robert Mangold & Sylvia Plimack Mangold
Massachusetts Cultural Council
 Cultural Facilities Fund
Henry McNeil

Hans & Kate Morris
Donald R. Mullen, Jr.
Susan & Leonard Nimoy
PaceWildenstein Gallery
Cynthia Hazen Polsky & Leon Polsky
Prospect Hill Foundation
Jock Reynolds & Suzanne Hellmuth
Lamson & Sally Rheinfrank
Saul & Hila Rosen
Eric Rudd
Dorothy & Frederick Rudolph
SABIC Innovative Plastics
Joan & Michael Salke
Philip Scaturro
David Schrader
Karsten Schubert
Patricia & David Schulte
Anna Marie & Robert Shapiro
Theodore & Mary Jo Shen
Ake & Caisa Skeppner
Richard Solomon/Pace Editions
W.L.S. Spencer Foundation
Carol & Bob Stegeman
Marion Stroud
James & Dana Tananbaum Family
Rachel & Jay Tarses
David & Julie Tobey
United Technologies Corporation
Jack & Susy Wadsworth
Waterman Excavating, Inc.
Angela Westwater
Williams College
Michele & Peter Willmott
Robert & Elisabeth Wilmers
Robert W. Wilson
Charlotte & David Winton
Anthony & Sally Zunino